全人教育の
歴史と展望

小原芳明

監修

100 Years of
Zenjin Education:
Footsteps into the Future

玉川大学出版部

全人教育の歴史と展望

全人教育 100 年

　1921（大正 10）年から始まり、オヤジさんは全国津々浦々講演を行ってきた。幼い頃に、國芳祖父と旅をした思い出もある。彼の心の底からの話しと笑いと涙ありの独特な話法は、多くの人たちからの賛同をもらい、多くの学校で「全人教育」を教育の柱の一つとして掲げてもらえるようになった。

　30 年ほど前の当時でも、全人教育を掲げている学校数は 2,500 あったと聞いている。1996（平成 8）年に学校を含めた多くの組織が意匠登録をしたが、本学園名は地名であること、そして全人教育は広く一般に普及している普通名詞という理由で共に登録に至らなかった。

　そう言えば、かつてアメリカで学んだ歴史の授業に西洋で全人教育（whole man education）が行われてきたとあったが、それは小文字で表示されていたので、そこでは普通名詞だったことを思い出した（今では man は使わず、being とか person としている）。

　また「全人」を「全入」と読み違えたり、「全ての人を教育」と解釈したのか、入試不合格はありえないことだと批判されたり、真善美聖健富だから学習は 6 分の 1 だけで良いと誤解されてきたことも、百年史の一コマである。

　私は国芳祖父とよく旅先や、あるいは夕食を共に取りながらの話しの中で、例えば、「温故知新」、「良薬口に苦し」、あるいは「過ちを改めざるを過ち」と言う、といったことを教えられた思い出がある。

　普通名詞と言われているが、本学にとっては提唱百年経った今も全人教育論の温故知新（今までを振り返り、そこから 21 世紀へ向けて何かを見出す）時とも言えよう。

　しかし、学校教育の在り方と社会の在り方（polity）は対応し符号している。そうすると一方では、大正 10 年に提唱された全人教育論は令和時代にとって「古臭い時代遅れ」と言われるかもしれない。また、今は VUCA（Volatile, Uncertain, Complex, Ambiguous）時代と言われているが、それでは全人教

育の考え方はこの時代に合わないと言えるのだろうか。スペイン風邪パンデミック、第一次世界大戦の時、大恐慌とその後の世界大戦の時も VUCA ではなかったのか。まさか Big Brother が差配する社会ならともかく、何時の時代においても社会は見通しが悪く、複雑に糾りあって、計画通りに行かずの状態であったはずである。

　そうであっても知識と技術の限界を知りながらも、その時代が持つ知識をもって課題解決に臨んできたのであり、これからも最先端の知識を駆使することに違いはない。社会は常に真理を求め、学問に力を入れるべきである。それに加えて、私たちが知識と技術を活用することの善悪を判断できる道徳観を備えていなければ、「智慧ある悪魔の暴走」を許してしまうことになろう。そして知識と技術の応用が新しい生活様式に資するだけなく、それが美しい社会作りへの貢献となることを是とする価値観も無くてはならないものである。

　今では、玉川のオヤジと言えば全人教育論提唱者と言われるようになった。また、玉川教育＝全人教育と評価されるまでになり、こうして百年を迎えることができたのは、実に多くの先輩教職員の努力の賜物である。ありがたいことです。

　終わりになるが、今年こうして全人教育論提唱して 100 年となる節目を迎えることを誰より喜んだのは提唱者の國芳祖父と、提唱とほぼ時を同じくして産まれた哲郎父であったであろう。

　今日の玉川教育の礎を確固たるものとしてくれた彼ら 2 人とその支えを担ってくれた諸先輩の労作に深い感謝を持ち。

2021 年（令和 3 年）1 月

玉川の丘にて

小原芳明

目　次

Contents

Part III　References

第 I 部

小原國芳における
全人教育の理論と実践

第1章

小原國芳の「全人教育」提唱への軌跡

はじめに

　小原國芳が「全人教育」を提唱したのは、1921（大正10）年8月8日、成城小学校主事時代のことであり、当年34歳であった。本章では、小原國芳の誕生から少年時代、鹿児島縣師範学校生徒時代、広島高等師範学校学生時代、香川縣師範学校教諭時代、京都帝国大学学生時代、さらに広島高等師範学校附属小学校理事（教頭）時代を経て成城小学校の主事として上京し、そこで全人教育を提唱するまでの約30年間に的を絞り、全人教育思想の胎動、さらには全人教育思想開花の様子に焦点を当て、「全人教育」提唱（結実）までの軌跡を追ってみることにしたい。

　なおその間、小原國芳は鹿児島縣師範学校卒業を間近にして、鰺坂家に養子に行っており、広島高等師範学校附属小学校理事（教頭）時代までは「鰺坂」姓を名乗っていた。よって本章では、節の見出し以外では「小原」という姓は使わず、「國芳」という名前で統一して論を進めていくことにする。

第 1 節　小原國芳における「全人教育」思想の胎動

（1）誕生から鹿児島縣師範学校入学までの道のり

　國芳は 1887（明治 20）年 4 月 8 日、鹿児島県川辺郡南方郷久志村に、小原茂七郎、ハセ夫妻の三男として誕生した。2005（平成 17）年 11 月の市町村合併によって、それまでの「川辺郡坊津町久志」が「南さつま市坊津町久志」と呼ばれるようになったことからも想像できるように、國芳誕生の地は薩摩半島の南西部に位置しており、西側は東シナ海に面するところにある。

　入り江が多いこの地は、船舶が停泊するには最適なところであり、季節風を選び、黒潮を利用して、古くから朝鮮や支那の人々が船でやって来た。久志地区の南部にある博多浦は古代から遣唐使船の寄港地としての他、遣明船、薩摩藩の密貿易拠点としても栄えたという。久志には江戸末期、さらに明治に入っても、中国文化の香りが漂っており、小さな集落ではあったが、漢方医が複数開業していた。

　漢方医だった 1 人、吉見玄珠（1790-1870）は、郷土の若者に読み書きを教えたという。吉見の診療所は、久志における「寺子屋」でもあった。吉見玄珠の一番弟子として薫陶を受けたのが小原茂右衛門であった。彼こそは國芳の父方の祖父であり、玄珠亡き後は、寺子屋の師匠を引き継いだ。学問だけでなく、絵にも、書にも、歌にも優れた才能を発揮した。國芳が誕生した頃、祖父は亡くなっていたが、祖母は、祖父の偉さを小さい國芳に話し、「お前が茂右衛門じいさんの跡取りぞ！」と励ました。國芳も次第に教育者を夢見るようになっていった。

　國芳は 1892（明治 25）年、久志尋常小学校に入学した。國芳が久志尋常小学校に入学し、最初に出会った先生が田實源之助であった。『小原國芳自伝——夢見る人』1・2（以下、『自伝』）のなかでは「源之先生」として登場してくる。田實は文科系の科目は得意であったが、理数系の科目はまったく苦手で、算数など正比例はできても反比例はできないので、「反比例校長」のあだ名がついていた。子供たちと一緒に理科の実験に興じては、酸素がブクブク出てくるのを見て、ともに喜んだらしい。物知りの教師ではなかった

が、子供たちと一緒に学んでくれる教師であった。

　1896（明治29）年3月に久志尋常小学校を優秀な成績で卒業した國芳は、その年の4月、同校の特置高等科へと進んだ。特置高等科に進んで2年目、1898（明治31）年の9月、母ハセが突然亡くなった。國芳11歳の時であった。1番下の弟、末武が生まれてまだ半年しか経っていなかった。金山で失敗し、酒に溺れる夫を助け、子育てに一生懸命な母であった。國芳は後年『自伝』において、母の思い出を次のように書いている。「気丈夫な人でした。ネ小便のことで一度も叱ったことのない母でした。でも、ケンカは必ず勝てと、きつかった母でした。……だが、私どもが悪いことをした時、おわびすると、だまって、ただニコニコしとる母でした[1]」と。厳しさと優しさをあわせ持った母親だったようである。

　その頃、久志尋常小学校に鹿児島師範学校を卒業した鎌田という名の訓導が赴任し、國芳が在籍していた特置高等科の子供たちも教えた。鎌田は國芳の成績の良いのに驚いた。鎌田は指宿出身であった。鎌田はわずか10か月ほどで久志を去ることになったが、「成績がいいのに、こんな貧乏村の小さな学校へ入れておくのは惜しい」と言って、國芳を指宿へ連れて行くことになった。國芳は鎌田の家に下宿。指宿尋常高等小学校（現・指宿小学校）へ転入した。しかし、その年1899（明治32）年の12月、國芳は卒業まであと3か月を残したところで、指宿から故郷久志へと戻らざるをえなかった。

　國芳が久志へ戻って来たことを知った久志尋常小学校時代の恩師田實は、もう少しで卒業できるのだから、将来のためにも、続けて尋常高等小学校で学び、高等小学校の卒業資格を取得するように勧めた。そこで、國芳は枕崎の桜山尋常高等小学校（現・桜山小学校）へ転入することになった。1900（明治33）年の1月から3月までの約3か月間、國芳は往復6里（24キロ）の山道を枕崎まで通った。

　かくて、1900年3月21日、國芳は桜山尋常高等小学校を卒業することができた。同年4月に鹿児島第四尋常中学校（旧制の川辺中学校）が創設された。國芳としては中学校へ進学したかったのであるが、家庭の経済状況から進学を断念せざるを得なかった。同年6月、父茂七郎も死去。貧乏な生活のなかに、兄弟7人のみが残された。同年11月に、國芳は、官費で学べて、授業

料が免除される鹿児島郵便電信局、電気通信技術伝習生養成所へと入所することになった。この時、國芳は 13 歳であった。

1901（明治 34）年 5 月 31 日、鹿児島郵便電信局、電気通信技術伝習生養成所を無事に修了した國芳は、同年 9 月 7 日、大隅半島にある大浜電信局に配属になった。当時、大浜電信局における電報の取り扱い数は、1 日 1,000通をはるかに超えていた。1,500 余坪の土地に、局舎、倉庫、官舎等が建ち並ぶ壮観さに、土地の人々は「大浜御殿」と呼んだ。ここに勤務する約 50名の職員は全国から選抜された電信技術のエリートたちであった。

この大浜電信局は、1903（明治 36）年 4 月、肝属郡大根占村城元へ移転し、「大根占電信局」と改称された。官舎ができるまで、職員は民家へ下宿することになった。そこで國芳は、大根占電信局から近い前田政行宅に下宿した。國芳が前田宅に下宿している間に、前田家の娘が鹿児島縣師範学校女子部（後の鹿児島縣女子師範学校）への進学を目指すことになり、國芳がその娘の家庭教師をおおせつかった。このことが契機となって國芳は、自分も師範学校に入って「先生になろう！」と決心した。家が貧乏で上級の学校への進学ができず、教育者になる夢を諦めていた國芳であったが、前田家の娘の受験勉強を手伝うなかで、寺子屋の師匠だった祖父茂右衛門のような立派な教育者になろう、という夢が甦って来たのであった。大根占の前田宅は、國芳にとって「教育者」になるという夢が具体的に動き出す舞台裏となったのである。やがて國芳は鹿児島縣師範学校を受験、みごと合格して、1905（明治 38）年3 月、大根占を去ることになった。

（2）真の教育を目指しての修業と実践

國芳が鹿児島縣師範学校本科第一部に入学したのは 1905 年 4 月のことであり、当年 18 歳であった。当時の師範学校は学費は無料とされながらも、全寮制で、軍隊的な命令と規律厳守のなかで教員養成がなされた。師範学校の軍隊式の生活については國芳は批判的であった。だが、教諭たちは素晴らしく、その教育内容には感銘を受けた。國芳が入学した頃の鹿児島縣師範学校は、野島藤太郎が校長、木下竹二が教頭であった。

師範学校の教諭たちに恵まれただけでなく、学校外においても國芳は生涯

における大きな出会いをすることになる。鹿児島市内で迎えた最初の日曜日、教会を見つけた國芳がおそるおそる玄関に近づいて行くと、1人の西洋婦人に出会った。その婦人とは宣教師のハリエット・M・ランシング（Lansing, H. M.）女史であった。「あなたは、はじめてですね。さあ、おはいりなさい。師範学校の生徒さんですね」と、女史は心優しく案内してくれた。國芳は後に『自伝』において次のように書いている。「その時の心やさしい温かさ、とうとう私の一生が支配された出来事なのです[2]」と。ランシング女史は、初めての出会いにもかかわらず國芳を見込んで、次の週から小学生の日曜学校を手伝わせ、「私のムスコです」と他人に紹介するほどであった。

このランシング女史との出会いにより、さらに尾島真治牧師を知るようになった。尾島牧師から洗礼を受けた國芳にとって、キリスト教は生活の一部となり、この時以来、生涯をクリスチャンとして生き抜くことになった。

鹿児島縣師範学校を卒業した國芳は、1909（明治42）年4月、広島高等師範学校英語部へと進学することになった。鹿児島師範の恩師たちは「入学してもあまり勉強するなよ」と忠告したという。鹿児島師範入学前に、大隅半島の大浜や大根占で、海底電信係の激務をこなした國芳は、胸を患っていたからであった。当時の彼は身体が弱く、細かった。そこで國芳が身体を鍛えるために始めたのが「和弓」であった。

國芳は『自伝』のなかで次のように書いている。「弓道には、全く凝りました。英語科に入学したというよりか、弓道科か武道科に入学したという格でした[3]」と。國芳によれば、「静かな、且つ胸のひろがる運動として、毎日、弓を100本ずつ、日曜は500本引いたという[4]」。勉強も決して怠けたわけではなかったが、國芳にとって、長生きのためには健康こそが基本であった。「点数より身体だ。健康だ。長生きするんだ」と國芳はいつも心に思っていた[5]。國芳はこのような自分自身の体験から、教育上、身体の「健康」の大切さをしみじみ感じた。

國芳は、ここ広島高等師範学校において「音楽」の魅力も知った。その契機となったのが、音楽の教師であった吉田信太との出会いであった。國芳は『自伝』のなかで、「正式に音楽が好きになったのは、先生のオカゲです[6]」と書いている。吉田信太は「空も港も夜は晴れて……」で有名な日本の唱歌、

「みなと」の作曲者であった。

　4年間の広島高等師範学校での生活を通して、國芳は専門の英語を勉強しただけではなく、前述の通り、弓道に打ち込むことによって丈夫な身体を取り戻し、健康の重要さを実感した。また、吉田信太との出会いにより音楽の素晴らしさを知った。さらに、キリスト教への信仰も深まり、広島の教会の日曜学校で子供たちに説教することも、國芳の生活の一部となっていった。人間の形成には、学問だけではなく、芸術、宗教、さらには健康が大切であることを、身をもって確認した國芳であった。

　1913（大正2）年3月、國芳は、広島高等師範学校本科英語部を卒業。辞令に従って、同年4月、四国、高松の香川縣師範学校に教諭として着任した。当年26歳であった。香川縣師範学校における教育活動は、國芳にとって小学校の教員養成に携わる第一歩であった。鹿児島縣師範学校で問題だと感じたことを改革する、絶好の機会と思われた。國芳はその意気込みを『自伝』に次のように記している。「『ようし、やるぞ』という意気込みでの高松入り。……特別に香川の校長からの懇望で……[7]」と。

　結果的には、わずか2年半の香川縣師範学校教諭としての生活であったが、英語、教育史、心理学等の授業をこなしたばかりではなく、クラス担任をしたり、ボート部の顧問として生徒と瀬戸内海を回ったり、寮の舎監をやったり、信心深い生徒を12名選んで祈祷会を催したり、生徒と一体となって教育活動に明け暮れた、充実した日々であった。

第2節　小原國芳における「全人教育」思想の開花

（1）京都帝国大学哲学科での学び

　香川縣師範学校の教諭を辞した國芳は、1915（大正4）年9月、再び学生となって京都帝国大学文科大学（現在の文学部）哲学科に入学した。國芳は、28歳になっていた。

　当時の京都帝国大学文科大学哲学科の教授陣には、哲学講座担当者として西田幾多郎（当時45歳）、西洋哲学史講座担当者として朝永三十郎（当時44歳）、印度哲学史・宗教学講座担当者として松本文三郎（当時46歳）、倫理学講座

図1-1　京都帝国大学学生時代の國芳
　　　　写真提供：玉川学園

図1-2　小西教授（前列左端）と
　　　　ともに國芳（最後列中央）
　　　　写真提供：玉川学園

担当者として藤井健治郎（当時43歳）、美学・美学史講座担当者として深田康算（当時37歳）、教育学・教授法講座担当者として小西重直（当時40歳）などが居た。30代から40代の、若くてしかも実力者揃いの教授陣であった。國芳は『自伝』のなかに書いている。「全く、どこか、学問の王国の桃源に、ユートピアに飛び込むような気持ちで、若鷹のような溌剌さで、あこがれの京大哲学科に入学した[8]」と（図1-1、2）。

　國芳が籍を置いたのは、哲学科のなかの教育学・教授法講座であった。そして、國芳が3年次の1917（大正6）年12月、生涯にわたって深いかかわりを持つことになる波多野精一（当時40歳）が、宗教学（キリスト教）講座担当者として、京都帝国大学へやってきた。ドイツ留学中に原始キリスト教研究に触れ、1908（明治41）年に『キリスト教の起源』を著していた波多野が、京都帝大の宗教学講座の担当者として着任したことにより、「初めて専任者によるキリスト教の授業が行われることになった」という。

　國芳は、教育の内容として「学問」、「道徳」、「芸術」があるだけではなく、さらにその根底に「宗教」が欠くべからざるものとしてあることを確認したのであった。であるから、西田幾多郎がその著、『善の研究』（1911年、弘道館）において「学問道徳の極地はまた宗教に入らねばならぬようになる」と述べていることは、國芳の胸に強く響いた。

　國芳は教育の根本を深め、同時に教育の内容を確立するために、小西重直の「教育学」関係の授業に主軸を置きながらも、西田幾多郎の「哲学」関係の授業、朝永三十郎の「西洋哲学史」関係の授業、藤井健治郎の「倫理学」関係の授業、深田康算の「美学」関係の授業、さらには、遅れて就任した波多野精一の「宗教学」関係の授業に積極的に出席したのであった。

　國芳は後に、その著『全人教育論』（1969 年、玉川大学出版部）のなかで、京都時代に小西重直が談話の席で、「道徳的人格の、芸術学的人格の、哲学的人格の、宗教的人格のというが、それを打って一丸とした総合的人格、マア、文化的人格（Kulturcharakter）とでも云おうか、そんなものが欲しい。誰かそんな意味のものにあてた言葉を使った人はいないかね[9]」と、教育学専攻の学生たちに尋ねたことを述懐している。京都帝国大学哲学科における國芳の研究は、哲学、道徳、芸術、宗教という各論の研究と同時に、その教育的人間像である「総合的人格」の問題、そのような人を育てる「総合的教育」は如何に可能であるかという問題へと進んで行ったのであった。

（2）洛陽教会、ならびに京都南座における思索と体験

　鹿児島時代に洗礼を受け、広島、高松と教会に通い続けた國芳は、京都においても、日曜日には京都御所の近く、新島襄が創設した同志社大学に近い洛陽教会へと礼拝に出かけた。國芳が洛陽教会に通うようになった背景には、広島高等師範学校時代の恩師、栗原基の存在があった。栗原は広島高等師範学校で國芳たちを教えた後、旧制の第三高等学校（後の京都大学教養部）の教授となっていたのである。

　國芳は、栗原基の薫陶を受けつつ、さらには栗原の後を受けて、洛陽教会の「月報」の編集責任者にもなっている。否、國芳は「月報」の編集と併せて、随筆を執筆して自分の考えを発表する機会も得たのであった。1917 年 3 月、國芳は教会の月報「道しるべ」に一篇の随筆を寄稿した。京都帝国大学を卒業する 1 年 4 か月前のことであった。

　そこには「教化を残せ」と題して、次のように書いている。「……而して学校ではどうしても知に偏するのは止むをえませぬ。で、何處かで情意の教育をもやらねばなりませぬ。即、全人の教育が必要です。情意の教育、殊に

霊性上の修養となりますと中々困難です。しかしこれなくんば、人はアヤツリ人形と同じく空ッポです。……[10]」と。

　この時の主張は、学校で知育が中心となるのは仕方のないこと、しかし人間の教育を考える時、知育だけでは駄目で、情意の教育が必要である。つまり「全人の教育」が必要である。しかもこの中心にあるのは、「宗教教育」だというものであった。

　國芳は広島高等師範時代に音楽の素晴らしさを知ったが、京都ではさらに、演劇に着目する機会を得た。これも京都時代の大きな収穫の一つであった。國芳は、京都帝国大学で美学担当であった深田康算の教えを受けたことで、教育における芸術の重要性に理論的裏付けを得たが、家庭教師先の藤江夫人との出会いを通して、京都南座において観劇体験をすることができ、演劇に目覚めたのであった。これが、後に勤める広島高等師範附属小学校において、児童の演劇を「学校劇」と名づけることにつながっていくのである。このことについては、また後に詳しく見ることにしたい。

（3）卒業論文においての「全人の教育」論究

　京都帝国大学哲学科での3年間（当時の帝国大学は3年制であった）の学びの締めくくりとして、1918（大正7）年7月、國芳は、波多野精一や小西重直の指導を受けることによって、「宗教による教育の救済」と題する卒業論文を提出した。國芳が書き上げた卒業論文は、國芳の言葉に従えば「三百頁の美濃紙大の和綴じを五冊、千五百枚」であった。現在流の数え方をすれば、「四百字詰原稿用紙、約六百枚」といったところであろう。

　口頭試問は、波多野精一、小西重直の他に、倫理学の藤井健治郎が加わり3名が担当であった。京都帝大卒業から10か月後の1919（大正8）年6月、國芳はこの卒業論文を『教育の根本問題としての宗教』と改題して、東京の集成社から出版した。1頁490字（35字×14行）で500頁からなる大著であった。この本の冒頭には、「本書は京都帝大哲学科卒業の際の卒業論文です。教育と宗教。これは私の一生の研究題目、一生の事業であります」と書いている[11]。この版の内容は、ほぼ卒業論文の原本のままであった。

　この本は、その後1950（昭和25）年11月に大幅に手が入れられ、改版されて、

玉川大学出版部より初版として刊行された。だが、実はその際に、第 1 編から 1 つの章が省かれてしまっている。つまり、1919 年版の集成社版の第 1 編の本質論は、第 1 章「宗教論」、第 2 章「教育本質論」、第 3 章「教育の内容としての科学、道徳及び芸術と宗教との関係」、第 4 章「教育と宗教とに対する世人の謬見」の全 4 章から成り立っていたが、1950 年の玉川大学版の第 1 編の本質論は、第 1 章「宗教論」、第 2 章「教育の内容としての科学、道徳及び芸術と宗教との関係」、第 3 章「教育と宗教とに対する世人の謬見」の全 3 章から成り立ち[12]、旧版にあった第 2 章「教育本質論」が、新しい版では削られてしまっている。

　先に、1917 年 3 月、國芳は洛陽教会の月報「道しるべ」に随想を寄稿して、「全人の教育」が必要であることを述べたことに触れたが、実は、この第 2 章「教育本質論」の第 3 節「教育の成分」において、國芳は改めて「全人の教育」について論及したのであった。つまり、國芳は「吾人の要求する教育は全人の教育である。しかもそれは、バトラーの主張する心身的両方面を一にしたるものでなければならぬ。しかもそれは、混雑せるエレメントの集合ではなくて、統一的過程である[13]」と述べて、「全人の教育」、「心身的両方面」、「統一」という、後の國芳の「全人教育論」の鍵概念をここで表明したのであった。

（4）広島高等師範附属小学校での「学校劇」の実践

　京都帝国大学を卒業した國芳は、1918 年 8 月、母校広島高等師範学校に着任。主に高等師範附属小学校の理事（教頭）の仕事を命じられた。理事には、普段は定まった授業はなかった。だが、訓導たちが病気や出張等で止む無く欠席すると、國芳は喜んで授業を代講した。後に國芳は『自伝』において「私は、オカゲで、各学年、各教科、いろいろの修練をさせてもらいました。ホントに、ヒロシマの附属小学校の一年半は、私の教育学——理論と実際、学と術、思索と体験の融合、『反対の合一』のために、ホントに貴い期間でした」と書き、さらにその体験から「特に小学校教師は、ダ・ヴィンチや宮本武蔵みたように何でも出来ることだ、全人的教養が必要だと思うことです[14]」と教師論にも言及している。

　広島高等師範学校附属小学校において、國芳は教頭として積極的にいろいろな活動を展開したが、「学校劇」の名づけ親となり、その学校劇を上演したことは、日本の学校教育史上でも画期的なことであった。昭和時代の学校劇を推進した岡田陽の著、『ドラマと全人教育』（1985年、玉川大学出版部）によれば、明治以降の学校教育のなかでも、語学練習のための劇や、寸劇・対話劇・活人画といわれるようなもの、歌舞伎を模倣した劇などが、学芸会で演じられることはあったようであるが、それらはあくまで語学の練習のためであったり、また余興的な意味のものであったりして、それ自身はっきりとした教育上の主張を持つものではなかったという。

　広島高等師範学校附属小学校でも、当時「学芸会」は盛んだったようだし、音楽、朗読、対話等と併せて、「お芝居らしきもの」が出し物としてはあったようである。しかし、國芳が着任した翌年、その「お芝居」をもっと教育的な見地から徹底して行うことになった。先に触れたように、國芳自身がちょうど京都で、家庭教師先の藤江夫人から南座の顔見世興行を見させてもらったり、学友の松原寛からの感化もあって『演劇画報』なぞを毎月買って耽読しており、「全人の教育」を推し進めるには、「感性の教育」としての芸術教育の重要性を感じていたからであった。

　同僚の先生方の協力もあって、1年目に行った「水師営の会見」や「天の岩戸」は大成功に終わり、喝采を受けた。國芳は後に『自伝』において、「日本で『学校劇』という名のついた最初のものではなかったでしょうか」、「オカゲで日本の『学校劇』の名づけ親になれたワケです[15]」と振り返っている。

　1919年の秋、長田新が東京から澤柳政太郎博士の使いとして國芳を訪ねてきた。澤柳政太郎といえば、1897（明治30）年に旧制第二高等学校（後の東北大学教養部）、翌1898（明治31）年には旧制第一高等学校（後の東京大学教養部）の校長を務め、1906（明治39）年に文部次官、1911（明治44）年に東北帝国大学初代総長、1913年には京都帝国大学総長、1916（大正5）年には帝国教育会長を歴任するなど、当時の教育界の大御所的存在であった。その沢柳が1917年4月、東京の牛込原町に新教育の実験校として「成城小学校」を創立して校長を務めていた。初代の主事は藤本（平内）房次郎であったが、一身上の都合で辞めたため、主事職が空席になっていた。

　長田が「君、どうだ。一つ、私立を、一生涯やってみる気はないか」と澤柳校長の意向を伝えると、國芳は「行きますよ。成城ですね」と即答した。國芳は、その２、３か月前に、成城を参観する機会があって澤柳校長とも会っていたし、「成城小学校創設趣意」には心から共鳴していた。かくて 1919 年 12 月、國芳は広島を出て新天地の東京へと向かい、成城小学校主事に着任した。そして、それから２年後の 1921（大正 10）年８月、当時の東京高等師範学校（現・筑波大学）の講堂で開催された「八大教育主張講演会」において、それまでの思索と実践の結実として提唱したのが「全人教育」なのであった。

注

1）小原國芳『小原國芳全集 28　小原國芳自伝（１）—— 夢みる人』玉川大学出版部、1960 年、50 頁。
2）同上、149 頁。
3）同上、296 頁。
4）同上、256 頁。
5）同上、258 頁。
6）同上、285 頁。
7）同上、311 頁。
8）小原國芳『小原國芳全集 29　小原國芳自伝（２）—— 夢みる人』玉川大学出版部、1963 年、9 頁。
9）小原國芳『全人教育論』玉川大学出版部、1969 年、130 頁。
10）鰺坂國芳「教化を残せ」『道しるべ』第 17 号、1917 年、1 頁。
11）鰺坂國芳『教育の根本問題としての宗教』集成社、1919 年、巻頭言。
12）小原國芳『教育の根本問題としての宗教』玉川大学出版部、1950 年、目次。
13）鰺坂國芳『教育の根本問題としての宗教』集成社、1919 年、83 頁。
14）小原國芳『小原國芳全集 29　小原國芳自伝（２）—— 夢みる人』玉川大学出版部、1963 年、126 頁。
15）同上、135 頁。

第2章

小原國芳の全人教育論
——その提唱と展開

はじめに

　「全人教育」を日本で初めて提唱したのは、玉川学園・玉川大学の創立者、小原國芳（1887-1977）である。小原は 1921（大正 10）年 8 月 8 日、八大教育主張講演会において、予定されていた演題「文化教育の主張」を変更し、「至って平凡な名前　全人教育[1]」と題して語り始めた。当時彼は、私立成城小学校の現場で働く教師（主事）であった。民間の教員研修に相当する講演会に集まった大勢の教師たちを前に、彼は詰め込み型の偏った当時の教育を批判し、「真実の教育[2]」のあるべき姿を「全人教育」と名づけて発表したのであった。その反響は大きく、「全人教育」という言葉は広く世の中に普及していった。今では『広辞苑』をはじめ、一般的な国語辞書のなかで「全人」や「全人教育」がごく普通の言葉として掲載されている。それどころか、「全人教育」は今、教育界でもっとも重要な言葉の一つになったと言っても過言ではない。「全人教育」や「全人的」といった言葉は、全国の学校（幼小中高大）の教育理念や方針などを表現する際に広く用いられているのである[3]。日本の教育界でその育成課題の中核にある「生きる力」も、中央教育審議会によっ

て「[生きる力]は、全人的な力[4]」と明言されている。

　このように「全人教育」や「全人的」という言葉は広く普及している。しかしその一方で、元来、これが小原に由来することなど、今や「知らない時代[5]」に突入した感さえある。たとえば、「全人力」、「全人教育 2.0」等々、小原のコンテクストから離れて、自由な意味合いで使用されるケースも数多くみられる。

　いわば一般名詞化したこれらの言葉を誰がどのように使おうと自由ではないか、との異論があるかもしれない。本章も「これが正しい全人教育だ」などと閉鎖的・教条主義的に主張しようとするものではない。そうではないが、「全人教育」は小原によって提唱され、彼のもとで実践され、100 年の歳月を重ねた言葉である。またこれだけ教育界で普及した言葉である。その「ことわけ」の始原へと遡ることは無益ではなかろう。「全人教育」が小原によって、どのようなコンテクストで提唱され、どのような意味合いで使用されたのか、それを確認する作業は、「全人教育」を継承・発展させていく上で有益な基盤づくりとなろう。

　小原が提唱し、彼の学び舎で実践されてきた「全人教育」の理論・実践の全体を把握することは、もとより浅学のおよぶところではない。本章は、小原國芳による全人教育論のテクストに基づき、その提唱と展開の一端を把握しようとするささやかな試みである。なお、史料の引用にあたり、漢字は新字体に、仮名は現代仮名遣いに、合字は仮名に改めた。

第1節　全人教育論のテクスト

（1）2つのテクスト

　小原國芳による全人教育論のテクストには、八大教育主張講演会の速記録による 1921 年の「全人教育論」と 1969（昭和 44）年の「新しい『全人教育論[6]』」の 2 つがある。両者の間には約半世紀近くの隔たりがみられる。前者は 30 代半ばの小原が世に向かってはじめて「全人教育」の必要を叫んだ「いわゆる必要論」であり、「若き日の貴重な記録」であった[7]。一方、後者は晩年の小原がそれまで成城・玉川と実践し続けてきた全人教育の「内容を盛って

みた[8]」ものである。確かに分量において前者が56頁に対し、後者は114頁とほぼ倍増している（『小原國芳全集』版での比較）。両者の内容的な特徴については次節以降で扱う。ここでは「全人教育論」の２つのテクストについてごく簡単に解説をしておく。

（2）「全人教育論」（1921年）のテクスト

「全人教育論」（1921年）のテクストには、同年発表された２つの異なるバージョンが存在している。まず一つは、八大教育主張講演会を主催した大日本学術協会版『八大教育主張』（1921年11月刊、図2−1）の「全人教育論」である（以下、「協会版[9]」）。もう一つは小原が勤めた成城小学校内・教育問題研究会の雑誌『教育問題研究』（1921年10月発行、図2−2）に掲載された「全人教育」である（以下、「成城版[10]」）。世に出た順番からいえば「成城版」が先である。小原は「成城版」において「学術会からも講演録が出るそうで、重複するけれども筆にする[11]」と記している。両者の比較の詳細は紙幅の都合で割愛するが、「成城版」のテクストも講演会の速記録に基づいている。つまり「協会版」のゲラに手を入れたものと考えられる。また、両者は文体・構成ともにほぼ同じでありながら、タイトルが異なる。「協会版」のタイトルは「全人教育論」であり、「成城版」は「全人教育」である。「協

図2−1　『八大教育主張』（1921年）

図2−2　『教育問題研究』（1921年）

会版」はその後、大日本学術協会版『八大教育批判[12]』（1923年）が使用する基本テクストとなった。なお「協会版」の「全人教育論」は、後に旧字・旧仮名を現代表記に改めた復刻版『八大教育主張』（玉川大学出版部、1976年）にも掲載されている[13]。一方、「成城版」の「全人教育」も同様に現代表記に改められて『小原國芳全集15　教育論文・教育随想（１）』（玉川大学出版部、1964年）に同じ「全人教育」のタイトルで掲載され、さらに晩年の著作『全人教育論』（1969年）に「二、全人教育」として再録された。

（3）「全人教育論」（1969年）のテクスト

　一方、1969年の新しい「全人教育論」は、晩年の小原自身がまさしく「昭和四十四年八月に出した新しい『全人教育論』[14]」と位置づけた著作『全人教育論』（玉川大学出版部、1969年、図２-３）に掲載されたものである。その目次を示すと、「序」、「一、全人教育論」、「二、全人教育」（1921年の「成城版」）、「三、価値体系論」、「結び」となっている。この「一、全人教育論」が1969年初出の、まさに新しいテクストである。なお「三、価値体系論」は「大正十三年秋刊行[15]」の『教育の根本問題としての哲学』から一部転載されたとしている（書誌情報に誤りがあり、刊行は大正12年である[16]）。

　なお、小原は『全人教育論』（1969年）に対して、さらに翌年10月、「改

図２-３　『全人教育論』初版（1969年）

図２-４　『全人教育論』（改訂）

版するに際して」を追加し、「改版増補いたしました[17)]」と書き記している。ただし、奥付に「改版」の表示はみられず、書誌情報においても改版扱いされていない点、注意が必要である。表紙の帯には「改版増補版」ではなく「改訂増補版」と印字されている（図2-4）。また、この「改訂増補版」の「版」表示は、あくまで1969年のままである。「改訂増補版」では「三、価値体系論」が「一、全人教育論」に組み込まれて消失している。その後の版はすべて、この「改訂増補版」に基づいている。『小原國芳全集33　全人教育論・宗教教育論・師道』（玉川大学出版部、1975年：以下、「全集版」）に掲載された新しい「全人教育論」も「改訂増補版」を収録している。なお、「全集版」の「全人教育論」には、小原自身による「『全集』に加えるに際し」が挿入されており、これは生前の小原が目を通した決定版とみなすことができる。小原の死後出された『小原國芳選集3　全人教育論・思想問題と教育』（玉川大学出版部、1980年）の「全人教育論」も「全集版」を底本にしている。よって、以下の論考で小原晩年の新しい「全人教育論」（1969年）を扱う際は、この「全集版」（図2-5）を使用する[18)]。

　なお、小原國芳の全人教育論のテクストとして、現在、もっとも入手しやすいものは1994年に改版された図2-6の『全人教育論』（玉川大学出版部、1994

図2-5　『小原國芳全集33
全人教育論・宗教教育論・師道』

図2-6　『全人教育論』改版

年：以下、「改版」）である（書誌情報として、正式に改版扱いされている[19]）。これも前述の「改訂増補版」を底本にしている。特筆すべきは、これには小原國芳の娘婿・岡田陽の「改版に際して——学生諸君へ」が加えられた点である。岡田によれば「本書は、先生の教育に対する基本理念を今日の若い諸君に理解しやすくするため、文章表現の末節を多少手入れさせていただいたものである[20]」という。このほか「小原國芳の『全人教育論』の英訳がほしい、という英語圏からの要求[21]」もあり、英日対訳（*Kuniyoshi Obara's Theory of Zenjin Education*）が 2003 年、玉川大学出版部から刊行されている。この日本語部分は岡田による「改版」を踏まえ、当時の『全人教育論』改訂編集委員会が「実際に『全人教育論』を輪読し、文字言葉の背景にある小原先生の意図を汲み、今日的に解釈し、最低限度、日常語に直すように努め[22]」たものである。

　以上、小原國芳における全人教育論のテクストについて概略を紹介した。小原國芳の全人教育論に関する研究として、彼の没後、1970 年代末に日本とドイツの研究者によって、それぞれ博士論文が上梓されている[23]。今世紀に入って、大正新教育運動への関心の高まりとともに、国内外でも小原に関する研究論文や著作が発表され続けている[24]。一方、小原のテクストに関する学術的精査を経た批判版の登場は、今後の重要な課題として残されている。

第2節　小原國芳における最初の全人教育論（1921 年）

（1）八大教育主張講演会の概要

　歴史的観点から捉えれば、小原國芳による「全人教育」の提唱は、世界的な新教育運動のコンテクストに位置づけられる。新教育運動とは 19 世紀末から 20 世紀の初頭、とりわけ 1920 年代をピークとして登場した近代教育批判の運動であった。日本では明治時代、近代国家の建設と連動して欧米から近代の学校制度、教授法、教具などを受容し、いわゆる画一的で詰め込み型の知育偏重の教育が全国に広まっていた。しかしその後、大正デモクラシーの自由主義的な風潮のもと、特に第一次世界大戦後、このような近代教育への反省・批判が浮上してくることになる。新教育運動は現象面でみると、たとえば成城小学校をはじめ、多くの新学校の設立となって具現化した。それ

はまるで「新しいぶどう酒は、新しい革袋に入れるものだ[25]」（マタイによる
福音書9章17節）の教えのごとくである。新教育運動の展開は新学校の設立
と連動したのであった。さらに現職教員向けの講習会や講演会を刷新する動
きもまた、新教育運動を特徴づけた。その代表的な出来事が1921年8月に
開催された八大教育主張講演会である。この講演会は大正新教育運動を象徴
する画期的な出来事として教育史上に位置づけられている[26]（図2-7）。

　八大教育主張講演会は、当時の「八種の新教育主義」を代表する8人の人
物たちを8月1日から8日まで毎日一人ずつ講師に迎えた「革新的講習会」で
あった[27]。これは民間の大日本学術協会が主催したもので、現在でいえば現職
教員向けの講習会であった。ただし、当時の無味乾燥な講習会を批判し、打破
する新企画のイベントとなった[28]。1921年8月の八大教育主張講演会に登壇し
た8人と、同年6月の広告に掲載された演題は次の通りである[29]。

　すなわち、1日目は及川平治（兵庫県明石女子師範学校主事）の「動的教育
の要点」、2日目は稲毛詛風（稲毛金七、創造社経営『創造』主筆）の「真実
の創造教育」、3日目は樋口長市（東京高等師範学校教授）の「自学教育の根柢」、
4日目は手塚岸衛（千葉県師範学校主事）の「自由教育の真髄」、5日目は片
上伸（早稲田大学教授）の「芸術教育の提唱」、6日目は千葉命吉（広島県師

図2-7　『教育学術界』（第44巻第1号、1921年、口絵）
　　　　に掲載された講演者
注：小原は下段左端

範学校主事）の「衝動満足と創造教育」、7日目は河野清丸（女子大学校主事）の「自動主義の教育」、そして最後の8日目は小原國芳（成城小学校主事）の「文化教育の主張」であった[30]。小原は、当初、主催者側が提示していた演題「聖愛教育の真髄[31]」を気に入らなかった。その後、前述のように「文化教育の主張」との演題が広告掲示されている。しかし、講演の当日、「今、私は聖愛教育でいかず、文化教育であき足らず、いろいろと考えた揚句、全人教育とした[32]」と新たな演題を発表した。これが日本ではじめて「全人教育」が世間に向けて提唱された瞬間となった。

　なお、講演会記録『八大教育主張』（大日本学術協会、1921年）に掲載された際のタイトルを順番に挙げれば、「自学教育論」（樋口）、「自動教育論」（河野）、「自由教育論」（手塚）、「一切衝動皆満足論」（千葉）、「創造教育論」（稲毛）、「動的教育論」（及川）、「全人教育論」（小原）、そして「文芸教育論」（片上）であった[33]。

（2）講演以前の全人教育論——『教育の根本問題としての宗教』（1919年）

　小原は1921年8月8日、「連日二〇〇〇人以上の聴衆を集めた[34]」といわれる講演会の最終日に、はじめて「全人教育」を掲げて「二時間有半[35]」の熱弁をふるった。しかし、大日本学術協会から講演記録を依頼されていた風塵子なる人物[36]は、当日の小原の講演について「一度ならず何度も聴いたことがある」とし、さらに「話す事柄も材料も大抵同じようなことである。而もそれでいて何度きいても面白い[37]」と評している。これは小原が以前から同様の思想について語っていたことを示唆している。

　小原は講演の約3年前、「宗教による教育の救済」（1918年）と題する卒業論文を京都帝国大学に提出した。論文の審査委員は、小西重直（教育学）、藤井健治郎（倫理学）そして波多野精一[38]（宗教学）であった。小原にとってはじめて学術的精査を受けたこの論文は、翌年、『教育の根本問題としての宗教』（集成社、1919年）と改題して出版された。本書について、土山牧民は「書物全体に流れる思想はまさしく小原全人教育論そのものである[39]」と評している。

　『教育の根本問題としての宗教』の初版第1篇「本質論」第2章「教育本

質論」において、小原は「真の教育」とはいかなるものかを追求し、教育を
毒する「従来の教育の定義」を「改造」せんと企てる[40]。彼は従来の教育に
ついて、それは「一方に偏したる」教育であり、「教育の一面」に過ぎない
「不完全な教育」だと批判し[41]、「心身の調和せる発達」へ向かう包含的な「全
人の教育」の必要を説くのである[42]。さらに小原は従来の偏向教育を批判し、
人間の「文化、教養」の全般を重視する。しかも本書が宗教を主題にしてい
るとおり、小原はこの「文化、教養」の根底に宗教がなければ「真の文化〔、〕
教養」（〔　〕内は筆者）にならないと宗教の必要を説く[43]。続く本書第２編「関
係論」において小原は、「文化、教養」の全般を扱うべく、知育、徳育、美
育、体育を宗教とのかかわりにおいて論じていく。小原にとって「真の教育」
とは、「真の自己」となる「宗教的境地」へ至ることであった。その「宗教
的境地」においては「知育も、徳育も、情育も、生活もすべてが融合してい
る。私の真の教育、真の教授とは、この境地をいう[44]」と述べている。また、
「教育は『全人』を以て『全人』を感化陶冶する作業[45]」と定義し、「その人
そのもの」、「その人の特質であり個性」を「人格」と捉え、それをまた「全人」
と置き換えている[46]。そして「人格の完成」とは「全人の充実そのもの」、「自
己展開そのもの」であると述べていくのである[47]。なお、小原は生前、晩年
の著作『師道』（玉川大学出版部、1974年）において、教師は「小利口な専門
家ではなく、実に崇い全人でなければなりませぬ」と述べ、「全人的理想の
教師」の条件を展開している[48]。まさに、「教育は『全人』をもって『全人』
を感化陶冶する」との思想は、彼の処女作から晩年の著作まで一貫していた
といえよう。

　『教育の根本問題としての宗教』に現れた全人観と教育観については、こ
こまでに留めるが、後に八大教育主張講演会で披露することとなる小原の思
想は、宗教を軸としてすでに現出していたことがわかる。八大教育主張以前
の講演で彼が「話す事柄も材料も大抵同じようなこと」になったとしても不
思議ではなかったわけである。

（3）講演時の「全人教育論」（1921年）

　八大教育主張講演会は「革命的講習会教育学術研究大会[49]」と銘打たれ、

広報された。講演会を主催した尼子止水は、「現今我が国に於ける教育教授改造主義の八新人を以てし、その趣意精神の存する所、主義主張の拠って来る所の論述開陳を乞い[50]」と開催趣旨を述べている。講演者８人に期待されていたのは「八種の新教育主義[51]」の開陳とそれをめぐっての討論であったわけである。小原を除く７人の論者たちはそれぞれ「動的」、「創造」、「自学」、「自由」、「文芸」、「衝動」をキーワードとして語った。しかし、このように特定の主義主張をそれぞれ強調せんとする「革命的講習会」において、むしろそうした一面的な主義主張を批判する立場に立っていたのが、小原の包括的な「全人教育」の主張であった。特定の主義主張に偏することは「真の教育」をゆがめる「ウソの教育[52]」であると考える小原は、実はこの「革命的講習会」の一翼を担いながら、講習会の趣旨を批判的に捉えてもいたわけである。一面性を強調する新教育の主義主張の並ぶなかで、「全人教育」という小原の演題は、何ら過激さのない、革命的どころか、むしろ反革命的・脱革命的なものであり、小原自身がいうように「至って平凡[53]」であった。聴衆も彼の主張を「穏健[54]」だと理解したのである。

　小原による講演の主題が「全人教育」の提唱にあることは言を俟たない。しかし、そもそもなぜ「全人教育」を提唱したのか、その「ねらい」が理解されないと提唱の意義も不明確になろう。すでに『教育の根本問題としての宗教』において、小原は当時の教育を「不完全な教育」と捉え、「真の教育」のあるべき姿を追求していた。それが八大教育主張講演においても貫かれている。彼は「ウソの教育」の特徴をあげ、それを批判し、「真実の教育」の姿を「全人教育」として高調するのである。

　小原が解する「ウソの教育」は「或る一方にのみ偏した教育[55]」である。たとえば、「入学試験準備教育」に偏する功利主義的な知育偏重教育や、「体育奨励といえば明けても暮れても体操ばかりやることと早合点[56]」する極端な体育偏重教育など、小原は次々と批判していく。さらに何か特定の教授・学習法（たとえば「分団式」）や主義主張（たとえば「自由教育」、「自学主義」、「児童中心主義」など）を極端に信奉することも批判の対象となる[57]。八大教育主張講演会自体、主催者の尼子から「現今我が国に於ける教育教授改造主義の八新人」による「主義主張」を求められていた[58]。つまり各論者が一面的

な主義主張に偏する危うさを内包した講演会であったともいえる。「何々主義といって狭いイズムの世界に蟄居することを何よりも嫌う[59]」小原は、演題について迷い「いろいろと考えに考えた揚句、全人教育とした[60]」のであった。小原にとって「全人教育」は特定の主義主張を表現するために用いられたものではなかったのである。その意味で彼は講演会で異色の立場にあった。彼にとって「或る一方にのみ偏した教育」の対極に立つ「真実の教育」とは、いずれにも偏向しない「中庸[61]」に立つ教育であり、それを表現せんとしたのが「全人教育」なのであった。

　しかし結局は、「全人教育」もまた偏った教育の一種ではないか。小原はこうした異論を想定し、あえて「全人主義[62]」という言葉も使い、「全人主義」は確固たる見識のない野放図な「無主義無定見」ではなく「無主義の主義」だと述べ、「名は何でもよい」と言い切る[63]。さらに正しいものならば一切を取り入れる「包摂主義[64]」だとも述べていく。さらに講演のちょうど中間に差し掛かり、小原は「すべて形容詞は、或る限定を与えることである」ので、結局「人の教育 Menschenerziehung なる一語に、簡単ではあるが無限の深い意味を自ら感ずることが出来た」と述べ[65]、彼は「全人教育」を「実に分かり切ったように簡単ではあるが、『人』の教育であります。人らしい人を作ること、否、人らしい人に助長させることである。外に教育はないのである。外にあってはならぬのであります[66]」と高調するに至る。前述したように、聴衆は小原の主張を「穏健」と評価した。また、小原の語りの魅力も取りざたされた[67]。しかし一方で「要する所よくわからなかった[68]」と評する者もいた。

（4）講演時の「価値の体系」論

　さて、ここからは「協会版」に基づいて、当日の小原の主張に関して、そのねらい、学術的根拠となる「価値の体系」論、小原が念頭においた全人教育をめぐる2つの論点の順で解説していく。

　まず、小原が提示した「価値の体系」論を取り上げる。彼は講演の最初の方で「教育するには生きた『人』が入る[69]」と述べ、この「人」の分析から教育内容を根拠づけ、方向づける「価値の体系」を提示していく。人は心（精神）

と身（身体）からなる。それゆえ心育と身育が必要である。心（精神）においては「論理の世界、倫理の世界、芸術の世界、宗教の世界の四つが展開される」ので、それに応じて心育は「真育、善育、美育、聖育の四方面」から構成される[70]。その他、私たちが実際に生きていく上で必要となる「手段」として、「経済、制度、軍事、交通、政治、法律、農工商等」にかかわる「実際の教育」も不可欠だとしている[71]。これに身育としての体育をあわせると6方面の教育となる。生きた「人」を「人らしい人」・「真人間」（つまりは「全人」）へと育む教育にはこれら6方面のすべてが必要だと説くのである[72]。そして講演の最後に「要するにすべてが『人』から出発して欲しい。そして『人』に到達することを願望とせねばならないのです[73]」と締めくくる。特筆すべきは、小原が人間論と教育論を展開する際に、まず、「人」そのものから出発し、その分析から教育を根拠づけ、方向づける「価値の体系」を導き出している点である。

　小原は八大教育主張講演会を迎える前、東京から遠く離れた壱岐島で講習会をしていた。講演前日の夜、東京の自宅に戻ったところ身重の妻・信が「急に身体に異常を呈し[74]」たため、徹夜で看病することとなった。講演当日の朝、病院へ妻を送り届け、その足で講演会場に駆けつけている（その日、令息哲郎が誕生）。小原自身講演のなかで「睡眠不足で朝飯すら取ることが出来ません。頭がガンガンいたしまして申すことは纏まって居らぬかも知れません[75]」と述べている。聴衆のなかには、「学術的に整頓された御講演として承ることは出来なかった[76]」との批判もみられた。しかし、少なくとも小原が講演で語った人間論と教育論の核となる「人」の分析、「価値の体系」の提示、そして6方面の教育へ至る論理は首尾一貫したものであった。

（5）想定される誤解をめぐって

　さらに小原は講演のなかで、想定される誤解をいくつか論点としてとりあげている。ここでは2つ挙げておく[77]。まず1つ目は、「根本問題や思想」と「方法論」の対立問題である。教育実践を改善するには、まず、その根本にある思想問題の何たるかを知るべきとする立場と、方法論に知悉すべきとする立場が拮抗していた。小原は当時、前者の立場に立つ人物とみられていた。し

かし、講演のなかで彼は、「『根本問題や思想丈けでよい』とは決して曰はぬ」と述べ、「日本の先生方が根本ばかりやって方法を軽視される時代が来たら、その時は又方法論を高調しようと思うのです[78]」と主張している。彼はここでも「中庸」の重要性を説くのである。しかし、講演後、彼の全人教育論は方法論が不十分と指摘された[79]。この問題への応答は晩年の新しい「全人教育論」（1969年初出）でなされていくことになる。

　2つ目の論点は、「全人教育」と「個性尊重の教育」に関するものである。「個性尊重の教育」とは、成城小学校がその趣意書で「我校の希望理想」の筆頭に掲げていたものである[80]。この学校は、1917（大正6）年、2度の帝大総長を務めた教育界の大御所・澤柳政太郎が創立した日本の新教育運動を代表する私立学校であった。澤柳に嘱望されて広島師範学校附属小学校を辞し、成城小学校の主事となった小原は、「〔澤柳〕先生に見出していただいたことは全く、私一生の運の開けです[81]」（〔　〕内は筆者）と述懐している。小原は澤柳の教育理想に共鳴し、教育活動に邁進していたのである。しかし、成城の「個性尊重の教育」に関しては、自分のことしか考えない「我利我利主義」の人間や、好きなことばかりをやる「社会生活の出来ない」人間を育ててしまうのではないかとの誤解があったとしている[82]。小原はこのような誤解に対して、「吾々の要求する個性尊重とはそんな皮相なものではない[83]」と批判し、「個性尊重の教育」が、決して社会生活と矛盾しないと、次のように説明している。

　　各個人はこの無限大の過去から無限大の永劫に亘る無限時間の中に於てただ一回的の出現であります。過去にも未来にも我と同一者の出現を許さないのです。しかも我ならでは成し得ざる貴いサムシングが与えられて居るのです。その物が発展し伸びない時に、それ丈け宇宙の完全が壊されるほど貴いものを有して居るのです。各自は実に宇宙完成の一員であると教えて呉れます。そこです。それを発見した時に彼は真に幸福でありましょう。喜び勇んで憤起することが出来ましょう。宇宙も為に美しくなりましょう。世界もそれ丈け幸福になりましょう。……だから決して社会生活と何等の矛盾もないのです[84]。

　ところで、小原が今回提唱したのは「全人教育」であった。それは「個性尊重の教育」といかなる関係にあるのか。それは「個性尊重の教育」と矛盾するのではないか。この論点を挙げる理由について小原は、「全人教育と個性尊重とは丁度正反対で、大きな矛盾ではないかと思われる方もありはせぬかと思われますから[85]」と述べている。これは後述する新しい「全人教育論」（1969年）においても繰り返される論点であり、小原の「全人教育」を理解する上で必須の重要事項となっている。結論から言えば、小原は「私達の真に要求する個性尊重の教育は、実に私の主張する全人教育」だと主張し、その理由を次のように説明している。

　　　私達は、子供の有するすべてを、天から授かったすべてのの[ママ]性能を出来る丈け順当に伸ばすことを願とするのです。だからそれは全人教育である。しかもそのすべてがよく伸びれば伸びる程、各自の天地がよく現れるのである〔。〕即ち各自の真面目が、換言せば個性が発揮されるのである。即ち個性尊重の教育である[86]。（〔　〕内は筆者）

　ここには小原の言う「全人教育」と「個性尊重の教育」との不可分の関係が説明されている。全人教育において前述した6方面の教育が行われ、各人の性能の「すべてがよく伸びれば伸びる」ほど、「図書も七点、体操も七点、唱歌も七点、算術も七点[87]」といった没個性化はおこらず、得手不得手、興味関心の深浅など、各人の個性があらわになってくると彼は考えているのである。

　とはいえ、「全人」と「個性」の関係についてまだ釈然としないものがある。小原はこの講演で「全人」を語る際、「whole man[88]」を使用している。この「whole（全…、全体の）」をどのように解釈するかが鍵であろう。西田幾多郎の愛弟子で小原の後輩にあたる高山岩男は、「私も『全人』『全人教育』の理念に立つものである[89]」と述べ、ドイツの哲学者ヴィルヘルム・ディルタイ（Wilhelm Dilthey）も「全人」を強調する哲学者であると指摘した上で、「小原、ディルタイの『全』の理念には、なお解明されていないものが残っていると思う[90]」と主張している。高山によれば、「『全』は『多』と次元の異な

るものである。全は多を超越したものであり、多が一によって統一せられる
もの、つまり多と一との統合である[91]」という。しかし、「全」という言葉
はそれ自体、多義的でわかりにくい。土山牧民は「全人」という場合、この「全」
が「全部人（the total man）」の全か、「完全人（the perfect man）」の全か、「全
体人（the whole man）」の全かによって「全人」の意味する所が変わってく
ることを踏まえ、小原の「全人」概念の解釈を試みている[92]。

　小原の良き理解者の一人であった三井浩は、小原の解する全人を「個性的
全人」と解釈した。三井は「個性」と全人における「全」との関係について、「個
性とは単なる特殊性ではなく、個における全のあり方なのである[93]」と見事
に説明し、「教育は全ての人が愛の原理によって秩序づけられた個性的全人
となることを目的としなければならない[94]」と主張する。小原自身、最晩年
の著作『師道』において、三井の「個性的全人」に関する箇所を引用し、「三
井博士が説いて下すっているとおりだと思います」と評価している[95]。

第3節　晩年の新しい全人教育論（1969年）

　この節では、小原の「全集版」に依拠して、晩年の新しい「全人教育論」（1969
年初出）の思想内容を見ていくことにする。前述したように、小原は後年、
八大教育主張講演会における「全人教育論」（1921年）が「いわゆる必要論」だっ
たのに対して、この新しい「全人教育論」では「いささか全人教育の内容を
説きました[96]」と述べている。執筆された分量もほぼ倍増している。記述内
容の項目は「価値体系論」、「教育理想の帰趨」（「一、宗教教育」、「二、芸術教育」、
「三、道徳教育」、「四、学問教育」、「五、健康教育」、「六、生活の教育、富の教育」）、
「全人教育と関係深い諸問題」（「一、全人教育と反対の合一」、「二、全人教育と
個性尊重の教育」、「三、労作教育」）、「教育の結論としての教師論」となった。
小原における最初の「全人教育論」（1921年）と比較すると、「価値体系論」
の完成版が登場すること、全人教育の内容論（「教育理想の帰趨」に該当）の
分量が増え、特に「生活の教育・富の教育」の項目立てがなされたこと、さ
らに「労作教育」が新たな項目として登場していることが挙げられる。以下
では、この新しい「全人教育論」の特徴を追っていくことにしよう。

（1）小原の全人観

　まず、晩年の新しい「全人教育論」（1969年初出）で特筆される点は、冒頭に「全人」の定義が登場することであろう。小原はこう述べている。すなわち、「教育の内容には人間文化の全部を盛らねばなりませぬ。故に、教育は絶対に『全人教育』でなければなりませぬ。全人教育とは完全人格即ち調和ある人格の意味です[97]」と。小原はこれまで「全人」という言葉を用いる際、直接的にその定義を明示していなかった。ここで初めて、しかも冒頭で彼の全人の定義が登場することになる。ただし、表現上の問題が若干生じている。それは「全人教育とは完全人格即ち調和ある人格の意味です」の箇所である。この原文は「全人教育＝完全人格即ち調和ある人格」となっていて読者を混乱させる。岡田陽による「改版」は、この点を修正し「全人とは完全人格すなわち調和ある人格の意味です[98]」としている。ともあれ、小原は冒頭で全人を「完全人格すなわち調和ある人格」と明確に定義したわけである。しかし、「完全人格」とは何かについて、小原はここで直接論じていない。この文言を冒頭で読んだ読者は、「完全人格？　それは何か？　それは可能なのか？」と疑念を持つかもしれない。「それはどこも欠けることのない完全無欠の人格のことか？」、「そのような人格の完成など有限な人間に実現可能なのか？」、「それは没個性的なもので個性尊重と矛盾するのではないか？」等々、次々と疑問が浮かぶであろう。

　小原の全人教育論を理解する上で重要なことは、すでにこれまで彼が他の機会に論及してきたことの多くが前提に含まれていることである。「完全人格」に関しては、実のところ、すでに小原は処女作『教育の根本問題としての宗教』のなかで展開している。本書第2編「関係論」第4章「徳育論」において、小原は「人格」、「完全なる人格」を取り上げて論じている。まず「人格とは何ぞや」との問いかけから始め、その慣用を分析した上で、彼は「私はここに人格を定義して『人格とはその人の総量である』とする。実に人格とはその人そのものである。それが実にその人の特質であり、個性であるのである[99]」と説明している。彼は他の箇所で「各人の人格的色彩の差異[100]」という表現も用いており、人格はそもそも各人別々の個性的なものとの認識に立っている。そして「完全なる人格」については、「真の自我の中心 focus

に向かって統制されたるものが、完全なる人格なのである[101]」と述べている。わかりやすくいえば、各人が各人らしくある時、その人は小原の言う意味での「完全なる人格」者なのである。したがって「完全なる人格」は各人の自我を離れてあり得ず、むしろ各人の統制の在りように応じて個性的であることがわかる。

　こうした小原の「完全人格」観を踏まえて晩年の新しい「全人教育論」を読んでいくと、小原は別の表現を用いてその個性的な「完全人格」の在りようを複数の箇所で述べていることがわかるのである。たとえば、「各自は各自の独特の世界を実現しながら、しかも、そこに各自に完全境が成就される[102]」や、あるいはさらにわかりやすく、「竹は竹の、百合は百合の、松は松の本性を、太郎は太郎の、花子は花子の唯一無二の本領を発揮した時が最も美しい[103]」がそれである。そして、最初の「全人教育論」（1921 年）には「完全人格」の文言は登場しないものの、そこでも子供たち一人一人が、「自己らしいものを自己らしく出した時が最も完全であり最も美しいのであります[104]」と主張されていたことが確認できるのである。ここには小原が念頭におく「全人」の本質的特徴がわかりやすく表現されているとみることができよう。

　小原の全人観について、これまで「完全人格」に着目して確認してきた。次は「調和ある人格」についてみていくことにする。前述したように小原は全人を「完全人格すなわち調和ある人格」（傍点筆者）と表現している。つまり、「完全人格」と「調和ある人格」は同義で用いられているわけである。「調和」に関して小原は、コスモスの花を引き合いに出して次のように説明している。すなわち、「この六つの文化価値が、秋の庭前に整然と花咲いとるコスモス Cosmos の花のように、調和的に生長して欲しいのです[105]」と。「六つの文化価値」とは、価値体系論に登場する真・善・美・聖・健・富の６価値のことである（後述）。

　もともとコスモスはギリシャ語の原義で「整美、調和、秩序[106]」を意味する。コスモスの花弁は８枚あるのに６つの文化価値をコスモスになぞらえるとは、と評する向きもあるが、無論、これはあくまでも比喩であって、花弁と文化価値の一つひとつを一対一対応とする必要はない。我々はコスモスの花々を眺めたとき、それらはどれも同じコスモスだとわかるであろう。し

かし、よくよく観れば、どのコスモスも花びらの形や大きさや、それぞれに違いがあり、1つとして同じものはなかろう。つまり、どれにも個性があるわけである。それと同じで、人間も一人ひとり、同じ「人間」と呼ばれる存在でありながら、誰一人同じ人間はいない。誰もがみな違う個性を持った存在である。「調和」という言葉を使う場合も、小原は没個性的なものをイメージしていないことがわかるのである。

　ところで、「完全人格」や「調和ある人格」に登場する「完全」や「調和」は、一見、静止したイメージと結びつきやすい。しかし、小原の場合、これらは力動性を包蔵している。

　彼は、「対立、反対、矛盾」といった苦しい「二元の葛藤」を「人間の真相」だと捉えたのである[107]。一方で、このような「闘争そのものが、煩悶そのものが、進歩の前提[108]」（傍点筆者）ともみている。しかし、そうした「対立、反対、矛盾」に留まった状態は、彼が批判する何か特定の主義（イズム）に偏向している状態であり、彼はそれを「不真実です。死です[109]」と否定し、それを乗り越えた「合一」、「調和」の境地を求めるのである[110]。彼はその境地を先人の思想家たちにヒントを得て[111]、「反対の合一」と称し、「反対の合一ということを、全人教育の立場から特に大事にいたします[112]」としている（さらに実践レベルでは「二つを一つに[113]」を好んで用いている）。なお、小原の「反対の合一」観をめぐって、近年、批判的な研究も登場しているが[114]、彼の立場を理解するには京都帝国大学時代の学究と恩師からの影響、そして彼の処女作『教育の根本問題としての宗教』の思想を丹念に検討すべきである。紙幅の都合上、ここでは、小原の「反対の合一」観を理解する上で最良の手引きとなる鰺坂二夫の解釈を紹介するにとどめよう。鰺坂は次のように述べている。

　　反対の合一ということは、普通の形式論理ではなじまないばかりか、むしろ拒否される論理である。しかし、生そのもの、経験そのもの、とくに、人間形成という実践、行為に支えられた教育の場合には、一般的な形式論理を超えた生そのもの、行為そのものの成立つ別な論理が見られる。反対の合一というような矛盾的な事実が深い実在の根底を支えるのである[115]。

小原がいかなる立場から「反対の合一」を捉えようとしたのかを鯵坂は簡明に示しているといえよう。

（2）価値体系論の軌跡

小原の全人教育思想形成に「決定的な影響を与えた」と思われる「四人の思想家」について、三井善止は、西田幾多郎、朝永三十郎、小西重直、澤柳政太郎を挙げている[116]。この4人のうち、西田、朝永、小西は京大時代に小原が直接薫陶を受けた恩師たちである。小原は八大教育主張講演において、小西のことを話題にしている。ちょうど彼が京大を卒業して広島高等師範学校附属小学校に赴任する際、小西から次のように諭されたという。すなわち、「訓導諸君にウンと哲学的修養（広く哲学も道徳も芸術も宗教も含めての意味）をすることを勧めよ。どうしても何十年たっても不徹底なのは根本がシッカリして居ないからである[117]」と。その影響を受けて、小原自身「私も教育教授を深みへ深みへと努力した[118]」という。その後、広島高等師範学校附属小学校で開催された「第四回全国小学校教育研究会」（1918年11月8日から12日）の最終日、彼は「教育の根本問題としての真善美聖」と題し、まさに教育的価値の根本問題を取り上げて発表していた[119]。小原は八大教育主張講演においても、「人」の分析から出発して教育的「価値の体系」を論じ、「人」に必要な全人教育の在りようを、心育（真育・善育・美育・聖育）と身育、さらに生活に必要な「実際の教育」の6方面から展開した。このことは前節で指摘したとおりである。講演当時、すでに教育的価値に知悉した学的根拠を持つ全人教育の提唱を企図していた。しかし、発表時この点は着目されず、前述したように、むしろ「学術的には不成功」などと批判もされていたわけである。小原はその後も、この価値体系論を彫琢し続け、晩年の新しい「全人教育論」（1969年初出）で一つの完成をみることになる。

八大教育主張講演の段階で小原は「価値の体系」を図解しなかった（講演会の都合上、やむを得なかったのかもしれない）。しかし、その後に発表した価値体系論においては、必ず体系図を披露している。今回、確認した限りで、小原の価値体系図は、少なくとも3回、大きな変更が加えられていることがわかる。まず『修身教授の実際 下』（集成社、1922年）に登場するのが、

図2-8の価値体系図である[120]。これと同じものが『学校劇論』（イデア書院、1923年）と『教育の根本問題としての哲学』（イデア書院、1923年）にも登場する[121]。この体系図で特徴的なのは、絶対価値（真善美聖）と手段価値（健富）の区分がはじめて使用された点である。ただし、晩年の価値体系図（1969年）と比較すると、「身」の傘下に「生命保存」と「活動力」が入り、これらを共に「健」の価値で捉えている点、「富」の価値が「人」の傘下にあるものの、「身」の枠外に出され、新たな「生活」の傘下に入れられている点が特徴的である（図2-8、図2-10）。

　しかし、この体系図はその後、大きく変化する。それは『母のための教育学　上巻』（イデア書院、1925年）においてである（図2-9[122]）。この体系図で特徴的なのは、「富」の価値が「人」から引き離された点である。価値体系を「人」から説き起こす小原の考え方からすれば、この体系図は「生活」と「富」の扱いに問題が生じている（なお、『母のための教育学』における価値体系図は、後述する1969年版の体系図にしたがって後年改変されている[123]）。

　そして、晩年の著作『全人教育論』（玉川大学出版部、1969年）に登場する価値体系図が図2-10である[124]。この価値体系図によって、「富」価値は再び「人」から説き起こす価値体系図に組み込まれた。しかも、はじめて「富」

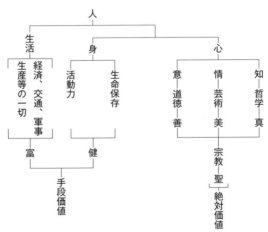

図2-8　価値体系図（『修身教授の実際　下』1922年）
出典：筆者作成

価値が「身」の傘下に位置づけられたのである。ただし、注意すべきことが
１つある。それは、本書において、この体系図が晩年の新しい「全人教育論」
（「一、全人教育論」）にはなく、「三、価値体系論」に別枠で掲載された点である。
「三、価値体系論」は前述したように『教育の根本問題としての哲学』から
抜き出されたものである。ただし、「三、価値体系論」に掲載された体系図は、
もともと『教育の根本問題としての哲学』に掲載されていた価値体系図と異
なり、新たなもの（図２-10）に差し替えられている。

　1970 年の「改版に際して」が付与された『全人教育論』「改訂増補版」では、
価値体系図が「一、全人教育論」内に組み込まれた。なお価値体系図に関して
は１点だけ軽微な追加がみられる。それは「活動力」内の「経済、交通、……」
に「政治」を加え「政治、経済、交通、……」とした点である[125]。以後、
この価値体系図が定番となるのである。

　なお、小原は価値体系図を説明するにあたり、多くの思想家に言及してい
る。「全集版」から、その主な人物を順を追ってあげてみると[126]、西田幾多
郎（「学問道徳の極致は宗教」）、プラトン（Platon:真善美の上に置かれる「最高善」）、
イマヌエル・カント（Immanuel Kant：プラトンを継承した「神聖性 Heiligkeit」）、
ヴィルヘルム・ヴィンデルバント（Wilhelm Windelband：「聖 das Heilige」）、価

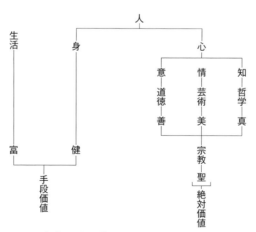

図２-９　価値体系図（『母のための教育学 上巻』1925 年）
出典：筆者作成

値体系を研究しているフーゴー・ミュンスターベルク（Hugo Münsterberg：価値間の位階的秩序は特に重視せず）、ハインリヒ・リッケルト（Heinrich Rickert：価値間の位階的秩序を重視）、ゲオルク・メーリス（Georg Mehlis：価値間の位階的秩序を排除）、京大時代の恩師・米田庄太郎（絶対価値と客観的価値を区別）などが登場する。小原の自伝によれば、彼は、京大時代「無論、西田先生の哲学と、米田先生の社会学だけは、特殊講義も演習も、三年間とも出席しました[127]」と述べており、京大在学時代（当時は3年間であった）、この両先生の薫陶を受けていた。また、西洋哲学史の朝永三十郎からは、彼の恩師・新カント学派のヴィンデルバントをはじめ、その影響を受けたリッケルトらの理想主義的文化主義哲学を学んだ。また、小西重直を介してパウル・ナトルプ（Paul Natorp）など文化的人格形成の思想も吸収していた。再び、八大教育主張講演の小原の言葉を挙げれば、小原は小西が話の席で「道徳的人格の芸術的人格の哲学的人格のというが、それらを打って一丸として綜合的人格、マア文化的人格 Kulturcharakter とでも云おうか、そんなものが欲しい[128]」と述べていたことに刺激を受けた。そして小原は、「私はその綜合的人格をこしらえるような綜合的教育と云おうか、全人教育といおうか、それが欲しいのである[129]」と全人教育論の構築へ踏み込んでいったのである。

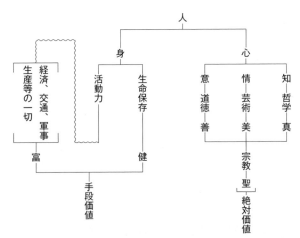

図2-10　価値体系図（『全人教育論』1969年）
出典：筆者作成
注：波線は筆者補足

その理論的支柱、学的根拠となるものが文化的・教育的な価値体系論であった。小原は次のように述べている。

　　さて、人間文化には六方面があると思います。すなわち、学問、道徳、芸術、宗教、身体、生活の六方面。学問の理想は真であり、道徳の理想は善であり、芸術の理想は美であり、宗教の理想は聖であり、身体の理想は健であり、生活の理想は富であります。教育の理想はすなわち、真、善、美、聖、健、富の六つの価値を創造することだと思います。
　　然して、真、善、美、聖の四価値を絶対価値と言い、健富の価値を手段価値と申します[130]。

　小原は先人たちの思想に学び、試行錯誤を重ね、この簡明なる価値体系論に到達した。特に「真、善、美、聖、健、富」は広く知られており、小原の全人教育といえば、ただちに「真、善、美、聖、健、富の価値を創造すること」と置き換えられるほどである。これは無論、間違いではない。しかし、価値体系論の構築へ向けた試行錯誤の末、彼が残した次のメッセージにも注目しておきたい。小原はこう述べている。

　　さて、幾多の大家の説を考えてみて、その間に不一致があることは私達に貴いものを教えてくれます。各自の個性、性情、気質、境遇がその相違を来たすのではないでしょうか。気随的でよいということはなくて、各自各自の価値体系を発見構成せねばならないということだと思います[131]。（傍点筆者）

　このメッセージは教育に真摯に向き合う人々に多くの示唆と励ましを与えるであろう。

（3）教育内容論の刷新① 絶対価値（真・善・美・聖）

　前述したように、小原は新しい「全人教育論」（1969 年初出）について、これまでよりも内容を充実させたとしており、分量も倍増している。詳細を

確認していくと、まず教育内容論については、これまで心育としての真育、善育、美育、聖育、身育としての体育、そして「実際の教育」の6方面としていた教育を、絶対価値に関する学問教育、道徳教育、芸術教育、宗教教育と、手段価値に関する健康教育、生活の教育・富の教育へと刷新している。そこで、これら各内容を一瞥しておこう。

　まず、学問教育を取り上げよう。小原の学問観はすでに八大教育主張講演で次のように表明されていた。すなわち、「生活の為の方便の為の学問教育といった功利主義や実際主義から脱却して、真理の為の真理、学問の為の学問、理科の為の理科、算術の為の算術といった立場にもっと立ち返って欲しい[132]」と。功利主義から脱却し、学問の純粋性を保つことを彼は高調している。新しい「全人教育論」においてもこの考えは継承され、さらに学問の純粋性を保持する学問教育論が展開される。その要点として、①学問の原義は「驚き、ふしぎ」であり、詰め込み・棒暗記・試験勉強で子供の「究知心、探求心、ふしぎ、驚きの心の芽」を枯らさないこと[133]、②「与える give する教育よりも、つかませる catch させる教育[134]」を重視すること、③「学問に対する燃ゆる情熱を与え、掘り方を会得させ、ツルハシを鍛えてやること[135]」が挙げられる。

　次に道徳教育の内容はどうか。小原は八大教育主張講演で師範学校による不自然な道徳教育を批判し、「意欲の貴い意味をもっと認めてほしい[136]」と述べ、道徳教育が人間の精神活動（知・情・意）のうち特に「意」にかかわる点を高調していた。さらには「子供のあの奔放な独我的な衝動生活」も「やがて理性的自由として発達すべき貴き芽生え」を包蔵すると、衝動の肯定すら掲げていた[137]。新しい「全人教育論」においては、戦後日本における修身科の廃止など、「全く行き過ぎてしまった」改革がもたらした「道徳の悲惨さ」、「出世病で毒せられた青少年たち」の登場を背景として、「道徳科の特設」が主張されている[138]。さらに道徳教育の意義として、①「人間人格価値の尊さ」を知ること、②「たしかな人生観を見出させる」こと、③「善の意義、悪の意味、悩み苦しみの深い意味」、「罪と懺悔の崇い意味」を了解すること、④「意欲と理性との葛藤」、「人間生活の矛盾と、苦悶の貴い意味」を知悉すること、⑤「美しい、正しい、たしかな永遠性のある人間像」を創

り出すこと、の5点が挙げられている[139]。

　3つ目として、小原の芸術教育論を語る上で特筆されるのは学校劇であろう。彼は八大教育主張講演の約2年半前、1919年2月、広島高等師範学校附属小学校の学芸会において日本初の学校劇（「天の岩戸」などで、学芸会の当日は「唱歌劇」と呼称された）を行った。当時すでに小原は「学校劇について」（1919年）と題する論考を発表し、「全人の教育という立場[140]」から「芸術教育」の必要性を説き、特に全人的な綜合芸術（音楽、絵画、建築、彫刻、舞踊、文学、さらに照明、音響効果まで取り入れた芸術）となる学校劇を高調していた。ただし、八大教育主張講演では、特に学校劇論を展開するわけでなく、冒頭で「芸術の世界に於て私共日本人は先進国に遅れて居る[141]」と後進性を批判するに留めている。そして「芸術なくして、美なくして、人生は丸で砂漠ではないでしょうか」と訴え、「人間」を人間らしく育成するために「ナゼ、よい劇、よい活動写真、よい音楽、よい絵画、よい小説を観せないのです？[142]」と問いかけている。このような芸術における鑑賞の意義について、小原はすでに『学校劇論』のなかで「享楽（鑑賞）と創作とは芸術活動の表現の二様式」であり、「突きつめて考えれば、……同じ活動である」と述べていた[143]。後年の新しい「全人教育論」（1969年初出）では、まず演劇に着目し、「演劇は具体的であるだけに人間形成には大きな力が与えられます[144]」とその意義を強調している。そして学校劇に対して、随分と迫害も受けてきたこと、演劇は「総合芸術であり、芸術の頂点ですのに！[145]」と彼の思いを吐露している。

　なお、現在もっとも入手しやすい岡田による『全人教育論』の「改版」では、46頁の1行目から9行目まで、『学校劇論』からの挿入がみられる。そこには小原の芸術観と芸術教育観が次のように明示されている。すなわち、「芸術活動そのものの一面」は「創作」、「創造」、「自己表現」、「個性の発揮」にある。特に「個性の発揮」は「自己統一の創造作用の実現」を意味している。「芸術教育の根本原理」は「全人的に人の性能を発揮せしめ、人格の創造的発動をなさしめんとする」ことにあると[146]。この箇所は「全人教育論」のオリジナルではないが、小原の芸術教育観が端的に表現されている。

　さらに小原の宗教教育観に立ち入ってみよう。価値体系論のなかで小原が

もっとも重要視しているのは「聖」価値である。ただし、価値体系論が如実に示しているように、学問も道徳も芸術も突き詰めていけば「聖」価値に通じていくとする立場に立っている。小原自身はクリスチャンであったが、彼が全人教育において説く宗教は、特定宗派の立場を表明したものではなかった。八大教育主張講演における小原は、聖育の話題に入った際、「これについては、先に『教育根本問題としての宗教』が出してあるし、多くを云う必要もありません」と述べ、学校教育（特に小学校教育）で宗教を無用とする吉田熊次らに対して「人の貴い霊の問題を度外視してどうして、『人』の教育が出来るのでしょう[147]」と反論している。

　小原の宗教観はすでに『教育の根本問題としての宗教』に明示されている。彼は宗教を次のように説明する。

　　　宗教とは「神と人との関係である」。……必ず宗教にはこの二つがなければならぬ。即ち宗教心または宗教意識には、主観と客観との両極がある筈である。主観とは自分のことで、客観とは宗教心の対象のことで、人力以上の者、即ち、神とか仏とかいうものである。この対象に向い、この対象を確と把え、この対象に関係し、知解をなし、信仰をなし、或は種々感激することが宗教である。即ち宗教とは一種結び付けられたる状態である。主観の客観に固く結び付いた状態を信仰状態というのである[148]。

このように特定宗派によらず、開かれた宗教観に立つ小原は、後年の新しい「全人教育論」において、公立学校で宗教教育ができないとする立場を批判して、次のように述べている。

　　　さて、公立学校では宗教教育は出来ないと、よく申します。とんでもないことです。宗教教育における私の願いは、どこまでも、「宗教教育」であって、「宗派教育」ではありませぬ。人間共通の宗教教育であり、根本問題を要望しとるのです。魂の教育なのです。宗教的薫化はいくらでも、どこででも出来ます。音楽で美術で、特に、演劇で。文学で、歴史で。

理科や算数では特に。いわんや、お茶で、生花で、体育で登山で[149]。

　小原が全人教育論において語る宗教教育は、特定の宗派や特定の宗教的教義の教育ではなく、まさに全人教育の実践そのものである。人間文化の諸般、人や自然に「深刻な興味」を抱き、利害打算を超えて「全我」的にかかわること、「深い敬虔の念」を抱くこと、「人格が人格を対象とする全精神の活動[150]」。これらを通じて、「心霊の清浄化[151]」、「物慾の清浄化[152]」が生じていく。心が清められていく。このことが、彼においては「聖」価値の世界、宗教的境地につながっている。小原が玉川学園の入学式で子供たちに語った「きれいな心[153]」こそ、宗教教育の目指す核心であったと言える。

（4）教育内容論の刷新② 手段価値（健・富）

　以上の絶対価値（真・善・美・聖）の世界とともに重要なのが、手段価値（健・富）の世界である。旺盛な精神活動は後者によって支えられている。まず、「身」を対象とする「体育」について八大教育主張講演では、まだ健康のための体育という視点は前面に出ていない。むしろ、講演の主題となる偏った教育批判のコンテクストが強調されている。彼は「中庸」を欠いて、朝から晩まで運動ばかりさせている「運動狂い学校」を例に、「運動が過ぎては甚だしく毒です[154]」と指摘している。ただし、「何だか私には一番体育が開拓されて居ないように思われます[155]」とも述べている。後年、小原は健康のためにもっともよい体操としてデンマーク体操を見出した。1931（昭和6）年9月、デンマーク体操の一行を招へいし、玉川学園で披露した。新しい「全人教育論」において小原は、デンマーク体操の思想を取り入れて、「健康体育」を主題に論じている。体育の目的は「優勝旗でも、メダルでも、レコードでも、カップでもない」、「手段と目的とを混同してはなりませぬ[156]」と主張する。そして体育が目指しているのは「強靭なる体力、長い生命、調和せる身体、そして巧緻性だ[157]」と喝破する。

　もう一つの手段価値「富」について、八大教育主張講演では、まだ具体的な価値の問題としてまとめられていなかった。前述したように、心育（真育、善育、美育、聖育）と身育（体育）の「その外に」（ルビ筆者）、私たちが実際

に生きていく上で必要となる「手段」として、「経済、制度、軍事、交通、政治、法律、農工商等」にかかわる「実際の教育」も不可欠だと短く語るに留まっていた。ただし、「実際の教育」は「経験の教育[158]」とも置き換えられている。これは当時まだ明示されていなかった「労作教育」につながる表現でもあり、小原の「実際の教育」観は、後の「生活の教育、富の教育」と「労作教育」へと分岐する以前の分水嶺として注目される。後年の小原は、新しい「全人教育論」のなかで、精神活動の不可欠の手段として健康を要求するように、「生きるためにパンを要求する[159]」と述べる。小原の生涯をひもとくと、彼は少年時代に貧しさのなかで辛酸をなめている。それゆえ金銭問題への関心が高いように思われるかもしれない。しかし、むしろ彼は富を広義にとらえている。彼は「旺盛なる精神活動」の手段となるものすべてを「富」と捉える。「発明、工夫、交通、政治、外交、産業、軍事、法律等一切に広義に於ける富なる名称を冠します[160]」と。しかし、富自身に意味はなく、それをいかに用いるかが重要となる。このような富の考え方を代表する思想家として、小原は、オックスフォード大学で美術講座の初代教授も務めた「万能の天才[161]」、イギリスの評論家・篤志家ジョン・ラスキン（John Ruskin）を引き合いに出す[162]。さらに「日本教育の恐ろしい欠陥」として、「富のための富、儲けんがための教育」に堕している点を挙げ、「物欲の奴隷たる惨状」と批判している[163]。「生活の教育、富の教育」の課題は、富を世のために生かすような「富の消費の仕方を、富のマコトの意味[164]」を教えることである。

　以上、ごく簡単に小原晩年の新しい「全人教育論」で主張された絶対価値（真善美聖）と手段価値（健富）にかかわる6方面の教育内容を一瞥した。1点だけ注意しておきたいのは、小原はこれらを個々別々に分断された6つの教育とはみていないことである。彼は単に宗教教育、芸術教育、道徳教育などを行うだけでは人間が偏頗になると考えた[165]。6方面の教育を、小原は全人へ向けた有機的連関のなかで捉えているのである。

（5）教育方法論の展開

　八大教育主張講演後の小原評のなかに、彼の方法論の弱さを指摘する声があったことは、すでに指摘した通りである。一方、彼は決して方法論を軽視

していたわけでなく、世の中が根本問題にのみ偏るならば、むしろ方法論を高調するとさえ述べていた。ただし、この講演での小原の立場は明らかに「根本問題」寄りであったことは事実である。講演の最後は「方法論」の見出しで締めくくってはいるものの、「人」の本質に根ざした方法であれば「何でもよい」としている。特定の具体的な方法は提示していない。そして最後に「方法の根本精神」の把捉が重要であり、まず「人」から出発して欲しいと、根本問題の探究を促して終わる[166]。しかし約半世紀後の新しい「全人教育論」においては、新たな展開がみられる。それは「労作教育」の登場である。

　労作教育という言葉は、小原の価値体系図のどこにもみられない。しかし、「実に教育の根本は労作教育にあります[167]」、「労作教育は実に、聖育、知育、徳育、美育、生産教育、健康教育の綜合全一なのであります[168]」と彼は高調する。6方面の教育がまさに有機的に連関する知行合一の優れた実践方法が、この労作教育なのである。小原は当初、命名に苦労したようである。『玉川塾の教育』（玉川学園出版部、1930年）によれば、彼は「体験の教育」や「体得の教育」なども面白いと思ったが、「働くことは万人の喜びであり、誇りであり、義務であると思う私は、『労』の字も使いたい[169]」（傍点筆者）と考え、「『作』は作業の作ではなくて、創作の作にしたい[170]」（傍点筆者）と記している。小原の「労作」観がここに端的に示されている。「労」は確かに働くこと、労働と関連はしている。しかし、単に労働することではなく、それを彼は創作の意味にしたいと述べているのである。しかし、労作教育に対して「労働搾取だ[171]」といって反対する人もいたようである。後年の新しい「全人教育論」で、小原は「働くことは万人の喜びであり」の箇所を「労しむことは万人の喜びであり」（傍点筆者）に変えている[172]。労作において重要なことは、東岸克好が指摘するように「わが事としての目的活動[173]」になり得るか否かであろう。「わが事として」という当事者意識、「百見は一労作に如かない[174]」といった身体性の重視、そして創作へつながる目的活動か否かが、労作になり得るか否かの試金石と考えらえる。

　労作の場面は特定の場所、分野に限定されない。彼は『玉川塾の教育』において、ヨハン・ハインリヒ・ペスタロッチー（Johann Heinrich Pestalozzi）

の3H（Head、Heart、Hand）に関連し「頭で働くか手で働くか、足で働くか胸で働くか、ペンか、鋤か、ハンマーか、ソロバンか[175]」と記している。労作の場面は多様である。彼は「学習の労作化[176]」についても語り、晩年の新しい「全人教育論」では「多方面の労作場面」として「自由研究」も挙げられている[177]。小原が玉川学園で取り組んできた「自由研究」は、今日世間一般でイメージされるような浅薄なものではない。玉川学園小学部による『自由研究の實際』（玉川出版部、1947年）によれば、自由研究がまず大切にしているのは「凡ては私からであるという教育の第一原理である自発活動[178]」である。研究問題の選択も、科目区分にとらわれず、子供自らが直接選ぶことが大切にされた。教師に求められていたのも、子供にもっとも効果的能率的な方法を教えることなどではなく、むしろ子供自らが工夫し創造できるような援助を与えることであった[179]。「自己らしいものを自己らしく」発揮することを願う小原の全人教育思想が、ここに明瞭にあらわれている。「学校も、ホントに、みなが喜ぶほどの種類の労作場面を用意してやるべきだと思うのです[180]」との小原の主張は、多様性や個別最適化が求められる現代において益々重要なメッセージとなろう。

第4節　「ホントの教育」を求めて

　小原は八大教育主張講演を終えた2年後、『理想の学校』（内外出版株式会社、1924年）のなかで「『八大教育』の何のと大ゲサに吹聴されたり広告された[181]」当時を振り返り、「私の講演の速記録位を見て、あれが私の教育論の全部かのように思って批判」されたと述べた上で、「『全人教育』とは、私の教育論の全体ではないのです[182]」、「何とも名のつけられない、ただホントの教育より外に何もないのです[183]」と反論している。小原は偏った教育を批判し、「真実の教育」を表現するために「全人教育」という言葉を選んで講演に臨んだ。講演のなかで彼は、自らの「全人教育」の主張もまた偏った教育のように誤解される危険性を自覚しつつ、「無主義の主義」、「名は何でもよい」とさえ述べていたのであった。まさに、この「何とも名のつけられない、ただホントの教育」の追求は、その後、玉川学園の実践のなかで展開

していった。学園には「教育十二信条」（全人教育、個性尊重、自学自律、能率高き教育、学的根拠に立てる教育、自然の尊重、師弟間の温情、労作教育、反対の合一、第二里行者と人生の開拓者、24時間の教育、国際教育）があるが[184]、これらはいずれも小原が実践とともに把捉していった「ホントの教育」、「真実の教育」を捉えるパースペクティブ（観点）とみることができる。

　晩年の小原は「全人教育」について、どのように語っているだろうか。彼は1973（昭和48）年8月、東京で開催された「世界教育連盟（World Education Fellowship: WEF）」主催の国際会議、「世界新教育会議」において、「師道」と題する講演を行った。この連盟は1921年に「新教育連盟（New Education Fellowship: NEF）」として創設され、世界の新教育運動を牽引してきた国際的な組織である。当時日本支部（「世界教育日本協会」、現在の「世界新教育学会」）の会長を務めていた小原は、8月13日、最後の講演者として、世界中から集まった教育理論家・実践家を前に、あらためて「全人教育」について語り、「教師は『全人』であらねばなりません[185]」と「全人的理想の教師[186]」論を展開した。そして自らの教職人生を振り返り、「私は60年たって、私の全人教育は正しかった、間違って居なかったと、つくづく感謝して居ます[187]」と総括している。

　小原國芳が「全人教育」を提唱して100年をむかえた。21世紀を生きる私たちの現前には、「誰一人取り残さない」世界の実現を目指すSDGs（持続可能な開発目標）や人間中心の未来社会（Society 5.0）へ向けた取り組みなど、新たな課題が次々と立ち現れている。教育界でも「誰一人取り残すことのない、公正に個別最適化された学び」の実現が求められている。新型コロナウイルス感染症の世界的大流行という未曽有の事態に遭遇し、先行き不安定な時代（VUCA時代）を生きる私たちにとって、あの「変化の激しいこれからの社会を［生きる力］」の育成を掲げた日本の教育は今、ますますその重みを増している。一人一人が真に「自己らしいものを自己らしく」発揮することが自他の真の「幸福」へつながると確信し、「真実の教育」、「ホントの教育」を求め続けた小原國芳の思想と実践の軌跡は、これからも私たちの羅針盤として、また帰還すべき教育の原点として生き続けるであろう。

注

1) 小原國芳「全人教育論」樋口長市・河野清丸・手塚岸衛・千葉命吉・稲毛金七・及川平治・小原國芳・片上伸『八大教育主張』大日本学術協会、1921年、308頁。

2) 同上、311頁。

3) たとえばインターネットで「全人教育」を検索してみれば、容易にこのことが確認できる。小原芳明は「『全人教育』を教育方針として掲げている学校は、公立と私立あわせて一、七〇〇校ほどにもなるそうです」と述べている（小原芳明『教育の使命』玉川大学出版部、2019年、17頁）。

4) 中央教育審議会「21世紀を展望した我が国の教育の在り方について──子供に［生きる力］と［ゆとり］を（第一次答申）」1996年（https://www.mext.go.jp/b_menu/shingi/chuuou/toushin/960701e.htm、最終閲覧日：2020年10月21日）。

5) 小原芳明『教育の使命』玉川大学出版部、2019年、17頁。

6) 小原國芳「全人教育論」『小原國芳全集33　全人教育論・宗教教育論・師道』玉川大学出版部、1975年、6頁。

7) 同上、6-7頁。

8) 同上、6頁。

9) 小原國芳「全人教育論」樋口長市他『八大教育主張』大日本学術協会、1921年、305-370頁。

10) 小原（鯵坂）國芳「全人教育」『教育問題研究』第19号、1921年、1-53頁。

11) 同上、3頁。

12) 尼子止水・真行寺朗・岡田怡川・滝沢北州共編『八大教育批判』大日本学術協会、1923年。

13) 小原國芳「全人教育論」小原國芳他『八大教育主張』玉川大学出版部、1976年、253-295頁。

14) 小原國芳「全人教育論」『小原國芳全集33　全人教育論・宗教教育論・師道』玉川大学出版部、1975年、6頁。

15) 小原國芳『全人教育論』玉川大学出版部、1969年、183頁。

16) 小原國芳『教育の根本問題としての哲学』イデア書院、1923年参照。本書はその後、『小原國芳全集4　教育の根本問題としての哲学』（玉川学園大学出版部、1954年）として再版されている。

17) 小原國芳「改版するに際して」『全人教育論』玉川大学出版部、1969年（9刷、1972年）、4頁参照。

18)「全人教育論」（1969年）とする表記法は、書誌情報の版表示に基づく。しかし、それのみならず、小原晩年の新しい「全人教育論」が初出した歴史的な年を銘記する意味でも用いている。土山牧民も『小原國芳選集3　全人教育論・思想問題と教育』（玉川大学出版部、1980年）の「解題」で、掲載される「改訂増補版」について「此の度の、「小原國芳選集」に加えられる『全人教育論』は、昭和四十四年（一九六九）即ち、小原國芳の極く晩年の作である」と、同様の表記法を使用している（土山牧民「解題」小原國芳『小原國芳選集3　全人教育論・思想問題と教育』玉川大学出版部、1980年、119頁）。

19) 小原國芳『全人教育論』改版、玉川大学出版部、1994年。

20) 岡田陽「改版に際して──学生諸君へ」小原國芳『全人教育論』改版、玉川大学出版部、1994年、183頁。

21) 小原國芳著、小原芳明監修、ダグラス・トレルファ英訳、*Kuniyoshi Obara's Theory of Zenjin Education*（『英日対訳全人教育論』）玉川大学出版部、2003年、7頁。

22) 同上、137頁。

23) Tsuchiyama, B., *Kuniyoshi Obara and the Concept of "The Whole Man"*, Tokyo: Tamagawa University Press, 1979; F. Ehmcke, *Die Erziehungsphilosophie von Obara Kniyoshi. Dargestellt an der "Erziehung des ganzen Menschen". Ein Beitrag zur Erziehung in Japan*, Mitteilungen der Gesellschaft für Natur- und Völkerkunde Ostasiens (OAG) Band LXXII, Hamburg 1979.

24) たとえば、橋本美保・田中智志編著『大正新教育の思想——生命の躍動』東信堂、2015年。H. Sakuma, "Kuniyoshi Obara's *Zenjin education at Tamagawa Gakuen*". Y. Yamasaki and H. Kuno (ed.), *Educational Progressivism, Cultural Encounters and Reform in Japan*, London& New York: Routledge, 2017, pp. 93-108. K. Obara, "West Meets East. A Well-Rounded Education versus an Angular Education in Japan". In: *Espacio, Tiempo y Educación*, vol. 5, 2018, pp. 101-122.

25) 『聖書　聖書協会共同訳』日本聖書協会、2018年、（新約聖書）15頁。

26) 橋本美保・田中智志編著『大正新教育の思想——生命の躍動』東信堂、2015年、165頁。

27) 吉田熊次「八種の教育主張について」『教育学術界』第44巻第1号、1921年、4頁。

28) 講演会の広告には「各講演者の主張する所を聴いて、然る後大に質疑討究に時間を費し、極力其の長短を攻究せんと欲す」と書かれている。その他、日中の見学と討論終結後の余興の予告も記されている（『教育学術界』第43巻第3号、1921年、折込広告、および『学校教育』第8巻第96号、1921年、折込広告参照）。

29) 同上。

30) ただし広告で発表者は「鯵坂國芳」と表示されている。講演当日の名前が小原だったため、別人ではとの戸惑いもみられた。たとえば猿木興平は「私は前から鯵坂先生の御話を聞きたいと思って居た所が小原さんと変わって居られましたので之は人違ったか知らんと思って落胆した所が図らずも先生の御活発なる講演を聞きまして非常に喜びました」と述べている（猿木興平「第五討論」『教育学術界』第44巻第1号、1921年、80頁）。

31) 『教育学術界』第43巻第2号、1921年、261頁。

32) 小原國芳「全人教育論」樋口長市他『八大教育主張』大日本学術協会、1921年、308-309頁。

33) 樋口長市他『八大教育主張』大日本学術協会、1921年参照。

34) 橋本美保・田中智志編著『大正新教育の思想——生命の躍動』東信堂、2015年、166頁。ただし、8月8日に実際何人集まったのか、正確なところは不明である。

35) 風塵子「教育学術研究大会奇録」『教育学術界』第44巻第1号、1921年、216頁。

36) 橋本美保によれば、風塵子は「尼子から記録係を任された佐藤浩悠とみられる」（橋本美保「八大教育主張講演の歴史的意義」『東京学芸大学紀要総合教育科学系』第66巻第1号、2015年2月、62頁）。

37) 風塵子「教育学術研究大会奇録」『教育学術界』第44巻第1号、1921年、216頁。

38) 波多野精一が京都帝国大学に赴任したのは、小原が最終学年にあたる3年生の時であった（当時は3年制）。小原はすでに卒業論文に取り組んでいた。後年、彼は当時を述懐して、「ご指導を受けたわずか一年の間に、私は〔波多野〕先生の偉大さに、すっかり打たれてしまいました」と述べている（小原國芳『教育一路』日本経済新聞社、1976年、64頁、〔　〕は筆者が補足）。小原は自らを波多野の「弟子」と公言している（小原國芳「波多野先生の思い出」松村克己・小原国芳編『追憶の波多野精一先生』玉川大学出版部、1970年、226-227頁）。

39) 土山牧民「解題」小原國芳『小原國芳選集3　全人教育論・思想問題と教育』玉川大学出版部、1980年、120頁。

40) 鰺坂國芳『教育の根本問題としての宗教』集成社、1919 年、74 頁。

41) 同上、82 頁。

42) 同上、83 頁。

43) 同上、100 頁。

44) 同上、254 頁。

45) 同上、282 頁。

46) 同上、293 頁。

47) 同上、293 頁。

48) 小原國芳『師道』玉川大学出版部、1974 年、48 頁。

49) 広島高等師範学校教育研究会編集『学校教育』第 8 巻第 96 号、1921 年、折込広告参照。

50) 尼子止水「巻頭之辞」『教育学術界』第 44 巻第 1 号、1921 年、1 頁。

51) 吉田熊次「八種の教育主張について」『教育学術界』第 44 巻第 1 号、1921 年、4 頁。

52) 小原國芳「全人教育論」樋口長市他『八大教育主張』大日本学術協会、1921 年、329 頁。

53) 同上、308 頁。

54) 渡邊政盛「第七討論」『教育学術界』第 44 巻第 1 号、1921 年、81 頁。同様に越川彌榮「教育学術研究大会所感……革命的講習会に臨みて」『教育学術界』第 44 巻第 1 号、1921 年、113 頁。

55) 小原國芳「全人教育論」樋口長市他『八大教育主張』大日本学術協会、1921 年、324 頁。

56) 同上、313 頁。

57) 同上、313 頁。

58) 尼子止水「巻頭之辞」『教育学術界』第 44 巻第 1 号、1921 年、1 頁。

59) 小原國芳「全人教育論」樋口長市他『八大教育主張』大日本学術協会、1921 年、309 頁。

60) 同上、308-309 頁。

61) 同上、322 頁。

62) 同上、323 頁。

63) 同上、323-324 頁。

64) 同上、325 頁。

65) 同上、337-338 頁。

66) 同上、338 頁。

67) たとえば小林古蹊は、小原の講演について「私はあの講演に於てあの情熱に溶かれて居たのであったろう」、「私はただ愉快に、胸をおどらして詩人の詩をきいていたのであったんだろう」と回想している（小林古蹊「教育学術研究大会にのぞみて」『教育学術界』第 44 巻第 1 号、1921 年、145 頁）。井上卓美は「……会員を感激せしめられ、連日の聴講に飽いてゐた精神を刷新せられた」と述べている（井上卓美「教育学術研究大会所感」『教育学術界』第 44 巻第 1 号、1921 年、165 頁）。なお、小原の「全人教育論」における「語り」に関する研究として、皇紀夫「小原國芳『全人教育論』のレトリック」（『臨床教育人間学』第 4 号、2002 年、5-19 頁）が挙げられる。皇は「語りにおける言葉の仕掛け（レトリック）とそれを効果的に演出して聞き手を楽しませる技法、つまり聞き手に『美妙の感覚を起さしむ』『美術』という新しい口術のジャンルを教育の世界に開いて見せた人物として、あるいは教育言説の戦略的技法（Attitude、方法）を創作した人物として、あるいはまた、通俗教育と呼ばれてきた分野の先駆者として、小原を再解釈すること」を提示している（同上、17 頁）。

68) 渡部盛政「教育学術研究大会所感——所謂新進諸家講演の批評」『教育学術界』第 44 巻第 1 号、

1921 年、120 頁。

69）小原國芳「全人教育論」樋口長市他『八大教育主張』大日本学術協会、1921 年、310 頁。

70）同上、350 頁。

71）同上、350 頁。

72）同上、350 頁。

73）同上、369 頁。

74）小原（鰺坂）國芳「全人教育」『教育問題研究』第 19 号、1921 年、3 頁。

75）小原國芳「全人教育論」樋口長市他『八大教育主張』大日本学術協会、1921 年、305 頁。

76）渡邊政盛「第七討論」『教育学術界』第 44 巻第 1 号、1921 年、81 頁。

77）この他、講演のなかで小原は、彼が当時勤務していた成城小学校の教育に対して、（教師の
サボタージュや傍観を容認する意味での）児童中心主義や自由主義のレッテルが貼られて
いたとし、それも誤解だと弁明している（小原國芳「全人教育論」樋口長市他『八大教育
主張』大日本学術協会、1921 年、325-326 頁）。

78）小原國芳「全人教育論」樋口長市他『八大教育主張』大日本学術協会、1921 年、330 頁。

79）たとえば『八大教育批判』では、全人教育論の「短所」の「第一」として、「方法論に積極
的新性と妥当性ある見解を示さぬこと」が挙げられている。さらに「根本問題には、見るべく、
聴くべき点がありながら、方法論には、何等氏独自なものがない」と批判されている（尼
子止水他共編『八大教育批判』大日本学術協会、1923 年、461 頁）。

80）「私立成城小学校創設趣意」によれば、「我校の希望理想」として、「一、個性尊重の教育　附、
能率の高い教育」、「二、自然と親しむ教育　附、剛健不撓の意志の教育」、「三、心情の教
育　附、鑑賞の教育」、そして「科学的研究を基とする教育」が挙げられている（澤柳政太
郎『新装版　教育論抄』新潮社、2015 年、161-165 頁参照）。

81）小原國芳『小原國芳全集 29　小原國芳自伝──夢みる人（2）』玉川大学出版部、1963 年、
219 頁。

82）小原國芳「全人教育論」樋口長市他『八大教育主張』大日本学術協会、1921 年、342 頁。

83）同上、342 頁。

84）同上、343 頁。

85）同上、341 頁。

86）同上、342 頁。

87）同上、337 頁。

88）同上、337 頁。なお、近年では "the whole man" よりも "the whole person" が使用され
ている。この点については、次の文献を参照のこと。小原國芳著、小原芳明監修、ダグラス・
トレルファ英訳、*Kuniyoshi Obara's Theory of Zenjin Education*（『英日対訳全人教育論』）
玉 川 大 学 出 版 部、2003 年、17 頁。H. Sakuma, "Kuniyoshi Obara's *Zenjin* education at
Tamagawa Gakuen". Y. Yamasaki and H. Kuno (ed.), *Educational Progressivism, Cultural
Encounters and Reform in Japan*, London& New York: Routledge, 2017, p. 93.

89）高山岩男『教育哲学』玉川大学出版部、1976 年、364 頁。

90）同上、364 頁。

91）同上、366 頁。

92）B. Tsuchiyama, *Kuniyoshi Obara and the Concept of "The Whole Man"*, Tokyo: Tamagawa
University Press, 1979.　土山牧民「全人教育論をどう理解するか」小原哲郎編『全人教育
の手がかり』玉川大学出版部、1985 年、67-69 頁参照。

93）三井浩『愛の場所──教育哲学序説』玉川大学出版部、1974 年、152 頁。

94）同上、152 頁。

95）小原國芳『師道』玉川大学出版部、1974 年、47-48 頁。

96）小原國芳「全人教育論」『小原國芳全集 33　全人教育論・宗教教育論・師道』玉川大学出版部、1975 年、7 頁。

97）同上、13 頁。

98）小原國芳『全人教育論』改版、玉川大学出版部、1994 年、10 頁。

99）鰺坂國芳『教育の根本問題としての宗教』集成社、1919 年、293 頁。

100）同上、29-30 頁。

101）同上、294 頁。

102）小原國芳「全人教育論」『小原國芳全集 33　全人教育論・宗教教育論・師道』玉川大学出版部、1975 年、26 頁。

103）同上、106 頁。

104）小原國芳「全人教育論」樋口長市他『八大教育主張』大日本学術協会、1921 年、343 頁。

105）小原國芳「全人教育論」『小原國芳全集 33　全人教育論・宗教教育論・師道』玉川大学出版部、1975 年、17 頁。

106）同上、17 頁。

107）同上、101 頁。

108）同上、101 頁。

109）同上、102 頁。

110）同上、102 頁。

111）小原は「全人教育論」の中で「反対の合一」を語る際、ジョルダーノ・ブルーノ（Giordano Bruno）、ヘラクレイトス（Herakleitos）、ゲオルク・ヴィルヘルム・フリードリヒ・ヘーゲル（Georg Wilhelm Friedrich Hegel）などを引き合いに出しているが、そこで彼は特に各思想内容を厳密に追及しているわけではない。

112）小原國芳「全人教育論」『小原國芳全集 33　全人教育論・宗教教育論・師道』玉川大学出版部、1975 年、100 頁。なお、小原は既に『教育の根本問題としての宗教』（1919 年）の中で「反対の合一」を取り上げており、八大教育主張講演（1921 年）の中でも語っている（鰺坂國芳『教育の根本問題としての宗教』集成社、1919 年、345 頁。小原國芳「全人教育論」樋口長市他『八大教育主張』大日本学術協会、1921 年、321 頁）。

113）同上、99-106 頁参照。

114）小原が八大教育主張講演（1921 年）で語った「反対の合一」について、「ニコラウス・クザーヌス（Nicolaus Cusanus 1401-1464）が用いた言葉であり、また矛盾対立する二項が合一することではなく、有限者の人の観点からは、たとえば『悪』と見えるが、無限者の神においては『善』である、という『対極の一致』である。人と神は同一の地平に位置していないので、coincidentia oppositorum は、小原がいうような『対立』『矛盾』ではない。また、小原が求める二元の一元化は、つきつめていえば、人が神になることを求めることであるから、古代ギリシア的に考えるならありうるが、キリスト教的に考えるならありえない。それは、神をまったく畏れない涜神行為である。小原は『対極の一致』をまったく理解していない」と批判されている（橋本美保・田中智志「第 5 章　八大教育主張の教育理念──愛に連なる生命」橋本美保・田中智志編著『大正新教育の思想──生命の躍動』東信堂、2015 年、188 頁）。一言だけするなら、小原は確かに「日本キリスト教会（改革派・

長老派）にて受洗した」クリスチャンであった（小針誠「大正新教育運動のパラドックス ——通説の再検討を通じて」『子ども社会研究』第21号、2015年、31頁）。しかし、「反対 の合一」問題を彼は「キリスト教的」コンテクストで捉えたわけではない。この問題は彼 の全人教育論のコンテクストから理解すべきである。たとえばそれは彼の全人教育論におけ る「宗教教育」の主張が、特定宗派教育のコンテクストから離れているのと同様である。「神 をまったく畏れない涜神行為」との批判は当たらない。

115) 鰺坂二夫「反対の合一」『全人教育の手がかり』玉川大学出版部、1985年、23頁。なお、 小原自身、八大教育主張講演（1921年）の中で、「普遍即特殊、個性の中に完全境を有し、 調和の中に個性を有する。これが実在の真相である」（小原國芳「全人教育論」樋口長市他『八 大教育主張』大日本学術協会、1921年、345頁、傍点筆者）と、「個性」、「完全境」そして「調 和」を引き合いに出して、彼の「実在」観を示している。

116) 三井善止「小原國芳の全人教育思想」『全人教育通論Ⅰ・Ⅱ』玉川大学通信教育部、1988年、 75頁。

117) 小原國芳「全人教育論」樋口長市他『八大教育主張』大日本学術協会、1921年、329-330頁。

118) 同上、330頁。

119) 鰺坂國芳「教育の根本問題としての真善美聖」『学校教育』第6巻第67号、1919年、118-127頁。

120) 小原國芳『修身教授の実際　下』集成社、1922年、84頁。

121) 鰺坂國芳『学校劇論』イデア書院、1923年、7頁。小原國芳『教育の根本問題としての哲学』 イデア書院、1923年、498頁。

122) 小原國芳『母のための教育学　上巻』イデア書院、1925年、128-129頁。

123) 小原國芳『小原國芳全集5　母のための教育学』玉川大学出版部、1977年、90頁参照。

124) 小原國芳『全人教育論』玉川大学出版部、1969年、192頁。

125) 小原國芳『全人教育論』玉川大学出版部、1972年、23頁参照。

126) 小原國芳『小原國芳全集33　全人教育論・宗教教育論・師道』玉川大学出版部、19-24頁参照。

127) 小原國芳『小原國芳全集29　小原國芳自伝——夢みる人（2）』玉川大学出版部、1963年、84頁。

128) 小原國芳「全人教育論」樋口長市他『八大教育主張』大日本学術協会、1921年、324頁。

129) 同上、324頁。

130) 小原國芳「全人教育論」『小原國芳全集33　全人教育論・宗教教育論・師道』玉川大学出版 部、1975年、15頁。

131) 同上、24頁。

132) 小原國芳「全人教育論」樋口長市他『八大教育主張』大日本学術協会、1921年、354頁。

133) 小原國芳「全人教育論」『小原國芳全集33　全人教育論・宗教教育論・師道』玉川大学出版 部、1975年、65-66頁。

134) 同上、65頁。

135) 同上、65頁。

136) 小原國芳「全人教育論」樋口長市他『八大教育主張』大日本学術協会、1921年、355頁。

137) 同上、357頁。

138) 小原國芳「全人教育論」『小原國芳全集33　全人教育論・宗教教育論・師道』玉川大学出版 部、1975年、51-55頁。

139) 同上、55-56頁。

140) 鰺坂國芳「学校劇について」『学校教育』第6巻第69号、1919年、48頁。

141) 小原國芳「全人教育論」樋口長市他『八大教育主張』大日本学術協会、1921年、359頁。

142) 同上、360 頁。

143) 小原國芳『学校劇論』イデア書院、1923 年、14 頁。

144) 小原國芳「全人教育論」『小原國芳全集 33　全人教育論・宗教教育論・師道』玉川大学出版部、1975 年、44 頁。

145) 同上、44 頁。

146) 小原國芳『全人教育論』改版、玉川大学出版部、1994 年、46 頁。

147) 小原國芳「全人教育論」樋口長市他『八大教育主張』大日本学術協会、1921 年、362 頁。

148) 鰺坂國芳『教育の根本問題としての宗教』集成社、1919 年、2 頁。

149) 小原國芳「全人教育論」『小原國芳全集 33　全人教育論・宗教教育論・師道』玉川大学出版部、1975 年、38 頁。

150) 同上、34 頁。

151) 同上、36 頁。

152) 同上、43 頁。

153) 小原國芳『師道』玉川大学出版部、1974 年、45-46 頁。

154) 小原國芳「全人教育論」樋口長市他『八大教育主張』大日本学術協会、1921 年、351 頁。

155) 同上、352 頁。

156) 小原國芳「全人教育論」『小原國芳全集 33　全人教育論・宗教教育論・師道』玉川大学出版部、1975 年、76 頁。

157) 同上、76 頁。

158) 小原國芳「全人教育論」樋口長市他『八大教育主張』大日本学術協会、1921 年、365 頁。

159) 小原國芳「全人教育論」『小原國芳全集 33　全人教育論・宗教教育論・師道』玉川大学出版部、1975 年、25 頁。

160) 同上、26 頁。

161) 富士川義之「ターナー擁護者から先駆的なエコロジストへ——ラスキンの生涯と作品」ジョン・ラスキン『この最後の者にも・ごまとゆり』飯塚一郎・木村正身訳、中央公論新社、2008 年、4 頁。

162) ラスキンは富を「われわれが使用することのできる有用なものの所有」(124 頁) と捉え、もっとも裕福な人とは「自分自身の生の機能を極限まで完成させ、その人格と所有物の両方によって、他人の生の上に最も広く役立つ影響力をもっている人をいうのである」(158-159 頁) としている (以上、引用箇所はジョン・ラスキン『この最後の者にも・ごまとゆり』飯塚一郎・木村正身訳、中央公論新社、2008 年より)。

163) 小原國芳「全人教育論」『小原國芳全集 33　全人教育論・宗教教育論・師道』玉川大学出版部、1975 年、93 頁。

164) 同上、94 頁。

165) 同上、30 頁。

166) 小原國芳「全人教育論」樋口長市他『八大教育主張』大日本学術協会、1921 年、369 頁。

167) 小原國芳「全人教育論」『小原國芳全集 33　全人教育論・宗教教育論・師道』玉川大学出版部、1975 年、109 頁。

168) 同上、111 頁。

169) 小原國芳『玉川塾の教育』玉川学園出版部、1930 年、64 頁。

170) 同上、65 頁。なお、新しい「全人教育論」にも同様の記述が登場する、しかし、語尾は「創作の作なのです」に変化している (小原國芳「全人教育論」『小原國芳全集 33　全人教育論・

　　　　宗教教育論・師道』玉川大学出版部、1975 年、109 頁）。

171）小原國芳「全人教育論」『小原國芳全集 33　全人教育論・宗教教育論・師道』玉川大学出版
　　　部、1975 年、111 頁。

172）同上、109 頁。

173）東岸克好「労作教育実践の立場から」小原哲郎編『全人教育の手がかり』玉川大学出版部、
　　　1985 年、213 頁。

174）小原國芳「全人教育論」『小原國芳全集 33　全人教育論・宗教教育論・師道』玉川大学出版
　　　部、1975 年、109 頁。

175）小原國芳『玉川塾の教育』玉川学園出版部、1930 年、64 頁。

176）同上、250 頁。

177）小原國芳「全人教育論」『小原國芳全集 33　全人教育論・宗教教育論・師道』玉川大学出版
　　　部、1975 年、107 頁。

178）玉川小學部『自由研究の實際』玉川出版社、1947 年、9 頁。

179）同上、31-32、44 頁。

180）小原國芳「全人教育論」『小原國芳全集 33　全人教育論・宗教教育論・師道』玉川大学出版
　　　部、1975 年、110 頁。

181）小原國芳『理想の学校』内外出版株式会社、1924 年、1 頁。

182）同上、2 頁。

183）同上、3 頁。

184）玉川学園の教育十二信条の変遷については、次の文献を参照のこと。白栁弘幸「玉川学園
　　　教育十二信条の成立」『全人教育研究センター年報』第 2 号、2016 年、37-46 頁。

185）小原國芳「師道」皇晃之・益井重夫・二見剛史・岩田朝一・大志万準治・中森善治編『世
　　　界新教育会議報告書』世界教育日本協会、1974 年、152 頁。

186）同上、153 頁。

187）同上、157 頁。

第3章

全人教育の普遍妥当性

はじめに

　　純真なる児童観に立ち、進歩せる心理学の指導に基き、認識論の教え
に従い、しかも、国家社会の要求に応じ、以上の大原則を展開せんとせ
ば、そこに教師という個性から来る多少の相違はあろうとも、自ら大体、
相似せる道を辿るべきが当然と思うのです。形の末からの反目や議論で
なくて、根本義からの握手、精神からの協力があり、純真なる教育愛に
立ち返るならば、諸種の形式や法案は自ら一元に帰するのではないかと
すら考えられるのです[1]。

　かつて小原國芳が提唱し、玉川学園創設の根拠とした全人教育も、今や一
般に普及した結果、それを理念等に盛り込んだ学校・大学は多い。たとえば
「全人力、人間性の醸成、そしてあらゆる価値観から自由になり、新たな自
分を構築するという『個』の確立[2]」を、教育の強みとして挙げる大学があ
る。そして、グローバルに通じる「個」を確立するために、対話を通じて世
界基準の全人力を養い、真のリベラルアーツ教育の実践が不可欠とする。そ

の結果、その大学は学生に1年間の留学や寮生活を義務付け、卒業時には半数の学生がTOEIC900点を取得しており、就職率100％を掲げ、タイムズ・ハイヤー・エデュケーションによる世界大学ランキング日本版で注目されるに至った。

　しかし、これが本来の全人教育のあり方だろうか。「世界基準の全人力」という言葉からは、何か特定の尺度で測定が可能という印象を受ける。世にあふれる様々な能力は、総じて人為的（時として恣意的、作為的）に作られた尺度に依拠した達成度を示すことで、その者にとっていわば勲章のような機能を果たす。果たして、全人教育を通して育まれるものは、権威主義的象徴ともなり得る可視化された「力」や「資格」なのか。

　本学の根幹を成す全人教育とその実践に鑑みると、全人力という言葉は的を射た表現とは考えにくい。同様に、「世界基準の全人力」は、1年間の留学や寮生活、卒業時の「英語」の試験のスコアによって担保・保証されるものだろうか。むしろ、「世界基準」を英語という言語で推し量ろうとする姿勢からは、特定の国・地域あるいは団体（主に欧米）によってのみ承認、認証されたいという印象が払拭できず、如何なる国・地域においても当然のように享受される「普遍妥当性[3]」には到底至らない。

　そこで、古代ギリシアで生まれたエンキュクリオスパイデイア[4]、アルテスリベラレス[5]、セプテムアルテスリベラレス（セブンリベラルアーツ）[6]、そして、比較的現代において多用されているウェルラウンデッド教育[7]で挙げられる科目構成と小原が提唱する科目の趣旨とに見られる共通点に着目し、教育の理想を突き詰めると全人教育に至り、結果、全人教育こそが普遍妥当性を有する教育であることを論じたい。

第1節　リベラルアーツの歴史的展開

（1）エンキュクリオスパイデイア

　全人教育論の系譜を辿ると、その発祥の大本は古代ギリシアの自由人の知、つまり、知を愛し求める者[8]たちの営みにまで遡る[9]。古代ギリシアの自由人の教育[10]は、「健全な精神は健全な身体に宿る」という格言にみられるよ

うに、心と身体の調和と均衡を目指したカロカガティア（善美なる者[11]）という理念に基づき、普遍的な知識ばかりでなく人間の徳を育むことを目的とした、知育・徳育・体育を通した人間教育、人格教育を意味した。その具体的な課程は文芸（文法）、修辞（弁論）、弁証、体育、算術、幾何、音楽、天文などを取り込みつつ、ヘレニズム期には全人教育的な学環として広まった。この時期に、自由人の教育をエンキュクリオスパイデイアと言う呼称が生まれたとされる。

エンキュクリオスパイデイアのパイデイアは、パイデウエイン[12]という動詞から派生した名詞であり、動詞形には、①「子供を育てる」、②「教えて訓練する、教育する」、③「正しくする、矯正する」という意味があり、教育学[13]の語源でもある。そして、エンキュクリオスという形容詞は、エンキュクロス[14]という形容詞と同様に、①「循環的な、円形」、②「円環運動、周期的な」という意味がある。すなわち、エンキュクリオスパイデイアとは、教養あるいは学知の円環、つまり、円環的に配列された科目による人間教育が基本的な意味とされる。

その後、ローマにおけるストア派の学者らを中心に、ギリシア的なもの（エンキュクリオスパイデイア）からラテン的なものへと転換する道程において、共和制ローマの学者たちが使っていた「自由な学芸」のラテン語であるアルテスリベラレスが、リベラルアーツという名称の始まりとされる。共和制ローマ末期に活躍したマルクス・トゥッリウス・キケロ（Marcus Tullius Cicero）は、心の涵養と徳の形成に欠かせない学芸の重要性を、自由人にふさわしい諸学芸[15]や自由学問[16]といった表現を用いながら指摘している。ちなみに、キケロは、人間的教養[17]を養うために弁論、弁証、文法の三科[18]と算術、音楽、幾何、天文の四科[19]を具体的な科目として挙げていた。また、同時期に活躍した建築家マルクス・ウィトルウィウス・ポッリオ（Marcus Vitruvius Polio）は、建築家が建築に加えて学ぶ必要のある学科目として文法、絵画、幾何、算術、歴史、哲学、音楽、医術、法律、天文学を挙げている。

いずれにしても、総合的な知の錬成、総合性の協和がこの時代は重視されていたことがうかがえよう。ローマに生まれたリベラルアーツ[20]は、帝国の繁栄とともにあった自由を象徴するものであり、工芸、美術など広範な芸

術、建築、土木、医術、法賢慮といった実学を含めた総合学術であった。職業的技能を養う学びや教育と区別して、実用性から自由になった学芸という解釈によってリベラルアーツは語られることがあるが、古代ギリシアから共和制ローマにおける発展の経緯を見れば、実学を、知を愛し求める一線に連ねる自由こそが、もともとの概念の本懐といえる。

（2）セブンリベラルアーツ

　これから500年の時が流れた西ローマ帝国滅亡直後、マルティアヌス・カペラ（Martianus Capella）は『メルクリウスとフィロロギアの結婚、そしてセブンリベラルアーツ九分冊[21]』を世に送り出す。この著書のなかで挙げられた科目が、文法、修辞、論理、数論、幾何、天文、音楽の七科であり、ここにセプテムアルテスリベラレス（自由七科）と呼ばれるリベラルアーツの構成が具体的に示された。カペラによって規定された7つの学科構成は、かつてのラテンリベラルアーツに替わり、キリスト教のもとでの文化形成という色彩が強くなったセブンリベラルアーツの誕生を宣することになった。

　それから200年程は、学問的に取り立てて創造的な発展はみられず、8〜9世紀にかけてのフランク王カール大帝によるカロリングルネッサンス期には政策的な学問振興がなされ、セブンリベラルアーツはあらゆる学問に至るための教育の根幹として確固たる位置付けを得ることになった。と同時に、セブンリベラルアーツの形式化と固定化にもつながった時期でもある。その後に続くルネサンス運動の高まりと大学の誕生が、今日的なリベラルアーツへと変容を促すことになる。

第2節　今日におけるリベラルアーツ教育

（1）教養としてのリベラルアーツ

　これまで古代ギリシアから中世に掛けてのリベラルアーツの歴史的展開を概観したが、なぜリベラルアーツが一般教育、教養教育という今日的意味を有するに至ったか、もう少し説明を加えておこう。ラテン語で自由な学芸を意味したアルテスリベラレスは、エンキュクリオスパイデイアをさらにその

語源としていることは上述の通りである。エンキュクリオスパイデイアは学知（教養）の円環という直接的な意味合いを有するが、円環という表現は、その後様々なソフィスト（知恵ある者）の解釈を経て、「一般的な、普遍的な」という意味を与えられた。ここに、エンキュクリオスパイデイアを一般教育、教養教育と捉える考え方が成立する。そして、技能教育、専門教育と一般教育、教養教育との対比・対立の図式へと至るのである。エンキュクリオスに与えられた普遍的という言葉は、専門化のように特殊化された人間を想定しておらず、専門を意味するプロフェッショナルを目指すための教育とはその目的も目標も異なる。

（2）アメリカ型リベラルアーツ教育

　それでは、リベラルアーツを一般教育とする考え方は、教育の現場ではどのように具体化されているだろうか。本節では、アメリカ合衆国（以下、アメリカ）におけるリベラルアーツ教育を例として取り上げて検討してみたい。もちろん、アメリカ型リベラルアーツ教育とはいえ、その実態は多種多様であるため、比較的頻繁に例示されるものを紹介する。

　基本コンセプトとして「集中（1つの専門分野、主専攻）と分散（広く学ぶ一般科目あるいは一般教育、副専攻）」を掲げ、主専攻、副専攻、選択科目、一般教育で大学の卒業要件を構成とする場合が多い。

　また、アメリカ型リベラルアーツ教育の学修スタイルは、次の特性を有したものである。

　①学生の自己教育（主体的学修）とカリキュラムの選択構造
　②早期に専門を固定しない
　③専門科目の教養化（専門科目も教養の一部とする）
　④教育の社会性（一般教育で表現される）
　⑤批判的思考力・課題発見・解決力の育成等、知的営みのための基礎能力の育成
　⑥キャンパスライフ等の潜在的学修課程（全寮生活等を含む）

　特に、アメリカ型リベラルアーツ教育では、入学時には専攻が決められていないことがその特徴である。通常は２年次の間に専攻を決めるが、この専攻の決定は、専門学部における専門の決定とは意味が異なる。どちらかといえば、学修の過程における専門選択、つまり、「取り敢えずある専門分野を選択して深く学んでみる」という意味での選択[22]である。また、専門学部教育では学修の内容に重点が置かれるが、リベラルアーツ教育では学修内容よりは学修主体の育成が重視される。この考え方は、フンボルト大学理念にその源があるとされており、「学問は常に未だ完全に解決されていない『問題』として、たえず研究されつつあるものとして扱う」こと、そして、「教員も学生も共に自学自習することを学ぶ」ことが謳われている[23]。

　アメリカ型リベラルアーツ教育における専攻（学科専攻）の主要な狙いは、学生が何か１つの学問的思考様式を身に付け、自身の知的活動に自信を持つこと、そのために、学問との一体感を学生に体験させる機会を与え、深い学修を提供することにある。換言すれば、専攻学問の知識探求方法の基礎訓練を受けることで人間の知的営み（自由人の知）への本質的参加を促し、知識人としての自己認識を確立することが、アメリカ型リベラルアーツ教育における専門学修の位置付けである。専門科目の学修が、専門教育のためではなく、人格の形成を目的としており、これが、古代ギリシア、共和制ローマに生まれたリベラルアーツに通底する要素とも考えられよう。

　さらに、アメリカ型リベラルアーツ教育における一般教育として、多くの大学では、数学、物理、生物、外国語、文学、古典、西洋政治史、哲学史、文化史、国家の基礎と原理（公民などの社会科学系科目）に該当する科目の履修を設定している。この科目設定は、セブンリベラルアーツが発案された８〜９世紀頃から、変化がみられる。かつて含まれていた音楽（芸術）は文学や古典に取って代わられている場合が少なくはない。また、宗教（特にキリスト教）系の大学では、一般教育に宗教が含まれることもあり、これが第１節で触れたルネサンス運動やその当時の大学の誕生によってもたらされた今日的リベラルアーツの変容の１つの帰結である。

第3節　ウェルラウンデッド教育

（1）ウェルラウンデッド教育という新しい概念

　近年、アメリカでは、ウェルラウンデッド教育という言葉を用いてアメリカ型リベラルアーツ教育の新しい形態を表すことがある。その動きは、どのような背景から生まれたのだろうか。たとえば、アメリカの高等学校では、これまで国語、数学、科学、外国語、公民、経済、歴史、地理、芸術を主要科目としているが、これらをリベラルアーツ科目あるいはリベラルアーツカリキュラムとは認識していない。日本と同様、主要科目は一般的な科目構成つまり「誰しもが当たり前に学ぶべき科目」として浸透している。かつて謳われた知を愛し求める者たちのリベラルアーツは、自由七科という概念形成の過程を経て、現代では、特定の科目に限定した学びの枠組みとなっているのである。

　現状でもリベラルアーツ的な要素を反映した一般教育を受けているにもかかわらず、アメリカにおける就学前、初等、中等教育が芳しくない実態に鑑みて、2015（平成27）年12月10日、オバマ大統領（当時）は、民主・共和両党によって提案された「すべての生徒が成功する法[24]」に署名し、同法は連邦教育法として成立した。この法律の主軸は、初等中等教育における教育上恵まれない地域（学区）、優秀教員や校長の養成・研修、英語学習者、就学前教育などへの財政支援が盛り込まれていたが、同時に、ウェルラウンデッド教育カリキュラムの徹底が定められている。これにより、学校では、かつての主要科目に加え、時代の趨勢や潮流を反映して、読書、言語技術、随筆、技術、工学、コンピュータ科学、キャリア教育、技能教育、保健、体育といった科目を加えることで、生徒にとっての豊かな教育経験を実現しようと試みている。着目すべきは、古代ギリシアより綿々と続いて来たリベラルアーツという教育に、今後の不確実性の高い時代を生き抜くために必要な知識・技能の獲得という要素が加味されている点である。

（2）ハーバード大学が求める教育

　今後を生き抜くために必要な知識・技能の獲得と同時に、幅広く学ぶとい

うことは、この世界に存在する様々な学問（分野）について満遍なく学ぶことを意味しており、その思想をハーバード大学は志願者に向けたメッセージとして明示している。

　　高校教育とは、次の段階にある教育やその後の職業に向けた準備のためだけにあるものではなく、あらゆる分野における将来の学びの機会を無駄にしないよう備えるためにあります。特定の技能や情報を獲得すると同時に、あなたは、世界とそこに存在する数多の可能性に対する大局的な物の見方をも獲得しなくてはならないのです[25]。

　このメッセージは、早い段階で学びの可能性を限定することや、進学や就職のためだけに高等教育を位置付けてしまうことへの警鐘とも捉えられよう。裏を返せば、大学での学びもまた、可能性を模索するためにあるという大学側の思想が見えてくる。自由な学芸を忠実に体現するためには、最早定型となってしまった既存のリベラルアーツ教育では足らず、あえて「幅広い」と冠したとも推察される。

　さて、上記メッセージに続けて、ハーバード大学は、大学におけるリベラルアーツ教育の強い基礎を築くために、高校で履修を薦める科目一覧を提示している[26]。

①４年間の国語を通した世界古典文学の精読・多読
②４年間の外国語（１言語）
③２年間以上（３年間が望ましい）の歴史（アメリカ史、西洋史、そして１つの上級レベル科目）
④４年間の数学
⑤４年間の科学（物理、化学、生物、そしてその内１つの上級レベル科目）

　また、あくまでも大学入学後の科目履修において直接的に寄与することを示唆するデータを保有するため推奨科目として列記された上記科目以外にも、たとえば体育、美術や音楽といった科目についても同様に重視してい

ることが示されている。列記されなかった理由は大学が不要と判断したからではない点が強調されていることからも、ハーバード大学が高校生に求めるウェルラウンデッド教育とはリベラルアーツ教育と同義ではありながらも、更にその枠組みを拡げるという意図の込められた呼称と考えられるだろう。

第4節　小原國芳の考える教科

　それでは、小原は、全人教育を体現するためにどういった科目構成及び各科目の位置付けを考えていただろうか。ここでは、「教育改造論」（『小原國芳選集4　教育改造論・自由教育論』玉川大学出版部、1980年）を手がかりに、小原の各科に対する考えを紹介しよう。

　まず、修身についてだが、小原にとって修身は道徳と同義であり、「偏狭な国民道徳ことに愛国心を絶対に排斥する[27]」と述べているように、当時日本の学校に導入されていた修身とは内容が異なる点に注意が必要である。小原は、修身（道徳）を通して、根本問題の研究を提唱している。たとえば、「善とは、悪とは」といった道徳の本質を理解することが不可欠としている。また、授業で取り上げる徳目の解釈が的確であること、そのために道徳判断力の養成を重視している。これは、「自ら道徳を発見し道徳を創作し得る[28]」能力の養成を考えていた小原にとって、道徳は文明の推移とともに変容するものであり、したがって、古い道徳の型に詰め込むのではなく、子供たちの内心生活に触れ、教員と子供双方が同じ精神生活を共有することを求めている。

　次に、国語について、小原は、言語習得のみに重きを置くことを忌避し、文学としての価値、芸術的な意味を有したものとして考えている。特に国語科の教授に関しては、「文学の意味、文の構想、作者の個性、作中の人物の批判、文芸批評論、文の鑑賞[29]」に注力すべく、認識論の知識を求めている。この認識論の深い知識がないまま、形式や内容を議論させることは、三者三様の解釈を生むだけであり、本当の吟味、議論には到達できないとしている。こうした理由に加えて、語学は学問の武器という信条からも、国語力を重視している。

　実は、国語に関する主張に連動して、小原は外国文学とりわけ外国古典文

学の研究を推奨している。これは、「外国語を知らぬ人は母国語の理解はできない[30]」というゲーテの言葉を引用して外国語の素養を要求していることに依拠したものである。国内の現代文学をより深く論じるためには、その比較対象となる国外の文学を研究して得た知見が求められるという考えである。また、それを担当する外国人教員は「語学のためよりは、世界心の養成を主[31]」にするべき、と述べている。

　算術（算数・数学）に関しては、日常の計算に習熟する以上に、思考力の錬磨を主にすることを提案している。これは、プラグマティックな捉え方を浅薄と断じており、算数・数学の知識を、目先の結果を優先するような損得勘定に活用することに強く反対していることから明らかである。真理探究の思索生活が必要であり、小原にとっては創作能力や思考推究力が啓培されていれば、日常の計算は十分に可能とされた。しかし、日常計算の習熟を疎かにはせず、これに思考力の錬磨を加算することを提唱している点には留意されたい。あくまでも簡便法を教え込むのではなく、たとえば定理定則についても、実際に子供自身に発見創作させる機会を求めている。

　理科に関しても、小原はプラグマティックな目的で実施されている状況を憂えている。理科研究の対象が自然であることに触れて、その不可思議さや神秘性を探求することを求めている。理科の目的として、真理のための真理の追究を挙げている。同時に、科学の追究に付随して必要とされる動植物の犠牲について言及するなかで、科学を通して人間のおごりを戒め、犠牲となる実験用動植物に対する感謝、慈悲の重要性について授業を通して説くことを求めている。さらに、科学における哲学的批判的考察を要求しているように、絶対的に真理とされたものに対する懐疑という学的価値を謳っているのである。これが、学習者の態度や思考の固定化を回避する妥当な教授法としている。

　地理については、事象に対する理解を深める上で、修身や歴史と関連させることを求めている。教科横断的な授業の提案である。また、歴史については、事柄の記憶や羅列を排し、文明評論、時代精神の批判、人物の批判、社会構造機能、社会発展の理法の理解を求めている。特に、文化史、文明史、生活史を歴史の授業に取り込むことを提案している。さらに、「国民精神も

必要だが同時に人道的国際的良心も涵養してほしい[32]」という要求から、日本と世界の双方の地理・歴史に目を向ける教科のあり方を提唱している。最後に、小原は「現在を知り将来を知るために過去を学ぶ[33]」と述べているように、地理・歴史を通して、学習者が「いかに生きるか」を知る機会となることも求めている。

　芸術（美術、音楽）に関する小原の指摘は多岐にわたる。まず、技巧的・表現的形式ばかりが尊重されることに疑義を呈しており、むしろ、芸術的・内容的価値の重視を提案している。芸術が軽視される現状を嘆いており、したがって、芸術的価値の承認を強く要求するのである。また、腕を磨くことだけを追求する授業は、芸術の授業までには昇華されないと考えていることから、技能を重視する教授そのものにも疑問を投げかけている。さらに、芸術の教授にあたっては、芸術を科学的に捉えること、芸術を研究することの重要性を主張している。単に作品を綺麗な状態に仕上げて完成とするのではなく、内面にある本質を具現することが芸術の趣旨としている。

　体操（体育）については、体操、遊戯を通して運動好きを増やすことを求めている。これは、成人後の健康維持・促進にも理由があり、全人教育論では健価値として盛り込まれているように、人の営みが存続するためには心身の健全さが不可欠であるという考えに立った主張である。また、生理学を授業に付加することも提案している。これは、体育という教科の枠組みを超えて、保健衛生をも包括しようという試みとも考えられる。

　最後に、小原は男女ともに家庭の授業を通して、心理学、経済学、社会学、教育学（育児法を含む）、建築学といった内容に触れることを求めている。女子だけの教科という色を排除し、世に存在する種々の職業について考える機会を提供するという、いわば現代で言うところのキャリア教育の要素も盛り込んだ授業と推察される。

第5節　全人教育の普遍妥当性

　前節で紹介した小原の各科に対する考え方を全人教育の教育課程と便宜的に考えて、これまで紹介した古代ギリシアより今なお連綿としているリベラ

ルアーツ教育（およびウェルラウンデッド教育）との共通点を見てみよう。まず、全人教育を通して育まれる全人とは調和、均整、（反対を合一した）統合の状態にある者を指すが、それはつまり、古代ギリシアにおけるカロカガティアであり、共和制ローマにおける学芸やフマニタス、つまり人間性や人間的教養を備えた者であり、ハーバードが謳うウェルラウンデッド教育を通して育まれた者である。いずれの教育においても、目標に据えられた人物像は非常に近似したものと考えられる。

　また、その教育を実現するために挙げられた具体的な科目についても、共通項が多く見受けられる。古代ギリシアにおいて人格形成に必要な科目として文芸（文法）、修辞（弁論）、弁証、体育、算術、幾何、音楽、天文等が挙げられていたが、これらは、その後、自由七科（文法、修辞、論理、数論、幾何、天文、音楽）でも踏襲されている。科学の進歩に伴って学問分野がより細密化するという時代的な変遷を経て、現代のアメリカ型リベラルアーツ教育の構成としては7科目を超えた科目数になって新たに宗教が加わり、音楽の代わりに文学が芸術系の科目としての役割を担うなどの若干の変更は確認されるものの、人間的教養として必要な科目構成の基本概念は不変といえよう。

　比較的近年になって普及し始めたウェルラウンデッド教育においても、フマニタスの概念は息衝いており、たとえば、ハーバード大学が、世界古典文学、外国語、歴史、数学、科学、音楽、美術、体育等を高校教育段階に求める科目として挙げていることからもうかがえる。加えて、社会構造の変容に伴い、これまで科目として扱われることがなかった分野の科目化（例：コンピュータ科学）が幅広い教育において展開されてはいるが、その理由はあくまでも人格教育、人間的教養の追求の一環から派生したことである。

　小原が考えた科目構成には、哲学としての道徳（当時は修身）があり、国語とそれを補完するための外国語、芸術（とりわけ本学では音楽）、体操（訓育的要素を盛り込んだ体育）、算術（算数・数学）、科学、社会（地理・歴史、政治等）がそれに続く。加えて、小原は、男女ともに家庭を学ぶことも強く求めている。これは、パイデイアに加えてテクネーをもその範囲に収めようとする小原の貪欲さとも受け取れるが、人間らしく生きるための教育に生活のあり方を知る科目が必要という考え方は、決して理解に難しくはないだろう。

　エンキュクリオスパイデイア、アルテスリベラレス、自由七科、リベラル
アーツ教育、ウェルラウンデッド教育、そして全人教育のいずれにも、人間
のあり方を模索する久遠の探究心が如実に反映されている。長い歴史のなか
で、人類が真摯に、そして愚直に人間の普遍妥当な教養について思案を重ね
た結果、今の時代にもその概念が脈々と受け継がれている事実は、教育とい
う活動が人間にとって必要不可欠という何よりの証左であろう。

第6節　名を冠さない教育

　リベラルアーツの語源であるエンキュクリオス・パイデイアは、円環的に
配列された科目による人間教育が基本的な意味とされることを第2節で述べ
た。また、リベラルアーツ教育の考え方を起点として、さらに多くの科目を
範囲に収めるウェルラウンデッドには、元来、「活発な、円熟した、均整の
取れた、幅の広い」という意味が与えられている。そして、小原は全人を円
でイメージしている。つまり、古今東西、理想とする教育を追究した結果、
行き着いたものは円を描く教育、つまり、全人教育であったといえる。
　実は、小原が理想とする教育に全人教育の名を冠することは普遍妥当性の
妨げになる、と「玉川塾の教育」において述べている。その一節を紹介して、
本章の締め括りとしよう。

　　　一体、教育に名前なぞがあってよいのでしょうか。何式教育とか、何
　　的教育とか、何主義教育とか、旗印があってよいのでしょうか。……つ
　　まり主義ということは、……換言すれば他を否定することですから。
　　　……私のかねがねいう所の全人教育ということすら偏したともいえる
　　し、……更に更に偏屈な何式、何的、何主義教育というものはどうして
　　も一方に偏して、ホントの教育から非常に縁遠いものなのです。いわん
　　や、（中略）更に外観の美を誇っているような教育は甚だしきウソの教
　　育なのです[34]。

　このように、煌びやかな文言を多用しながら特定の枠組みを押しつけるか

のような教育に対して強く非難を述べつつも、自身の教育、思想、概念について説明するためには名が必要であり、小原はそこに苦心しつつ、究極としては名前なくして思惟の内容のみを訴求することを理想とした。古代ギリシアから続く理想の教育（ホントの教育）は、様々な名前を授かりながらも、その本質は普遍妥当であり、自然と「一元に帰する」のだろう。これからも、小原が渇望した「一宗一派にとらわれない、主義主張に毒されない、一時の流れや傾向、個人の主義やすき好みに促われない全的な、古今東西を貫く、永劫に普遍妥当性を有する堅実な[35]」マコトの教育、ホントの教育が本学から発信され続けることを期待し、筆を置きたい。

注

1) 小原國芳「玉川塾の教育」『小原國芳全集11　秋吉台の聖者本間先生・玉川塾の教育』玉川大学出版部、1963年、182頁。
2) タイムズ・ハイヤー・エデュケーション「世界標準の『全人力』教育でグローバルリーダーを育成する」2019年3月27日（https://japanuniversityrankings.jp/college/00010/，2021年1月5日閲覧）。
3) この概念については、次の文献を参考にした。中村清「文化の個性と普遍性について」『宇都宮大学教育学部紀要第1部』第48号、1998年、75-78頁。
4) ギリシア語では、enkyklios paideiaと表す。
5) ラテン語では、artes liberalesと表す。
6) ラテン語では、septem artes liberalesと表す。
7) 英語では、well-rounded educationと表す。
8) ギリシア語では、philo sophiaと表す。
9) 本節の執筆にあたり、次の文献を参考にした（五十音順）。①田村恭一「教養の概念とその理論」『上武大学経営情報学部紀要』第32号、2008年、19-38頁。②馬場浩平「百科事典と教養市民の間——18世紀以降のドイツで発展した社交文化における知の受容をめぐって」『METROPOLE』第35号、2015年、1-16頁。③半田智久「セブンリベラルアーツとはどこから来た何ものか」『お茶の水女子大学人文科学研究』第6巻、2010年、149-160頁。④山田耕太「ギリシア・ローマ時代のパイデイアと修辞学の教育」『敬和学園大学研究紀要』第17号、2008年、217-231頁。⑤山田耕太「リベラルアーツ教育の基礎としての作文教育——古代ギリシア・ローマ時代の『プロギュムナスマタ』について」『敬和学園大学研究紀要』第28号、2018年、1-16頁。
10) 主に言葉を用いる職業人を意味する自由人の教育がパイデイアと呼ばれていたことに対し、職人や奴隷を意味する非自由人の教育をテクネー（技術）と呼ばれ、区別されていた。
11) ギリシア語では、kalokagathiaと表す。
12) ギリシア語では、paideueinと表す。
13) 英語では、pedagogyと表す。
14) ギリシア語では、enkýkliosと表す。

15) ラテン語では、artes, quae sunt libero dignae と表す。

16) ラテン語では、doctrina liberalis と表す。

17) ラテン語では、humanitas と表す。

18) ラテン語では、trivium と表す。

19) ラテン語では、quadrivium と表す。

20) これをその後出現するセブンリベラルアーツと差別化するためにラテンリベラルアーツと呼ぶ場合がある。

21) 原題は、*De nuptiis Philologiae et Mercurii et de septem artibus liberalibus libri novem* となる。

22) したがって、一度選んだ専門に、自分の生涯を重ね合わせることではない。

23) 絹川正吉「リベラルアーツ教育と学士学位プログラム」『高等教育研究』第 8 集、2005 年、16 頁。

24) 英語では、the Every Student Succeeds Act と表す。本項の執筆にあたり、次の文献を参考にした。① Jimenez, L. and Sargrad, S. *A Well-Rounded Education: Rethinking What Is Expected of High Schools*, Center for American Progress, 2018. ② Minnesota Department of Education, "Overview: Well-Rounded Education" (https://www.google.com/url?sa=t&rct=j&q=&esrc=s&source=web&cd=&ved=2ahUKEwiEurSpzaLwAhUZfnAKHTSoBacQFjAAegQIBBAD&url=https%3A%2F%2Feducation.mn.gov%2Fmdeprod%2Fidcplg%3FIdcService%3DGET_FILE%26dDocName%3DMDE058763%26RevisionSelectionMethod%3DlatestReleased%26Rendition%3Dprimary&usg=AOvVaw1EEB3H7cajFCIC-3kxyKcy, 2021 年 1 月 5 日閲覧). ③北野秋男「現代米国のテスト政策と教育改革」『教育学研究』第 84 巻第 1 号、2017 年、27-37 頁。

25) 次のサイトより文章を翻訳した。Harvard College, "Guide to Preparing for College" (https://college.harvard.edu/guides/preparing-college, 2021 年 1 月 5 日閲覧)。

26) 同上。

27) 小原國芳「教育改造論」『小原國芳選集 4　教育改造論・自由教育論』玉川大学出版部、1980 年、153 頁。

28) 同上、153 頁。

29) 同上、156 頁。

30) 同上、158 頁。

31) 同上、213 頁。

32) 同上、168 頁。

33) 同上、168 頁。

34) 小原國芳「玉川塾の教育」『小原國芳全集 11　秋吉台の聖者本間先生・玉川塾の教育』玉川大学出版部、1963 年、220 頁。

35) 同上、196 頁。

コラム1

歌に始まり歌に終わる
──玉川の音楽教育が語るもの

　ギネス世界記録にも認定されている、「世界でもっとも歌われている曲」は誰でも一度は口にしたことのある『Happy Birthday to you』。この原曲は『Good Morning to All』という幼稚園で歌われる朝の挨拶の歌であった。この曲を作ったヒル姉妹の妹ミルドレッド（Mildred Hill）は幼稚園の先生、姉のパティ（Patty Hill）はその園長である。誰かのために誕生日を歌で祝福するという素晴らしい習慣は、この曲がなければ世界に根付かなかったであろう。何故なら、この歌が誰でもすぐに覚えられ、簡単に口ずさむことができるからである。極めて簡易な歌詞であり、たった8章節の短い曲だからである。もし何ページもある大曲で、楽譜を見なければ歌えないような歌詞の長い歌であったら、歌い終わる前にケーキに立てたロウソクが燃えつきそうである。実は玉川学園の生活のなかで扱う歌は、覚えやすく、誰もが口ずさめる「簡易さ」が重要なキーワードとなっている。玉川学園がこれだけ歌にあふれる環境となったのも様々な工夫が施された教材が豊かにあるからである。

　玉川学園の音楽教育の特徴を述べる時、「生活音楽」をおざなりにすることはできない。玉川学園において「生活音楽」は音楽のカテゴリーを表わすだけではなく、玉川学園の音楽教育のあり方を示す、理念を内包するものと

して捉えるべきである。この「生活音楽」が定着する過程において玉川独自の「教材」が大きな役割を果たしてきた。「生活音楽」の土壌を築いたのは他でもなく『玉川学園校歌』を作曲した岡本敏明である。草創期の玉川において岡本は「音楽の生活化」を提唱していた。これは創設者小原國芳の「音楽は絶対に、われわれの生活に融け込んだものでありたいのです[1]」という期待に岡本が手探りで模索し、必死に答えようとした結果であり、やがてこれが岡本の目指す音楽教育の根本理念となったのである。開校当初の玉川学園は、生徒が道を作り、肥溜めを運び、畑を耕すといった、まさに労作教育の実践の場であった。こうしたなかで「『岡本君、だから泥臭くならないためにも歌を沢山与えてよ』しつこいほどの小原先生の要求に私も子供たちが飛びついてうたえる歌、うたっている内に自然に合唱になる歌、そんなものを暗中模索しながら何曲作ったか数えきれない[2]」と随筆のなかで述べている。

　岡本は随所で「音楽の生活化はまず輪唱から[3]」と主張していた。岡本敏明は日本において「輪唱」の教育効果を誰よりも高調していた人物であり、輪唱の代名詞ともいえる『かえるの合唱』は岡本によって全国の子供に紹介されたのである。1947（昭和22）年、日本における最後となる国定教科書に教科書編纂委員に任命された岡本が教材として掲載したことによって瞬く間に全国の子供たちに広まった。しかしそれよりも以前に玉川学園では愛唱されていた歌だったのである。玉川っ子必携の歌曲集である『愛吟集[4]』の昭和17年版には、すでにライン地方の民謡として掲載されている。岡本が教科書に『かえるの合唱』を紹介した際、玉川大学出版部発刊の『全人』において次のように述べている。

　「おなじみの《蛙の合唱》が四年教材となったことは日本音楽教育の大飛躍である。いずれ又ゆっくり書きたいと思っているが〈蛙の合唱主義〉の音楽の教育で今後の音楽教育は百八十度の転回が可能である[5]」。一見すると、とるに足らない子供のあそび歌として、その価値を見落としてしまいそうになる歌であるが、この一文から岡本がいかに「輪唱」に大きな期待を込めて教材として採択したのかがわかる。この「かえるの合唱主義」が示す意味を紐解くと、「生活音楽」が何を目指していたのかが明らかになってくる。

　開校間もない1930（昭和5）スイスからヴェルナー・チンメルマン（Werner

Zimmerman）という教育学者が玉川学園を訪れた。すっかり玉川学園の教育に魅了されたチンメルマンはそれから半年も滞在したのである。その間、自らヴァイオリンやピアノを弾いて多くのヨーロッパの歌を子供たちに教えてくれた。『かえるの合唱』もそのなかにあった。輪唱の面白さを直感した岡本は言語の歌詞をそのまま訳詞として施すのではなく、輪唱によって生まれるハーモニーを演奏者が感得しやすくするために日本語の歌詞をあえて作詞としてつけた。重要な点は、原曲の歌詞の意味を正確に伝えようとはせず、ハーモニーの楽しさを演奏者が感じやすくすることを優先させたところにある。岡本は「徳性ノ涵養」として手段的に取り組まれた唱歌教育や、戦時中の「国民的情操の醇化」としての訓練的な芸能科音楽に対して批判的な立場を貫いていた。音楽は手段ではなく音楽そのものの喜びを感得できるものでなければならないと強く考えていたのである。「唱歌は言葉による作用を重視しすぎた結果、歌詞が確直になりしたがって音楽の自然と相離反し、旋律も歌詞に引きずられて硬直してしまふ[6]」と説明している。また、自身が編纂した『輪唱のたのしみ』の解説では「音楽の構成美を味わうためには歌詞は意味のないラララ……でもいいのです。……歌いやすくすること、原曲のリズムをいかすことなどには、目に見えない苦心を払っているつもりです[7]」と述べている。つまり岡本にとって歌詞は重要でなく、輪唱の醍醐味であるハーモニーを楽しめる教材として輪唱の効果に大きな期待を寄せていた。しかも標題にはとらわれず、音だけの芸術、すなわち純音楽、絶対音楽を味わえなければならないという明確な信念を持っていた。このような輪唱を日常的にしかも数多く触れていくことが相対音感を涵養し、『ハレルヤコーラス』や『第九』の演奏にも発展するのだと考えていたのである。節まわしの面白さだけに固執する日本の音楽教育に対し、和音のなかで歌う面白さ（和声的な音楽の面白さ）、旋律のやりとりの面白さ（対位法的な音楽の面白さ）を追求することができるように導くべきであると主張している[8]。

　また、「日本の教科書の輪唱の歌詞には四節も五節も付いているものがありますが、正直のところ、一節でたくさんです：歌詞が長すぎたり、かたくるしかったりするので、教室だけの輪唱になってしまうのです[9]」と述べ歌詞の面白さと同時に覚えやすさの重要性について説いている。

歓 迎 の 歌

岡本 敏 明 作詞
アメリカ民謡
岡本 敏 明 編曲

譜例1　歓迎の歌

　玉川学園校歌と同等に玉川っ子は誰でも必ず歌える歌がある。『歓迎の歌』（譜例1）である。「♪ランラ　ランラ　ラン」と先導者が声をかけると、たちまち子供たちは条件反射的に歌が口を衝いて出てくる。このメロディはもはやユニバーサル・スタンダードといえる『幸せなら手をたたこう』のメロディが元となっている。玉川学園では編入生や実習生、来園したお客様を必ずこの歌で歓迎する。お互い初対面の緊迫したムードはこの『歓迎の歌』によって一気に和むのである。譜例1にある通り、歓迎する人の名前をモジュール・パーツとして歌詞に取り込むことができる。重要なことはグラウンドや体育館など、どのようなシチュエーションであってもすぐに歌えることである。岡本は「伴奏がなければ歌がはじまらないようでは音楽の生活化はいつまでたっても望まれない[10]」と述べ、生活のなかで取り組みやすい教材の工夫を尽くしたのである。

　「歌に始まり歌に終わる」という玉川ではおなじみの標語は、音楽の授業にとどまらず、生活のあらゆる場面で年中歌を歌うという意味にもとれるが、

譜例２　夜が明けた

譜例３　さよなら

文字通り玉川学園の生活は歌から始まる。小学部の児童はグラウンドで自由に遊びながら始業前を過ごしている。すると体操の音楽が聞こえ始め子供たちは遊んでいた各々の場所でその場飛びが始まる。音楽に合わせ一連の体操が教員による指示もないなか、児童が主体的に取り組む。体操が終わり、聴こえてくるのが『夜が明けた』（譜例２）の前奏である。この10小節の輪唱は２つのコードによるきわめて単純な和声進行であるが、輪唱であるためアインザッツ[11]を規定する必要がない。指揮者が合図する必要もなく、各々が遊んでいたそれぞれの場所からこの輪唱を歌いながら朝会隊形に並ぶので

ある。むしろ歌い出だしが揃わない方が輪唱としてハーモニーを生み、演奏が豊かになる。たった10小節の曲であるため、繰り返しも終始も朝会隊形の並び具合に即して自在にコントロールできるのである。しかもこれは習慣化されていることにより、教員が大きな声で指示を出さなくても子供たちは歌いながら整然と朝会隊形に並ぶのである。このような場面で毎日取りあげても飽きてしまって、形骸化する心配がないのは「簡易」であることと、輪唱による音楽の本質的な楽しさがあるからであり、玉川を一歩出るとこのような教材は教育現場で意外と普及していない。

　帰りの会は1日の振り返りを行う重要な学級活動の時間であるが、時には深刻な話にもなる。しかし「歌」の力がどのような時も、たちまち健全な雰囲気を取り戻してくれる。玉川の終会では最後に必ず『さよなら』（譜例3）を輪唱して解散するのである。この教材も8小節。2小節のモチーフのなかで初めの3拍目から次の小節に向かってドミナント[12]からトニック[13]を繰り返す。この和声進行を感覚的に無意識のうちに子供たちは感得しているのである。この和声感覚は古典的な西洋音楽であればどのような大曲にも共通する和声構造の基本であり、こうした経験の繰り返しが、合唱や吹奏楽の全国大会でも定評の「玉川サウンド」を生み出していると考えられる。『かえるの合唱』を皮切りに戦後の教科書に各学年3〜4曲輪唱が掲載されるようになったが、岡本はそれでは不十分であると主張している。「子供ははだしで歌ひたいのである。歩き乍ら、仕事しながら歌って居たいのである[14]」と述べ、「春の輪唱、桜の輪唱、おひなさまの輪唱、登山の輪唱、秋の輪唱、雪の輪唱というように、児童生徒の生活に即した輪唱を数多く用意して、音楽の生活化、生活の音楽化[15]」を図ろうとしたのだ。

　日本においては知らない人がいないほど認知度の高い『かえるの合唱』であるが、実は母国ドイツではあまり知られていない。むしろアメリカでは『フロッグソング』という曲名でジャパニーズ・トラディッショナル・ソングとして広まっている。さらに興味深いのは、かえるの鳴き声を表す歌詞の部分が国内においても、様々な鳴き声で親しまれていることである。これは楽譜を見ながら歌詞を間違えずに歌うという堅苦しい音楽としてではなく、岡本の望んだ通り、歌が音楽室を飛び出し、子供の遊びのなかで、口伝えに広ま

り親しまれていることを意味している。「かえるの合唱主義」は充分に輪唱の面白さを全国に広めることはできたであろう。しかし岡本が本当に広めたかった理想とは、紛れもなく現在の玉川学園にもしっかりと根付いている「生活音楽」の精神なのである。「Happy Birthday to you」のような世界中の生活に自然にとけ込む歌を玉川学園から生み出したいものである。

注

1）玉川大学玉川学園「玉川学園の生活音楽」（https://www.tamagawa.jp/introduction/enkaku/history/detail_15668.html、2020 年 12 月 4 日閲覧）。

2）岡本敏明「岡本先生と私たち」『私の履歴書』岡本先生を偲ぶ会、1983 年、7 頁。

3）たとえば岡本敏明編『輪唱のたのしみ』音楽之友社、1957 年、46 頁。

4）玉川学園編『愛吟集』玉川大学出版部、1942 年。

5）岡本敏明「新音楽教科に現れた諸傾向」『全人』7 月号、1947 年、14 頁。

6）岡本敏明「家庭と音楽」『全人』5 月号、1939 年、65 頁。

7）岡本敏明編『輪唱のたのしみ』音楽之友社、1957 年、142 頁。

8）岡本敏明「輪唱論」『教育音楽』4 月号、1956 年、102 頁。

9）岡本敏明編『輪唱のたのしみ』音楽之友社、1957 年、46 頁。

10）岡本敏明「感動の音楽 生活の音楽」『全人』1 月号、1966 年、15 頁。

11）オーケストラあるいは合唱で、ある声部が長い休止ののちに再度演奏を始めること。フーガの主題の入り（海老澤敏・上参郷祐康・西岡信雄・山口修監修『新編音楽中辞典』音楽之友社、2006 年）。

12）日本では「属音」ともいう。他のどの三和音よりも決定的な形でトニックに解決する。いわゆる属調といわれるドミナントの調性的機能は、トニックを準備するためのもっとも強力な手段となるばかりか、調整音楽のもっとも多用される調的対象を生むのである（ジョージ・グローヴ『ニューグローヴ世界音楽大辞典 11』柴田南雄・遠山一行総監修、講談社、1994 年）。

13）長短調組織において、調の主要な音であり、その音名がその調の名称として用いられる音のこと。日本では「主音」ともいう（ジョージ・グローヴ『ニューグローヴ世界音楽大辞典 11』柴田南雄・遠山一行総監修、講談社、1994 年）。

14）岡本敏明「家庭と音楽」『全人』5 月号、玉川大学出版部、1939 年、66 頁。

15）岡本敏明『実践的音楽教育論』カワイ楽譜、1966 年、9 頁。

第 II 部

世界的視野から見た
全人教育の展望

第4章

クルト・ハーンと全人教育
──経験の場としての学校

はじめに

　クルト・ハーン（Kurt Hahn）と小原國芳は、ともに20世紀に顕著な広が
りをみせた教育改革運動のなかに位置している。彼らの教育学的思考と行動
は、互いに近接し、似ているといわれる。全人教育の中心にある「全人（whole
person）」というモチーフが、2人の教育者を結びつけている。本章では、
まず最初にクルト・ハーンの伝記をひもとき、人物像と業績に迫っていく。
経験と経験作用について考えることがもっとも重要であることが示されるだ
ろう。他方で教育機関のあり方についての新たな批判的観点にも触れる。次
の第2節では、クルト・ハーンの業績を世界の教育との関連のなかに位置づ
けていく。平和、人権、国際理解といったモチーフが、クルト・ハーンにとっ
て重要であったことが示されるだろう。加えて教育機関にかんするクルト・
ハーンの革新的な視点についても紹介する。クルト・ハーンは批判的に時代
を見極め、明確な原則に基づいて田園教育塾に関する彼独自の考え方を構築
したのである。最後の第3節では、全人教育という教育プログラムに貢献し
たクルト・ハーンの教育学について概説する。さらに小原の教育学との簡潔

な比較を行い、経験を通しての学習という考え方に着目していく。

第 1 節　クルト・ハーン——伝記的アプローチ

　クルト・ハーンは 1886(明治 19)年 6 月 5 日にベルリンで生まれた。1974(昭和 49) 年 12 月 14 日、バーデン・ヴュルテンベルク州南部のヘルマンスベルクで死去した。クルト・ハーンは、政策について考え、行動することに関心を持った教育者として世界的に知られている。クルト・ハーンの伝記[1]については、すでに様々な文献があるので、ここでは、ハーンの業績の中身をいくつか紹介したい。その主な目的は、教育思想と教育政策的な行動の両方におよぶクルト・ハーンの重要性を、詳細かつ体系的に検討する価値について示すことにある。

　全体として、教育学と政策との絡み合いが、ハーンの伝記において基本的な役割を果たしている。このことは何よりも、ドイツ帝国最後の首相であるバーデンのマックス (Max von Baden) 王子や、イギリスのプリンス・コンソートであるフィリップ王子 (Prince Philipp) との親密な関係に表れている。クルト・ハーンは「フィリップに考えることを教えた男[2]」である。クルト・ハーンの政策的な見解は、基本的には民主主義的な共存の考え方によって形成されていた。一方では、平等、普遍的な人間の尊厳、人類全体の承認といった基準が、彼の民主主義概念の中心にあった。他方で、彼は統治力を持つエリートの育成を民主主義社会の重要な課題と考えていた。このエリートに期待されていたのは、自らの人生と社会全般に対する包括的な責任に基づいて考え、行動することであった。しかし、民主主義の発展は、様々な文明の病に直面し、危機に瀕していた。ハーンが確認したのは次の 6 つの社会病、すなわち、体力の欠如、自発性と冒険心の衰え、想像力の衰え、職人技の衰え、自己鍛錬の衰え、そして思いやりの心の衰えであった。社会はそれゆえ、教育学的な考え方や教育方針を変えることで、この問題に対処する必要があった。

　民主主義へと参画する、その伝記的背景を考えてみると、ハーンは第一次世界大戦後に生じたドイツの政治体制の断絶と特に深くかかわっていたことがわかる。国家社会主義を明確に否定したハーンは、1933 (昭和 8) 年に短

期間、逮捕され、その後、イギリスに移住した。ハーンが国家社会主義に反対したのは、確かにユダヤ人としての出自が影響しているが、根本的には彼の基本的な政治的立場と民主主義への参画によって決定づけられていた。ハーンは 1933 年以前から、すでに国家社会主義への強い拒否感をあらわにしていた。1932（昭和 7）年 8 月、彼はこう書いている。「ザーレムは中立でいることはできない。SA や SS と協力しているザーレム連盟のメンバーには、ヒトラーへの忠誠の誓いを撤回するか、ザーレムへの忠誠の誓いを撤回するかのいずれかを求める[3]」。教師あるいは生徒として彼の学校に参加することと、国家社会主義の愚かな原則とは相容れず、彼は移住し、ゴードンストウンに学校を設立した。この学校はやがて世界的な影響力を持つようになったのである[4]。

　彼の業績の意義を考えてみると、明確に次のように述べることができる。すなわち、クルト・ハーンが世界的に知られるようになったのは、ある種の教育学的思考と教育政策的な行動によるものであると。

　彼の教育学的思考については、2 つの点を強調できる。彼の中心思想の 1 つは、学習が基本的に自分の経験に支配されているとする見解にある。したがって、教育学は個人的に形成された経験をあらゆる教育の基盤とする方法を見い出す必要がある。

　2 つ目として、彼の教育学的思考の中心には、次のような洞察がある。すなわち、教育機関は経験を通しての学習過程を考慮しなければならない。ハーンによれば、教育は、したがって個人のロールモデルとあらかじめ用意された仕組みとの相互作用によってのみ機能する。

　教育政策については、特に 2 つの点が注目される。まず、ハーン自身がオルタナティブ・スクールの創設者として大成功を収めたことである。1919（大正 8）年、彼はバーデンのマックス王子の協力を得て、世界的に有名な学校であるシュロス・ザーレムを創設し、1920（大正 9）年 4 月に開校した。1932 年には、ザーレムの姉妹校であるビルクルホーフをシュヴァルツヴァルトのヒンターツァルテンに設立した。前述したように、ハーンは 1933 年にナチス・ドイツから逃れて移住した後、1934（昭和 9）年にスコットランドのゴードンストウンにイギリスのザーレム校を設立している。

　教育政策的な行動は自らの学校設立にとどまらず、彼の関心は国際的なネットワークの仕組みづくりにもおよんだ。この関心は、一方で、ユナイテッド・ワールド・カレッジのネットワークとなって表れた。ハーンは1960年代、その原型づくりに貢献している。とりわけ国際バカロレアは、地球市民のための教育というビジョンの実現をめざして大きな意義と成功を収めたネットワークである。ユネスコは1960年代後半にハーンの影響を受けて、この世界的に認められた学位資格を承認した。まさにそれは注目すべきサクセスストーリーで、「2020年12月現在、世界158か国の5,400校以上で、7,200以上のプログラムが提供されている5)」。

　教育学的思考と教育政策の考え方については、まずクルト・ハーンを世界の教育運動との関連で考察することによって、両方とも説明できる。われわれは彼が学校を改革志向的に理解していた点に着目する。学校にかんするクルト・ハーンの思想を見ていくと、彼は当時の重要な疑問に答えていた。それはたとえば小原一仁が日本の教育制度の発展について提示した次のような疑問である。すなわち、「最初の疑問は、日本の教育は変えられるのかということである。その答えは、変えられるが、それには日本人の教育イデオロギーに対するコペルニクス的革命が必要かもしれない、というものである。換言すれば、教育のオルタナティブな概念を考えることが不可欠である。第2の疑問は、その実行の方法と過程を問うものである。答えは、教育の本質に立ち返ること、つまり、日本の教育を取り巻く現状や価値観を取り払って、教育の本当の意味、真の目的、純粋な動機を考えることである。具体的には、日本人全体が、人を評価する際に、偏差値、学歴そして（あるいは）職業など、目に見える、相変わらず表面的で偏った情報によって評価する傾向から、全体としての人間を観る人物評価へと、思い切ったパラダイムシフトを行わねばならない6)」。

　この「全体としての人間」という概念は、第3節で扱っていく。クルト・ハーンの教育学は、ホリスティックな全人教育へ向けた刺激を生み出した。経験による学習の考え方に焦点を当てていくことにする。

第2節　世界の教育との関連におけるクルト・ハーン

　クルト・ハーンの業績は、教育学において世界的な広がりをみせた改革運動の、ある概念を考えることで初めて理解できる。まず、「新教育」というものの基礎的な解釈について説明することが有益である。ここでは、世界教育連盟（World Education Fellowship）の元会長ヘルマン・レールス（Hermann Röhrs）が展開した区分を参考にすることができる。この点で極めて重要なのは、レールスが「新教育」の概念に政策上の対比を導入したことである。この対比においてレールスは、従来、教育改革を担ってきた個々の人々やプログラムの範囲内で、その内側から相違点を明らかにしている。レールスは、国際主義の観点と、それを呼び起こす平和教育への取り組みに打ち込むことを、新教育の重要な基準とした。しかし外側から見れば、学習者自身の権利を主張し、それぞれの時代精神に対する批判的な態度によって、新教育の異なる形態が重なり合う。「新教育は、人類に奉仕するための継続的かつ国際的な運動を体現するものであり、自己活動的で責任ある発展の原則にしたがって教育の進歩を促すものである[7]」。「新教育」は、つねに「教育学的な地方主義[8]」と対立し、「経験と知識の国際的な地平を批判的に包摂する[9]」ことによって構成される。結局、これは新教育の役割というものを教育的援助による世界批判の理論として理解する倫理的アプローチ[10]である。

　今日の「個性」と「グローバル化」の間の緊張関係は、この万人共通のラベルが持つ多様な意味を表している。新教育は、このような倫理的観点から、まさしく次の2つの規範的方向性において、この緊張関係に関与する。それは、個人——特に、個々の姿をしたすべての人間——が、世界を舞台に開花する権利を持つとする方向と、この開花、展開には「平和」を特徴とする枠組みが必要だとする方向である。この教育学的理解に基づく平和とは、単に戦争がないということだけではない（それ自体には計り知れない価値があるにせよ）。さらに、この教育学的理解は、まさに個性というあらゆる人間の権利に言及している。それを少なくとも寛容の態度で認めて、それなりの敬意を払う文化のなかで平和を叶えていく社会集団の実現を目指している。

　今日、「新教育」の真価が問われているが、それはもともと倫理的な性質のもので、規範的な用語でいえば、グローバル化との関連で行われる教育学的な文化批判のなかに見出される。新教育の精神に基づく教育学的な文化批判の発展には、多様でありながら相互に関連する問題が含まれている。たとえば、ユネスコの活動やその「万人のための教育」プログラム、「世界教育連盟（WEF）」の活動、さらには 1989（昭和 64）年の「子供の権利条約」のような文書などがある。普遍的な人権を学習者の権利に変えるための教育学的アプローチ、特に子供の権利を政策的に実現することは、グローバルな教育概念あるいは持続可能な学習の人間学的な位置づけを確固なものとするための努力と同様に、この分野に属している。その意味で、地球市民のための教育にかかわっているのである。

　ヘルマン・レールスは、特にクルト・ハーンの業績について、それは「本物の」新教育的アプローチを完成したことにあると考えた。この「本物の」新教育という基準は、究極的には 2 つの機能を果たしていた。それは外部との差異化を構成すると同時に、新教育自体の内部で批判的な区別を可能にさせている。

　この基準により、新教育の内部を省みて区別することが可能となる。たとえば、学習者志向、あるいはオルタナティブな形の学校教育の模索など、ある種の教育学的な指針を共有しつつも、弱者や傷つきやすい人を擁護する教育を社会政策的な基本姿勢へと転換するのに失敗した取り組みが複数存在したりする。それゆえレールスが新教育の指導原理として明確に述べたのは、次の点である。「まったく明白なことだが、新教育の考え方は、ウィリアム・ジェームズ、ピエール・ボヴェ、マリア・モンテッソーリ、クルト・ハーン、フリードリヒ・ヴィルヘルム・フォースター、エリザベート・ロッテンなどにみられるように、平和教育とのかかわりを活性化する[11]」。レールスは、特にクルト・ハーンにかんして、国際主義の観点——そしてそれを呼び起こす平和教育の輪郭を描く取り組み——が、多様な新教育の考え方を区別するための不可避の基準を形成しているとしている。換言すれば、ある実践や理論が本物の新教育に数えられるかどうかは、この国際主義的で同時に平和主義的な態度をどの程度共有しているかによって決まるということである。レールスの考えでは、教育の取り組みが政策的な思想に転換されてい

ない場合、新教育の帰結は理論と実践の両方において未完の断片のままとなることを意味している。しかし、そうであるならば、教育学は国際的な状況内でのコミュニケーションにふさわしく開かれたものでなければならない。

　クルト・ハーンは、レールスにとって、「本当の」、「真の」新教育を代表する重要な人物であることがよくわかる。クルト・ハーンは、自分の学校を国際理解ならびに国際的な責任を果たすための構成要素と考えていた。ザーレムの学校からユナイテッド・ワールド・カレッジズに至るまで、ハーンの次のような教育思想と行動が浸透している。すなわち、我々は皆、この地上に生きる人間である。だから、他者の異質さに身をさらさなければならない。他者の異質さに触れる経験を積み重ねたところで、その異質さがなくなるわけではない。しかし、その異質さが私の馴染みのあるものの一部となり、その結果、私は彼らと世界を分かち合うことができる。このことをクルト・ハーンは、いわゆるザーレム法に定式化した。このザーレム法とともに、世界市民という考えが教育実践のなかへと取り入れられている。ハーンが重視していたのは、地球市民へ向かう途上にある全人である。次に挙げられた原則は、たとえば寄宿制学校のシュロス・ザーレム校やゴードンストウン校、並びにユナイテッド・ワールド・カレッジに至るまで、今なお、今日の教育実践を基本的に導いている。

1　子供たちに自分自身を発見する機会を提供せよ。
2　子供たちに勝利と敗北を体験させよ。
3　子供たちが自分たちに共通する事柄に打ち込める機会を提供せよ。
4　静かな時間のために配慮せよ。
5　ファンタジーを鍛えよ。
6　競争は重要だが、それに支配的な役割を持たせるな。
7　裕福で権力のある両親を持つ子女を軟弱な特権意識から救済せよ[12]。

　このように、地球市民としての教育は、望ましい人格理想と結びついているが、クルト・ハーンにとって、その全体的な考え方は、世界的なプラグマティズムと結びついている。ハーンはこの人格理想を、個人の好み、人間の尊厳

の尊重、普遍的な道徳的法則への自己投入といった緊張状態の場において定義している[13]。ハーンによれば、子供は「社会的、政治的、技術的なあらゆる面で自国を理解する（必要がある）。それは、やがて道徳的に責任ある大人になるために他ならない[14]」というのが教育の主な目的である。ハーンは、「現代の都市環境[15]」の危険性と、道徳性に良い影響を与えるとされるスポーツや社会参加を通じた教育を対比させている。このように、ハーンが計画する教育学的な「救済策」は、若者が「衰退の犠牲者」になるのを防ぐための４つの戦略を提供している。この４つの要素は、ハーンが日々の学校生活に取り入れたいと考えているもので、次のようなものである。

1　週に４回、午前中に行われるアスレチック・ブレーク、
2　土曜日の朝に行われるプロジェクト、
3　３学期に数回の遠征、
4　午後は救助活動に専念[16]。

　ハーンによると、他者の方を向くには、社会を構成する相手の方を向くには、海であれ山のなかであれ、危険な状況にある他の人間に責任を果たす経験が必要である[17]。他者に向かうことで、他者を同じ人間として認識し、責任を負うという一般的な感覚を促すことが期待されている。これらの要素は、最終的にコスモポリタン的な意識として市民意識の開発を意図した「体験的療法[18]」の一部である。人類自体の一部である人間に対する責任こそが、あらゆる教育の究極の目標である。

　クルト・ハーンは、このような教育学的・政策的設定を、機関としての学校や学習に対する異なる解釈のなかへと取り入れた。この独特の仕方で世界の教育を考え、我々はまず機関としての学校について振り返ってみることにしよう。クルト・ハーンにとって、学校は認知的な知識を伝達するだけの場ではないということが重要である。学校とは、何よりも社会的な学習の場であり、社会組織のなかでどのように振る舞うかを学ぶ場なのである。

　学校を社会的な学習と行動の場として考える時、我々は文化的所産に目を向ける。つまり、文化的所産とは文化から生まれた産物であり、同時に文化を

維持するために不可欠なものでもある。この叙述から２つの問いが生まれる。

　まず第１の問いは、「学校のなかでは何が起こるのか？」である。これは最初の、しかも明白な問いかもしれないが、最後の問いではない。我々は、学校という場で何が起こるのかを問うだけでなく、次のような問いかけをすることもできる。

　すなわち、第２の問いは、「学校を通じて何が起こるのか？」である。この問いは異なる方向へ向かっている。前述の問いの観点を他のやり方で再構成すると、社会的学習が学校のなかでどのように起こるのか、そして社会的学習が学校を通じてどのように起こるのかを区別できる。

　クルト・ハーンの教育学を参考にすれば、この２つの視点を次のように結びつけることができる。すなわち、「学校という場を通じての社会的学習が、学校という場のなかでの社会的学習を形作る」。間違いなく、「学校」は学習の計画と統制によって特徴づけられる。しかし問題は、この計画と統制が、どのように、どこで、いかなる手段で行われるかである。学校は、特別なタイプの学習にかかわっている。学習の過程は日常生活のなかで、テレビの前で、仲間のなかで、そのほか、様々な場面で生じる。結局のところ、学校には特に優れた特徴がなければならない。

　学校というものは、単純に人間が学習する準備を整えて学ぼうと決意するから存在しているわけではない。むしろ、学習は統制され、先導されている。この先導は異なる次元で、特定の内容を通じて、特定の機会と特定の時間に行われる。

　言い換えれば、次のようになる。すなわち、

・学習内容が設計され、選択され、
・学習機会もまた設計され、選択され、そして両方とも限られた学習時間のなかで実現される。
・学習の方法と内容は、意図的に決められるか、あるいは少なくとも許容された範囲から成り立つ。

　「学習」とそれを先導するものを学校の中心に据えて概念化すると、おお

むね次のような見解に同意できる。すなわち、教師と学習者の相互作用による学習過程を統制する公式のシラバスは存在するが、それだけではない。シラバスは確かに存在するが、それ以上のものも存在している。何か他のものが、「さらに」学習過程を先導するものが存在している。この「さらに」を隠そうとするのは、クルト・ハーンの意味でも、浅はかで、稚拙なことだろう。学校という場で学習過程の統制について考えるなら、それはシラバスに沿って作業することだけを意味しているわけではない。

　学習はむしろ、おそらくは知識を構造的に伝達する組織化された教室の外でも行われる。では、学習はその時どのように記述できるのか。学習にはつねに特定の内容、特定の機会、特定の時間が必要だと仮定すると、次のような区別が可能である。学校のなかで行われる学習の様態は、3タイプに分けられる。そこでの学習とは、意図なく起こるものではなく、意識的に形作られたり、あるいは少なくとも、そこまではよいと認められているもののことである。すなわち、方向性としては、次の3タイプの学習がイメージできる。

　（a）第1に、狭義に理解される学習は、教授して知識を伝達することによって行われる。教師は教室の前方やグループの前に立ち、あるいは別の形で、与えられた期間内に特定の科目を提供したり、詳しく説明したりする。この点で教師中心の授業も、グループワークあるいは自由作業も突き詰めれば違いはない。学習は、この時点では専門的な訓練を受けた教師の指導のもと、あらかじめ指示され、決定された特定の題材に直接触れる様々な形式によってつねに統制されている。

　（b）第2に、学習は様々な形の「社交」を組織することによって行われる。ここでいう社交とは、学校の枠組みのなかで意図的に設けられた機会のことであり、つねに学習のための教育的な魅力を含んでいる。たとえば、クラス会や学園祭、時間と内容が限定されたグループのプロジェクト、長期的な研究グループ、スクールカフェ、遠足やクラス旅行などがある。これらの社交形式のルール、つまり意図的に形成された社会的空間に適用されるルールを学習する必要がある。教室で行われる教育には、同年齢、同じ興味、あるいは他の形式で構成されたクラスであっても、一段と組織された社会的空間がある。1つの学習団体として、学習用に、そのような人との交わりを編成す

るが、その編成には後で議論される学習への要求が含まれている。

　（ c ）第3に、学習は、たとえば社会的、時間的そして空間的枠組みを拘束し、それゆえ統一して行われるあらゆる形態の学校行事に重みを与える服装で行われる。我々はよく、説明する際に「服装と同じように」といった言葉を使う。学校の「習慣」にも、教育学的に利用可能な学習への誘い（いざな）が含まれている。たとえば、運動場での生徒の行動を取り上げてみよう。この行動は、間違いなく、解読するのが難しい多くの要因に影響されている。しかし、表に現われる行動パターンは、ある程度変更できるし、教育的に導くこともできる。このことを過小評価してはならない。習慣の概念は、社交よりも明らかに抽象的で、それゆえ把握するのが難しい。社交の機会は意識的にデザインされるが、習慣はどういうわけか学校に持ち込まれたり、あるいは学校でみつけられたりする。しかし重要なことは、習慣も変えることができるということである。「人種差別のない学校」のような取り組みを考えてみると、「学校」のような機関における社会的共存のルールは、決して変えられないものではないし、自然に与えられたものでもないことが明らかになる。この場合もルールの変更は可能であり、特に今日ではその必要性が強く感じられる。わかりにくい習慣であっても、変えることができる。

　教える過程で明らかになるのは、学習は決して公式に承認された教材や、あるいは担当者としての教師によってのみ導かれるものではないということである。学習は、社会的なルールによって著しく共同決定される。要するに教科や教師だけでなく、社会的状況もまたその社会形態において学習をコントロールしているといえる。このことは社交や習慣の場合には当然のことかもしれないが、教えるという行為にも適用できる。その主たる考え方は次のようなものである。すなわち、人間は知識を獲得し、今度は人間を教育する行動を身に付けていく。これは特に、あらかじめ設定された仕組みのなかで起こる[19)]。重要なのは、場というものが単に抽象的で非現実的な形で存在するだけではなく、それ自体、物理的な形となっても現れることである。社会的なルールが染み込んだこの物理的な場が、学習を導くのである。デザインされた、あらかじめ形作られた場というものは、しかも教育機関と変わらない。学習者にとって機関は、機関としての学校は重要である。機関としての

学校、社会的な学習と行動の場としての学校には、その社会形態があらかじめ与えられているだけでない。学校は変えられるものでもある。このことは極めて重要で、これらの仕組みは、程度の差こそあれ、すぐにでも形づくることができる。

　個人の教育と構造的な教育との関係を明らかにすることは、田園教育塾の特別な性質を理解する上でも、またクルト・ハーンの立場からも、必須の条件である[20]。個人の教育と構造的な教育の評価と配置は、まさに田園教育塾における、また田園教育塾による特別な教授法の基礎となるものである。クルト・ハーンは、学校は教育の場であり、教育は人格形成であるとするヘルマン・リーツの基本的な考え方を引き継いだ[21]。ハーンはヘルマン・リーツを「近代ドイツのもっとも偉大な教育者[22]」と称した。田園教育塾における理想の教育者は誰かという問いには、2つの相互に関連した方法でしか答えられない。田園教育塾の鍵となる教育者には、一方で、ある種のタイプの教師が必要であり、他方ではある種の構造的な配置が必要である。明白なのは次の点である。すなわち、田園教育塾が行う教授活動の特質は、個人と周囲の構造との緊張関係から生じていることである[23]。田園教育塾の社会的空間は確かに（徹底的に）事前に設定された環境であることが観察される。しかしながら、その観察から、田園教育塾の社会的空間は権威主義的で、全体としてみれば完全に大人中心主義的な構造に違いない、などということにはならない。田園教育塾は、むしろ、子供たちや青年たちに、個性的な人格形成のための「自然な」空間を提供することに明確にかかわっているのだと理解されることを望んでいる。

　この基本的な考え方は、教育というものが本質的には人間の直接的な（相互）行動に依存するものの、それにまったく限定されていないことを示唆している。それはむしろ、学習の過程を導くにあたり、教育的刺激を構造へと、意識的に選択され構築された構造へと向けていくということである。田園教育塾はそれゆえ、とりわけクルト・ハーンの場合、彼が選択し形成した社会・文化的環境で構成されているのである。個人と周囲の構造との関係というよりも、むしろ緊張関係が、田園教育塾の教育学的特徴を理解するための解釈学的な鍵となる。彼は自分の学校施設が、子供たちや青年たちの成長のため

の「自然な」空間の提供にかかわっていると認められることを望んでいた。その構造を選択し、デザインした教育的効果は、スタッフが望んだ「人格」の発達と調和していなければならない。道徳性の教育といった教育学上の主張と、それに続く、まさにこの道徳性の教育に焦点を当てた学校構想は、個人と構造の間の模範となるような相互作用によってのみ達成できるというのが、その基本的な考え方である。この方法は、もっぱら子供たちや若者たちの人間としての全体性や完全性を重要視している。教師自身も、最終的にはデザインされた環境内の社会を構成する規範構造の一部となる。彼らの役割は、価値観とそれに呼応する態度の良い模範となることである。

第3節　クルト・ハーンと彼の全人教育にかんする教育学的プログラム

　小原一仁は、小原國芳が主導する人間観を次のように述べている。「小原は人間を二元論的に心と体に分け、6つの価値観を絶対価値（真・善・美・聖）と手段価値（健康・富）に区分した。（中略）真、善、美、聖は、人間の精神的、霊的な相に直接関わるものであり、本質的な価値であるから、絶対的価値に含まれる。反対に、健や富は、絶対価値を実現し維持するためにのみ必要で役立つという事実から、手段価値に数えられる[24]」。全人教育とは、人間の尊厳というものをその人間の完全性において完全に尊重することであり、この考え方は、子供たちや青年たちを扱う際にも適用されるべきである。子供たちや青年たちは完全な人間であり、何らかの欠陥を持った存在ではない。このように、子供たちや青年たちを「全体的な、完全な人間」としてとらえることは、現代の全人教育における「教育十二信条」の核心的な考え方である「自学自律」を理解することにつながる[25]。全人教育を実践し、個人の教育と構造的な教育を相互に関連させることは、主として、幼稚園、学校、あるいは大学などの教育機関を、自己省察的な経験が準備される環境として理解することを意味する。

　全人教育に対するクルト・ハーンの貢献を理解するために、まず第1に思い浮かぶことは、この経験学習の概念を一般的に定義することである。次にクルト・ハーンの教育の考え方が、この経験学習の過程をいかに実現したか

を示していく。まずはじめに観察できるのは、子供たちや青年たちが世界を適切に利用できるようになるには、まさしく、ほとんどが間接的なやり方を取らねばならないし、実際にそうしていることである。直接経験できるもの、自分の近くで経験できるものは、社会に入っていくために必要な学習のほんの一部に過ぎない。この観察はたいてい「間接経験」として分類される。しかし、上に述べた事実を評価すれば、多くの異なった結果が生じる。ある人にとって、間接経験はまさに文化発展がもたらす最初の罪を表している。教育小説『エミール』に描かれたルソーの教育的ユートピアがその好例である[26]。直接経験を重視するルソーは、幼少期や青年期の学習刺激が不確かな時は、身をもって体験されなければならないとしており、エミールが窓ガラスを割った後の罰の場面に、それは象徴的に表れている。これに反対の立場では、「間接経験」は必要であるばかりか、高度な文化水準の恩恵でさえあると主張される。手に負えないほどの量と質の情報が、個人にとってはその個人の発達のために、また社会にとってはその文化的な発展のために、利用できるといわれている。たとえ個人はこの豊富な情報を徐々に処理し、内面化することしかできないにせよ、それは我々の文化の計り知れない豊かさを象徴しているといわれる。それゆえ、代理となる情報を提供する間接経験は現代社会の文化水準を維持するために不可欠であると、その積極的な機能を認識しなければならない。「経験を通しての学習」は、このように賛否両論のみられる主張である。学校の機能と役割をめぐって、特に1900年頃から、一方で学習教科と生活との隔たりが、他方で学習目的に見受けられる生活からの乖離が、大きな問題となっていた。クルト・ハーンの学校観や全人教育学では、子供たちや青年たちの「人間らしい全体性」を支援しつつ、経験を通しての学習と、その経験のために刺激を与えることが中心的な役割を果たしている。多様な方法での学習は、学校のなかで、また学校の助けを借りて可能となるべきであろう。次のような人間学的前提は、経験を通しての学習が特に学校において相応しい学習形態であるとする考え方の支柱となっている。すなわち、

・我々はなすことによってのみ学ぶ。
・我々は自分で何かをすることによってのみ学ぶ。

ということである。

　特にヴァルトラウト・ノイベルト（Waltraud Neubert）は、ヴィルヘルム・ディルタイ（Wilhelm Dilthey）やヘルマン・ノール（Herman Nohl）を参考にしながら、彼女の学位請求論文「教育学における体験」（1930年）において、これらの言説を証明しようとした。この論文では、「我々はなすことによってのみ学ぶ」との前提に立ち、「体験による学習」と「作業による学習」の2つを学習の基本的な形態として区別している[27]。体験は主に感情に影響を与え、作業は主に意志に影響を与える[28]。しかし、その根底にあるのは、体験と作業の両方に共通する原理であり、すなわち直接性、学習者と学習対象との一体性、そして自己活動性である。

　学習の体験的側面、つまり自分が直接関与し、影響を受けることを強調することは、学習内容に少なくとも2つの結果をもたらす。一方では、学習者の体験が学習過程にとって重要な意味を持つため、学習内容がすぐ上滑りしてしまう。その体験がなければ、学習は淡白で二次的なものにとどまり、最終的には効果がないといわれている。しかし他方で、前述した言説が意味しているのは、可能とされる学習内容が価値の観点から評価されることである。この論理によると、体験できないものは、必然的に格下の学習対象となる。したがって、ノイベルトはまず、芸術、文学、歴史、数学、宗教教育のような科目に、体験型の教授法がうまくいく可能性を見ているのである[29]。これは、教育学的に統制された学習が、体験を重視した学習の側面をどのように正当化できるのか、また、体験学習はどの程度まで行うべきなのかという根本的な問題を提起している。

　アンドレアス・フリットナー（Andreas Flitner）は彼の著書『教育の改革』のなかで、「最近の学校は、これまで以上に書物と学習の学校になっている[30]」と述べ、学校での学習に新たな直接性を求めている。教授分析の観点からは、クラウス・プランゲ（Klaus Prange）が彼の著書『授業の構造形式[31]』のなかで、授業や作業と並ぶ3つの教育形態の1つとして経験を通しての学習を挙げている。彼は、教師の観点から、学校の授業中のいくつかの場面は、すでにいつでも授業自体の経験を伴っていることを強調し、したがって経験をどのように扱うかについて特別な方法論が必要であると主張している。しかし、こ

れはむしろ例外的なことであり、少なくとも例外的であるべきだろう。

　「経験を通しての学習」という原則は、学校を直接的に、また間接的に統制された学習過程の集合体と見なす理解にとって、特に重要である。この関係では、学校における教育的・体験的状況のデザインが中心的な意味を持つ。さらに、課外活動において学校と環境をどのように組み合わせるかが重要である。クルト・ハーンに続いて、イェルク・ツィーゲンスペック（Jörg Ziegenspeck）は、たとえば山あるいは海辺といった自然の役割を強調する教育形態として、「体験教育」を開発した。ツィーゲンスペックは、体験教育を「伝統的で確立された教育機関に代わるもの、補完するもの[32]」と明確に理解している。

　ヒルデガルト・ティーゼン（Hildegard Thiesen）は、クルト・ハーン教育学に関する広範な研究の中で、クルト・ハーンの業績における、あらかじめ形成された環境を媒介する間接的な教育活動の特異性と多様性を詳細に示している。ティーゼンは、ハーン教育学を「構成と接続の間の教育環境[33]」のデザインと表現している。彼女は、ハーンの教育学的業績を、教育活動が主に「環境」を介して間接的に行われる教育学的生態学のモデルと表現している。「一方で、ハーンは教育的な意図を持って環境を設定し、環境を作り、環境を構成している。他方で、彼は教育目標をすでに存在する環境と接続する。（中略）教育環境を提供するためのハーンのやり方の一つひとつが、教育を受けるべき人々をその『環境』との関係に導くことを意図している[34]」。この革新的で影響力のある主張が示しているのは、教育の構造理論とそれに関連する解釈学的アプローチの妥当性を、まさにハーンの学校教育学を考察することによって明らかにできることである。

　このように、クルト・ハーン教育学の基本は、「非個人的なものを含む[35]」「教育環境の解釈学」であり、教育過程の生態学的・構造的な理解を重視する。教育は、人間が説明する指示的、直接的な活動だけでなく、環境を意識的に利用することで、構造的、間接的に作用する。ハーンによれば、環境を扱うとき、「特定の環境の選択、デザイン、あるいは創造を、特定の教育的意図をもって導くことは可能であり、また必要である[36]」ことに気づくのである。ハーンは、「自分の思想と創造力のすべてを、生徒たちを関係づけよ

うとする『環境』の方に[37]」向けている。ティーゼンによれば、クルト・ハーンは、環境が意図的に存在するようになる３つの方法として、第１に構成、第２に接続、第３にその２つの観点の組み合わせを区別しているという。彼女は、クルト・ハーンの教育目標に対するこの説得力のある解釈を、共学、奨学金制度、訓練計画、そして最後にもっとも複雑な「環境」である救急隊を分析することによって示している[38]。クルト・ハーンは「『環境』の効果の自動化[39]」までをも想定しているのか、また「教育過程の柱となる教科の軽視[40]」がみられるのではと、教授学上では異論もありえるだろう。

　クルト・ハーンの教授学は、文化批判を取り入れながら、工業化した現代における人間の状態の熟考を目指している。ハーンの教育目標は、「人間性の救済と回復[41]」である。これによると、「力の増大ではなく、力の維持であり、開発ではなく、開発によるダメージの防止、あるいは少なくとも抑制である[42]」としている。この教育的意図は、特に思春期において劇的で根本的なかたちを迎える。たとえばハーンは、思春期の青年たちの生活実態のなかで、社会のダメージと青年たちが抱える脅威とが悲惨なほどにぶつかり合うと述べている。ハーンはこの点で、教育の仕事と医療の仕事を比較している。ティーゼンによれば、診断、治療そして治療目標の各段階が区別できるという[43]。ハーンの立場の特徴は、文化批判を「適度な[44]」程度にとどめていることにある。限度を知らない過激な文化批判はあってはならないだろう。思春期にはすでに、むしろ与えられた境遇に身を置き、それに対処する術を身につけるべきである。

　このような教授上の戦略をとる理由は、学校卒業資格の交換と相互承認を促進するグローバルな資格付与の考え方にある。傘下の組織は、非営利財団としての役割を果たし、参加校が関連する基準に準拠しているかどうかを検証する。無論、個々のシラバスは、参加校のプロフィールに応じて異なる。学校での学習をグローバル・ネットワーキングへと方向づけることが目指しているのは、資格を共有し、それによって他の生徒たちとのつながりを経験することである。このようにして、クルト・ハーンが教育学上の基本的関心事としていた、子供たちや若者たちが責任ある世界市民となるように教育することが、実際に地球規模で広がっていったのである。人格の概念を指導原

理とすることが、やがて普遍的な妥当性を持つようになる。ハーンによれば、この原理は世界中のあらゆる地域の教育学を統合するものである。これは学校を知識の伝達や学習者の認知能力の向上のみに限定しようとするアプローチとは正反対のものである。人格のことを考えるということは、この世界の市民としてのあらゆる面を含んでいるのである[45]。

注

1) Röhrs, H. *Kurt Hahn*, Routledge, 1970., Ziegenspeck, J. W. and Hahn, K., *Erinnerungen-Gedanken-Aufforderungen. Beiträge zum 100 Geburtstag des Reformpädagogen*, Lüneburg, 1987., James,T., "Kurt Hahn and the Aims of Education", 2000 (http://www.kurthahn.org/wp-content/uploads/2016/04/james_final.pdf)., M, Knoll., "School reform through experiential therapy: Kurt Hahn-an effiacious educator", 2011 (https://files.eric.ed.gov/fulltext/ED515256.pdf).

2) BBC News, "Kurt Hahn: The man who taught Philip to think", 2016 (https://www.bbc.com/news/magazine-35603975).

3) Hahn, K. and Michael, K. (Eds.), *Erziehung und die Krise der Demokratie. Reden, Aufsätze, Briefe eines politischen Pädagogen*, Stuttgart, 1986, p. 54.

4) Ibid., pp. 67.

5) International Baccalaurate, "Facts and figures" (https://www.ibo.org/about-the-ib/facts-and-figures/).

6) Obara, K., "West Meets East. A Well-Rounded Education versus an Angular Education in Japan", *Espacio, Tiempo y Educación*, Volume 5, 2018, p. 110.

7) Röhrs, H., "Die Internationalität der Reformpädagogik und die Ansätze zu einer Welterziehungsbewegung", In: Lenhart, D. and Lenhart, V. (Eds.), *Die Reformpädagogik auf den Kontinenten*, Ein Handbuch, 1994, p. 14.

8) Ibid., p. 20.

9) Ibid., p. 19.

10) Koerrenz, R., *Reformpädagogik-eine Einführung.*, Paderborn, 2014, chap. 5., Koerrenz, R., "New Education-Historical Aspects and Recent Significance", *The Journal of the World Education Fellowship*, Volume 100, 2019, pp. 73-85. を参照。

11) Röhrs, op. cit., p. 20.

12) Schule Schloss Salem, "Salem Laws"(http://www.salem-net.de/privatschule-internat/vertiefendes/salemer-gesetze.html).

13) たとえば Hahn, K., *Erziehung zur Verantwortung. Reden und Aufsätze*, Stuttgart, 1958, pp. 9.

14) Ibid., p. 17.

15) Ibid., p. 30.

16) Ibid., p. 74.

17) Ibid., p. 77. を参照。

18) Ibid., p. 78., Ziegenspeck の前掲書も参照。

19) Dreeben, R., *Was wir in der Schule lernen*, Frankfurt/M, 1980. を参照。

20) Koerrenz,R., *Hermann Lietz-Einführung mit zentralen Texten*, Paderborn 2011., J. Yamana, "Die Struktur der "Übersichtlichkeit" des Landerziehungsheims Haubinda. Zur Interpretation des "Schulstaat"-Konzepts von Hermann Lietz", Zeitschrift für Pädagogik, 42, 1996, pp. 407-421. を参照。

21) Lassahn, R. (Ed.), Lietz, H., *Schulreform durch Neugründung. Ausgewählte Pädagogische Schriften*, Paderborn 1970., Koerrenz, op. cit.

22) Hahn, op. cit., p. 55.

23) この教授活動の説明として、例えば次のイエナ・プランの学校モデルを参照のこと。R. Koerrenz, Reform (ing) Education. The Jena-Plan as a Concept for a Child-Centred School. Paderborn 2020.

24) Obara, op. cit., p. 115., Sakuma, H. "Kuniyoshi Obara's *Zenjin* Education at *Tamagawa Gakuen*". In:Y, Yoko & K, Hiroyuki (Eds.), *Educational Progressivism, Cultural Encounters and Reform in Japan*, Routledge, 2017, p. 105. を参照。

25) Sakuma, op. cit., pp. 101ff. を参照。

26) Rousseau, J.-J., *Emil oder Über die Erziehung*, Ed. by Ludwig Schmidt. Paderborn 1971. を参照。

27) Neubert, W., *Das Erlebnis in der Pädagogik*, Lüneburg 1990, p. 64.

28) Neubert, ibid., p. 65.

29) Neubert, ibid., pp. 41ff. を参照。

30) Flitner, A. & Doris. K., *Reform der Erziehung. Impulse des 20. Jahrhunderts*, Piper Verlag GmbH, 2001, p. 96.

31) Prange, K., *Bauformen des Unterrichts*. Bad Heilbrunn 1986. を参照。

32) Ziegenspeck, op. cit., p. 95.

33) Thiesen, H., *Kurt Hahn-Pädagogische Umwelten zwischen Konstruktion und Anknüpfung*, Garamond, 2006. を参照。

34) Ibid., p. 82.

35) Ibid., p. 74.

36) Ibid., p. 62.

37) Ibid., p. 188.

38) Ibid., pp. 231ff.

39) Ibid., p. 189.

40) Ibid., p. 321.

41) Ibid., p. 155.

42) Ibid., p. 176.

43) Thiesen, op. cit., p. 135. を参照。

44) Hahn, K., *Reform mit Augenmaß. Ausgewählte Schriften eines Politikers und Pädagogen*, Klett-Cotta, 1988. を参照。

45) 本稿は、ドイツ・イエナ大学教育文化研究所の Sarah Ganss (M. A.) がドイツ語から英語に翻訳したものである。

国際バカロレアと全人教育
—— Learner Profile に着目して

はじめに

　玉川大学・玉川学園の総合パンフレットの最後のページに日本の学校には珍しく「アクレディテーション」が記載されていて、国際バカロレアの認定を受けていることが紹介されている（図5-1）。日本ではまだ広く知られていないが、アクレディテーションは教育の質保証のために政府から独立している第三者機関が行う制度である。学校の教育が学外の視点から見ても価値あるものであるかを示し、どこのアクレディテーションを受けているかで信用度が高まる。この章では教育の世界基準であるといわれている国際バカロレアと玉川の教育とのつながりをみていきたい。

　10年ほど前から日本では「グローバル人材育成」が注目されるようになった。2011（平成23）年に「グローバル人材育成推進会議」が設置され、その中間まとめで、育成すべきグローバル人材に求められる資質・能力が以下のように示された[1]。

　　要素Ⅰ：語学力・コミュニケーション能力

要素Ⅱ：主体性・積極性、チャレンジ精神、協調性・柔軟性、責任感・
　　　　使命感

要素Ⅲ：異文化に対する理解と日本人としてのアイデンティティー

　当時の内向き志向の日本の若者が、留学を目指すように、グローバル人材の育成のために、そして、教育改革推進のために「高校卒業時に国際バカロレア資格を取得可能な、又はそれに準じた教育を行う学校を 5 年以内に 200校程度へ増加させる」と文科省が発表した[2]。多くの日本の教育関係者がこのとき初めて「国際バカロレア」を知った。

第 1 節　国際バカロレアとは

　国際バカロレア機構（International Baccalaureate Organization：以下、IB）は 1968（昭和 43）年に設立された非営利の教育財団で、本部はスイスのジュネーブにある。4 つの国際教育のプログラムを開発し、それらを実施する学校を IB ワールドスクール（IB World School：以下、IB 認定校）として認可する組織である。学校を経営しているのではなく、学校と協力し、IB 認定校を認可し、国際的な資格を付与する認可団体である。現在、世界中の国や地域に 5,000 校以上の IB 認定校が存在し、IB の使命のもと教育活動を行っている。

　　国際バカロレア（IB）は、多様な文化の理解と尊重の精神を通じて、より良い、より平和な世界を築くことに貢献する、探究心、知識、思いやりに富んだ若者の育成を目的としています。
　　この目的のため、IB は、学校や政府、国際機関と協力しながら、チャレンジに満ちた国際教育プログラムと厳格な評価の仕組みの開発に取り組んでいます。
　　IB のプログラムは、世界各地で学ぶ児童生徒に、人がもつ違いを違いとして理解し、自分と異なる考えの人々にもそれぞれの正しさがあり得ると認めることのできる人として、積極的に、そして共感する心をもって生涯にわたって学び続けるよう働きかけています[3]。

図5-1　IB ワールドスクールに使用が許される IB 認定校ロゴ
出典：International Baccalaureate, "Logos and programme models"
(https://www.ibo.org/digital-toolkit/logos-and-programme-models/、2020 年 12 月 30 日閲覧)

　この IB の使命に共感する学校が IB 認定校を目指す。世界各地の IB 認定校は、所在している国や在籍児童生徒の数や文化的背景、そして学校が置かれている政治的、経済的、社会的な状況が大きく異なっていても、この使命に記されている教育の理念に基づいて、同じ方向を目指しているのである。

第2節　IB の学習者像とは

　IB の使命を行動として表し、子供の姿に落とし込んだものが IB の 10 の学習者像である。その人物像とその説明は以下の通りである（図5-2 [4]）。

　　探究する人：私たちは、好奇心を育み、探究し研究するスキルを身につけます。ひとりで学んだり、他の人々とともに学んだりします。熱意をもって学び、学ぶ喜びを生涯を通じて持ち続けます。

　　知識のある人：私たちは、概念的な理解を深めて活用し、幅広い分野の知識を探究します。地域社会やグローバル社会における重要な課題や考えに取り組みます。

　　考える人：私たちは、複雑な問題を分析し、責任ある行動をとるために、批判的かつ創造的に考えるスキルを活用します。率先して理性的で倫理的な判断を下します。

　　コミュニケーションができる人：私たちは、複数の言語やさまざまな方

法を用いて、自信をもって創造的に自分自身を表現します。他の人々や他の集団のものの見方に注意深く耳を傾け、効果的に協力し合います。

信念をもつ人：私たちは、誠実かつ正直に、公正な考えと強い正義感をもって行動します。そして、あらゆる人々が持つ尊厳と権利を尊重して行動します。私たちは、自分自身の行動とそれに伴う結果に責任を持ちます。

心を開く人：私たちは、自己の文化と個人的な経験の真価を正しく受け止めると同時に、他の人々の価値観や伝統の真価もまた正しく受け止めます。多様な視点を求め、価値を見いだし、その経験を糧に成長しようと努めます。

思いやりのある人：私たちは、思いやりと共感、そして尊重の精神を示します。人の役に立ち、他の人々の生活や私たちを取り巻く世界を良くするために行動します。

挑戦する人：私たちは、不確実な事態に対し、熟慮と決断力を持って向き合います。ひとりで、または協力して新しい考えや方法を探究します。挑戦と変化と機知に富んだ方法で快活に取り組みます。

バランスのとれた人：私たちは、自分自身や他の人々の幸福にとって、私たちの生を構成する知性、身体、心のバランスをとることが大切だと理解しています。また、私たちが他の人々や、私たちが住むこの世界と相互に依存していることを認識しています。

振り返りができる人：私たちは、世界について、そして自分の考えや経験について、深く考察します。自分自身の学びと成長を促すため、自分の長所と短所を理解するよう努めます。

　IBの学習者像に示されている10の人物像は、IB教育の全人的（ホリスティック）な性質を反映していて、好奇心や思いやりといった資質を育み、知識やスキルを発展させることの重要性を強調している。また認知的発達だけではなく、児童生徒の社会的、感情的、身体的な健全性に注意を払い、児童生徒が自分、他者、そして周辺の世界に敬意を払うよう確実に学ぶことを強調して[5]いる。

図5-2　IB学習者像ポスター

出典：International Baccalaureate, "Brochures, flyers and posters"
（https://www.ibo.org/digital-toolkit/brochures-flyers-and-posters/、2020年12月30日閲覧）

　子供はこの10の属性のすべてを兼ね備えることを目指す。IBの学習者像は、理念を学習者に期待する21世紀型の学習成果の理想の姿に置き換えたものである。この学習者像は教育の長期的ビジョンを表すものであり、学校や教師を突き動かし、動機付けを高め、努力を焦点化するのに役立つ理想の学習者像である[6]。この点は小原國芳が「『全人教育』の意味は、子供たちをこの完全なる境地に到達させるということ[7]」と記していることと重なる。また、IBの理想は国際的な視野を持つ人間の育成であり、その国際的視野を持つということは、即ち、この10の属性を持ち合わせることである。IBの「国際的視野を持った」人材は、いわば政府の目指す「グローバル人材」のIB版でもあり、結局のところIBの学習者像と全人教育と政府のグローバル人材の3つは目指すところは同じであるといえるのではないだろうか。

第3節　IBの4つの教育プログラム

　IBの教育理念を具現化し、IBの学習者を育てるためにIBは4つの教育プログラムを提供している[8]。
　最初、1968年に設置されたのが、日本では1番知名度の高いディプロマ・

プログラム（以下、DP）である。対象年齢は 16 歳から 19 歳で、日本では高校 2 年生と 3 年生で実施する大学進学準備の 2 年間のプログラムである。6 科目の学習と批判的思考力やリサーチスキルを育てる「知の理論」や「課題論文」と、社会とのつながりや実際の社会での体験を重視する「創造性・活動・奉仕」の領域の学びがその特徴である。世界共通の最終試験を受験し、45 点満点のスコアを活用して大学を受験をする。DP は学習内容等が規定されているカリキュラムである。

　次いで 1994（平成 6）年に開発したのが、中等教育プログラム（以下、MYP）である。対象年齢は 11 歳から 16 歳で、小学校 6 年生から高校 1 年生までの原則 5 年間のプログラムである。8 教科の学習と学際的な学びや実社会での奉仕活動がその特徴で、社会のあり方に関して、既存の教科の枠組みを超えた理解を構築していくことを目指す。MYP 修了後は DP へ進級する者もいる。MYP は学習内容の規定はなく、指導言語も自由に設定できるカリキュラムフレームワークである。

　さらに 1997（平成 9）年に開発したのが初等教育プログラム（以下、PYP）である。対象年齢は 3 歳から 12 歳で、連続した 2 年以上のプログラムとして小学校や幼稚園や保育所でも実施が可能なカリキュラムフレームワークである。合科学習を基本とし、探究の単元から構成される探究のプログラムを通して、子供は身近な話題を糸口に社会の問題に気付き、考え、発信していくことを目指す。PYP を修了した者のなかにも MYP へと進級する者もいる。

　そして、最近開発したのが 2012（平成 24）年に始まったキャリア関連プログラムである。対象年齢は DP と同じである。DP は大学進学を目指す生徒向けであるが、CP は大学進学予定者のみならず幅広い層の生徒たちのニーズに対応すべく DP 2 科目とキャリア関連学習を組み合わせたプログラムである。

　このように DP 単独のプログラムとして始まった IB の教育は、現在では 3 歳から 19 歳まで、国や学校が異なっても一貫して IB 教育を受けることができるようになっている。

表5-1　IB の教育プログラムの特徴

IB が提供する国際教育プログラム			
理念	IB の使命		
育てたい学習者像	10 の学習者像		
プログラム	Primary Years Programme	Middle Years Programme	Diploma Programme	Career-related Prgogramme
略称	PYP	MYP	DP	CP
日本語名称	初等教育 プログラム	中等教育 プログラム	ディプロマ プログラム	キャリア関連 プログラム
対象年齢	3〜12 歳	11〜16 歳	16〜19 歳	16〜19 歳
ねらい	国際的視野の育成		
カリキュラムと フレームワーク	探究単元から 構成される 探究プログラム	8 教科 グローバルな文脈	6 科目とコア 「知の理論」 (TOK)	2 科目と キャリア関連学習
指導の方法	6 つの指導のアプローチ （探究、概念、文脈、協働、インクルーシブ、評価を重視した指導）		
学習の方法	5 つの学習のアプローチのカテゴリー （思考、リサーチ、コミュニケーション、社会性、自己管理のスキル）		
評価の方法	内部評価	内部評価 オプション 外部評価 (e アセスメント)	内部評価 外部評価 (最終試験)	内部評価 外部評価 (最終試験)
体験を通した 学習	行動	奉仕と行動 (SA)	「創造性・活動・ 奉仕（CAS）」	奉仕学習
集大成 プロジェクト	発表会	コミュニティ プロジェクト／ パーソナル プロジェクト	「課題論文(EE)」	振り返り プロジェクト

出典：各プログラムのカリキュラムモデル（https://www.ibo.org/digital-toolkit/logos-and-programme-models/、2020 年 12 月 30 日閲覧）より筆者作成。

第4節　IB における指導と学習

　IB の教育における指導は 4 つのプログラムに一貫した（以下、指導のアプローチと呼ぶ）特徴を持つ（表5-1）。

1　探究学習を基盤とした指導：児童生徒がそれぞれ独自に情報を入手し、独自の理解を構築することを重視する。

2　概念理解に重点を置いた指導：各教科の理解を深め、つながりを見出し、新しい文脈へと学びを転移できるようになるために概念を探

究する。

3　地域的な文脈とグローバルな文脈において展開される指導：実際の文脈と例を用いて、新しい情報を自分の体験や周囲の世界に結びつけて消化することを児童生徒に奨励する。

4　効果的なチームワークと協働を重視する指導：児童生徒間のチームワークと協働を促すだけではなく、教師と生徒の協働関係もこれに含む。

5　学習への障壁を取り除くデザイン：多様性に価値を置き、インクルーシブな指導を行う。児童生徒のアイデンティティーを肯定し、全ての児童生徒が適切な個人目標を設定して追求できるよう、学習機会を創出することを目指す。

6　評価を取り入れた指導：評価は学習成果の測定だけでなく学習の支援においても重要な役割を果たす。また、効果的なフィードバックを児童生徒に提供することの重要性も、このアプローチでは認識されている[9]。

　IB教育では生涯学習者を育成する目的で学習のアプローチ（以下、ATL）、学び方を学ぶためのスキルの発達を目指す[10]。

1　コミュニケーションスキル
2　社会性スキル
3　自己管理スキル
4　リサーチスキル
5　思考スキル

　指導と学習のアプローチの根底には「実際に行い経験することによって学ぶ」という体験を通じた学習が重要視され、PYPでは学習のプロセスの成果としての「行動」、MYPでは「行動としての奉仕活動」、DPでは「創造性・活動・奉仕（CAS）」の活動、そしてCPではサービスラーニングである「コミュニティーと奉仕活動」として位置づけられている[11]。

第 5 節　IB と玉川学園

（1）IB 教育のパイオニアとしての玉川学園

　玉川学園では 2009（平成 21）年に MYP の認定を受け IB 認定校の仲間入りをし、2010（平成 22）年に DP 認定も受けた。2009 年の認定は学校教育法第 1 条に規定されているいわゆる一条校では国内第 2 号である。政府が 1979（昭和 54）年より、大学入学資格に関し、学校教育法に基づき、国際バカロレア資格を有する者で 18 歳に達した者を、高等学校を卒業した者と同等以上の学力があると認められる者として指定[12]したが、長い間、日本における IB 校の認定はインターナショナルスクールに限られていた。それは言語の壁があったことと日本の学校が外部からの認定や評価を受ける体質がないことに起因すると推測できる。

　IB の公式言語は英語とフランス語とドイツ語である。今でこそ、文部科学省と IB の協力によりデュアル・ランゲージ・ディプロマ・プログラム（通称「日本語 DP」）が立ち上がり、IB 発行の指導の手引き集の多くが日本語訳されているが、玉川学園が認定を目指した当時は、一条校としての認定第 1 号だった加藤学園暁秀中学・高等学校がわずかに先を行っているだけで、資料を読み解くだけでもかなり手探りの取り組みだったと考える。また、日本の学校には馴染みの薄い、外部機関から認定や評価を受けることで教育の質保証を希求するアクレディテーション（適格認定）という事後評価の制度を活用したのも当時としてはかなり先進的な取り組みだったはずである。IB 認定校になるためには「プログラム基準と実践要綱」という手引きに記載されている認定要件を読み解き、該当する取り組みを特定し、可視化し、資料化し、要件充足の証拠として提出することが必要であり、多くの時間と労力を要する。このような状況のなかで IB の認定を目指し、達成したことは、小原國芳の「教育に対して何ごとも惜しまない姿勢」の現れと感じる。現在では一条校の IB 認定校の数は 4 つのプログラム併せて 45 校となっている[13]。多くの学校にとって玉川学園は道なき道を切り拓いてくれた良きお手本であることは間違いない。

（2）　IB の教育と玉川の全人教育のつながり

　国際バカロレア機構の設立のきっかけは、世界中のインターナショナルスクールに共通する悩みであった[14]。1962（昭和 37）年にジュネーブで開催されたインターナショナルスクール会議において、共通の課題が議論され、世界共通の高校卒業資格を設置することが合意され、「国際バカロレア」と命名された。同年、ドイツの教育学者のクルト・ハーンがイギリスに後の最初の IB 認定校となったアトランティック・カレッジを創立[15]。クルト・ハーンと言えば、玉川学園が加盟している国際的な私立学校の連盟であるラウンド・スクエアを創設し[16]、その後は野外体験教育の発展に寄与し[17]、玉川学園の玉川アドベンチャープログラム（TAP）の原点となったことが思い起こされる。玉川学園と IB の発展の歴史が交差する「ご縁」の 1 つである。また、1962 年に IB 構想を練った教員がもっとも影響を受けた教育学者が1896（明治 29）年にシカゴ大学付属実験学校を開校して進歩主義の教育を実践したジョン・デューイ（John Dewey）と 1921（大正 10）年にサマーヒル・スクールを開校し自由教育思想の実践を行った A・S・ニイル（Alexander Sutherland Neill）である[18]。これは、小原國芳が玉川学園を開校し、全人教育の実践を行ったのと同じ時代である。教育学者が自ら提唱する教育のあり方を実践するために学校を開校し、教育改革を推進し始めていたこともまた「ご縁」であり、玉川学園が一条校としては 2 番目に認定を受けたのは偶然ではなく必然だったと思うのである。

　玉川の全人教育と IB の理念、学習者像、指導と学習のアプローチには多くの共通点がみられる。まず、玉川の全人教育では真・善・美・聖・健・富の 6 つの価値、その理想を実現するため 12 の教育信条と玉川の魅力、特徴をモチーフとして表したピクトグラム（図5-3）がある。それが IB 教育の使命と学習者像（図5-4）と同じように、単なるスローガンとして黒板の上に掲げられているだけではなく、教育活動のあらゆる場面で意識化されていて、学校と教員、児童生徒から大学生、院生までが、活動のあり方を模索する際に必ず立ち戻る道しるべとなっている点である。これは教育組織として確固たる信念があることを示し、それらを文字やイメージなどで多元的多面的に包括的に伝え、有機的なつながりを持って人々の心に伝わっていくこ

図5-3　玉川ブランドピクトグラム
出典：玉川大学 玉川学園「玉川大学について」
（https://www.tamagawa.jp/introduction/
brand/、2020 年 12 月 30 日閲覧）

図5-4　IB 学習者像ロゴ
出典：International Baccalaureate, "Logos and
programme models"
（https://www.ibo.org/digital-toolkit/logos-and-
programme-models/、2020 年 12 月 30 日閲覧）

とを可能にしている。

　IB の学習者像はすなわち、各プログラムを通して育てたい学習者の姿で
あるが、これは、実は、設立当初からあったのではない。もとは「PYP 学
習者像」という名称であった。IB の学習者像は 2006（平成 18）年に、1997
年に PYP が設置された当時から採用していた「PYP 児童像」（図5-5）か
ら発展的にすべての IB のプログラムに採用されたものである[19]。現在では
欠かせない IB の学習者像が小学校教育を発祥としている点も、玉川学園が
大学の附属学校としてではなく、初等中等教育から発展したことと重なるよ
うに思う。また、「児童像」から「学習者像」に変更する際に唯一変更した
のが現在の「バランスのとれた人」である。これは PYP の児童像時代には
「健康な人」となっていた。「バランスのとれた人」となっても、「私たちの
生を構成する知性、身体、心のバランスをとることが大切」とした[20] ことは、
小原國芳が人間形成に必要な 6 つの価値のなかに「健」を位置付け、「人間
には心と身体の両面が認められ」、「身体のために生命保存と精神活動の源泉
となる健康を要求した[21]」のと同じ思いがこめられているのではないだろう
か。

　「バランスのとれた人」という学習者像を見るたびに思い出す、『全人教育
論』の一節がある。「肥桶も担げばピアノも弾け、掃き掃除もすればお茶や
生花もでき、雑巾も縫えば絹の着物もしたてられ、ドブ溝もさらえば第九シ

WHAT DO WE WANT STUDENTS TO LEARN?
Student Learning Outcomes
Students will be:

Inquirers
Their natural curiosity will have been nurtured, their sense of wonder and love of learning will be sustained throughout their adult lives and they will have acquired the skills necessary to conduct purposeful, constructive research.
Thinkers
They will exercise initiative in applying thinking skills critically and creatively to make sound decisions and solve complex problems.
Communicators
They will be able to receive and express ideas and information confidently in more than one language, including the language of mathematical symbols.
Risk-takers
They will approach unfamiliar situations without anxiety and have the confidence and adoptability to explore new roles, ideas and strategies. They will be courageous and articulate in defending those things in which they believe.
Knowledgeable
They will have spent their time in our school exploring themes which have global relevance and importance. In so doing, they will have acquired a 'critical mass' of significant knowledge.
Principled
They will have sound grasp of the principles of moral and ethical reasoning.
Caring
They will show sensitivity towards the needs and feelings of others and have developed a sense of responsibility and personal commitment to action and service.
Open-Minded
They will respect the views, values and traditions of other individuals and cultures and be accustomed to seeking and considering a range of points of view.
Healthy
They will understand the importance of physical and mental balance and personal well-being.
Reflective
They will be accustomed to examining their own learning, and analysing their personal strengths and weaknesses in a thoughtful, constructive manner.

図5-5　PYP 児童像

出典：International Baccalaureate Organization, *History of the Primary Years Programme*, International Baccalaureate Organization, 2013, p. 28.

ンフォニーも歌え、薪割りもすれば絵も描くし、ソロバンもはじくがお経も繙ける玉川っ子[22]」という記述である。IB でいえばこれは、自己管理をしながら自分で探究もできるが協働での学びも楽しみ、エビデンスを持って提案もできるが自分でも行動をし、極めてローカルな文脈と広くグローバルな視点もあり、自分の言語的文化的アイデンティティーを大事にしながら他者の価値観も尊重し、多くの問いを立てるが多くの課題解決も試み、文系理系や主要科目・実技科目という区別なくすべての教科を大事にしつつも学際的な学びで統合や再構成を堪能する IB っ子とでもなるだろうか。このバランスが二項対立の世界を超え、高次の思考を促進し、深い学びへと学習者を誘う点が共通していると言える。

「PYP 児童像」という名称も「IB の学習者像」となり、「児童生徒像」としなかったことに大きな意味がある。IB の教育では、教師も成長する「学習者」と捉えるからである[23]。IB の学習者像は子供だけではなく、教師、保護者を含めてすべてのステークホルダーを学習者と捉え、全員に向けて IB の

学習者像は学習者の理想形を示すものでもあり、国際的視野の獲得を目指す子供と大人の人生の旅路において迷った時に頼りになる地図なのである[24]。小原國芳も「全人」を「完全なる境地」とし理想として語っている[25]。玉川の丘で育った者は、卒業した後も、この6つの価値観の実現を目指している。そのような卒業生に私は多く出会ってきた。玉川学園の全人教育も、IB教育も目指すところがはっきりしているからこそ逆向き設計ができる。そして、その精神を教育活動の特定の時間ではなく、すべての時間や活動にひたひたと浸透させるべくカリキュラムマネジメントが可能になる。その結果、教え方や学び方などを超越した、玉川やIBで育った者の生き方へと昇華されていくように思うのである。

　つねに理想を追い求めるという姿勢の現れとして、IBの教員は定期的にIB主催の研修に参加して、授業の質の向上を目指す。研修では教師の振り返りが求められる。IBの単元指導案には教師の振り返り欄がある[26]。IBの学習者像は単なる理念を人物像に変換しただけではなく、教員が自身の授業や教育活動を振り返る際に活用できる共通の言語を提供し、振り返りの検討をより深いものにすることを可能にするのである。IBの学習者像は「PYP児童像」ではない。『全人教育論』のなかで、よき教師は「自己を磨き、子どもたちとともに進む教師」であり、「ドイツで最初の教師養成学校の校長となったディースターヴェーグ」から「進みつつある教師のみ人を教える権利あり」と学んだことが記されている[27]。玉川とIBの教育においては、子供と一緒に学び続ける教師がいなければ教育が成り立たないという、この同じ教師観が展開されている。

　IBの学習者像のなかに探究する人があり、IBの教育の特徴にも探究学習があり、あらゆる場面で探究が奨励されている。知識を探究するのではない。IBの探究においては知識があるという前提のもと、構成主義の教授法で認識されているように、子供がすでに持っている知識を引き出す学習経験を提供し、振り返りと統合の機会をつくり、生徒が継続的に知識を発達させ、理解し、その知識をより広い文脈へ転移・応用させることを重視している[28]。そして、探究するのは発達させる知識である概念と呼ぶ「生徒が世界を理解し、今後の学習や学校の枠を超えた人生で成功するために活用するこ

とのできる、普遍的な原則」である[29]。この概念を理解するために子供は学び方のスキルである ATL を使いながら、課題を特定し、解決する手段を創造していく。教師が投げかける様々な問いに対する答えを探るなかで、自分自身で問いを立て、探究を深めていく。これを通して、永続的な概念の理解に到達する[30]。全人教育も「知識とはお互いが総合するのです。構成するのです。ただ単に模写されるのではなくて、各人が組み立てるのです、構成するのです、創造するのです[31]」と構成主義的な考えに根差している。そして、IB の教育の探究学習は、小原の言葉に代えると「教師は教え子に、学問に対する燃ゆる情熱を与え、学問の掘り方を会得させ、探究の力を鍛えてやること」ことになるのである[32]。さらに、「疑問は真理探究の原動力」と明記し、「自由研究」の提案[33] に至ったことは、IB が各プログラムの集大成として、MYP で「パーソナル・プロジェクト」を、DP で「課題論文」を設定したことと重なる。自由研究は巷の学校では名称だけが今でも利用されていて、研究のあり方に関する指導などは伴わないのが残念であるが、玉川学園では、現在でも小原の「自由研究」が「学びの技」として息づいていて、毎年開催される探究型学習発表会は見ごたえのある行事である。

　IB の学習者像の「考える人」、「信念をもつ人」、「思いやりのある人」に「行動」という用語が使用されている。IB の教育で探究とともに重要とされるのが「行動」と「振り返り」であり、「構成主義的な考え方に基づき、質問すること（探究）、実行に移すこと（行動）、考えること（振り返り）の相互作用を通じて、さまざまな意見やものの味方が尊重される開かれたクラス」を目指す[34]。「IB の学習者は家庭や教室、学校、地域社会、そしてより広い世界で行動」とされているが、「行動」には、サービスラーニング（奉仕活動を通じた学習）が含まれている。「探究」、「行動」、「振り返り」、それぞれ単体の学習では達成できない、この３要素から成るダイナミックな学習経験を通じて、「学び合う者たちのコミュニティー」が複雑でグローバルな課題に取り組めるよう」になると考える[35]。これはまさに全人教育の労作である。「苦しみ、作り、体験し、試み、考え、行うことによって得られる[36]」ものは IB の「探究」、「行動」、「振り返り」の探究サイクルから得られるものと一致するのではないだろうか。知識として現代の社会における大小様々な葛

藤や軋轢を知った時、それを知識としてのみ終わらせず、解決の糸口になるような行動を起こす義務が生まれる。知り得たものの義務を果たすことがより良い世界、より平和な世界をもたらすと IB では考える。労作教育とのかかわりの深い6つの価値のうちの「富」も経験が我々にもたらすリソースであり、それを共有することがより豊かな人間形成と社会福祉をもたらすのではないかと考える。キャンパスに入る時に目にする「人生の最も苦しい、いやな、辛い、損な場面を／真っ先に微笑を以って担当せよ」という玉川のモットーと心を洗うが如くの噴水によって毎朝、この人間としてのあるべき姿を再確認するのである。

第6節　そしてこれから

　時代も国も異なるところで生まれた IB において「全人」や「全人教育」という用語は資料のなかで頻繁に使われている。ホール・パーソン、ホール・チャイルドやホリスティック教育といった英語の訳語である。IB は日本の学校への普及を見越して、2008（平成20年）年夏に指導の手引きなどの日本語翻訳に着手した。その時、翻訳プロジェクトに参加していたのが当時玉川大学学術研究所准教授であり IB のアジア太平洋地域の日本・韓国代表であったバーナード恭子氏、そして現在、教育学研究科で IB 教員養成を担当している教育学研究科のカーティス・ビーバーフォード教授、学術研究所所属のカメダ・クインシー准教授と私であった。後者2名とは今では玉川大学大学院教育学研究科で IB 教員養成を担当する同僚であるが、当時はそれぞれ別の職場から集められて、他のメンバーとともにプロジェクトに参加し、IB の基本用語の翻訳をした。その時、議論となったのは「全人教育」という玉川の教育を表す用語を IB の用語として使用するのが適切か否かという点である。玉川色が強すぎるのではないかと時間をかけて他の訳語を探したものの、代わりの適切な訳語がみつからず、「全人教育」を採用した。現在も手引きには「全人教育」の文字がみられる。全人教育と IB 教育がぴったり重なっているだけではなく、時代も国も言語も違うところで生まれたにもかかわらず、その2つが出会えたことは感動的ですらある。

　玉川学園の全人教育と IB との関係は発展し続けている。2009 年の玉川学園中学部・高等部での MYP の認定から始まり、2010 年高等部における DP の認定、同年からは玉川大学における国際バカロレア AO 型入学審査制度の開始、そして、2014（平成 26）年から大学院教育学研究科における IB Educator Certificate（IB 教員認定証）取得要件を満たす IB 研究コースの設置と続いた。現在中学部・高等部の下部組織である IB クラスが 2021（令和 3）年の春には IB テヴィジョンとして位置付けられることが決まっている。また、時期を同じくして、IB 教員養成のコースがどこからでも、現職のままでも受講できる完全オンラインコースの開講の準備も進んでいる。これは玉川学園の持つ「内在的しなやかさ[37]」の証明であり、IB の学習者像の「挑戦する人」としての取り組みである。玉川学園が IB との絆を重視した全学的な取り組みにより、全人教育を通してより平和な、より良い世界の実現を目指す学びのコミュニティーの中心で末永くあり続け、また創設者の理念を守り、玉川学園のアイデンティティの維持と発展への貢献につながることを願っている。

注

1 ）グローバル人材育成推進会議「グローバル人材育成推進会議中間まとめ 2011 年（平成 23 年）6 月 22 日」7 頁（https://www.kantei.go.jp/jp/singi/global/110622chukan_matome.pdf、2020 年 12 月 30 日閲覧）。

2 ）同上、11 頁。その後、「未来投資戦略 2018──『Society 5.0』『データ駆動型社会』への変革」（平成 30 年 6 月 15 日閣議決定）において「国際バカロレア認定校等を 2020 年度までに 200 校以上（2016 年度：101 校＜候補校含む＞）」と訂正された。

3 ）国際バカロレア機構「国際バカロレア（IB）の教育とは？」2019 年（2019 年 11 月に発行の英文原本 *What is an IB education?* の日本語版）。

4 ）国際バカロレア機構「国際バカロレア（IB）の教育とは？」2017 年（2013 年 8 月に発行、2015 年 6 月および 2017 年 4 月改訂の英文原本 *What is an IB education?* の日本語版）。

5 ）同上、4 頁。

6 ）International Baccalaureate Organization, *IB learner profile booklet*, International Baccalaureate Organization, 2006, p.1.

7 ）小原國芳・小原芳明（監修），ダグラス・トレルファ（英訳）*Kuniyoshi Obara's Theory of Zenjin Education*『英日対訳全人教育論』玉川大学出版会、2003 年、43 頁。

8 ）International Baccalaureate Organization, "Programmes"（https://www.ibo.org/programmes/、2020 年 12 月 30 日閲覧）.

9 ）国際バカロレア機構「国際バカロレア（IB）の教育とは？」2019 年、7 頁。

10）同上、8 頁。

11）国際バカロレア機構「一貫した国際教育に向けて」2014 年、33 頁（2008 年 9 月に発行の英文原本 *Towards a continuum of international education* の日本語版）。

12）文部科学省 IB 教育推進コンソーシアム「日本における IB 教育」（https://ibconsortium.mext.go.jp/ib-japan/、2020 年 12 月 30 日閲覧）。

13）International Baccalaureate Organization, "Find an IB World School"（https://www.ibo.org/programmes/find-an-ib-school/、2020 年 12 月 30 日閲覧）.

14）Peterson, A., *Schools Across Frontiers: The Story of the International Baccalaureate and the United World Colleges*, Open Court Pub. Co., 1987, pp.15-17.

15）International Baccalaureate Organization, "The history of the IB"（https://www.ibo.org/globalassets/digital-toolkit/presentations/1711-presentation-history-of-the-ib-en.pdf、2020 年 12 月 30 日閲覧）.

16）Round Square, "RS History and Heritage"（https://www.roundsquare.org/being-round-square/who/our-history-and-kurt-hahn/、2020 年 12 月 30 日閲覧）.

17）Outward Bound, "HISTORY"（https://www.outwardbound.net/history/、2020 年 12 月 30 日閲覧）.

18）International Baccalaureate Organization, "The History of the IB"（https://www.ibo.org/globalassets/digital-toolkit/presentations/1711-presentation-history-of-the-ib-en.pdf、2020 年 12 月 30 日閲覧）.

19）International Baccalaureate Organization, *IB learner profile booklet*, International Baccalaureate Organization, p.1.

20）International Baccalaureate Organization, *IB learner profile booklet*, International Baccalaureate Organization, p.28.

21）小原國芳・小原芳明（監修）、ダグラス・トレルファ（英訳）*Kuniyoshi Obara's Theory of Zenjin Education* 『英日対訳全人教育論』2003 年、玉川大学出版会、27 頁。

22）同上、117 頁。

23）国際バカロレア機構「一貫した国際教育に向けて」2014 年、27 頁。

24）International Baccalaureate Organization, *IB learner profile booklet*, International Baccalaureate Organization, p.2.

25）小原國芳・小原芳明（監修）、ダグラス・トレルファ（英訳）*Kuniyoshi Obara's Theory of Zenjin Education* 『英日対訳全人教育論』2003 年、玉川大学出版会、43 頁。

26）国際バカロレア機構「MYP——原則から実践へ」2016 年、66 頁（2014 年 5 月発行、2014 年 9 月改訂の英語原本 *MYP: From principles into practices* の日本語版）。

27）小原國芳・小原芳明（監修）、ダグラス・トレルファ（英訳）*Kuniyoshi Obara's Theory of Zenjin Education* 『英日対訳全人教育論』2003 年、玉川大学出版会、129 頁。

28）国際バカロレア機構「MYP——原則から実践へ」2016 年、83 頁。

29）同上、18 頁。

30）同上、73-74 頁。

31）小原國芳・小原芳明（監修）、ダグラス・トレルファ（英訳）*Kuniyoshi Obara's Theory of Zenjin Education* 『英日対訳全人教育論』2003 年、玉川大学出版会、55 頁。

32）同上、51 頁。

33）同上、125 頁。

34）国際バカロレア機構「MYP——原則から実践へ」2016 年、13 頁。

35）同上、13-14 頁。

36）小原國芳・小原芳明（監修）、ダグラス・トレルファ（英訳）*Kuniyoshi Obara's Theory of Zenjin Education*『英日対訳全人教育論』、2003 年、玉川大学出版会、106 頁。

37）Breaden, J. & Goodman, R., *Family-run Universities in Japan*, Oxford University Press, 2020, p.6. より翻訳。

ラウンドスクエアと全人教育
—— IDEALS に着目して

はじめに

　玉川学園は創立以来、「12 の教育信条」の 1 つに国際教育を掲げて力を入れてきた。2021（令和 3）年 4 月現在では初等中等教育段階で 8 か国、15 の提携校を持ち、毎年 300 人前後の児童生徒を海外の学校へ派遣したり受け入れたりしている。2005（平成 17）年には日本の学校として初めて、世界の学校連盟であるラウンドスクエア（Round Square）にも加盟している。

　本章では、そのラウンドスクエアを通して全人教育について考え、国際教育のあり方を探りたい。

第1節　クルト・ハーンとラウンドスクエアの歩み

　ラウンドスクエアは、IDEALS（Internationalism, Democracy, Environmentalism, Adventure, Leadership, Service）を理念とした人間教育を目指し、それを実現するために様々な国際交流活動、体験学習や課題解決学習等を実践する学校が集まった世界規模の学校連盟である。2020（令和 2）年では、世界約 55 か国、

約220の学校が加盟しており、玉川学園は2005（平成17）年、日本で最初に認定されたメンバー校である。

（1）クルト・ハーンの教育

ラウンドスクエアの創立には、ドイツの教育者クルト・ハーン（Kurt Hahn, 1886-1974）が密接にかかわっている。クルト・ハーンはドイツのザーレム校、スコットランドのゴードンストウン校を創立し、これら2つの学校がラウンドスクエア誕生に大きな役割を果たすことになる。

20世紀になると、それまでの教師中心、暗記中心の教育を批判し、豊かな自然の中で子供の自発的な学びを尊重し、人間性をバランスよく育てる全人教育を目指した新教育運動が盛んになった。この運動は、1889（明治22）年、イギリスのセシル・レディ（Cecil Reddie）によるアボツホルム校の創立が始まりだといわれている。アボツホルム校[1]は、「都市の悪影響から逃れた田園の地に、単に知的、身体的な面だけでなく、全人格の形成を目指した学校、教師と生徒による一大家庭をなす共同体としての学校の創設を図った[2]」。

クルト・ハーンはこの新教育運動の流れのなかで1920（大正9）年、ドイツに田園教育塾としてザーレム校を創設した。田園教育塾の目的は、「託された子供たちを、身体と精神において健康で力強く、肉体的、実践的、科学的、芸術的に有能で、明晰かつ鋭敏に思考し、温かく感じ、勇気を持って力強く意欲する、調和的で自律的な性格の持ち主であるドイツの若者へと教育すること[3]」であるとヘルマン・リーツ（Helman Lietz）は述べている。さらにクルト・ハーンは1934（昭和9）年にはスコットランドにゴードンストウン校を創立した。彼は、子供たちには人生について学習させる必要があり、そのためにはいろいろな刺激的で挑戦的な体験が必要であることを説いた。また生きる上で不可欠な勇気と思いやりを持つためにリーダーシップを発揮し、奉仕する活動が重要であるとした。クルト・ハーンは1941（昭和16）年にはゴードンストウン校の野外教育活動を発展させた、世界初のアウトドア教育のための組織であるアウトワード・バウンド・スクール（OBS）を創設[4]。1962（昭和37）年にはユナイテッド・ワールド・カレッジ（UWC）の最初の学校であるアトランティック・カレッジを創設し、1968（昭和43）

年の国際バカロレア（IB）設立に大きく貢献している。

　ドイツの哲学者オットー・フリードリヒ・ボルノー（Otto Fridrich Bollnow）はその著書のなかに、新教育運動で活躍した教育者たちについて次のように書いている。「それは一連の偉大な教育者たちの姿であり、ドイツではまた、田園塾の設立者として教育を硬化した形から解放した、ヘルマン・リーツ、パウル・ゲネープ、グスターフ・ヴィーネケン、クルト・ハーンである。彼らは本質的には同じ世代の者たちであり、この流れのなかのおそらくは最後の者として、小原國芳は立っている[5]」。これは小原國芳が目指した全人教育と、クルト・ハーンの田園塾教育が、新教育運動の流れのなかで教育を硬化した形から解放したという点で同じ方向を向いていたことを示している。

（2）ラウンドスクエアの歴史

　1953（昭和28）年、ギリシャ・イオニア諸島のケファロニア島で大地震が発生した。翌1954（昭和29）年、ドイツ・ザーレム校の呼びかけにスコットランドのゴードンストウン校とギリシャのアナヴリタ校の教員・生徒が加わり、被災地復興に向けての労作キャンプが実施された。クルト・ハーンの教育理念が、これらの学校にそのような行動を起こさせたのである。このケファロニア島での労作体験や交流が大変有意義なものであったので、これらの学校はその後も交流活動を継続することの必要性について話し合いを続けた。そしてそれは月日の流れとともにクルト・ハーンの教育理念を共有する世界的な学校連盟設立案に発展した。1966（昭和41）年、クルト・ハーンの80歳の誕生日を祝うためにドイツのザーレム校に集った8つの学校の校長たちによって準備が進められ、1967（昭和42）年、ゴードンストウン校を会場に、アナヴリタ校（ギリシャ）、ザーレム校（ドイツ）、ゴードンストウン校（スコットランド）、ボックスヒル校（イングランド）、バティスボロー校（イングランド）、アセニアン校（アメリカ）の校長、理事長、そしてクルト・ハーンが集まって最初のカンファレンスが開催された。その直後にスイスのエイグロン・カレッジもメンバーに加わっている[6]。

　この学校連盟は当初「ハーン・スクール・カンファレンス」という名称案

図6-1　ゴードンストウン校のラウンドスクエア
提供：ラウンドスクエア本部

が候補に挙がっていたそうである。しかしこれには、クルト・ハーン自身が反対しており、最初の会議が開かれたゴードンストウン校の施設の名称である「ラウンドスクエア[7]」（図6-1）から「ラウンドスクエア・カンファレンス」と呼ばれることになる。

　その後ラウンドスクエアの理念や活動は世界中の多くの学校の支持を得て、2020年には約55か国、220校が加盟する学校連盟に成長している。

第2節　IDEALSと全人教育

　ラウンドスクエアの教育理念はInternationalism、Democracy、Environmentalism、Adventure、Leadership、Serviceの6つから成り、それぞれの頭文字をとって、IDEALSと呼ばれている[8]。

（1）Internationalism：国際性の尊重

　ラウンドスクエアの学校は、生徒に国際性を身につけさせ、国際理解を促進することを目指している。自国のアイデンティティ、文化、伝統、遺産を大切にしながら、他国や他地域のそれらとの類似点や相違点を発見し、それらを受け入れる態度を育むために、世界中の学校の生徒や教

師の交流活動を実施している。近年では、地理的な境界を越えたデジタルコミュニケーションの成長が、この相互理解につながっている。様々な背景の若者たちが種々の交流活動や協働作業を通して、世界に通用するスキルと態度を身につけ、国際理解を深め、国際性を高めることが世界の平和につながっていく。

「『地球は、われわれの故郷である』とは、スイスのチンメルマン博士が1949年、2度目の来園をした時の言葉。宇宙時代にはいった今日、この言葉があらためて思い出されます。地球がすべての人々の故郷になるためには真の世界平和を実現しなくてはなりません。（中略）教育というものは、教室の中だけで行われるものではなく、地球上のあらゆるところが、宇宙のすべての場所が教育の現場でなければなりません。学生、生徒の国際交流はもとより、先生たちの交流にもつとめました[9]」。小原國芳はこのように述べている。また、「われわれが要求する世界国家は、それぞれの国家が益々その特色を発揮すればそれと同時に世界がそれだけ豊富になって行く意味のものです[10]」、「国際的の広さ。『広く知識ヲ世界ニ求』むる襟度をもって、隣国の人たちにはもとより、世界人に接してほしい。また、親しまれる親しさを持ってほしい[11]」とも述べている。玉川学園の12の教育信条に「国際教育」が位置付けられていることからも、玉川学園の教育とラウンドスクエアの考え方が国際性を尊重するという点で一致していることがわかる。

（2）Democracy：デモクラシー

ラウンドスクエアの学校は、生徒たちにデモクラシーの精神を身につけるように奨励する。それは平等、公平、正義について考え、思考と言論の自由を大切にし、公共の義務や他人のニーズを理解しながら充分な情報の共有、効果的な話し合いを経て、正しいことを進んで行う態度を身につけることである。それができるようになるためには、責任感を持ち、自立かつ自律していることが必要である。ラウンドスクエア国際会議等では、世界中の様々な文化背景を持つ生徒たちが協働しながら課題をみつけ、解決する方法について話し合い、ディベートやディスカッショ

ンを重ね、それを実行するための手段について意思決定し、アクション
を起こすまでのプロセスを経験する。それが将来の民主的な地球市民を
育てることにつながるのである。

　小原國芳はデモクラシーについて以下のように書いている。「デモクラシー
ということは、根本に宗教が、神が、慈悲が、愛が生きていなければなら
ないのだということを切実に、為政者に、国民に、教育者にわかってほし
い。デモクラシーということを決して、浅薄に法制的に考えないで頂きた
い[12]」、「われわれの教育は、個人主義対社会主義、国家主義対世界主義、理
想主義対現実主義、自由主義対法則主義という、いみじき対立、反対、矛盾
です。しかも、これが実に人間の真相なのです。(中略)ゼヒ、お互相応の協調、
調和、合一、歩み寄り、落合がなくてはなりませぬ[13]」。

　このような言葉からは、デモクラシーが安易な多数決などによる物事の決
定手段ではなく、真、善、美、聖を追求するためのより高次な行動プロセス
であると語っているように読める。そしてそれはラウンドスクエアが目指す
デモクラシーの考え方と重なっている。

（3）Environmentalism：環境保護

　　ラウンドスクエアの学校は、生徒たちに環境保護の精神を身につける
　　ことを奨励する。地球における私たちの居場所について知り、私たちの
　　環境を形作る様々な要因や環境への影響について理解し、環境問題への
　　取り組みにおいて実践的な役割を果たすことを目指す。環境の美しさ、
　　複雑さ、壊れやすさを知ることを通して、環境への感謝の気持ちを持つ
　　ことを大切にする。そして持続可能なコミュニティーを構築し、地球の
　　将来を守ることへ向けて感じ、考え、行動できるようにする。

「森の一隅にはチャペルが欲しい。朝と夕べには鐘がなる。未明に殿堂に
集まりたい。薄暗い中に、ローソクがかすかに神秘の光を放っている。その
中で、静かに黙祷したい。誰かが聖句を読む。堂の奥からコワイヤが歌う。
夕べには、夕べの鐘と共に、『今日も送りぬ主につかえて』と歌いたい。感

謝したい。静かに、静かに、森のチャペルの中に。あるいは流水のほとりに。木の根に。小鳥の歌に和して、幸いに得た新しい広い敷地は、まさに、それにふさわしい、何という幸福だろう！[14]」。小原國芳は、このような自然環境を教育の理想の場とした。そしてそこでは、「でき得べくんば、自らが食するコメも麦も、芋も野菜も自ら作りたい。利潤のためよりも、むしろホントにコメ一粒の貴さを、葉っぱ一茎のありがたさを、汗の崇さを、芽生えのうれしさを、土の意味、自然の美しさを、神の恵みの有難さを……知る[15]」ことを大切にした。玉川学園の自然環境のなかでの労作教育は、環境に対する意識を高め、持続可能な社会を目指す態度を育む。

（4）Adventure：アドベンチャー

　　　ラウンドスクエアでは、自分の限界を越えて挑戦し、試行錯誤と成功体験を通して自己肯定感を得ることをアドベンチャーという。このアドベンチャーを経験するために、ラウンドスクエアの学校では、生徒に各自のコンフォートゾーンからリスクを冒してでも一歩外へ踏み出すような活動を用意する。不測の事態に直面したり、潜在的な失敗に直面したりすることもあるが、あらゆる状況で勇気をふるい、挑戦し、粘り強さを発揮することでその挑戦を達成することを奨励する。これは野外活動のなかで効果的に実践されることに疑いはないが、それ以外にも生徒はスピーチ、パフォーマンス、メンタルチャレンジ、新しい趣味やスキルの習得等、カリキュラム内外の様々な機会のなかで個々の目標を設定して挑戦することができる。このようなアドベンチャー精神は、人生の開拓者として必要な資質・能力である。

　玉川学園は創立以来、挑戦することを大切にしてきた。小原國芳がこの丘に学校をつくり、教育を始めたこと自体がアドベンチャーであったし、創立以来今でも、その開拓者精神が大切にされている。

　玉川学園がスキーを教育に取り入れたことも、このアドベンチャー精神育成の考え方に通じる。「上野発。夜行。行く先は福島県の沼尻というところだというのです。目が覚めると川桁駅！　すごい吹雪！　全く形容のできな

いスゴさ！　オーケストラそのままの乱舞の花ビラ。森も、畑も、電柱も、煙突も、家々も、雪と戦っとるようなのです。サツマ生まれの私には全く、はじめての驚異でした。これだ！　これだ！　これに東京の子供たちをブッつけてやるんだ！[16]」小原國芳は、この厳しい吹雪のなかで生徒がそれぞれの目標に向かって挑戦し、心と技を磨くスキーを大切にした。そして生徒の「どうせ習うなら世界一に習いたい」という一言で、当時世界のアルペンスキー界第一人者であったハンネス・シュナイダー（Hannes Schneider）をオーストリアから招聘したことは、日本スキー界の歴史のなかでも有名な話である。

　また2000（平成12）年には、玉川アドベンチャープログラム（TAP）がスタートしている（第7章参照）。これは、アメリカのプロジェクト・アドベンチャー（PA）をベースに玉川オリジナルのプログラムとして実施している。プロジェクト・アドベンチャーは、イギリスのアウトワード・バウンド・スクールから派生したプログラムであり、アウトワード・バウンド・スクールの創設者は、ラウンドスクエアを創立したクルト・ハーン（Kurt Hahn）である。玉川学園のアドベンチャー教育は、まさにラウンドスクエアのアドベンチャー教育と同じルーツを持ち、同じ目的に向かって若者のアドベンチャー・スピリットを育てている。

（5）Leadership：リーダーシップ

　　ラウンドスクエアが考えるリーダーというのは、責任感と正義感を備え、仲間に対する思いやりの気持ちを持ちながら、チームが成功するために考えたり行動したりすることができる人材である。そのためにリーダーは状況分析能力、意思決定力、説得と交渉の力、そして創造的な問題解決能力等のスキルを身につけている必要がある。リーダーが課題に対してアイディアを集め、方向性を定めて仲間とビジョンを共有し、謙虚にしかし自信を持ってダイナミックな行動を起こすことで、チームのメンバーは貢献に価値を感じ、努力と成果に誇りをもつことができるようになる。

　ラウンドスクエアでは、カンファレンスやサービスプロジェクトなどの

様々なアクティビティにおいて生徒が企画から運営、振り返りまでを行い、リーダーとしての資質を身につけるための訓練を積んでいる。

　小原國芳は聖書マタイ伝5章の「あなたがたは地の塩である。世の光である」の一節を大切にした。現学長、学園長の小原芳明も、12 年生の卒業式では高校卒業後の人生の指針としてこの句を用いて訓示を述べている。玉川学園では、全人教育を通して世の中のリーダーを育てることを創立以来目指してきたが、一人ひとりが発揮すべきリーダーシップは、この聖句の教えが大前提になっている。

　また、生徒のリーダーシップを育てるためには、教師が世の中のリーダーであるべきことを小原國芳は説いている。教育者は「世のリーダー、警醒者、木鐸でなければなりません。時の政治家や一般民衆をも指導し得る力量も教師には育って欲しいものです[17]」。

（6）Service：奉仕

　ラウンドスクエアの学校では、生徒の身近なところから広く世界のなかで個人やコミュニティーに起きている課題や問題を深く理解し、そこにどのようなサポートが必要なのかを慎重に見極めた上で、誠実にかつ創造的に責任ある社会的行動をとることができるような奉仕の精神と実行力を育てる。そして自主的な奉仕活動を通じて、地域社会やより広いコミュニティーとかかわり、生徒個々は成長する。そのような成長のために、ラウンドスクエアは国際的な奉仕プロジェクトを提供し、様々な国のメンバー校の生徒を集めて、異文化のチームで労作をする機会を提供している。毎年の国際会議でも、必ず日程のなかに、サービス・デーが用意されていて、生徒は種々の奉仕活動を行っている。

　「ペスタロッチが身を以て強調した通り、実に教育の根本は労作教育にあります。額に汗を流し、労しむことは万人の喜びであり、誇りであり、義務だと思います。『作』は『作業』の作ではなく、創作の作なのです。合わせて『労作』と名づけたのです[18]」。この労作を通して、「正直、忍耐、克己、節制、共同、友情、忠実、勇敢、快活、奮闘、独立独行、奉仕、感謝……等

の諸徳が修練[19]」されると小原國芳は述べている。玉川学園が教育の根本に据えている労作教育を通して、奉仕の精神、感謝の心が養われる。玉川学園の校門には、「人生の最も苦しい、いやな、辛い、損な場面を、真っ先に微笑を以って担当せよ」というモットーが掲げられているが、これはまさにラウンドスクエアが目指す奉仕の精神を表している。

第3節　IDEALS を支える資質・能力

（1）ラウンドスクエア・ディスカバリー

　ラウンドスクエアが学校連盟として誕生して約50年が経過し、多くの加盟校によって IDEALS の理念に基づいた様々な活動が繰り広げられてきた。近年、加盟校の教員やラウンドスクエア本部のメンバーが話し合いを重ね、これからの時代に IDEALS に基づいて身につけるべき 12 の資質や能力（表6-1）が具体的に示された（2015〈平成 27〉年）。これらはラウンドスクエア・ディスカバリー[20]と呼ばれており、加盟校は生徒たちがこれらのディスカバリーを身につけるための教育活動や加盟校同士の交流を実施している。

（2）活動の実際

　玉川学園は、2005（平成 17）年、日本で最初のメンバー校としてラウンドスクエアへの加盟が認められて以来、毎年 9 年生が参加するジュニア・カンファレンスや 10 ～ 12 年生が参加する国際会議に代表生徒を派遣している。そこでは約 1 週間、より良い世界を目指して話し合われる様々なディスカッションに参加し、アドベンチャーの体験や、奉仕活動なども経験する。また、ラウンドスクエアの加盟校が企画するサービスプロジェクトに参加し、世界各地での奉仕活動に加わった生徒も多くを数える。加盟校との国際交流活動も盛んに行われ、今まで数多くの生徒を派遣し、また世界中の加盟校から生徒の受け入れを行ってきた。その生徒たちと一緒に探究課題に取り組む授業等も実施している。

　9 年生から 12 年生を対象にした学内のラウンドスクエア実行委員会も組織的に活動を行っている。約 100 名の生徒が所属するこの委員会では、国際

表6-1　ラウンドスクエア・ディスカバリーの12項目

Communication Skills：コミュニケーションスキル
相手のアイディアをよく聞き、自分の意見を相手と共有し、お互いに敬意をもって意見交換することで相互理解を深める。今日のデジタル社会では、様々なコミュニケーションツールを効果的に活用することが重要である。
Inquisitiveness：好奇心
真実を追求するために継続的な探究を行う。興味を持ち、調べ、質問し、仮定し、疑問を抱き、批判的にしかし建設的に判断し、正解のない課題の解決にも挑戦する。探究の旅それ自体が学習のプロセスである。
Appreciation of Diversity：多様性の尊重
国籍、人種、民族、文化、宗教、社会経済階級、障害の有無、性別などに関係なく、すべての個人を包摂的に受け入れる寛容さと強さを持つことが、差別や偏見を乗り越えることにつながる。そして公平な社会を築くことにつながる。
Ability to Solve Problems：課題解決能力
情報に基づいて論理的に、また批判的、創造的に考えて、課題に取り組み状況に応じて最善の解決策を見つける能力。
Sense of Responsibility：責任感
自分自身、隣人、コミュニティー、社会に対する道徳的義務を認識し、正義感を持ってその義務を果たす。間違いを認識し、修正し、間違いから学び、自分の行動の説明責任を果たし、自分の努力と行動に誇りを持っている。
Commitment to Sustainability：持続可能性への取り組み
自分の周りの環境を認識し、自然、エネルギー、廃棄物、食品、汚染等について理解しながら、責任を持って地域の、そして地球の修復のために節約、再利用、リサイクルなどの行動をとり持続可能な社会を目指す。
Tenacity：粘り強さ
課題に直面した時に、それに忍耐強く取り組み、その過程から学び、試行錯誤することができる。
Courage：勇気
恐怖、痛み、危険、不確実性に立ち向かう意欲と能力。この勇気が、正しい行いを可能にする。
Self-Awareness：自己認識
自分自身について知り、自分の人格や価値、態度、強みと弱みや自分が生活する環境、文化などを理解する。これが世界について考え、世界との相互作用を生むためのより良い意思決定をもたらす。
Teamwork Skills：チームワークスキル
チームメンバーの長所と短所を認識し、個々の属性、スキル、および才能を組み合わせてチームのパフォーマンスを向上させる。
Inventiveness：独創性、創造性
新しいアイディアを生み出すための思考力、創造性、想像性、革新性。課題解決のために柔軟なアプローチが採れる。
Compassion：思いやり
国際性の高まりのためにも、環境保護と持続可能な社会のためにも、その根底には思いやりが必要。相手の感情、視点、意見を知り、それを共有して共感することが理解を深める。

出典：Round square, "ROUND SQUARE"（http://www.roundsquare.org, 2021年4月30日閲覧）
　　　および国際会議参加時のメモより筆者作成

会議形式で玉川学園版のラウンドスクエア・カンファレンス「たまがわ会議」を開催している。また、交換留学生の歓迎会や交流校とのオンライン交流、古着や学用品等を集めて発展途上国に送る活動など、様々な奉仕活動等を行っている。

　これらの諸活動を通して、ラウンドスクエア・ディスカバリーに示された資質・能力を育み、IDEALSの精神を身につけた生徒の育成を目指している。それはすなわち、「全人性」を身につけることにつながるのである。

注

1）アボツホルム校はラウンドスクエアのメンバー校で、現在玉川学園とも交流がある。

2）石橋哲成「新教育運動の展開と玉川学園の教育」2013年。

3）石橋哲成「新教育運動の展開と玉川学園の教育」2013年。

4）玉川学園のTAPが導入しているプロジェクト・アドベンチャーは、このアウトワード・バウンド・スクールの影響を受けてアメリカに作られた野外教育組織である。

5）ボルノー，O. F.、浜田正秀（訳）『哲学的教育学入門』玉川大学出版部、1973年、209頁。

6）Tacy, P., *IDEALS at Work*, Deerfield Academy Press, 2006.

7）ゴードンストウン校のラウンドスクエアは、1600年代にロバートゴードン卿が所有していた土地に真円に建てられた建造物で、学校が創設された後の1950年代に生徒の寮や教室として改修された。現在は教職員室、図書館としても使用されている。

8）以下、2字下げの解説については、ラウンドスクエアの公式ホームページ（https://www.roundsquare.org/being-round-square/what/ideals/）に掲載されている内容をベースに、要点を日本語に訳し、筆者が8年間ラウンドスクエアの国際会議等に参加した経験をもとに説明している。

9）小原國芳『教育一路』日本経済新聞社、1976年、120頁。

10）小原國芳『全人教育論』玉川大学出版部、1969年、139頁。

11）小原國芳「教育立国論」『小原國芳全集5　母のための教育学』玉川大学出版部、1980年、397頁。

12）同上、380頁。

13）小原國芳『全人教育論』玉川大学出版部、1969年、106、107頁。

14）小原國芳「理想の学校」『小原國芳全集8　理想の学校・教育立国論・道徳教育論』玉川大学出版部、1980年、443頁。

15）同上、412頁。

16）小原國芳『全人教育論』玉川大学出版部、1969年、87頁。

17）小原國芳『教育一路』日本経済新聞社、1976年、181頁。

18）小原國芳『全人教育論』玉川大学出版部、1969年、114頁

19）同上、115頁。

20）ROUND SQUARE, "Discover more.."（https://www.roundsquare.org/being-round-square/what/discoveries/,2021年3月2日閲覧）.

第7章

全人教育としての TAP
── OBS との関連で

はじめに

　小原國芳は、「真・善・美・聖・健・富」の6つの価値を調和的に創造することが人間形成には必要だとして全人教育を提唱し、その理想の実現のために12の教育信条を掲げたのである。玉川アドベンチャープログラム（以下、TAP）は、冒険教育の父と呼ばれるクルト・ハーンの教育哲学に影響を受けながら、全人教育と12の教育信条の具現的な教育実践の一翼を担い、社会に貢献し世界で活躍できる若者を育てている。詳細については以下の第1節から第4節を熟読して欲しい。

第1節　玉川アドベンチャープログラム（TAP）の背景

　TAP は 1999（平成 11）年 7 月、小原芳明（玉川学園園長・玉川大学学長）と米国の Project Adventure, Inc.（以下、PA, Inc.）のリチャード・プラウティ（Richard G. Prouty）代表との間で「非営利団体プロジェクトアドベンチャーと玉川学園は教育活動を通じて日米交流を促進する事業に協力して取り組む

ことに合意する」という協定を結んだことから始まった。

　2000（平成12）年4月、玉川学園は「行動する全人教育」のテーマのもとに全人教育研究所心の教育実践センターを発足させ、全人教育の具現化の1つとしてアドベンチャープログラムを導入した。そしてPA, Inc. とプロジェクトアドベンチャージャパンの協力を得て、玉川学園内に学校教育施設の屋外コースとしては日本初の ropes コースを設立したのである。同年8月にPA, Inc. から講師を招聘し、玉川学園・玉川大学の教師向けに Adventure Programming コースと Adventure in the classroom コースを合わせた研修を開催したのである。その内容を玉川学園の教育や日本社会に適応させ誕生したのが TAP である。

　2002（平成14）年4月には PA, Inc. 主催の創設30周年記念セレモニーにて「Project Adventure Award for Program Excellence」を受賞した。受賞理由は、小学部から高等部での TAP の取り組みが、子供たちの自尊感情を大切にしながら好奇心を育て、チャレンジ精神と豊かな心を育む海外の実践校として評価されたためである。

　2000年から2014（平成26）年までは玉川アドベンチャープログラムを小文字で "tap" と表記してきたが、2015（平成27）年より大文字の "TAP" に変更したことを踏まえ、本書で扱う「玉川アドベンチャープログラム」は混乱を防ぐためにすべて大文字の TAP に統一することとする。

（1）TAP のコンセプトと精神

　TAP ということばには以下の3つのコンセプトがあり、現在にまで引き継がれている。

① Tamagawa Adventure Program
　　全人教育を具現化するためにアドベンチャー教育を用い、チームで協力し人と支え合う体験学習を通して生きる力を身につける
② Teachers as professionals
　　教師としての専門性を発揮して、子供の可能性を促進する
③ tap

ノックをしてドアを開く（自己開示）、コツコツ叩いて自分の意思を発信する（自己主張）、自他の能力や資源を開発する・活用する・利用する

　活動の中心となるコンセプトは上記の①と③である。グループ活動を通し参加者が主体的に基礎的・汎用的能力等について体験学習するプログラムである。他者とのかかわりを通してコミュニケーション能力や信頼関係を構築する能力、課題解決能力やリーダーシップ能力等を養い、そこで気づき、感じ、学んだことを日常生活に応用・転用することが重要である。また他者が持っている力を発揮できるように支援できる能力、つまりファシリテーション能力の開発にも寄与している。

　さらにTAPには「I am（Inter-accountable mind）」という精神があり、これは「私は私である」という意味と同時に、「相互に責任を担う気持ち」が大切であることを意味している。この「I am」を尊重した上で様々なことに挑戦していこうとするのが「I am a challenger !」という精神であり、Challengerのなかには以下のような意味が込められている。

CH　：Challenge　　（挑戦する）
ALL　：Alternative　（全て／選ぶ余地がある）
EN　：Enrich　　　（豊かにする）
G　　：Growth　　　（成長）
E　　：Experience　（経験）
R　　：Respect　　　（尊重）

　つまり「I am a challenger !」とは、挑戦することにはすべて選ぶ余地があるが、相互に責任を担う気持ちを最大限に持ち実行していくことが前提である。その上で様々な挑戦をすることにより、経験が豊かなものになり人間的な成長が促進されていくものである。ただし、諸要因により直接的には活動に参加できず挑戦することを選択しない場合でも、I amの精神によって仲間のために何か協力できることでかかわり、お互いを尊重し合うことで「I am a challenger !」になる。たとえばチームで課題解決に取り組む際に、体

調不良などの理由で全体のパフォーマンスに影響がある時は、個人によって
は挑戦しないことを選択することがチャレンジの1つとも考えられる。その
代わりに、メンバーに励ましの声掛けやメモを取ったりすることでチームに
貢献するのである。

　我々には目に見えない心の領域（C-zone: 安全・既知、S-zone：緊張・未知、
P-zone：パニック）があり、安全な領域に他人が無断で踏み込んできたり、
強制的にその領域から出されてしまうと、心理的安全性が損なわれ委縮し、
自主的に挑戦することが困難になるのである。

　TAP は 12 名前後のグループや大人数の集団を目的と状況によって小グ
ループに分けて行う活動が中心である。グループや個人の目標に向かい、そ
れぞれの責任を果たす過程を通して体験学習を行うのである。知育に偏るこ
となく、なすことによって学ぶことを重要視する TAP は、参加者が体験か
ら得た気づきや学び、知恵や感性等を大切にするのである。

（2）TAP と 12 の教育信条

　小原國芳は全人教育の完成のために 12 の教育信条を掲げている。その内
の「労作教育」、「反対の合一」、「第二里行者と人生の開拓者」、「24 時間の
教育」、「国際教育」は、玉川学園の大きな特徴であり、さらに、TAP との
関連性が高いのは「労作教育」、「反対の合一」、「第二里行者と人生の開拓者」
である。

　小原の労作教育は「自ら考え、自ら体験し、自ら試み、創り、行うこと」
を意味し、「百見は一労作に如かず」と表現したのである。額に汗して「労
しむこと」と、それに作業の「作」ではなく創作の「作」を合わせて「労作」
とし、その本質は自ら進んで手伝う自発性であり心構えであるとした。石塚
清章は労作教育を「何かを成し遂げた体験こそが何かを成し遂げたくなる動
機の源[1]」と述べ、単なる作業ではなく自発性・行為性・創造性を伴うのが
労作であるとしており、TAP はこれを具現化したものといえる。森山賢一
は小林澄兄の労作教育思想研究の特質をまとめ、労作教育は「体験的学習を
推進していく上で重要な示唆を与えている[2]」とし、小原の目指す労作教育
と TAP の重要性を示している。

　玉川学園校歌の2番の歌詞は労作教育そのものである。「星あおき　朝^{あした}に学び」は、学ぶことや知ること、つまり「知」の大切さを表し、「風わたる野に鋤ふるう」は実際に身をもって行うこと、すなわち「行」の重要性を表している。そして「斯^かくて　吾等^{われら}人とは成らん」は、「知行合一」を表している。

　ここでは朝日が昇り、明るい内に勉学に励み、その後、汗水たらして労しむことの両方が大切であると述べられている。我々はこのようにして人となるのであり、知と行を兼ね備えた人を目指す精神が労作教育でありその重要性が謳われている。

　「反対の合一」とは相反する二面を1つにすることであり、知識と体験の合一や理想の自己と現実の自己との合一などを意味する。たとえば机上で学んだ知識や伝達の方法を知ることも重要であるが、実際に目と目を合わせ自分の思いや考えを伝え合わなければコミュニケーションは成立しない。知識と併せて直接的な人とのやり取りのなかで学ぶコミュニケーションが重要なのである。価値観の異なる他者とかかわりながら自分の価値観を磨き、多様性を認めながら自己を確立していくことも反対の合一である。TAPでは、課題解決を通しながら正反対の考えを1つにまとめ、合意形成を図る活動が豊富にある。

　玉川学園のモットーである「人生の最も苦しいいやな辛い損な場面を真っ先に微笑みを以って担当せよ」は、マタイ伝5章「山上の垂訓」に第二里行者の1節「人もし汝に一里の苦役を強いなば彼と共に二里行け」の影響を受けて小原が考案したものである。苦役を強いられた者は一里で開放されるが、イエスは次の一里も自らの意思で行けと説き、これを第二里行者として教育信条の1つとした。このことは、与えられた課題を超えて追及する逞しさや＋αへの挑戦こそ価値ある開拓であると捉えることもでき、その実践力はTAPのなかで培うことができる。個人として最大限に課題解決に努めることはもとより、他者との協働の上に目標を達成し、挑戦するレベルを自己決定し、失敗を恐れずに挑戦する姿勢こそが第二里行者と人生の開拓者であり、TAPはそれを具現化しているのである。

第2節　TAP の目的の変遷

　2000 年当時、教育界は多くの問題を抱え、そのなかでも特に子供たちの豊かな心を育む環境をいかに促進するかが課題の１つであった。そうした社会的状況に対応し、21 世紀の豊かな教育社会を創生するために TAP を導入し、玉川学園全体として取り組んだのである。

　発足当時の TAP は①強い心を育むプログラム（K-12 の教育活動）、②より望ましい人間関係を育成するためのプログラム（K-16 および教職員・一般の活動）、③国際社会で活躍する人材の「心」を育てるためのプログラム（K-16 の教育活動）を目的としていた。

　2015 年の改組により、玉川大学学術研究所心の教育実践センターから玉川大学 TAP センターとなり現在に至っている。TAP センターの目的は①全人教育の理念を基調に、体験を通して、心の豊かさや人間関係、リーダーシップを育成する教育活動の拠点とすること、②必要に応じ玉川学園の各学校および学外の教育諸機関にも門戸を開放し、その実践と、研究の成果を広く社会に提言し、わが国の教育諸活動の充実発展に寄与することである。

　①における「全人教育の理念」は、玉川大学での教育実践のなかでもっとも根源的なことであり、TAP の実践および開発には全人教育の理念がその基調になくてはならない。小原國芳は理想の教育の在り方を探求し続けた結果、情熱と苦難の体験から「全き人を育てる」という教育の姿を全人教育としたのである。そして「真（学問の理想）・善（道徳の理想）・美（芸術の理想）・聖（宗教の理想）・健（身体の理想）・富（生活の理想）」の６つの価値を調和的に創造することが人間形成には必要だとした。その全人教育の理想を実現させるために 12 の教育信条があり、さらに具現的かつ今日的な教育実践の一翼を担っているのが TAP である（表7-1）。

表7-1　12 の教育信条と TAP の関連性

12 の教育信条	TAP の学習理論
全人教育	調和のとれた人格形成のための教育 全体論的な教育アプローチ Tamagawa Adventure Program・tap Teachers as Professionals
個性尊重	お互いを最大限に尊重し合う集団の中の役割 Full Value・TAP-Commitent・多様性の受容
自学自律	自己決定権の尊重・自己指導力の育成 自らの意志で学びへの挑戦 I am a challenger！・Challenge by Choice
能率高き教育	学習スタイル 試行錯誤の探究学習の上での能率 多重知能（MI）に基づくアプローチ
学的根拠に立てる教育	体験学習理論・冒険教育・アドベンチャーの理論 社会心理学・教育心理学・人間性心理学 実在主義・発達の最近接領域・脳科学 ダイナミック・スキル理論・アクティブラーニング
自然の尊重	野外教育（冒険教育・環境教育） 雄大な自然自体が偉大な教育 子どもの本質を十分に発揮させるための教育
師弟間の恩情	ファシリテーターと学習者との関係性 参加者同士からも学び合う共同体 生徒指導（指導と支援）、特別活動
労作教育	体験学習、経験学習 総合的学習、アクティブ道徳教育 自発性・行為性・創造性 全人的理解（知的理解＋感性的理解＋身体的理解）
反対の合一	個と集団、理論と実践、知識と体験、理想の自己と現実の自己 価値観の受容と統合・正反合
第二里行者と人生の開拓者	自己冒険力 リーダーシップとフォロワーシップ、起業力 ＋αへの挑戦、実践力、キャリア教育
24 時間の教育	遠征型教育 リアルとオンラインのハイブリット教育 Any time, Any place
国際教育	異文化への尊重、国際交流 コミュニケーションスキル

出典：藤樫亮二・小原一仁「玉川学園におけるラウンドスクエアと玉川アドベンチャープログラム
　　　の重要性」『玉川大学学術研究所紀要』第 16 号、2010 年、7 頁より筆者作成

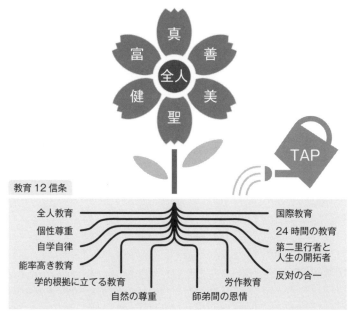

図7−1　全人の花と12の教育信条とTAP

出典：工藤亘「TAPの足跡とこれからの可能性──teachers as professionalsモデル開発を目指して」
『教育実践学研究』第19号、2016年、57頁より筆者作成

　図7-1の全人の花は、真善美聖健富の6つの価値を備え、調和のとれた全人を表しており、全人の花を育てる土壌には、栄養素である12の教育信条が必要である。全人の花が、困難な環境下でも逞しく成長するためには適応力や抵抗力、自己冒険力（自分自身で人生を開拓していく力）が必要であり、それらはTAPを通して獲得しやすいのである。TAPで得た能力や栄養素である12の教育信条で育った全人の花は、いつか各自のタイミングで開花し、やがて自己実現という実をつけるのである。

　TAPセンターの目的で述べられる「体験」とは、TAPで行われている個々の活動を指すものではない。玉川学園の内外を問わない自然のなかでの体験活動や遠征型の活動、美化労作を含めた環境の維持や保全活動、国籍や宗教を超え様々な人とかかわり、リーダーシップや価値観の多様性を学ぶ交流活動も含まれる。これらの体験を通して、コミュニケーション能力や対人関係能力、課題解決能力等の向上がみられるのである。

　また②における、「学外の教育諸機関にも門戸を開放」とは、一般企業やプロスポーツ、教員研修など、積極的に学外の教育諸機関との連携を図りながら教育現場で起こっている様々な事例や課題を協議し、省察しながら一般化できるように研究を進めることを指す。

　以上の解釈を踏まえTAPセンターは、自らが推奨している体験学習のサイクルに則り、その教育実践を振り返り、教育現場をはじめ実生活に応用・転用できるように一般化し、研究を積み重ねた成果や課題を公表していくことが使命である。特に教員養成に注力している玉川大学では、教職にかかわる人材養成の学修スタイルやモデル開発をすることが目的でもある。

第3節　クルト・ハーンの冒険教育とTAP

　TAPとプロジェクトアドベンチャー（PA）との関係については先述したが、PAの源流を遡るとアウトワードバウンドスクール（OBS）やクルト・ハーン（Kurt Harn）に行きつくことになる（第6章参照）。ハーンは、ユダヤ系ドイツ人の教育哲学者であり、冒険教育の祖と呼ばれている。ハーンはザーレム校、ゴードンストウン校、アバドビーにOBS等、多くの学校や組織を設立し、その教育哲学は世界中に影響を与え続けている（表7-2）。

　日本国内の学術論文探索CiNii Articlesで、キーワードを「クルト・ハーン」で検索した結果、8件が検出され国内でのハーンにかんする研究は限定的である。石川道夫は、ハーンについて「新教育運動の代表的な教育者の一人だ

表7-2　クルト・ハーンが設立した主な学校・組織

1920年	ザーレム校
1934年	ゴードンストウン校
1941年	アウトワード・バウンド・スクール
1956年	英国エディンバラ公国際アワード
1962年	アトランティック・カレッジ ユナイテッド・ワールド・カレッジ
1967年	ラウンドスクエア
1968年	国際バカロレア

出典：筆者作成

が、田園教育塾や労作教育、芸術教育、ワンダーフォーゲルなどの影に隠れてとかく我々の視界からこぼれ落ちがちである[3)]」と指摘している。しかし「冒険教育」をキーワードに検索すると57件が検出され、間接的ではあるがハーンの影響力は日本でも大きいといえる（2020年8月6日現在）。

　OBSの冒険教育プログラムは、英国の海運業で働く船乗りが第二次世界大戦中の北大西洋で生き残るためのトレーニングとして始まり、戦後、青少年教育プログラムとして世界中で導入されるようになったのである。OBSは、自然環境のなかでストレスフルな経験を通して自己の発達をとげることを目的とするプログラムである。1962（昭和37）年に米国コロラドにOBSが設立されたのを契機に短期間に顕著な発達を遂げ、OBSプログラムを修正した様々なアドベンチャープログラムが開発されたのである。

　ハーンの教育理念は、道徳的で正しい判断力を持ち、強い精神力を持った人間の育成であった。教育の目的について「人々に価値観を形成する経験を与え、意欲的な好奇心、くじけない精神、飽くなき追求心、そして最も重要な他者を思いやる心という資質を維持することです。若者に経験を積ませないことはとがめられるべき怠惰です[4)]」と述べている。

　厳しい身体訓練やサバイバル技術を修得し、実践する過程で生命の危険さに直面させ、生に対する正しい態度を育て、他人の生命を危険から救出する能力を養い、他人への奉仕の精神を培うことを目的としたのである。

　この思想をもとにOBSの根本方針は4つの柱（奉仕活動・自己信頼・熟練したモノづくりの技術・心身の健康と思いやり）、教育の5信条（冒険心あふれる好奇心・折れない精神力・不屈の追求心・自制心・思いやり）、ザーレムの7つの掟「①子ども達に、自己を発見する機会を与えよ、②子ども達に勝利と敗北を経験させよ、③子ども達に共通のものに没頭する機会を与えよ、④沈黙する時間を提供せよ、⑤ファンタジーをもって行動せよ、⑥競争は大切であるが、優先的な役割を持たせなければならない、⑦裕福で権力のある親の子女を特権的な意識から救い出せ[5)]」とされており、世界中のOBSに引き継がれている。OBSの使命は、非日常的なチャレンジという体験を通して、自己の中に秘められた可能性に気づき高めることである。

　ハーンは1967（昭和42）年にラウンドスクエアを設立し、Internationalism

（国際理解）、Democracy（民主主義の精神）、Environment（環境問題に対する意識）、Adventure（冒険心）、Leadership（リーダーシップ）、Service（奉仕の精神）の頭文字をとった「IDEALS[6)]」を教育の柱とした。玉川学園はラウンドスクエアの国際会議に 2004 年（平成 16）から参加し、翌年には日本で初めて正式なメンバー校として認定され関係を深めてきた。それを踏まえ玉川大学では「IDEALS」を人生における究極的な目標と定め、教育の基本理念としたのである。

　2015（平成 27）年 6 月に来日したドイツのラルフ・ケレンツ（Ralf Koerrenz）教授は、講演会のなかで「クルト・ハーンこそ、新教育の真の担い手であり、クルト・ハーンの思想や理念の根底にあるのは全人教育であり、その今日的な成果である国際バカロレアやラウンドスクエアが玉川学園とつながるのは自然な流れ」と主張した。これは、ハーンの教育哲学と TAP を含む玉川学園の教育実践との関係性を裏付けるものとなったのである。

第 4 節　TAP の使命

　これからの日本社会や世界を担っていく若者たちが、夢を叶えるまでの険しい道のりを積極的に歩んで行くためには自己冒険力を育む必要がある。そのために教師は、指導（子供の人間形成を目指し直接的・具体的に教師が働き

図 7-2　指導と支導の上での自己決定と自己実現

出典：工藤亘・藤平敦編著『生徒・進路指導の理論と方法』玉川大学出版会、2019 年、9 頁より筆者作成

かけること）と「支導（子供の主体性と目標を最大限に尊重し、教師と子どもとの双方向のやりとりを大切にした上で、子供一人ひとりや集団の特性や状況、プロセス等を的確に判断し、子供一人ひとりや集団の能力、特性を十分に発揮できるように支援しながら導くこと[7]）」によって子供たちがアドベンチャーをできる環境について理解しデザインする必要がある。

　図7-2は子供が自転車に乗り、自分の目的地（自己実現）に向かっているものである。しかし、自転車を乗りこなす過程では誰かの指導と支導を受け、乗り方や交通ルールを学ぶ必要がある。最初は補助輪を付けたり、誰かに補助をしてもらいながら試行錯誤を繰り返し、徐々に自分自身でバランスをとって自立できるようになる。そして次第にスピードのコントロールや方向転換が可能になると行動範囲が拡大し、自分が望む場所へ自力で向かうことが可能になるのである。親や教師がいつまでも主体となり指導のみをしていては、子供の主体性や生きる力は育まれないため、社会的自立が困難になるのである。

　TAPでのアドベンチャーとは「成功するかどうか不確かなことにあえて挑戦すること」であり、その結果として未知なる自分と出会い新たなる自分を創生していくことである。TAPで用いるアドベンチャーの理論とは、クルト・レヴィン（Kurt Zadek Lewin）の「場の理論[8]」を基底にしており、

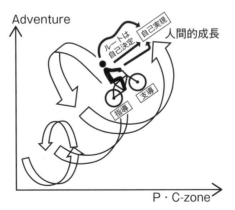

図7-3　アドベンチャーの理論と自己冒険力の関係性
出典：筆者作成

その公式は「A＝f（P, C-zone[9]）」である。A は Adventure（アドベンチャー）、P は Personality（個性・性格）、C-zone は Comfort-zone の略（周囲の人的・物理的環境が心身ともに安全な状況や領域）である。この理論では、個人の性格と C-zone の積によってアドベンチャーが促進され、その結果として人間的な成長につながると考えている（図7-3）。

　教師は子供自身に自己決定や試行錯誤をする機会を積極的に設け、指導と支導のバランスによって子供が自己指導力や自己冒険力を修得できるようにかかわる必要がある。ただしそのバランスが崩れどちらかに偏り、タイヤがパンクをすると子供がアンバランスとなり、自分の進みたい方向に行けないため、個に応じた指導と支導が必要となる。この自転車を乗りこなしていくプロセスにおいて「知情意が活性化し、頭と心と身体がフル動員されることによって、人としての知性や感性が磨かれ、見識が養われていく[10]」のである。

　玉川大学では全人教育の理念に加え、前出の IDEALS を人生における究極的な目標と定めた。2019（令和元）年、TAP センターでは公式なロゴを作成し、TAP センターの目標の実現のためにロゴの3色に IDEALS の意味を込めている。T（赤）は Leadership & Service、A（緑）は Adventure & Environment、P（青）は International Perspective & Democracy を表している（図7-4）。

　TAP は、若者たちが夢を叶えるまでの困難な道のりを積極的に歩んで行けるように支援し、専門知識や技術と同時に社会人としてふさわしい倫理観を身に付け、知識と心を豊かにするために存在するのである。TAP センターは、これらの使命を果たすために理論と実践（Theory and Practice = TAP）の往還と統合を続けていく。

図7-4　TAP ロゴ
出典：TAMAGAWA ADVENTURE PROGRAM「HOME（ホーム）」（http://tap.tamagawa.ac.jp/、2021年3月2日閲覧）

　玉川学園の教育の理念は、教育を通して昨日まで知らなかったことを知るようになり、そしてできなかったことをやり遂げることができるようになることである。小原國芳は人間を「生まれながらにして、唯一無二の個性を持ちつつも、万人共通の世界をも有する存在である」と定義した。玉川教育の使命はこの人間像を実現させることであり、日本社会さらには世界へ貢献する気概を持った人材を養成することである。

　以上を踏まえ、未知の苦難に対して玉川学園のモットーを実践できる気概のある人を育て、失敗を恐れずに挑戦していく「人生の開拓者」を育てていくことが玉川大学の使命であり、それを具現化するのがTAPである。

注

1）石塚清章「労作教育」『全人』第756号、2012年、22頁。
2）森山賢一「小林澄兄における労作教育思想研究の特質」『教育実践学研究』第15号、2011年、83頁。
3）石川道夫「クルト・ハーンとアウトワード・バウンド」『教育新世界』第27巻第2号、2001年、59頁。
4）英国エディンバラ公国際アワード「歴史と理念」（http://intaward-jp.check-sixcore.jp/history.php、2020年8月5日閲覧）。
5）ラルフ・ケレンツ、米山かおる訳「田園教育塾――ヘルマン・リーツとクルト・ハーンにおける基本理念と国際的責任」『玉川大学教育学部全人教育研究センター年報2015』第2号、2016年、16-17頁。
6）Tacy, P., *IDEALS at Work*, DEERFIELD ACADEMY PRESS, 2006, p.63.
7）工藤亘「teachers as professionals としての tap――『指導者』から『支導者（ファシリテーター）』へ」『教育実践研究』第16号、2012年、38頁。
8）クルト・レヴィン、外林大作・松村康平訳『トポロギー心理学の原理』生活社、1942年、21頁。
9）工藤亘「アドベンチャー教育におけるエッジワークと動機づけについての研究――アドベンチャーの理論を基にした教師の役割と C-zone に着目して」『教育実践学研究』第19号、2016年、40頁。
10）鹿毛雅治『授業という営み――子どもとともに「主体的に学ぶ場」を創る』教育出版、2019年、27頁。

玉川学園草創期の教育信条とその実践

　現在では 12 ある玉川学園（以下、本学）の教育信条ではあるが、草創期にはどういった考えに基づいて掲げられていたか。今回は小原國芳の著書『玉川塾の教育』をもとに紐解いてみよう。現在、本学には塾はなく、当時掲げられた教育信条およびその実践も時代とともに変容している。しかし、当時の小原の思想が綿々と今につながっていることもまた事実である。そこで、かつて小原が心血を注いだ教育実践から、未来の本学の教育実践を展望する一助となれば幸いである。

　小原は、日本の若者が「意気天を衝き天馬空をかけるような夢と幻に燃えねばならぬ二十ざかりを、投機的な打算的な功利的な試験準備にクヨクヨせねばならぬ[1]」ことを嘆き、「社会を学校にとり入れ、……他の介在物を中間に置きたくない[2]」と望み、「学校は社会の実相でありたい[3]」という理想の実現に突き動かされて玉川学園ならびに玉川塾を開校した。ちなみに、小原は、玉川塾を構想するに際し、園児（幼稚部）と児童（小学部）は家庭つまり親元から通学させることを理想とした。その理由として、第 1 に、子供時代は親を離れて良い教育は到底できず、かつ、温かい家庭で思う存分に甘えることが不可欠と考えたこと、第 2 に、如何に教員が努力、苦心しても、親の代わりは非常に困難であること、そして、第 3 に、健康等の責任を学校

が負うことの危険を考えると、安易に園児・児童を預かることはできないことを挙げている。一方で、中学生からの入塾を認めるにあたり、社会性の培養をその理由の1つに挙げている。

　では、これから現在本学が掲げる教育信条が、当時、どのような経緯で信条として掲げられるに至ったかを紹介したい。なお、現在の教育信条は、次の通りである——全人教育、個性尊重、自学自律、能率高き教育、学的根拠に立てる教育、自然の尊重、師弟間の温情、労作教育、反対の合一、第二里行者と人生の開拓者、24時間の教育、国際教育。これらすべてが開学当初から信条として明示されてはいなかったが、草創期の著書で小原の考えから推察することで、当時の玉川教育に思いを馳せてみよう。

第二里行者と人生の開拓者

　クラーク博士の言葉を引用しながら、大望心について小原は頁を割いて説明している。教育力は時間と必ずしも正比例ではないという考えを示した上で、教育力が目指すべきは何事かを開拓し得るパイオニアの輩出を望んでいる。加えて、ピラミッドの土台石という言葉を用いて、「知られざる善、報償を求めざる行、人生の損を喜んでいる人、第二里を行く人……の出現[4]」も求めている。これは、「受くるより与うるは幸なり」という境地のわかる子供、つまりは、「人生の最もいやな、最も苦しい、最も損な、最も辛い場面を、真ッ先に微笑を以て担当せよ[5]」というモットーが実行できる玉川っ子の姿である。

能率高き教育、学的根拠の上に立てる教育

　小原は、日本の教育は学課の連絡が無方針、無系統であること、法や制度による拘束が強いため年限の規定が厳格であること、したがって、授業の遅滞者と順調な者とが同じ歩調で進まざるを得ないことを批判している。これは、現代でいうところの習熟度別授業の積極的導入を謳ったものと考えられよう。その上で、小原は、年限撤廃を主張している。進度の速い者は規定の年限を待たずに進級、進学させ、遅滞者にはより時間を掛けて学ばせることを提案している。逓減の法則を引き合いに、その根拠を「子供一人一人に

対して最も適当な時期に、最も適する学科や進度を与えんが為[6]」、そして、順応性が損なわれない内に大学を卒業させ、「大学を出ても、卒業後二カ年ぐらいは見習小僧のつもりで働くほどの純真さがあり、若さある者[7]」が必要と考えたためとしている。加えて、1学級25名程度の少人数教育も提唱している。

学的根拠に立ち、能率高き教育の具体的な方法として、教員はまず教材（単元）の研究を経て、教材の系統を整理し、繰り返しを省き、内容を精選することで効率化を図ること、結果、生まれた余裕を応用等の時間に充てることを提唱しているが、特に単元の組み替えについては、現在も本学の一部の教科で行われていることを申し添えておこう。

個性尊重の教育（自己発見の教育）

小原は、個性が承認され尊重されないことを「希望を失わしめ、本人をして死に突き落とすと同じこと[8]」と考えている。また、「個性なきものは模倣であり、繰り返しであり、機械と等しい[9]」としつつ、各人の本質を発揮させることが教育の大乗でなければならず、かくして被教育者は、「自己の自己たる所以を、自己の何物であるかを、自己の生くべき道を、ホントの自己を発見し、開拓し得るくらい、うれしいことはない[10]」と述べている。そして、教育とは、「点数とか、卒業証書とか、知識の分量ではなくて、実に、各人に各人の本質を発見させること[11]」と結論付けている。

自学自律の教育、塾教育

教育は「分量や暗記、詰め込み、点数……不自然な拘束や繰り返し、無意味な歩調や反省なき教材[12]」を必要とはしないという考えに立ち、教育を通して「推理、判断、思考、敢行、想像、工夫、応用、発明等[13]」の諸能力とりわけ独創力の啓培、研究法の鍛錬、「学問に対する趣味……、知識に対する生き生きした欲求、驚異に対するデリケートな敏感、旺盛なる探究心、創作発見の喜び、そして真澄の鑑の如き学的良心[14]」の醸成、そして、「どんな困難な難問でもやッつけようという[15]」意思の涵養を目指すとした。この具体的実践として自由研究を挙げ、これに「全学科の総点数と同様の価値を

与えたい[16]」と述べている。

　また、小原は、学習する場所について「一斉的研究をする外は、全然自由[17]」としている。そして、時間割はなく、子供は先生と相談、質問して参考書を教えてもらう、レポート等を確認してもらう、共同研究に取り組むといった取り組みを紹介している。さらに、図書館は起床から就寝時間まで開館していたが、それは、図書館は学校の目玉であり、「大学のみならず、低学年から大いに図書館を利用するクセをつけて……図書館ずき、読書ずき、研究ずきの国民[18]」の輩出を目指したからである。

全人教養、反対の合一

　小原は、「一人の生徒に何でも彼でもやらせること、いわゆる八人芸の出来る人間を造り上げる[19]」寄せ木細工のような教育といった誤った解釈を正し、全人教育とは、「一つのものに調和統一された……止揚［aufheben］されたもの[20]」であると断言している。つまり、全人教育を通して育まれる全人教養とは、反対の合一（アウフヘーベン）の体現であり、具体的には、「物質と精神、天と地、汗と美、コヤシ汲みとピアノ、ソロバンとお経、お金とイデア、機械と理想、土地と哲学、貧しきと富めると……それらの一丸[21]」こそが真の全人教育の極地と主張している。

自然尊重の教育

　小原が成城学園や玉川学園の場所選定に何よりも苦心したと述べているように、学校の位置、子供の環境はもっとも重視した点であった。都市部で生活する子供の実態を嘆きつつ、「青天井の下に、森の木陰に、小川や海浜のさざなみのほとりに、堤の青草の上にいくらも金のかからぬ教室は無限に[22]」あると考えた。しかし、これは決して学校を社会と絶縁させ、温室育ちの子供を量産することを意味していない。むしろ、活きた社会と密接な交渉を持ちつつも、自然を尊重する環境にある学校では、教育学や教授法の前に必要とされる「心構えとまごころと生きた宗教と純真な児童観と子供心[23]」が存在すると考えたからである。なお、小原は、玉川学園の土地の選定について、以下の言葉を残している。

関八州を双眸に収め、房総半島に昇る朝日の崇高、眠りの朝霧の間に頭だけ波形に出している相模の連山、黄金色に紫色に紺碧につつまれて己が如く高く強かれと聳ゆる大山丹沢連山、さては千変万化の学園の丘陵、そこには、武蔵野の豊富な雑草、緑濃き松林、萌え出る雑木の若葉……東京から僅かに四十分にして、どうして、かかり大森林、大自然があろうとフシギに思われるほどの場所にブッつかった私は、たしかに、土地の選定だけでも、玉川教育の大成功だとほほえまざるを得ませぬ[24]。

労作教育

労作教育については、玉川塾での実践が多く紹介されているので、ここではそのいくつかに焦点を絞ってみよう。たとえば、学内で行われる農業活動は、「生産上からもですが、宗教上道徳上の修練や博物研究には貴い材料になっている[25]」とし、また、飼育については、「無味乾燥な標本やアイマイな挿絵なぞで到底生きた理科は出来るものではない[26]」という考えに立ち、中核的な活動として位置付けている。

しかし、労作教育を世の中に役立つ教育とする功利主義的かつ打算主義的な職業教育尊重論には真っ向から対立しており、労作教育を通して培われるものは自己発揮、自我実現であり、その帰結として世に役立つことがなされると考えている。小原の労作教育は、「打算と職業と功利と金とを超越した[27]」ものであり、それは、「常に『聖』が指導原理として君臨[28]」していることが不可欠であった。

師弟間の温情

玉川塾は、「学習の労作化、理論の実際化、概念の体験化、知識の証得、学問の生活化、理論と実際の合一[29]」を目標として誕生したが、その教育をなすために不可欠な要素として設備とともに、教師の存在を挙げている。

出来るだけ有能の士を！ しかも労作教育の熱愛者を！ 知識と工夫と技巧と熟練と……しかも、子供ずきで、教育ずきで！ 万事を焼き尽せる情熱の人を！ 骨惜しみやでない愛の人を！[30]

　契約書にある事項のみを業務と捉える教員のあり方に対する危機感とも捉えられるが、とりわけ欧米文化圏における契約主義に立脚する教員観は、小原の言う師弟間の温情から逸脱した考え方であろう。

国際教育（新日本文化建設者の養成）

　小原にとっての教育の狙いは「明るい、勇敢な、義を重んずる、正直な、清い、やさしい、人情深い、渋味のある、芸術的な、信心深い、礼儀正しい、シンミリした、聡明な、本来は人道的な、平和的日本人[31]」の養成としている。そこで、小原は、日本心を土台、苗床として、たとえば海外の精神を取り込むことを提唱し、「儒教を、仏教を、西洋文物を取り入れて、一つにして行く処に、たとえば外国の大学が他国の学問を毛嫌いする際に、我が国の大学が実に世界的国際的なのは何よりの美点[32]」と言って日本人の異文化に対する柔軟性、寛容性を指摘する。

　ただし、「何でも横文字でかいたものに心酔しすぎる欠陥[33]」にも言及しているように、日本における西洋中心主義、欧米コンプレックス、あるいは国家主義的、偏狭な考え方を持つ者には警鐘を鳴らしている。つまり、この中庸、バランス感覚を、小原は国際心と呼んでいる点に留意すべきであろう。

注

1）小原國芳「玉川塾の教育」『小原國芳全集11　秋吉台の聖者本間先生・玉川塾の教育』玉川大学出版部、1963年、185頁。
2）同上、187頁。
3）同上、400頁。
4）同上、232頁。
5）同上、236頁。
6）同上、239頁。
7）同上、240頁。
8）同上、242頁。
9）同上、242頁。
10）同上、243頁。
11）同上、243頁。
12）同上、246頁。
13）同上、246頁。
14）同上、247頁。

15）同上、247 頁。
16）同上、367 頁。
17）同上、374 頁。
18）同上、376 頁。
19）同上、252 頁。
20）同上、252 頁。
21）同上、253 頁。
22）同上、256 頁。
23）同上、260 頁。
24）同上、256 頁。
25）同上、354 頁。
26）同上、345 頁。
27）同上、390 頁。
28）同上、390 頁。
29）同上、371 頁。
30）同上、371 頁。
31）同上、210 頁。
32）同上、212 頁。
33）同上、212 頁。

第Ⅲ部
資料編

1　教育十二信条との親和性

12の教育信条	TAP	ラウンド・スクエア	国際バカロレア
全人教育	調和のとれた人格形成のための教育 全体論的な教育アプローチ	全人に関係する実践	ホリスティック教育（Holistic education）
個性尊重	お互いを最大限に尊重し合う集団の中の役割 多様性の受容	民主主義（人間に関する幅広い知識）	信念をもつ人 思いやりのある人
自学自律	自己決定権の尊重・自己指導力の育成 自らの意志で学びへの挑戦	修養と自身	探求する人 知識のある人 考える人
能率高き教育	試行錯誤の探究学習 多重知能に基づく学習スタイル		考える人 振り返りができる人
学的根拠に立てる教育	体験学習理論・冒険教育・アドベンチャーの理論 社会心理学・教育心理学・人間性心理学 実存主義・発達の最近接領域・脳科学 ダイナミック・スキル理論・アクティブラーニング		
自然の尊重	野外教育（冒険教育・環境教育） 雄大な自然自体が偉大な教育 子どもの本質を十分に発揮させるための教育	環境保護 冒険心	

師弟同行	ファシリテーターと学習者との関係性 参加者同士からも学び合う共同体 生徒指導（指導と支導） 特別活動	大人と生徒との協力	
労作教育	体験学習、経験学習 総合的学習 アクティブ道徳教育 自発性・行為性・創造性 全人的理解（知的理解＋感性的理解＋身体的理解）	奉仕 冒険心	思いやりのある人 挑戦する人
反対の合一	個と集団 理論と実践 知識と体験 理想の自己と現実の自己 価値観の受容と統合・正反合	民主主義（国内外情勢に対する自覚）	心を開く人 バランスのとれた人
第二里行者と人生の開拓者	自己冒険力 リーダーシップとフォロワーシップ 起業力 ＋αへの挑戦 実践力 キャリア教育	指導力	信念をもつ人
24時間の教育	遠征型教育 リアルとオンラインのハイブリット教育		
国際教育	異文化への尊重 国際交流 コミュニケーションスキル	国際性	知識のある人 コミュニケーションができる人 心を開く人 バランスのとれた人

2　名句抄（小原國芳『全人教育論』より）

以下は小原國芳『全人教育論』（改版、玉川大学出版部、1994 年）を底本とする。

1．全人教育の主張

　　教育の内容には人間文化の全部を盛らねばなりませぬ。故に、教育
は絶対に「全人教育」でなければなりませぬ。全人とは完全人格すな
わち調和ある人格の意味です。その人間文化を欠いただけ人間はそれ
だけ片寄ってしまうのです。今日、日本の多くの学校はほとんど偏頗
ではないでしょうか。あるいは、世界中、そうなのかも知れませぬ。

　　（中略）入学試験準備、棒暗記、詰め込み、カンニング、予備校、教
育ママ、準備塾、出世病………これらが、マコトの人間を破壊しとる
のだと思います（10 頁）。

2．教育の理想 —— 六つの文化価値の創造

　　さて、人間文化には六方面があると思います。すなわち、学問、道徳、
芸術、宗教、身体、生活の六方面。学問の理想は真であり、道徳の理
想は善であり、芸術の理想は美であり、宗教の理想は聖であり、身体
の理想は健であり、生活の理想は富であります。教育の理想はすなわち、
真、善、美、聖、健、富の六つの価値を創造することだと思います。

　　然して、真、善、美、聖の四価値を絶対価値と言い、健富の価値を
手段価値と申します（12 頁）。

3．調和的な成長 —— コスモスの花のように

　　この六つの文化価値が、秋の庭前に整然と花咲いとるコスモス Cosmos

の花のように、調和的に成長して欲しいのです。コスモス、これを中国の学者は「宇宙」とホンヤクしました。宇は空間、宙は時代。大哲カントも、宇宙は時間空間から成ると教えてくれました。そもそも、ギリシャ語の Kosmos という言葉は、整美、調和、秩序という意味をもっています（14頁）。

4．私の要求する「人」

　要するに、私は人間にその六方面を認めます。私の要求する「人」はこの六方面を備えた人間でありたいのです。という意味は、一般陶冶（いっぱんとうや）とでも云うような生ぬるいものではないのです。また個性を没却（もっきゃく）したような無味乾燥（むみかんそう）なものでもないのです。人間に真によき教育を施し、神より与えられたる自然をそのまま伸ばして行って、ただ、各自は各自の独特の世界を実現しながら、しかも、そこに各自の完全境が成就されるのではないでしょうか（23-24頁）。

5．ホントの教育

　私は一切の主義と主張を撤廃して、ただ「人」に帰りたいのです。「人に帰れ、人に帰れ」。ただ「人の教育」です。そこには自ら否応なしに、ホントの教育が生まれます。「人」それは発しては個人であり、社会人であり、国民であり、人類であり、神の子であり、人の子であり、腕は働くべく、頭は考うべく、美を慕い、善を行ない、しかも体系的秩序を有する一個の大宇宙です。しかも、各自が「天上天下唯我独尊（ゆいがどくそん）」、唯一無二の、全世界とも代えられない大宇宙なのです。その各宇宙が内的発展完成により各自の天性自然を発揮する時に、何物にも代えられない、竹は竹、松は松、菊は菊、菫（すみれ）は菫という独一無二の美しき完全境を生ずるのです。ジョットーの「一円」を描くことを念願とします。
　プラトンは調和は善だとしました。ペスタロッチは調和的発達を要

求しました。私もただ、ホントの「全人」になることを希います(28-29頁)。

6．宗教教育

　だから、宗教教育は、精神生活の全局を適当に発達させることなのです。一方面、一部分の啓発ではないのです。一切の精神生活を綜合したものの、啓培、成長、開発なのです。いうまでもなく、全人教育なのです。学問、芸術、道徳、産業、社会人事など一切に深刻な興味を有すると共に、宇宙の絶対者に対して深い敬虔の念を有する人こそ真に完全な宗教家であると言わねばなりませぬ。この人間生活の一切を綜合した精神状態が「宗教心」なのです。

　だから、われわれの宗教生活は詩的趣味でもなければ、神秘的安息でもなく、実に、人格が人格を対象とする全精神の活動そのものなのです。全人教育そのものなのです。これを忘れた知育偏重の今の日本の教育は、実に恐ろしい人間破壊のガンのようなものです（32頁）。

　さて、公立学校では宗教教育は出来ないと、よく申します。とんでもないことです。宗教的薫化はいくらでも、どこででも出来ます。音楽で美術で、演劇で、文学で、歴史で。理科や算数では特に。いわんや、お茶で、生花で、体育で登山で。「名山大沢は偉人を生ず」と申します。登山は身体鍛錬よりも、心霊の浄化です。スキーを特に、玉川で尊重する所以です。あの白雪皚々たる銀世界。無我無心の滑走。スキーは、むしろ宗教教育です（36頁）。

7．芸術教育

　そして、心の美しさ、温かい人間関係を有する人間らしい感情の教育を忘れてはなりませぬ。

私達が、ホントに人生と、自然と芸術とを享楽し、味わい、生き得るために。せめて人らしき生活を生活し得るために。芸術教育を必要とします（45頁）。

〔芸術活動そのものの一面は実に創作ということである。創造ということである。自己表現ということであり、個性の発揮ということであります。個性のなきものに生命はない。

そこには、自己の生活の統一、調整、総合が営まれねばなりません。それが完全なればなるほど完全なる自己表現、自己活躍が行われ、遺憾なき個性発揮となる。結局、個性発揮とは、自己統一の創造作用の実現です。自我の自由なる生長です。生命の増進。自我の解放です。芸術活動の貴さはそこに存します。人間の本具する芸術活動の力に信頼して、心身の成長を図り、全人的に人の性能を発揮せしめ、人格の創造的発動をなさしめんとするのが芸術教育の根本原理であります。ことに、子供の創造的本能、想像的本能、探究的本能、構成的本能というものを無視してはなりません。〕（46頁）

＊〔　〕内は小原國芳『学校劇論』から挿入されたものである。

8．道徳教育

イ、人間人格価値の尊さを万人が知って欲しいです。カントの人格擁護律は実に「汝自身の人格並びにすべての人格に於て、人間性の品位を尊敬せよ。而して、人格を常に同時に目的として用い、決して単に手段として用うること勿れ」と、いみじくも人間人格の厳粛なる尊さを教えてくれました。（中略）

ロ、たしかな人生観を見出させることです。喜びも哀しみも、楽しみも苦しみも、一切を超越した確乎たる人生観を。

ハ、善の意義、悪の意味、悩み苦しみの深い意味。罪と懺悔の崇い意味を了解して欲しい。

　二、道徳生活の意味を知悉（ちしつ）すること。意慾と理性との葛藤。「山中の賊は破り易し、心中の賊は破り難し」（王陽明）、人間生活の矛盾と、苦悶の貴い意味を知らしめねばならない。

　ホ、美しい、正しい、たしかな永遠性のある人間像を創り上げさせたいのです（53-54頁）。

9．学問教育

　学問教育については、全く、言語道断です。詰め込み、棒暗記、入学試験準備、出世病！　甚しきはカンニング！（58頁）

　そもそも、教育教授の態度はまず、二つにわかれます。teach するか、study させるかです。教授するか学習させるかです。与えるのか摑ますのかです。記憶や詰め込みを主とするか創意工夫を主とするかです。

　いうまでもなく、与える give する教育よりも、つかませる catch させる教育が尊いのです。教えこむ teach する教師は下の下です。学習させる教師、study させる教師でありたいのです。大学生を student と呼ぶワケを特に大学教授はわかっていて欲しいのです。暗記よりも発明工夫、詰め込むよりも創造すること、分量よりも「好き」にすることです（64頁）。

　大哲カントが「汝等は吾より哲学を学ぶべきにあらず、哲学すること philosophieren を学べ」と、きびしく教えてくれたことを、今の日本の大学教授はじめ、高校教師、否、中小幼の教師たちも心にキビシク感じて欲しいのです。学問に対する燃ゆる情熱を与え、掘り方を会得させ、ツルハシを鍛えてやることだと思います（64頁）。

ギリシャの昔、「学は驚きより始まる」と申しました。学問という言葉は驚き、ふしぎという言葉でした。（中略）詰め込みや棒暗記や試験勉強で、究知心、探求心、ふしぎ、驚きの心の芽を枯らしてはいけませぬ（65頁）。

10. 健康教育

いうまでもなく、体育の目的は、優勝旗でも、メダルでも、レコードでも、カップでもないのです。手段と目的とを混同してはなりませぬ。
私は、体育の目的は、強靭なる体力、長い生命、調和せる身体、そして巧緻性だと思います。そのためにはまず、生理学的知識。基礎としての体操（デンマーク体操では、基本体操と、整美体操と、巧緻体操との三つを平均してやっとることに敬意を払います）。そして、各種のスポーツ。特に、日本人たるために各種の武道のうち、少なくとも一つは選ばせたいです（77頁）。

さて、体育には、節制、礼儀、克己、勇敢、共同、忍耐等の実に尊い道徳訓練が錬磨されることが感謝です。だからこそ、やたらに勝負事や、賞品目あてや、興行化することを反対したいのです。基礎になる体操を尊重して、体操の国民化、体操の一般化、体育の清浄化を希うことです（96頁）。

11. 生活の教育、富の教育

われわれは生きねばならぬ人間です。「人はパンのみに生くるものにあらず」。然して、精神活動の不可欠の手段として健康を要求する如く、生きるためにパンを要求するのです。精神活動を有効に強大ならしむるために、そこには幾多の手段が必要です。発明、工夫、政治、外交、

産業、軍事、交通、法律等一切に広義における富なる名称を冠します。富価値も結局は手段価値です。しかも健価値と同様に、不可欠の価値です。決して富を軽視するものではありませぬ。何人にもまさりて私は富の力を認めるものです。否、旺盛なる精神活動を営まんとせばそれだけ大なる富を要求します。富は富自身には意味はありませぬ。それを如何に有益に用いるかにその価値を生じてきます。吾人は富の主人たるべきであって、富に使役されてはなりませぬ（23頁）。

広く、政治も産業も、経済も交通も、軍事も外交も、含めてのことです。富のための富ではなく、四つの尊い絶対価値を支えて、発達させ、啓培するための富です。

日本教育の恐ろしい欠陥は富のための富、儲けんがための教育、物欲の奴隷たる惨状です（98頁）。

12. 全人教育と反対の合一

われわれは尊く教えられて、反対の合一ということを、全人教育の立場から特に大事にいたします。

大胆で小心で、朗らかで淑やかで、快活でたしなみがあって気はやさしくて力持ちで、よく学びよく遊び（従来の教育は実に閑の教育を忘れました。正しく、楽しく、善く、遊ぶことを教えませんでした）、よく儲けて正しく費い（今までの教育は儲けることと貯えることと節約することを教えて、国家社会の為に大いに捧げることを忘れました）、これらの二面を一つにした花も実もある立派な紳士に仕上げたいのです。コヤシも担げばピアノも弾け、拭き掃除もすればお茶や生花もでき、雑巾も綴れば絹の着物も仕立てられ、どぶ溝もさらえば第九シンフォニーも歌え、薪割もすれば劇も絵も書もいたし、ソロバンもはじくがお経も繙ける玉川っ子にしたいのです（105頁）。

結局は、永遠に永劫不変の教育とは、あらゆる正反対の二つの一つ一つを一つにした一つのみがそれだと思うのです。その中心が実に自我なのです。その自我を広く、高く、深く、清らかに育て上げねばなりませぬ（108頁）。

13. 全人教育と個性尊重の教育

完全なる個性発揮が実によき全人教育なのです。竹は竹の、百合は百合の、松は松の本性を、太郎は太郎の、花子は花子の唯一無二の本領を発揮した時が最も美しいのだと思います。

実に教育とは、その全宇宙とも取りかえられない尊き自己を発見することであり、天の与え給う各人の天地を十分に生きることだと思います（111頁）。

考えてみれば、人間ほど個性差の大きいものはけだし、宇宙間にないと思います。何物ともかけがえのない本質を持っとる上に、質において、量において、深さにおいて、速度において、時期において、全く千変万化です。同じカリキュラムや、同じ時間割からが恐ろしい束縛ではありませんか（112頁）。

14. 労作教育

ペスタロッチが身を以って強調した通り、実に教育の根本は労作教育にあります。額に汗を流し、労しむことは万人の喜びであり、誇りであり、義務だと思います。「作」は「作業」の作ではなくて、創作の作なのです。合わせて「労作」と名づけたのです（114頁）。

　労作教育を「労働搾取」などといって反対する人たちがいます。マコトの教育を毒する恐しい悪解です。労作教育は実に、聖育、知育、徳育、美育、生産教育、健康教育の総合全一なのであります。私たちの心の念願は、ただホントの教育のためなのです。ホントの人間になることなのです。ホンモノを作り出すことなのです。ホントの教育への精進であり努力なのです（117頁）。

15.　教師

　教育は精一杯、触れることです。教師は水車です。生徒、学生の中に住むことです。共に生きることです。「君汲川流我拾薪」という淡窓先生の詩句は教育の秘儀です（56頁）。

　教育の結論は教師論です。生かすも死なすも、教師です。「人」です。制度も、理想も、カリキュラムも、教科書も、設備も、方法も………一切が「人」です、人！（121頁）

100 Years of Zenjin Education: Footsteps into the Future

100th Anniversary of Zenjin Education

Oyaji, or Good Father, toured all over Japan to give lectures, starting from 1921. I cherish my memory of accompanying my grandfather, Kuniyoshi Obara, touring, when I was a little boy. His speech, spoken from the heart and in a unique way which evoked laughter and tears, was supported by many people, and as a result, many schools upheld "*zenjin* education" as one of their pillars of education.

Even in those days, about 30 years ago, the number of schools which upheld *zenjin* education was reportedly 2,500. Many organizations including schools made design registration applications for *zenjin* education in 1996, but the application submitted by Tamagawa was not approved for registration because its name was a toponym and the term *zenjin* education was a broadly accepted common noun.

Now that I think of this, I recall the term *zenjin* education (whole man education) was indicated as a common noun written with lower-case letters when I learned about the education in history class in the U.S. (It is common now to use 'being' or 'person' instead of 'man.')

The hundred years' history of *zenjin* education saw behind-the-scenes episodes such as the Kanji characters "*zenjin*," meaning 'whole person,' being mistaken as "*zennyu*," meaning 'all enrolled'; the term *zenjin* being misinterpreted as to "provide education to any and all persons" and schools being criticized that they should not reject admission through entrance exam processes; and learning being misunderstood as only one-sixth worthwhile as it was a component of the six core values —— learning (truth), goodness (virtue), beauty (art), holiness (religion), soundness (health) and wealth (life).

My grandfather Kuniyoshi used to tell me about sayings such as "We can learn from the past to gain new perspectives," "Good medicine tastes bitter," and "Not correcting a fault is regarded as another fault" when we were traveling or having dinner together.

Although *zenjin* education is considered as a common noun, the theory of Zenjin Education was first advocated by Kuniyoshi Obara 100 years ago and now is the time for Tamagawa to learn from the past to gain new perspectives (reflecting on the past to shape the 21st century).

That being said, the setup of school education and that of society (polity) correspond to and coincide with each other. So, it may be the case that the theory of Zenjin Education advocated in 1921 would rather be regarded as "old fashioned and outdated" in the present time. In addition, we are said to be now living in a VUCA time: volatile, uncertain, complex, and ambiguous. Does this mean that the concept of Zenjin Education does not fit with the current time? I believe the times of Spanish flu pandemic, World War II and the Great Depression and the subsequent World War were also VUCA. Society might not be VUCA only if controlled by Big Brother; but in fact, in any era, society should have always had a foggy outlook, been entangled in a complicated manner and not operated in a planned manner.

Even so, society has always striven to solve issues with the current knowledge of the times while recognizing the limitation of knowledge and technology, and will make the full use of cutting-edge knowledge in the future as well. Society should always seek for the truth and focus on learning. On top of the foregoing, if we lack the morality to judge between right and wrong in making use of knowledge and technology, it would allow for a "runaway of the knowledgeable devil." Furthermore, it is essential for us to have the values which affirm that the application of knowledge and technology contributes not only to new ways of life but also creation of graceful society.

Now, Good Father of Tamagawa is known as the advocate of the theory of Zenjin Education. In addition, education at Tamagawa has come to be identified with Zenjin Education. My sincerest thanks are with so many senior school staff members whose efforts made it possible for us to celebrate the 100th anniversary of Zenjin Education.

Let me finish up this message by saying that nobody would be happier about our marking the 100th anniversary of the theory of Zenjin Education this year than my grandfather Kuniyoshi, who first advocated the theory, and my father Tetsuro, who was born just about the same time as the theory.

I would like to express my deep gratitude to those two, who solidified the foundation of Today's Tamagawa education, and efforts of all seniors who supported them.

January 2021

From the hill of Tamagawa
Yoshiaki Obara

Part I

Theory and Practice of Zenjin Education
by Kuniyoshi Obara

Chapter 1

Journey of Kuniyoshi Obara to the Advocacy of "Zenjin Education"

Introduction

Kuniyoshi Obara first advocated "Zenjin Education" in August 8, 1921, at the age of 34, when he was Director at Seijo Elementary School. This Chapter focuses on the period of about 30 years from the birth of Kuniyoshi Obara to the advocacy of Zenjin Education, highlighting the signs of burgeoning of the Zenjin Education concept and further blooming thereof, and thereby follows the journey to the advocacy (fruition) of "Zenjin Education."

In the period, Kuniyoshi Obara was adopted by the Ajisaka family just before graduating from Kagoshima Normal School and used "Ajisaka" as his surname until the time when he served the Elementary School Attached to Hiroshima Higher Normal School as a director (vice principal). Accordingly, Kuniyoshi Obara is referred to as "Kuniyoshi" without using "Obara" in this Chapter other than in headings of sections where applicable, for consistency.

1   Signs of Burgeoning of the "Zenjin Education" Concept of Kuniyoshi Obara

(1) From the birth to the admission to Kagoshima normal school

Kuniyoshi was born on April 8, 1887, in the village of Kushi, Minamikata, in the county of Kawanabe in Kagoshima Prefecture as the third son of Moshichiro and Hase Obara. As represented by the fact that it changed the name from "Bonotsucho-Kushi, Kawabe" to "Bonotsucho Kushi, Minami-satsuma city" in November 2005 through municipal merger, Kuniyoshi's place of birth is located southwest of the Satsuma Peninsula, the west side of which faces the East China Sea.

With so many ocean inlets and being optimal for vessels to be berthed, Korean and Chinese people have visited this place since ancient times taking the advantage of seasonal winds and the Kuroshio current. The port of Hakataura, located south of the Kushi district, has reportedly flourished as a port for trade with the Tang dynasty since medieval times. Even in the Meiji era, the scent of Chinese culture still hanged in the air in Kushi and there were multiple practitioners of Chinese medicine even it was a small village.

Genshu Yoshimi(1790-1870), one of these practitioners of Chinese medicine, taught how to read and write to young people in the town. Yoshimi's clinic served also as a *"terakoya"* (temple school) in Kushi. Moemon Obara, who studied under the teacher Genshu Yoshimi's top apprentice and took over charge of the teacher after Genshu's death, was the grandfather of Kuniyoshi on his father's side. He displayed his talents for studying but also painting, calligraphy, and poetry. Kuniyoshi's grandfather died before he was born, but his grandmother told little Kuniyoshi about how great his grandfather was, encouraging him, saying, "You are the successor of Grandpa Moemon!" Kuniyoshi gradually developed a dream of becoming an educator.

Kuniyoshi entered Kushi Ordinary Elementary School in 1892. The first teacher under whom Kuniyoshi studied at Kushi Ordinary Elementary

School was Gennosuke Tajitsu, who is mentioned as "Genno Sensei" in *Obara Kuniyoshi Jiden & Yumemiru Hito* (hereinafter referred to as "Autobiography"). Tajitsu was good at liberal arts subjects but totally poor in terms of science and mathematics subjects. His nickname was "Inverse Proportion Principal" because he could only handle arithmetic and direct proportion but not inverse proportion. He is said to have enjoyed science experiments together with children, like having fun with children watching oxygen bubbling up. He was not a type of knowledgeable teacher, but was a teacher who learned together with children.

Kuniyoshi graduated from Kushi Ordinary Elementary School with honors in March 1896 and entered the Specially Established Higher Course of Kushi Ordinary Elementary School in April of the same year. In the second year of the Specially Established Higher Course, Kuniyoshi's mother Hase suddenly died in September 1898, when he was 11 years old. His youngest brother Suetake was only six months old at that time. She worked hard raising children while helping her husband, who failed at his business in goldmines and came to drink heavily. Kuniyoshi wrote memory of his mother later in his "Autobiography" as follows: "She was an incredibly determined person. She never scolded children for bed-wetting. But she was strict and told us that we had to win a fight. On the other hand, if we did something wrong and we said sorry, she said nothing but just smiled to us[1]." Hase seems to have been a mother who was strict yet affectionate.

Around that time, a teacher named Kamata, who graduated from Kagoshima Normal School, was assigned to a post at Kushi Ordinary Elementary School and also taught children in the Specially Established Higher Course in which Kuniyoshi was enrolled. Kamata was astonished at Kuniyoshi's excellent academic performance. Kamata was from Ibusuki, and when the time Kamata left Kushi in about only 10 months after the assignment, allowed Kuniyoshi to accompany Kamata to Ibusuki saying that it was a pity for Kuniyoshi, with such an excellent performance, to study in such a small school in a poor village. Kuniyoshi boarded with Kamata and transferred to Ibusuki Ordinary Higher Elementary School (later Ibuki Elementary School). However, in December of that year, 1899, three months before his graduation, Kuniyoshi had no choice but to go back from Ibusuki to his old town, Kushi, for some reason unknown.

Tajitsu, Kuniyoshi's former teacher at the time when he was in Kushi Ordinary Elementary School, who learned that he came back to Kushi, suggested that Kuniyoshi continue studying in an ordinary higher elementary school for the sake of his future, as there was only a little time left before the graduation, and obtain a higher elementary school diploma. Following the advice, Kuniyoshi enrolled in Sakurayama Ordinary Higher Elementary School (current Sakurayama Elementary School) in Makurazaki. For about three months from January to March 1900, Kuniyoshi went to school in Makurazaki taking a 24 km round trip along mountain paths each time.

Finally, Kuniyoshi graduated from Sakurayama Ordinary Higher Elementary School on March 21, 1900. In April of the same year, Kagoshima Fourth Ordinary Junior High School under the old education system (current Kawanabe Junior High School) was established. Kuniyoshi wished to advance to junior high school but the household economic situation did not allow him to do so. In June of the same year, his father Moshichiro also died. Seven brothers were left in poverty. In November of the same year, Kuniyoshi entered Telecommunications Technology Students Training School of Kagoshima Post and Telegraph Office, which allowed students to study at government expense and exempted them from tuition. Kuniyoshi was 13 years old at this point in time.

Kuniyoshi successfully completed the course in Telecommunications Technology Students Training School of Kagoshima Post and Telegraph Office on May 31, 1901, and was assigned to Ohama Telegraph Office in Osumi Peninsula on September 7 of the same year. At that time, the number of telegrams handled at Ohama Telegraph Office was way over 1,000 per day.

Local residents called the office "Ohama Palace" for its spectacular view of the land of over 1,500 tsubo (about 4958.7 square metres) lined with offices, warehouses, official residences, etc. About 50 employees working at the office were the elite in telegraph technology selected from across Japan.

This Ohama Telegraph Office relocated to Shiromoto in the village of Onejime in the Kimotsuki county in April 1903 and renamed its name to "Onejime Telegraph Office." The employees needed to stay at houses of citizens until the time when their official residences were ready. Kuniyoshi boarded with Masayuki Maeda, who lived close to Onejime Telegraph Office. During this time of his stay at Maeda's, a daughter of Maeda decided to advance to the Female Section of Kagoshima Normal School (later Kagoshima Female Normal School), and Kuniyoshi was asked to be a tutor for her. This event served as an opportunity for Kuniyoshi to decide to enter a normal school and become a teacher. Coming from a poor family, Kuniyoshi could not advance to higher learning and gave up his dream of becoming an educator, but this dream of becoming a great educator like his grandfather Moemon, who taught at a *terakoya*, came back to him while he helped Maeda's daughter for her entrance exam. The house of Masayuki Maeda in Onejime was the place where Kuniyoshi started specifically to move toward his dream of becoming an "educator." Kuniyoshi subsequently took the entrance exam for Kagoshima Normal School, successfully passed it and left Onejime in March 1905.

(2) Study and practice with aspiration for genuine education

Kuniyoshi entered the Regular Course First Section of Kagoshima Normal School in April 1905, when he was 18 years old. Normal schools at that time offered free tuition, required all students to live in school dormitories and trained teachers-to-be under the military-like command line and strict discipline. Kuniyoshi was critical of such way of living at the normal school, but the teachers were great and Kuniyoshi was strongly impressed by the education. The principal of Kagoshima Normal School was Fujitaro Nojima and the vice principal was Takeji Kinoshita, when Kuniyoshi entered the school.

Kuniyoshi was blessed with teachers in the government-funded normal school, and further in November of the same year, outside the school, he had a significant encounter with someone. On the first Sunday in Kagoshima city, Kuniyoshi found a church, and when he approached the entrance respectfully, he met a woman from a Western country. It was Ms. Lansing, who was a missionary. "We haven't met before, have we? Please come in. You seem to be a student at the normal school," Ms. Harriet M. Lansing said as she guided Kuniyoshi kind-heartedly. Kuniyoshi later wrote in his "Autobiography" as follows: "Her warmth, her kindness. It was an event which decided my whole life[2]." Ms. Lansing just met Kuniyoshi for the first time, but asked him to assist Sunday school for elementary school students starting from the next week with confidence in him, and she even introduced him to others saying he was her son.

This encounter with Ms. Lansing led Kuniyoshi to be acquainted with Pastor Shinji Ojima. The Christian faith became part of the life of Kuniyoshi, who was baptized by Pastor Ojima, and he lived his whole life as a Christian thereafter.

After graduating from Kagoshima Normal School, Kuniyoshi advanced to the English Department of Hiroshima Higher Normal School in April 1909. His former teachers at Kagoshima Normal School reportedly advised him to "not study too hard after entering the school." It was because Kuniyoshi had trouble in his lungs after working hard as an undersea telegraph operator in Ohama, Osumi Peninsula and in Onejime, before entering Kagoshima Normal School. In those days, Kuniyoshi was thin and weak. Kuniyoshi started practicing the "Japanese art of archery" to build up his body.

Kuniyoshi wrote in his "Autobiography" as follows: "I came to be into Japanese archery so much. It was more like I entered the department of Japanese archery or the department of martial arts rather than the department of English[3]," He also said: "I drew 100 bows each day as a quiet activity which allowed my lungs to expand. Or 500 bows on Sundays[4]." He would not neglect his study, but health came before anything else for Kuniyoshi to live longer. "My body matters more than scores. I need to be healthy. I want to live a long life[5]," Kuniyoshi always told himself. Kuniyoshi felt the importance of "health" keenly from the perspectives of education and body based on his own experience.

Kuniyoshi also became aware of the appeal of "music" in his days at Hiroshima Higher Normal School. This was resulted from the encounter with Shinta Yoshida, a music teacher. Kuniyoshi wrote in his "Autobiography" that he thankfully came to love music earnestly because of the teacher[6]. Shinta Yoshida is the composer of the Japanese song "*Minato* (Port)," which is famous for the lyrics "*Sora mo Minato mo Yoru ha Hare te......* (The sky and the port are clear in the night......).""

During the four years when he was in Hiroshima Higher Normal School, Kuniyoshi studied English as his major subject, and on top of it, as mentioned above, regained strong body by throwing himself into the Japanese art of archery and realized the importance of health. In addition, he came to know of the wonderfulness of music thanks to the encounter with Shinta Yoshida. Furthermore, Kuniyoshi deepened the Christian faith and made it part of his life to preach to children in Sunday school of a church in Hiroshima. Kuniyoshi realized through his own experience that not only learning but also art, religion and health are of importance for the development of a person.

Kuniyoshi graduated from the Regular Course English Department of Hiroshima Higher Normal School in March 1913. In April of the same year, Kuniyoshi assumed a position as a teacher of Kagawa Normal School in Takamatsu in Shikoku in accordance with an appointment order. He was 26 years old at the time. The teaching activities which Kuniyoshi engaged in at Kagawa Normal School were the first step for him to take part in training elementary school teachers. It seemed a golden opportunity for him to implement reforms which solve the issues he found in Kagoshima Normal

School. Kuniyoshi wrote the determination in his "Autobiography" as follows: "I moved to Takamatsu with the determination 'I'll do it!' ...... I received a special invitation from the principal in Kagawa ......[7]"

His life as a teacher at Kagawa Normal School ended in a rather short period of time, two and a half years. However, he not only held classes of English, education history, psychology and others, but also spent productive days closely with students, devoting himself to teaching activities such as assuming a position of homeroom teacher, traveling around the Seto Inland Sea with students as the head of the boat club, serving as a dormitory superintendent and holding prayer meetings with select religious 12 students.

2　Blooming of the "Zenjin Education" Concept of Kuniyoshi Obara

(1) Study in the Department of Philosophy at Kyoto Imperial University

After leaving the position as a teacher at Kagawa Normal School, Kuniyoshi became a student once again in September 1915, and entered the Department of Philosophy at the College of Letters, Kyoto Imperial University (later the college of Literature, Kyoto University). Kuniyoshi was 28 years old then.

Professors of the then Department of Philosophy at the College of Letters, Kyoto Imperial University included Kitaro Nishida, who was in charge of the philosophy course (45 years old at the time), Sanjuro Tomonaga, in charge of the Western philosophy history course (44 years old at the time), Bunzaburo Matsumoto, in charge of the Indian philosophy history and religious studies course (46 years old at the time), Kenjiro Fujii, in charge of the ethics studies course (43 years old at the time), Yasukazu Fukada, in charge of the aesthetics and aesthetics history course (37 years old at the time) and Shigenao Konishi, in charge of the pedagogy and teaching methodology course (40 years old at the time), among others. They were all in their 30s or 40s, young and well-qualified professors. Kuniyoshi wrote in his "Autobiography" as follows: "In fact, I entered the Department of Philosophy at Kyoto Imperial University, which I

Fig. 1-1. Kuniyoshi at the time when he
was a student at Kyoto Imperial
University
Photo courtesy of Tamagawa Academy

Fig. 1-2. Kuniyoshi (in the last row, in
the middle) with Professor
Konishi (in the front row, on the
lefthand side)
Photo courtesy of Tamagawa Academy

had long admired with a sense of somewhat like jumping in to a paradise of a learning kingdom, or a utopia, and with so much energy like a young hawk[8]." (Fig. 1-1 and Fig. 1-2).

Kuniyoshi enrolled in the pedagogy and teaching methodology course of the Department of Philosophy. In December 1917, when Kuniyoshi was in the third year of the course, Seiichi Hatano (40 years old at the time) assumed a position in charge of the religious studies (Christianity) course of Kyoto Imperial University. Hatano was exposed to early Christianity research while he was studying in Germany and authored Kirisutokyo no Kigen in 1908. As he took charge of the religious studies course of Kyoto Imperial University, it was said that Christianity class was provided by a specialist for the first time.

Kuniyoshi confirmed that education entailed not only "learning," "morality" and "art" but also "religion" as the underlying essential component. As such, the statement of Kitaro Nishida, "learning and morality shall ultimately reach religion," in his book *Zen no Kenkyu* (1911, Kodokan) struck the chord of Kuniyoshi strongly.

In order to deepen the foundation for and establish the content of education at the same time, Kuniyoshi, while placing the primary focus of his study on Shigenao Konishi's "pedagogy" classes, actively attended Kitaro Nishida's "philosophy" classes, Sanjuro Tomonaga's "Western philosophy history" classes, Kenjiro Fujii's "ethics studies" classes, Yasukazu Fukada's "aesthetics" classes, and further, "religious studies" classes of Seiichi Hatano, who came in later.

Kuniyoshi later recalled in his book *Zenjin Kyoiku Ron* (1969, Tamagawa University Press) that Shigenao Konishi asked a question to students majoring in pedagogy in a conversation in the days at Kyoto Imperial University, saying, "We talk about moral personality, artistic personality, philosophical personality or religious personality. But I want a comprehensive personality combining all of them, let's say, something like cultural personality (*Kulturcharakter*). Have any of you used a word that has that kind of meaning[9]?" Kuniyoshi's study in the Department of Philosophy at Kyoto Imperial University advanced to the direction of not only each subject of philosophy, morality, art and religion but also to the direction of an issue of "comprehensive personality," an ideal form of an educated person, and an issue of the possibility of "comprehensive education" to develop such a person.

(2) Contemplation and experience in Rakuyo Church and Kyoto Minamiza Theatre

Having been baptized during his days in Kagoshima and made regular visits to churches in Hiroshima and Takamatsu, Kuniyoshi, also in Kyoto, visited Rakuyo Church located closed to the Kyoto Imperial Palace and Doshisha University founded by Jo Niijima to give worship on Sundays. Motoi Kurihara, who was a former teacher of Kuniyoshi when he was in Hiroshima Higher Normal School, influenced Kuhiyoshi and he began visiting Rakuyo Church. Kurihara became a professor at the Third High School under the old education system (later the College of Liberal Arts, Kyoto University) after teaching Kuniyoshi and other students at Hiroshima Higher Normal School.

Kuniyoshi studied under Motoi Kurihara and even succeeded the position of editor in chief of Rakuyo Church's "Monthly Report" from Kurihara. Rather, Kuniyoshi obtained an opportunity to not only edit "Monthly Report" but also publish his thought through essays. In March 1917, Kuniyoshi contributed an essay to the Monthly Report "Michishirube." It was a year and four months before his graduation from Kyoto Imperial University.

Under the title "Pass the Enlightenment," his essay goes like this: "...... And, it is unavoidable that schools overemphasize knowledge. So, education on the emotion and volition must also be provided somewhere. In other words, education for the whole person is necessary. Education on the emotion and volition, or cultivation of the spirituality in particular, is quite difficult. However, without such education, people would become vacant like a puppet[10]."

His assertion in this essay was as follows: It is unavoidable that school focuses on intellectual education. However, when it comes to education of a person, intellectual education only is not enough, and education on the emotion and volition is necessary. In other words, "education for the whole person" is necessary. Moreover, "religious education" is at the core of this education.

Kuniyoshi came to know of the wonderfulness of music in his days at Hiroshima Higher Normal School, and in Kyoto, he further gained an opportunity to turn his attention to drama. It was another significant harvest he obtained in his days at Kyoto Imperial University. Kuniyoshi gained theoretical support on the importance of art for education through his study under Yasukazu Fukada, who took charge in the aesthetics course at Kyoto Imperial University. Kuniyoshi also had an opportunity to see a play in the Kyoto Minamiza Theatre through his acquaintance Ms. Fujie, for he worked as a tutor for the Fujie family, which led him to become interested in drama. This event led him to name children's drama "school drama" when he was working for the Elementary School Attached to Hiroshima Higher Normal School later. This matter will be discussed later in more detail.

(3) Discussion on "education for the whole person" in bachelor thesis

As the culmination of what he learned through his three years in the Department of Philosophy at Kyoto Imperial University (they provided three-year programs at the time), in July 1918, Kuniyoshi submitted the bachelor thesis titled "Shukyo ni yoru Kyoiku no Kyusai" under the instruction of Seiichi Hatano and Shigenao Konishi. The volume of the bachelor thesis written by Kuniyoshi was, according to Kuniyoshi, "five Mino paper-sized 300-page books bound in Japanese style. 1,500 sheets of paper in total." It would be equivalent to "approximately 600 sheets of 400-character manuscript paper" if converted based on the current way of calculation.

The oral examination was carried out by three professors: Seiichi Hatano, Shigenao Konishi, and Kenjiro Fujii. In June 1919, 10 months after his graduation from Kyoto Imperial University, Kuniyoshi published the bachelor thesis modifying its title to *Kyoiku no Konpon Mondai toshite no Shukyo*, through a publisher Shuseisha in Tokyo. It was actually a great work, consistin of 500 pages (490 characters a page). At the top of this book, he wrote: "This book is based on my bachelor thesis for my graduation from the Department of Philosophy at Kyoto Imperial University. Education and religion. These are my research subjects for the whole life, my lifelong projects[11]." This edition was almost the same as the original bachelor thesis.

Subsequently, this book was thoroughly revised and the first print of the new edition was published by Tamagawa University Press in November 1950. In fact, in this new edition, one chapter was omitted from Part I. More specifically, in the 1919 edition published by Shuseisha, Part I "Discussion of Essence" consisted of the following four chapters in total: Chapter 1: "Discussion of Religion"; Chapter 2: "Discussion of Essence of Education"; Chapter 3: "Relationship Between Science, Morality and Art and Religion as the Content of Education"; and Chapter 4: "Misunderstanding of the General Public on Education and Religion." On the other hand, in the 1950 edition published by Tamagawa University Press, Part I "Discussion of Essence" consisted of the following three chapters in total: Chapter 1: "Discussion of Religion"; Chapter 2: "Relationship Between Science, Morality and Art and Religion as the Content of Education"; and Chapter 3: "Misunderstanding of the General Public on Education and Religion." As seen above, Chapter 2: "Discussion of Essence of Education" in the old edition was removed in the new edition[12].

It was already mentioned that Kuniyoshi asserted that "education for the whole person" was necessary in his essay contributed to Rakuyo Church's Monthly Report "Michishirube" in March 1917. In fact, in Section 3: "Components of education" of this Chapter 2: "Discussion of Essence of Education," Kuniyoshi discussed "education for the whole person" once again. More specifically, Kuniyoshi stated: "Education I demand is the education for the whole person. In addition, the education must be oriented toward both aspects of body and mind in an integrated manner as asserted by Butler. Furthermore, it is an integrated process rather than a group of mixed elements[13]." Here, Kuniyoshi expressed the key concepts of his later "Zenjin Kyoiku Ron," namely, "education for the whole person," "both aspects of body and mind" and "integration."

(4) Practice of "school drama" at Elementary School Attached to Hiroshima Higher Normal School

After graduating from Kyoto Imperial University, Kuniyoshi assumed a position at Hiroshima Higher Normal School, his alma mater, in August 1918. He was ordered to concurrently serve as a director (vice principal) of its attached elementary school. As a director, he did not take charge of predetermined classes on a regular basis. However, when any other teacher had to be absent for illness, business trip or any other reason, Kuniyoshi happily substituted for them and conducted the class. Kuniyoshi later wrote in his "Autobiography" as follows: "Thankfully, I had the chance to train myself for all grades, and all subjects. Indeed, my one and a half years at the Elementary School Attached to Hiroshima Higher Normal School was so valuable for my pedagogy —— for fusion of theory and practice, knowledge and technique and contemplation and experience, or 'uniting opposites.'" In addition, based on this experience, he also discussed his argument on teachers, stating that elementary school teachers needed to be capable of doing everything like Leonardo da Vinci and Miyamoto Musashi or they needed to be educated as a whole person[14].

As vice principal at the Elementary School Attached to Hiroshima Higher Normal School, Kuniyoshi actively developed various activities. The facts that he produced the name of "school drama" and such school dramas were performed were landmarks in history of school education in Japan. According to the book authored by Akira Okada, who promoted school dramas in the Showa era, *Drama to Zenjin Kyoiku* (1985, Tamagawa University Press), dramas for the purpose of practicing a language, skits, dialogue-driven dramas and so-called tableaux vivants and dramas imitating Kabuki, among others, seemed to have been performed as school plays in the course of school education in the Meiji era and thereafter. But, these were reportedly performed only for the purpose of practicing language or entertainment, and they themselves did not make a clear educational point.

"School plays" seemed to have been popular at the Elementary School Attached to Hiroshima Higher Normal School as well at the time, and "a sort of theatricals" seemed to have been played as an attraction along with music, dramatic readings, dialogues, etc. Starting from the year following Kuniyoshi's appointment, however, it was decided that such "theatricals" should be performed intensively from a more educational viewpoint. As is already mentioned, Kuniyoshi worked as a tutor for the Fujie family and had a chance to see Kaomise (all-star cast) performance in the Minamiza Theatre in Kyoto thanks to Ms. Fujie. In addition, he bought Engeki Gaho every month and was absorbed in reading it, due partly to the influence from Kan Matsubara, who was a fellow student. As such, he himself felt the importance of art education as "education of sense" for the promotion of "education for the whole person."

The plays performed in the first year, "Suishiei no Kaiken" and "Ama no Iwato," were a great success and received applause thanks to cooperation by his colleague teachers. "I think they were the first that were named 'school drama' in Japan. Thanks to them, I am said to be the one who produced the name 'school drama' in Japan," Kuniyoshi later recalled in his "Autobiography."

In fall of 1919, Arata Osada visited Kuniyoshi from Tokyo on behalf of Dr. Masataro Sawayanagi. Masataro Sawayanagi was a leading figure in the then educational circles, who successively held positions as a principal at the Second High School under the old education system (later the College of General Education, Tohoku University) in 1897 and at the First High School under the old education system (later the College of Arts and Sciences, the University of Tokyo) in 1898, the following year; Vice Minister of Education in 1906; the first president at Tohoku Imperial University in 1911; president at Kyoto Imperial University in 1913; and the head of Imperial Educational Society in 1916. Sawayanagi founded "Seijo Elementary School" in Ushigome-Haramachi, Tokyo, in April 1917, as a school for experimenting new education and was serving as the principal. The first director Fusajiro Fujimoto (Hirauchi) resigned from office for a personal reason and the post of director was vacant.

When Osada told him about an offer from Principal Sawayanagi, saying, "Well, we wanted to see if you might be interested in devoting your whole life to a private school," Kuniyoshi immediately responded to the offer, "Of course I am. To Seijo." In fact, Kuniyoshi had an opportunity to tour Seijo Elementary School two or three months before this meeting and met Principal Sawayanagi during the visit. Kuniyoshi empathized with the "purpose of founding Seijo Elementary School" from the bottom of his heart. Consequently, in December 1919, Kuniyoshi left Hiroshima and stepped into new endeavors in Tokyo to assume the position of director at Seijo Elementary School. Two years later, in August 1921, as a fruition of his contemplation and practice up to this point in time, Kuniyoshi advocated "Zenjin Education" in the "Hachidai Kyoiku Shucho Koenkai (Eight Educators Educational Advocacy Conference)" held in the lecture hall of then Tokyo Higher Normal School (current University of Tsukuba).

Notes

1) Kuniyoshi Obara, *Obara Kuniyoshi Zenshu 28: Obara Kuniyoshi Jiden-Yumemiru Hito(1)*, Tamagawa University Press, 1960, p. 50.

2) Ibid., p. 149.

3) Ibid., p. 296.

4) Ibid., p. 256.

5) Ibid., p. 258.

6) Ibid., p. 285.

7) Ibid., p. 311.

8) Kuniyoshi Obara, *Obara Kuniyoshi Zenshu 29: Obara Kuniyoshi Jiden-Yumemiru Hito(2)*,Tamagawa University Press, 1963, p. 9.

9) Kuniyoshi Obara, *Zenjin Kyoiku Ron*, Tamagawa University Press, 1969, p. 130.

10) Kuniyoshi Ajisaka, "Kyouka wo Nokose" in *Michi Shirube*, Vol. 17, 1917, p. 1.

11) Kuniyoshi Ajisaka, *Kyoiku no Konpon Mondai toshite no Shukyo*, Shuseisha, 1919, foreword.

12) Kuniyoshi Obara, *Kyoiku no Konpon Mondai toshite no Shukyo*, Tamagawa UniversityPress, 1950, a table of contents.

13) Kuniyoshi Ajisaka, *Kyoiku no Konpon Mondai toshite no Shukyo*, Shuseisha, 1919,   p.83.

14) Kuniyoshi Obara, *Obara Kuniyoshi Zenshu 29: Obara Kuniyoshi Jiden-Yumemiru Hito(2)*,Tamagawa University Press, 1963, p. 126.

15) Ibid., p. 135.

Chapter 2

Theory of Zenjin Education of Kuniyoshi Obara
—— Advocacy and Development Thereof

Introduction

The first advocate of "Zenjin Education" in Japan was Kuniyoshi Obara (1887–1977), the founder of Tamagawa Academy & University. Obara gave a lecture in the Eight Educators Educational Advocacy Conference on August 8, 1921, changing the pre-determined lecture title from "Advocacy of Cultural Education" to "Zenjin Education, Which Is a Totally Ordinary Name[1]." At that time, he was a teacher (director) working on the front line of a private elementary school, Seijo Elementary School. In front of a large number of teachers who attended the Advocacy Conference, which can be seen as a private teacher training session, he criticized the then education, which was unbalanced and heavily focused on cramming knowledge into students, and presented the ideal form of "true education[2]" naming it "Zenjin Education." It went viral and the term "*zenjin* education" came to be known widely to the public. Now, *Kojien* and other general Japanese dictionaries include the terms "*zenjin*" and "*zenjin* education" as ordinary terms. Rather, it is not an overstatement to say that *"zenjin* education" has now become one of the most important terms in the educational circles. The terms *"zenjin* education" and *"zenjin teki"* are widely used by schools (kindergartens, elementary schools, junior high schools, high schools and universities) for describing their educational philosophy, policy and the like[3]. *"Ikiru chikara* (zest for living)" is a term which is currently placed at the core of the development theme by the educational circles in Japan, and the Central Council for Education clearly states that the "'zest for living' is *zenjin teki* (whole-person) power[4]."

As exemplified by the foregoing, the terms *"zenjin* education" and *"zenjin teki"* are widely spread. On the other hand, however, it seems that we have now entered the "age in which people are unaware[5]" that these terms are originally from Obara. There are a large number of cases observed that *zenjin* is used freely with a meaning out of the context in which Obara used it, for example, *"zenjin* power" and *"zenjin* education 2.0."

There may be arguments that these terms, which can be said to have become common nouns, should be freely used by anyone. This paper does not intend to argue what "authentic Zenjin Education" is close-mindedly and dogmatically. Still, because "Zenjin Education" was advocated by Obara and practiced under his direction, and the term has a 100 years of history, which has become a common term that is used in the educational circles, it should be useful to trace back to "the origin." Confirming in what context Obara advocated "Zenjin Education" and how he used the term should be a beneficial foundation in succeeding and developing *"zenjin* education."

Our superficial knowledge may not allow us to understand the theory and practice of "Zenjin Education," which was advocated by Obara and practiced at his schools, in its entirety. This Chapter modestly intends to understand the advocacy and development of the education, even in part, based on the texts of the theory of Zenjin Education written by Kuniyoshi Obara. In citing terms in this paper in Japanese from the materials, old Kanji characters are modified to new Kanji characters, old Kana characters are modified to modern Kana characters and Kana ligatures are modified to Kana characters.

1   Texts of the Theory of Zenjin Education

(1) Two texts

There exist two texts as the theory of Zenjin Education by Kuniyoshi Obara: one is "Zenjin Kyoiku Ron" in 1921, which is based on the stenographic notes from the Eight Educators Educational Advocacy Conference; and the other is "new 'Zenjin Kyoiku Ron'[6]" in 1969. There is an interval of about half a century between the two. The former was a "so-called argument of necessity," in which Obara in his mid 30s argued for the necessity of "Zenjin Education," or a "precious record when he was young[7]." On the other hand, in the latter, Obara in his later years "incorporated the details[8]" of Zenjin Education he had continued to practice at Seijo Elementary School and Tamagawa. The volume has almost doubled from 56 pages for the former to 114 pages for the latter, indeed (comparison based on the numbers of pages in *Obara Kuniyoshi Zenshu*). The characteristics of the content of both of them will be discussed in the following section and onwards. Here, I will provide simple commentaries on the two texts of "Zenjin Kyoiku Ron."

(2) Text of "Zenjin Kyoiku Ron" (1921)

There are two different versions of the text of "Zenjin Kyoiku Ron" (1921). They were published in the same year. One version is "Zenjin Kyoiku Ron" in Hachidai Kyoiku Shucho (published in November 1921; Fig. 2-1) published by the Dai Nippon Academic Association , which sponsored the Eight Educators Educational Advocacy Conference (hereinafter referred to as the "Association Version[9]"). The other version is "Zenjin Kyoiku" published in the magazine *Kyoiku Mondai Kenkyu* (issued in October 1921; Fig. 2-2) of the Educational Issue Research Association of Seijo Elementary School, for which Obara worked (hereinafter referred to as the "Seijo Elementary School Version[10]").

The "Seijo Elementary School Version" was the first in terms of order of publication. "I heard that the Academic Association is planning to publish a record of the lectures, so it would be redundant. Still, I am going to write this one[11]," Obara wrote in the "Seijo Elementary School Version." Detailed comparison of the two versions is omitted for the sake of reducing the number of pages of this paper, but the text of the "Seijo Elementary School Version" is also based on the stenographic notes from the Advocacy Conference. In other words, it is assumed that Obara made some alterations on a galley proof of the "Association Version." In addition, both versions are written in almost the same style and uses almost the same composition, but have different titles. The title of the "Association Version" is "Zenjin Kyoiku Ron" and that of the "Seijo Elementary School Version" is "Zenjin Kyoiku." The "Association Version" subsequently became the basic text used in *Hachidai Kyoiku Shucho Hihan*[12] (1923) published by the Dai Nippon Academic Association. Later, "Zenjin Kyoiku Ron" as the "Association Version" was published again in the reprinted edition of *Hachidai Kyoiku Shucho* (Tamagawa University Press, 1976), in which old Kanji and Kana characters were modified to modern characters[13].

Fig. 2-1. *Hachidai Kyoiku Shucho* (1921)

Fig. 2-2. *Kyoiku Mondai Kenkyu* (1921)

On the other hand, "Zenjin Kyoiku" as the "Seijo Elementary School Version" was published again under the same title "Zenjin Kyoiku" in *Obara Kuniyoshi Zenshu 15: Kyoiku Ronbun / Kyoiuku Zuiso (1)* (Tamagawa University Press, 1964), being modified into modern characters, and further, published once again as "II Zenjin Kyoiku" in the book *Zenjin Kyoiku Ron* (1969) in his later years.

(3) Text of "Zenjin Kyoiku Ron" (1969)

The other new one, "Zenjin Kyoiku Ron" in 1969, was published in the book *Zenjin Kyoiku Ron* (Tamagawa University Press, 1969; Fig. 2-3), which was exactly positioned by Obara himself in his later years as "new 'Zenjin Kyoiku Ron' he released in August 1969[14]." Its table of contents is as follows: "Introduction," "I Zenjin Kyoiku Ron," "II Zenjin Kyoiku" (the "Seijo Elementary School Version" in 1921), "III Kachi Taikei Ron," and "Conclusion." "I Zenjin Kyoiku Ron" here is the very new text of "released in 1969 for the first time. "III Kachi Taikei Ron" is explained as partly reprinted from *Kyoiku no Konpon Mondai toshite no Tetsugaku*, which was published in fall of 1924[15] (the year is

Fig. 2-3. *Zenjin Kyoiku Ron*
(First Edition, 1969)

Fig. 2-4. *Zenjin Kyoiku Ron* (Revised)

mistaken in the bibliography; the correct year is 1923[16]).

Obara further added "In renewing the edition" in October of the following year to *Zenjin Kyoiku Ron* (1969). He wrote, "The edition was renewed and additions and supplementations were made[17]." However, attention should be paid to the points that there is no indication of "renewed edition" in the publication information and it is not treated as a renewed edition in the bibliography as well. The print on the book band on the front cover says "revised edition with additions and supplementations" instead of "renewed edition with additions and supplementations" (Fig. 2-4). In addition, the indication of "edition" in this "revised edition with additions and supplementations" is still 1969. In the "revised edition with additions and supplementations," "III Kachi Taikei Ron" was incorporated into "I Zenjin Kyoiku Ron." Subsequent editions are all based on this "revised edition with additions and supplementations." "Zenjin Kyoiku Ron" newly published in *Obara Kuniyoshi Zenshu 33: Zenjin Kyoiku Ron / Shukyo Kyoiku Ron / Shido* (Tamagawa University Press, 1975; hereinafter referred to as the "Zenshu Version") is also the "revised edition with additions and supplementations." "In adding to 'Zenshu'" is inserted by Obara himself to "Zenjin Kyoiku Ron" in the "Zenshu Version," and thus, this can be regarded as the definitive edition run through by Obara when he was alive. "Zenjin Kyoiku Ron" in *Obara Kuniyoshi Senshu 3: Zenjin Kyoiku Ron / Shiso Mondai to Kyoiku* (Tamagawa University Press, 1980) issued after the death of Obara is also based on the "Zenshu Version." Accordingly, when mentioning Obara's new "Zenjin Kyoiku Ron" (1969) in his later years in the following discussion, the "Zenshu Version" (Fig. 2-5) shall be used[18].

Out of the texts of the theory of Zenjin Education of Kuniyoshi Obara, the most easily available one is *Zenjin Kyoiku Ron* (Tamagawa University Press, 1994; hereinafter referred to as the "Renewed Edition") shown as Fig. 2-6, the edition of which was renewed in 1994 (officially treated as the renewed edition in the bibliography[19]). This is also based on the aforementioned "revised edition with additions and supplementations." The addition of "In renewing the edition – for students" by Akira Okada, Kuniyoshi Obara's son-in-law to this one is worthy of special mention. According to Okada, "Minor modifications have been made to phrases in this book so that the basic philosophy of education of Mr. Obara can be easily understood by today's young students[20]." In addition, in response to "demand for English translation of *Zenjin Kyoiku Ron* of Kuniyoshi Obara from English speakers[21]," an English/Japanese side-by-side translation text (*Theory of Zenjin Education*) was published by Tamagawa University Press in 2003. For the Japanese part, "members of the Revision and Editorial Committee of *Zenjin Kyoiku Ron* have made efforts to revise *Zenjin Kyoiku Ron* to everyday language to the minimum extent possible by actually reading the book in turns, maintain the underlying intentions of Mr. Obara for the words and phrases and interpreting the text to suit the present times[22]" based on the "Renewed Edition."

This concludes the summary of the texts of the theory of Zenjin Education of Kuniyoshi Obara. As research on the theory of Zenjin Education of Kuniyoshi Obara, doctoral theses have been published by Japanese and German researchers in the late 1970s after Obara's death[23]. Since the

Fig. 2-5. *Obara Kuniyoshi Zenshu 33*

Fig. 2-6. *Zenjin Kyoiku Ron*
(Renewed Edition)

beginning of this century, research papers and books on Obara have been published one after another in Japan and overseas in step with growing interest in the Taisho New Education Movement[24]. On the other hand, an advent of commentary versions after academic scrutiny on Obara's texts remains a future important issue.

2 First Theory of Zenjin Education of Kuniyoshi Obara (1921)

(1) Overview of Eight Educators Educational Advocacy Conference

From the historical perspective, the advocacy of "Zenjin Education" by Kuniyoshi Obara is positioned in the context of the worldwide New Education Movement. The New Education Movement is a movement of criticizing modern education emerged at the end of the 19th century and continued to the beginning of the 20th century, peaking in the 1920s in particular. In Japan, modern school systems, teaching methodology, teaching tools and the like were received from Europe and the U.S. in the Meiji era in connection with the construction of a modern state, and education which is known for the uniform style heavily focused on intellectual education cramming knowledge into students spread throughout the country. Subsequently, however, in the liberal atmosphere of Taisho Democracy, after World War I in particular, reflection and criticism concerning such modern education have taken place. In terms of phenomena, the New Education Movement took its concrete shape for example in incorporation of many new schools including Seijo Elementary School. It was just as the parable of "New wine must be put into new wineskins[25]" (Gospel of Matthew 9:17) taught. The development of the New Education Movement was connected with incorporation of new schools. In addition, the New Education Movement was also characterized by moves towards remodeling seminars and lecture meetings for current teachers. The representative event was the Eight Educators Educational Advocacy Conference held in August 1921. The Advocacy Conference is positioned as a landmark event in education history which represents the Taisho New Education Movement[26].

The Eight Educators Educational Advocacy Conference was an "innovative seminar" in which the then eight representatives of "eight types of new educational theories" were invited one by one for each day, from August 1 through August 8[27]. It was sponsored by the Dai Nippon Academic Association in the private sector like a today's seminar for current teachers. And what was more, it criticized boring seminars in those days and presented itself as a new style event[28]. The eight lecturers who were invited to the Eight Educators Educational Advocacy Conference in August 1921 and their lecture titles announced in the ad in June of the same year were as follows[29]:

Day 1: "Key Points of Dynamic Education" by Heiji Oikawa (director at Hyogo Akashi Female Normal School); Day 2: "Creation of Truth education" by Sofu Inage (Kinshichi Inage; editor in chief of *Sozo* operated by Sozosha); Day 3: "Foundation of Self-Learning Education" by Choichi Higuchi (professor at Tokyo Higher Normal School); Day 4: "Essence of Free Education" by Kishie Tezuka (director at Chiba Normal School); Day 5: "Advocacy of Art Education" by Noburu Katakami (professor at Waseda University); Day 6: "Impulsive Satisfaction and Creative Education" by Meikichi Chiba (director at Hiroshima Normal School); Day 7: "Self-Moving Education" by Kiyomaru Kono (director at Japan Women's University); and Day 8 (final): "Advocacy of Cultural Education" by Kuniyoshi Obara (director at Seijo Elementary School)[30]. Obara declined the lecture title "The Essence of Education by Sacred Love[31]" which was initially announced by the sponsor. After that, as mentioned above, the lecture title "Advocacy of Cultural Education" was announced in the ad.

However, on the day of the lecture, he announced a new lecture title, saying, "Now, I did not go ahead with education by sacred love, I was not satisfied with cultural education and, after much consideration, I decided to go with Zenjin Education[32]." This was the very moment when "Zenjin Education" was advocated to the public for the first time in Japan.

In order of the titles listed in Hachidai Kyoiku Shucho (Dai Nippon

Fig. 2-7. The lecturers printed on *Kyoiku Gakujutu Kai* (Vol.44,
Issue No.1, Dai Nippon Acodemic Association, 1921,
frontispiece)
Note: Obara is in the bottom row, far left.

Academic Association, 1921), the Advocacy Conference record, "Theory of Self-
Learning Education" (Higuchi); "Theory of Self-Moving Education" (Kohno);
"Theory of Free Education" (Tezuka); "Theory of Education by Impulsive
Satisfaction" (Chiba); "Theory of Creative Education" (Inage); "Theory of
Dynamic Education" (Oikawa); "Theory of Zenjin Education" (Obara); and
"Theory of Education by Art and Literature" (Katakami)[33].

(2) Theory of Zenjin Education before the lecture ── Kyoiku no Konpon Mondai toshite no Shukyo (1919)

On August 8, 1921, on the final day of the Advocacy Conference, which
reportedly "attracted at least 2,000 people in the audience for consecutive
days[34]," Obara harangued the audience on "Zenjin Education" for the first
time, for "two and a half hours[35]." A person named Fujinshi[36], who was asked
by the Dai Nippon Academic Association to record the lectures, commented
on the lecture of Obara of that day, saying, "I have already heard of what he
talked more than once. The topics and anecdotes were almost the same. Even

so, it is still interesting no matter how many times I have listened to it.[37]" This comment suggests that Obara had already talked on similar thoughts.

About three years before the lecture, Obara submitted the bachelor thesis titled "Shukyo ni yoru Kyoiku no Kyusai" (1918) to Kyoto Imperial University. The thesis review committee members were Shigenao Konishi (pedagogy), Kenjiro Fujii (ethics studies) and Seiichi Hatano[38] (religious studies). This thesis, which underwent academic scrutiny for the first time for Obara, was published in the following year with the revised title, Kyoiku no Konpon Moncai toshite no Shukyo (Shuseisha, 1919). Bokumin Tsuchiyama commented on this book that the underlying thoughts for the entire book was precisely Obara's theory of Zenjin Education itself[39].

In Part I "Discussion of Essence," Chapter 2: "Discussion of Essence of Education" of the first edition of *Kyoiku no Konpon Moncai toshite no Shukyo* (Religion as the Fundamental Problem of Education), Obara pursued what "genuine education" was and intended to "alter" the "traditional definition of education" which harmed education[40]. He criticized traditional education as being "unbalanced," only "one aspect of education" and "incomplete[41]", and explained the necessity of comprehensive "education for the whole person (the underline is added by the author)" in which "mind and body develop in harmony[42]". Obara further criticized traditional unbalanced education and placed emphasis on "culture and enlightenment" in their entirety of a person. In addition, as is the fact that the subject of this book is religion, Obara explained the necessity of religion stating that "genuine culture [and] enlightenment" (the word within the parentheses is added by the author) must have religion at the root of "culture and enlightenment[43]". In the following Part II "Discussion on Relationship" in this book, Obara discussed intellectual education, moral education, beauty education and physical education in terms of the relationship with religion with the aim of arguing about "culture and enlightenment" in their entirety. For Obara, "genuine education" meant reaching a "religious state" which is "genuine oneself." "In the 'religious state,' everything from intellectual education, moral education, affective education to livelihood is integrated. When I say genuine education or genuine pedagogy, I mean this state,[44]" he wrote. In addition, he defined education as work of inspiring and cultivating a "whole person" by another "whole person[45]," and considered "the person themselves" and "the essential quality and individuality of the person" as "personality" and further paraphrased them as a "whole person[46]." And he went on to state that "perfection of personality" was "nothing else but enhancement of a whole person" and "nothing else but development of oneself[47]." In the book *Shido* (Tamagawa University Press, 1974), a work of his later years, Obara stated that a teacher "must be a truly noble whole person rather than a clever expert," arguing the conditions of "ideal teachers under the concept of whole person[48]." Indeed, his thought that "education is inspiring and cultivating a 'whole person' by another 'whole person'" was consistent from his first book to the book in his later years.

I am going to leave it there for now concerning Obara's views on whole person and education expressed in *Kyoiku no Konpon Mondai toshite no Shukyo*, just pointing out that Obara's thought which was later presented in the Eight Educators Educational Advocacy Conference had already been expressed with religion at the core. So, it is no wonder that his "topics and anecdotes were almost the same" in lectures he delivered before the Educators Educational Advocacy Conference.

(3) "Zenjin Kyoiku Ron" at the time of the lecture (1921)

The Eight Educators Educational Advocacy Conference was advertised with a slogan "Revolutionary Seminar as a Pedagogical Research Conference[49]." Shisui Amako , who held the Advocacy Conference, stated the purpose of holding the event as follows: "We invited eight new advocates who are arguing for education and pedagogy innovation in Japan at present, asking them to present and discuss their purposes, spirits and arguments[50]." The eight lecturers were expected to present their "eight types of new educational theories[51]" and have discussions on them. The seven lecturers excluding Obara had their respective keywords for their lectures: "dynamic," "creative," "self-learning," "free," "art and literature" and "impulsive." However, in the "revolutionary seminar" which emphasized each specific theory in such a manner, Obara's comprehensive argument for "Zenjin Education" rather stood on the position of criticizing such one-sided arguments. Obara, who believed that overemphasizing specific arguments was "fake education[52]" which distorted "genuine education," was actually critical of the purpose of this "revolutionary seminar" in part, while playing his role in it. Among the assortment of arguments for new education which emphasized only one side, Obara's lecture title "Zenjin Education" was not sensational at all, and was anti-revolutionary or beyond revolutionary rather than being revolutionary. As Obara himself described it, it was "totally ordinary[53]." And audience found his argument "moderate[54]."

It goes without saying that the subject of this lecture of Obara was to advocate "Zenjin Education." However, the significance of the advocacy would become unclear if the fundamental "aim" of advocating "*Zenjin* Education" is not understood. Obara had already had a view in *Kyoiku no Konpon Mondai toshite no Shukyo* that education at that time was "incomplete," and he sought for the ideal form of "genuine education." This view was also followed through in the lecture at the Eight Educators Educational Advocacy Conference. He listed characteristics of and criticized "fake education" and stressed that "Zenjin Education" was the form of "true education."

For Obara, "fake education" means "education unbalancedly weighted towards only one given aspect[55]." Obara criticized such education giving a succession of examples such as utilitarian intellectual education unbalancedly weighted towards "education preparing for entrance exams," and education extremely unbalancedly weighted towards physical education which "misinterprets encouragement of physical education as doing gymnastic exercises day in and day out[56]." He further criticized acts of extremely espousing some specific teaching or learning methodology (for example, "dynamic group instruction") or arguments (for example, "free education," "self-learning theory," "children-oriented theory," etc.)[57]. The "eight new advocates who are arguing for education and pedagogy innovation in Japan at present" were required to present their "arguments" at the Eight Educators Educational Advocacy Conference by Amako, who held that conference[58]. In other words, the Conference can be said to have entailed the risk of each lecturer being unbalancedly weighted towards a one-sided argument. Obara, who "disliked, more than anything else, settling down in a narrow world of some principle calling it a whatever theory[59]," was at a loss what lecture title to use, and "after much consideration, he decided to go with Zenjin Education[60]." For Obara, "Zenjin Education" was not something that was used to express a specific argument. In that sense, he stood out in the Conference. For him, "true education," the complete opposite of "education unbalancedly weighted towards only one given aspect," meant education which is not weighted towards anything but takes the "golden mean[61]," and he intended to express such education as "Zenjin Education."

In the end, however, "Zenjin Education" is another type of unbalanced education, isn't it? Obara anticipated such an objection and made his point by using a term "whole person theory[62]" and stating that the "whole person theory" was not about a messy "lack of principle and aim" without a solid view but was a "theory of no-ism," and flatly stated that whatever name could be used to describe it[63]. He also stated that it was an "inclusive theory[64]" in which anything was incorporated as long as it was right. Moreover, when the lecture approached just about halfway, Obara said, "All adjectives bring about some kind of limitations. Therefore, I was able to feel the simple but limitless and deep meaning of the term *Menschenerziehung*, or education of people, myself[65]." And then he came to a point which he stressed, saying, "It is so obvious and simple that 'Zenjin Education' is education of 'a person'; or creation of a person as a human, or rather, helping a person to develop as a human. There is no other education. There must be no other education[66]." As mentioned above, the audience evaluated Obara's argument as "moderate." In addition, the audience also talked about the appeal of Obara's way of speaking[67]. On the other hand, however, some of the audience commented that they were not sure what was the key point[68].

(4) The theory of "value system" at the time of lecture (1921)

Now, I am going to explain the aim of Obara's argument on that day based on "Zenjin Kyoiku Ron" (1921) which is the Dai Nippon Academic Association Version, the theory of the "value system" which served as the academic basis therefor, and two points of issue concerning Zenjin Education which Obara kept in mind, in order.

First, I go through the theory of the "value system" presented by Obara. At the beginning of the lecture, Obara stated that "education involves a living 'person'[69]," and presented the "value system" which served as the basis for and set the direction of the content of education based on analysis of the "person." A person has mental (mind) and physical (body) aspects. Therefore, education of mind and education of body are necessary. For the mental aspect (mind), the four worlds, namely, "the world of logic, the world of ethics, the world of art and the world of religion are developed," and accordingly, education of mind consists of "the four aspects, namely, truth education, goodness education, beauty education and holiness education[70]." He argued that "practical education" concerning "economy, system, military affairs, transportation, politics, law, agriculture, industry and commerce, etc." was also indispensable as other "means" necessary for us to live our real life[71]. The foregoing plus physical education as education of body constitute six aspects of education. Obara explained that all of these six aspects were necessary as education for a living "person" to develop them to be "a person as a human" or "decent person" (in other words, "whole person")[72]. At the conclusion of the lecture, he said, "The bottom line is that I want 'a person' to be placed as a starting point for everything, and that the goal which must be aspired for is becoming 'a person'[73]." What is worthy of special mention is that, when Obara developed his arguments on human beings and education, he first started from "a person" themselves and, based on the analysis, drew the "value system" which served as the basis for and set the direction of education.

Before attending the Eight Educators Educational Advocacy Conference, Obara held a seminar in Iki Island located far away from Tokyo. After he came home in Tokyo the night before the Conference, his wife Nobu, who was pregnant, "suddenly felt something wrong with her body[74]," and he looked after her, staying up all night. He stopped by at a hospital in the morning of the Conference to send her there and then rushed to the venue of the Conference (his son Tetsuro was born on that day). Obara said during the lecture, "I couldn't sleep enough last night and even couldn't have breakfast this morning. I have banging headache so I may not be able to organize my talk[75]." Some of the audience criticized it saying that it was not acceptable as an academically organized lecture[76]. However, at least, Obara's analysis on "person," which was the core of his arguments on human beings and education, presentation of the "value system" and logic to lead to the six aspects of education explained in the lecture were consistent.

(5) Anticipated misunderstands

In the lecture, Obara further talked about anticipated misunderstandings as some points of issue. Here, I list two of them[77]. The first issue is conflict between "fundamental issues and thoughts" and "methodology." There were competing positions concerning improvement of educational practice: one was to first understand the fundamental thought issues and the other was to be completely familiar with the methodology. Obara was deemed to be in the position of the former at the time. "I would never say 'just fundamental issues and thoughts will do'," he remarked, however, in his lecture. "If the day will come when teachers in Japan focus only on fundamentals and underestimate

methodology, then I will place an emphasis on methodology once again[78]."
Here, he again explained the importance of the "golden mean." However,
after the lecture, it was pointed out that methodology for his theory of Zenjin
Education was insufficient[79]. Response to this issue was provided in his new
"Theory of Zenjin Education" in his later years (first published in 1969).

The second point of issue concerns "Zenjin Education" and "education
in which individuality is respected." "Education in which individuality is
respected" was at the top among the "aspirations and ideals at our school"
listed in the founding prospectus of Seijo Elementary School[80]. This school was
founded in 1917 by Masataro Sawayanagi, a leading figure in the educational
circles who had served as president at two Imperial Universities, and was a
private school which represented the New Education Movement in Japan. In
response to Sawayanagi's request, Obara resigned from the Elementary School
Attached to Hiroshima Normal School and assumed the position as a director
at Seijo Elementary School. "It was so lucky of me that new path of my life
began when Dr. [Sawayanagi] recruited me[81] (The words with in the brackets
[ ] are added by the author)," recalled Obara. He empathized with the ideal
education that Sawayanagi upheld and devoted himself to teaching activities.
However, it is said that there was misunderstanding in regard to "education
in which individuality is respected" at Seijo Elementary School that such
education might develop "selfish" people who only think about themselves or
people "incapable of social life" who do only things they like[82]. Obara criticized
such misunderstanding saying, "Respect for individuality we demand is not
such a superficial thing[83]," and explained it as described below, claiming that
"education in which individuality is respected" would never contradicts social
life.

Each individual comes into being only once in this infinite time
spanning from the unlimited past to the unlimited future. There was
and will be nobody identical with myself to be allowed to come to being.

And each of us is granted something valuable which is achievable only by ourselves. The thing we have is so valuable that if the thing is not developed or grown, the completeness of the cosmos is destructed to that extent. It teaches us that each of us is indeed a part that constitutes the cosmos. It lies in there. When one finds it, they will be truly blessed. One will be able to brace oneself with joy and courage. One will find the cosmos beautiful for it. The world becomes more blessed to that extent. ...... Therefore, there is no conflict whatsoever with social life[84].

Now, what Obara advocated on this occasion was "Zenjin Education." What is its relationship with "education in which individuality is respected"? Does it conflict with "education in which individuality is respected"? Obara explained the reason for talking about this point of issue by saying, "Zenjin Education and respect for individuality are totally opposite to each other, and I guess that there may be people who think that they render significant conflict[85]." It is a point of issue which is also repeated in new "Zenjin Kyoiku Ron" (1969) described below, which is an important matter indispensable for understanding Obara's "Zenjin Education." As it turns out, Obara asserted that education in which individuality was respected that they truly demand was indeed Zenjin Education that he advocated, explaining the grounds thereof as follows:

> We hope to develop everything children have, every gift sent to them from heaven, in due course to the extent possible. Therefore, it is Zenjin Education. Moreover, if all of such things develop more and more, innate abilities of each of them are demonstrated better[.] So, the earnestness, or individuality, of each of them is exerted. So, it is education in which individuality is respected[86] (The words within the brackets [ ] are added by author).

The inseparable relationship between Obara's "Zenjin Education" and "education in which individuality is respected" is explained here. He believes that, if the aforementioned education in the six aspects is provided under Zenjin Education and "all of" gifts of each person "develop more and more," the individuality of each person, such as strengths and weaknesses, degrees of interest in various things, would come out, without a lack of individuality, such as "7 scores for reading, 7 scores for gymnastic exercises, 7 scores for singing and 7 scores for arithmetic, being caused[87]."

That being said, the explanation on the relationship between "zenjin (whole person)" and "individuality" is not yet completely satisfactory. When Obara talked about "*zenjin*" in this lecture, he used the term "whole man[88]." The key would be how to interpret the word "whole (as *zen* or *zentai no* in Japanese)." Iwao Koyama, Kitaro Nishida's favorite student and Obara's junior in school, remarked, "I also stand on the idea of 'whole person' and 'Zenjin Education'[89]," and, upon pointing out that Wilhelm Dilthey, a German philosopher, also emphasized "whole person," argued that the idea of "*zen*" of Obara and Dilthey had matters yet to be elucidated[90]. According to Koyama, "'Whole' and 'many' are in different dimensions. Whole transcends many, and integrates many into one. In other words, whole is integration of many and one[91]." That being said, the term "*zen*" per se is ambiguous and is not easy to understand. Bokumin Tsuchiyama attempted to interpret the concept of Obara's "*zenjin*," taking into account that, when the term "*zenjin*" is used, the meaning of "*zenjin*" changes depending on whether this "*zen*" refers to "*zenbu-jin* (the total man)," "*kanzen-jin* (the perfect man)" or "*zentai-jin* (the whole man)[92]."

Ko Mitsui, one of Obara's supporters, interpreted Obara's whole person as an "whole person with individuality." Mitsui effectively explained the relationship between "individuality" and a whole person's "wholeness" saying, "Individuality is not mere uniqueness but is how wholeness is achieved in an individual[93]." He also said, "Education must aim a goal where all people become a whole person with individuality who is organized based on the principle of love[94]." Obara himself recognized this in his book *Shido* in his last years, and wrote, "I agree to the explanation by Dr. Mitsui" with a citation to Mitsui's explanation concerning "whole person with individuality[95]."

3 New Theory of Zenjin Education (1969) in His Later Years

In this Section, I am going through Obara's thoughts in the new "Zenjin Kyoiku Ron" in his later years (first published in 1969) based on the "Zenshu Version." As mentioned above, Obara later stated that, while "Zenjin Kyoiku Ron" (1921) at the time of the Eight Educators Educational Advocacy Conference was "so-called argument of necessity," he "explained the content of Zenjin Education to some extent[96]" in his new "Zenjin Kyoiku Ron." The volume has almost doubled. The sections of the discussions were as follows: "Theory of Value System," "Consequences of Educational Ideals" ("I Religious Education"; "II Art Education"; "III Moral Education"; "IV Learning Education"; "V Health Education"; and "VI Livelihood Education / Wealth Education"), "Zenjin Education and Relevant Various Issues" ("I Zenjin Education and Uniting Opposites"; "II Zenjin Education and Education in Which Individuality Is Respected"; and "III Rosaku Education") and "Discussion on Teachers as a Consequence of Education." As compared with his first "Zenjin Kyoiku Ron" (1921) advocated by Obara, "Theory of Value System" became the complete version, the volume of discussion on the content of Zenjin Education (discussed in "Consequences of Educational Ideals") increased and "Livelihood Education / Wealth Education" became an independent section in particular, and further, "Rosaku Education" was added as a new section. Now, let us go through the characteristics of this new "Zenjin Kyoiku Ron."

(1) Obara's view on whole person

First of all, the point worthy of special mention concerning new "Zenjin Kyoiku Ron" in his later years (first published in 1969) is that there is a definition of "whole person" at the beginning. Obara states as follows: "Everything in human culture must be incorporated in the content of education. Therefore, education absolutely must be 'Zenjin Education.' Zenjin Education means a perfect personality; in other words, personality in harmony[97]." Up to this point in time, Obara had never expressly and directly defined the term "whole person" when he used it. Here, for the first time, and at the beginning of the book, his definition of whole person appeared. However, a minor expression issue occurred where he wrote "Zenjin Education means perfect personality; in other words, personality in harmony." This original sentence means that "Zenjin Education equals to perfect personality; in other words, personality in harmony." This would cause confusion to readers. The "Renewed Edition" modified this point to "a whole person means perfect personality; in other words, personality in harmony[98]." Regardless, Obara clearly defined "whole person" at the beginning of the book as "perfect personality; in other words, personality in harmony." However, Obara does not provide direct explanation on what "perfect personality" is. Reading the statement at the beginning of the book, readers might have questions: "Perfect personality? What is that? Would it be possible?" A succession of questions could arise such as "Does that refer to flawless personality?," "Would perfection of such personality be ever possible for humans who have limitations?" and "Wouldn' it be a lack of individuality, which contradicts with respect for individuality?"

An important fact in understanding Obara's theory of Zenjin Education is that the theory is premised on many of the discussions he has already presented in other opportunities. In fact, Obara already explained "perfect personality" in his first book *Kyoiku no Konpon Mondai toshite no Shukyo*. In Part II "Discussion on Relationship," Chapter 4 "Discussion on Moral Education" in this book, Obara discussed "perfect personality." He first started with a question "What is personality?," analyzed the common usage of it, and then explained, "Here, I define personality as follows: 'Personality is the entirety of that person.' Indeed, personality is the person themselves. It is indeed the essential quality and individuality of that person[99]." He used an expression "differences in personal tendency between people[100]" in another part; he was under the perception that personality basically has individuality and is different for each person. In regard to "perfect personality," he wrote, "The thing that is controlled toward the center (focus) of genuine selfhood is the perfect personality[101]." To put it in an easy-to-understand manner, when a person is being who the person is, that person has "perfect personality" in the meaning defined by Obara. Accordingly, "perfect personality" would never be independent from the selfhood of each person; rather, it has individuality which corresponds to how each person is controlled.

If we read his new "Zenjin Kyoiku Ron" in his later years in light of Obara's such view on "perfect personality," we can see that Obara has stated what "perfect personality" with individuality is at multiple places using different expressions. Such expressions include, for example, "Each person will realize the unique world of their own, and further, achieve the state of perfection there[102]," and, in an even more easy-to-understand manner, "When bamboo, lily or pine demonstrates their own true nature, or when Taro or Hanako fulfills their own unique potential, that is the time when they are most beautiful[103]." And, it can be seen in the first "Zenjin Kyoiku Ron" (1921) that, although the term "perfect personality" is not used, Obara has asserted that each and every one of children "is most perfect and beautiful when they demonstrate how they are in a unique manner of their own[104]." It is deemed that, here, the essential characteristics of the "whole person" which Obara kept in mind were expressed in an easy-to-understand manner.

So far, Obara's view on the whole person has been reviewed with a focus on "perfect personality." Now I move on to review of "personality in harmony." As mentioned above, Obara expressed the whole person as "perfect personality; in other words, personality in harmony (the underline is added by the author)". This means that "perfect personality" and "personality in harmony" are used as having the same meaning. Obara explained "harmony" as follows, referring to cosmos flowers. "I want these six cultural values to grow in harmony like cosmos flowers blooming orderly in front yards in fall[105]." The "six cultural values" refer to truth, goodness, beauty, holiness, soundness and wealth as discussed in the theory of the value system (as described below).

The original meaning of cosmos in Greek is "beautifully arranged, harmony and order[106]." Some people complains about six cultural values being likened to cosmos which has eight petals, but of course this is just a metaphor and there is no need that each petal corresponds to each cultural value. When we see cosmos flowers, we would know that they are the same flowers, cosmos. However, if we have a close look at them, cosmos flowers have different shapes and sizes of petals and other differences to each other, and there would never be any two the same. In other words, each cosmos flower has their individuality. As is the case with the foregoing, each of humans is called the same "human" but no one is the same. Each and every one has different, their own individuality. Even when he uses the term "harmony," Obara does not have the image of lacking individuality.

Now, "perfect" and "harmony" as in "perfect personality" and "personality in harmony" are apparently tied to a still image. However, for Obara, these words contain dynamics.

He deemed that agonizing "ambivalence" like "conflict, opposition and contradiction" was the "real situation of humans[107]." On the other hand, he also deemed that such "struggle itself, or agony itself is the precondition for development[108] (the underline is added by the author)". However, remaining in such a state of "conflict, opposition and contradiction" is a state unbalancedly weighted towards a specific argument (principle), which Obara criticized. Obara denied it saying, "It is untrue. It is a death,[109]" and sought for the state of "uniting" or "harmony" which gets over the foregoing state[110]. Taking a hint from philosophers of ages past[111], Obara called the state "uniting opposites, (the underline is added by the author)" and said, "I will consider the uniting opposites particularly paramount from the standpoint of Zenjin Education[112]." (He used the phrase "unify the two to one[113]" preferably in practice.) Research critical of Obara's argument of "uniting opposites" emerged in recent years[114]. In order to understand his standpoint, thorough examination should be carried out on his academic activities while at Kyoto Imperial University, influence from former teachers and his thoughts presented in the first book *Kyoiku no Konpon Mondai toshite no Shukyo*. For the sake of reducing the number of pages of this paper, here, I just introduce the interpretation by Tsugio Ajisaka, which would be the best guidance in understanding Obara's argument of "uniting opposites." Ajisaka stated as follows:

Uniting opposites does not suit to be ordinary formal logic, or rather, a logic that is unacceptable. However, in the case of education which is supported by life itself, experience itself and practice and acts of developing humans in particular, a different logic can be formed in which life itself and acts themselves are established beyond the general formal logic. The contradictory fact of uniting opposites lays the ground for the depth of reality[115].

Ajisaka can be said to have clearly and briefly indicated Obara's standpoint for explaining the "uniting opposites."

(2) Path of the theory of the value system

Zenji Mitsui listed the names of Kitaro Nishida, Sanjuro Tomonaga, Shigenao Konishi and Masataro Sawayanagi as the "four thinkers" who were deemed to have "exercised a decisive influence over" the formation of Obara's thoughts on Zenjin Education[116]. Among them, Nishida, Tomonaga and Konishi were former teachers under whom Obara studied when he was at Kyoto Imperial University. Obara talked about Konishi in the lecture at the Eight Educators Educational Advocacy Conference. According to Obara, Konishi encouraged him as follows when he graduated from Kyoto Imperial

University and was about to leave for the position at the Elementary School Attached to Hiroshima Higher Normal School: "Tell teachers to do academic study (widely including philosophy, morality, art and religion) hard. They are still somewhat superficial even after many decades because their foundation is not solid enough[117]." Influenced by Konishi, "I myself studied education and teaching hard, getting immersed deeper and deeper[118]," Obara said. After that, on the final day of the "Fourth National Elementary School Education Research Conference" (from November 8 to November 12, 1918) held at the Elementary School Attached to Hiroshima Higher Normal School, he made a presentation titled "Truth, Goodness, Beauty and Holiness as the Fundamental Problem of Education," discussing exactly the fundamental problem of educational values[119]. Also in the lecture at the Eight Educators Educational Advocacy Conference, Obara discussed the educational "value system" starting with analysis of "a person," and explained what Zenjin Education necessary for "a person" is based on the six aspects of "practical education" necessary for education of mind (truth education, goodness education, beauty education and holiness education), education of body and livelihood. This is as already pointed out in the previous section. At the time of the lecture, Obara already had the

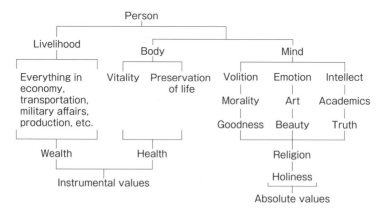

Fig. 2-8. Value system diagram (*Shushin Kyoju no Jissai Ge*, 1922)
Source: Created by the author

intention to advocate Zenjin Education which has the academic basis fully predicated on educational values. However, attention was not paid to this point at the time of the presentation, and rather, as mentioned above, there was even a criticism describing the presentation as "academically unsuccessful." Obara continued to elaborate the theory of the value system after that, presenting one of the completed forms in new "Zenjin Kyoiku Ron" in his later years (first published in 1969).

Obara did not present the illustrative "value system" in the lecture at the Eight Educators Educational Advocacy Conference. (There may have been an unavoidable reason for the convenience of the Conference.) However, in the theory of the value system he later made public, he always presented system diagrams. As far as I confirmed this time, Obara's value system diagrams went through major modification at least three times. First, the value system diagram in Fig. 2-8 appeared in *Shushin Kyoju no Jissai Ge* (Shuseisha, 1922)[120]. The same diagram also appeared in *Gakko-Geki Ron* (Idea-Shoin, 1923) and *Kyoiku no Konpon Mondai toshite no Tetsugaku* (Idea-Shoin, 1923)[121]. This system diagram is characterized by the use of categories with absolute values (truth, goodness, beauty and holiness) and instrumental values (health and

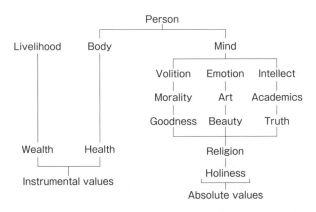

Fig. 2-9. Value system diagram (*Haha no Tame no Kyoiku-gaku Jo*, 1925)
Source: Created by the author

wealth) for the first time. As compared with the value system diagram (1969) in his later years, however, this diagram is characteristic in such a manner that "preservation of life" and "vitality" was placed under the category of "body" and these were deemed a part of value "health" altogether, and the value "wealth" was placed under the category of "person" but placed outside of "body," and placed under the new category "livelihood" (Fig. 2-8 and Fig. 2-10).

However, this system diagram is changed significantly later. The change appeared in *Haha no Tame no Kyoiku-gaku Jokan* (Idea-Shoin, 1925) (Fig. 2-9)[122]. This system diagram is characterized by the separation of the value "wealth" from "person." Considering Obara's approach to explaining the value system starting from "person," this system diagram has an issue in the handling of "livelihood" and "wealth." (In later years, the value system diagram in *Haha no Tame no Kyoiku-gaku* is modified as per the system diagram in 1969 as described below[123]).

And, the value system diagram appeared in the book *Zenjin Kyoiku Ron* (Tamagawa University Press, 1969) in his later years is in Fig. 2-10[124]. In this value system diagram, the value "wealth" was again moved under "person" as the starting point for explaining the diagram. In addition, the value "wealth" was placed under the category of "body" for the first time. However, there is one point requiring attention, which is that, in this book, this system diagram was separately included in "III Theory of Value System" rather than in new "Zenjin Kyoiku Ron" ("I Theory of Zenjin Education") in his later years. As mentioned above, "III Theory of Value System" was reprinted from *Kyoiku no Konpon Mondai toshite no Tetsugaku*. However, the system diagram included in "III Theory of Value System" was not the value system diagram originally included in *Kyoiku no Konpon Mondai toshite no Tetsugaku*, but instead, replaced with the new diagram (Fig. 2-10).

In *Zenjin Kyoiku Ron* (revised edition with additions and supplementations) to which "In renewing the edition" in 1970 was added, the value system diagram was incorporated into "I Theory of Zenjin Education." It should be noted that one minor addition is observed in the value system diagram. More specifically, "politics" was added to "economy, transportation, ..." in "vitality," making it to "politics, economy, transportation, ...[125]". From then on, this value system diagram has become the standard.

Obara mentioned many philosophers when he explained the value system diagram. Here is the list of the major philosophers in order who were mentioned in the "Zenshu Version[126]": Kitaro Nishida (religion as the ultimate of learning and morality); Plato ("ultimate goodness" placed on top of truth, goodness and beauty); Immanuel Kant ("holiness (Heiligkeit)" inherited from Plato); Wilhelm Windelband ("sacred (das Heilige)"); Hugo Münsterberg researching on value systems (not particularly focused on the hierarchy between values); Heinrich Rickert (focused on the hierarchy between values); Georg Mehlis (excluded the hierarchy between values); Shotaro Yoneda, a former teacher when Obara was at Kyoto Imperial University (distinguished absolute values and objective values). According to Obara's Autobiography, he attended at least philosophy class of Professor Nishida and sociology class of Professor Yoneda, including special lectures and seminars, during the three years[127] as a matter of course when

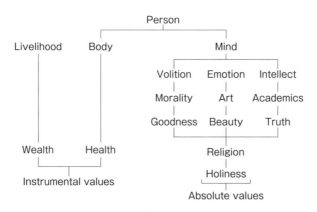

Fig. 2-10. Value system diagram (*Zenjin Kyoiku Ron,* 1969)
Source: Created by the author
Note: The wavy line is a supplementation made by the author.

he was at Kyoto Imperial University. Obara studied under these two teachers when he was at Kyoto Imperial University (for three years). In addition, Obara studied idealistic culturalism philosophy of Neo-Kantian Windelband as well as Rickert and others, who were influenced by Windelband, under Sanjuro Tomonaga in the field of Western philosophy history one of whose former teachers was Windelband. Obara also absorbed thoughts of Paul Natorp, etc. on the formation of cultural personality through Shigenao Konishi. Citing Obara's statement in the lecture at the Eight Educators Educational Advocacy Conference again, Obara was inspired by what Konishi said in a conversation: "We talk about moral personality, artistic personality, philosophical personality or religious personality. But I want a comprehensive personality combining all of them, let's say, something like cultural personality (*Kulturcharakter*)[128]." Subsequently, Obara stepped into establishment of the theory of Zenjin Education, saying, "I want something like comprehensive education, or Zenjin Education, which creates the comprehensive personality[129]." The theoretical pillar or the academic basis for the foregoing was the cultural and educational theory of the value system. Obara stated as follows:

> Now, I think there are six aspects in human culture, namely, learning, morality, art, religion, body and livelihood. The ideal for learning is truth, the ideal for morality is goodness, the ideal for art is beauty, the ideal for religion is holiness, the ideal for body is health and the ideal for livelihood is wealth. The ideal for education is to create the six values of truth, goodness, beauty, holiness, health and wealth.
>
> And I call the four values of truth, goodness, beauty and holiness as the absolute values and the values of health and wealth as the instrumental values[130].

Obara reached this clear and brief theory of the value system after studying thoughts of predecessors and through trial and error. "Truth, goodness, beauty, holiness, health and wealth" in particular are widely known to the extent that Obara's Zenjin Education is immediately rephrased as creating "values of truth, goodness, beauty, holiness, health and wealth." This is of course no mistake. However, I would like to turn our attention to Obara's message below after trial and error for the establishment of the theory of the value system. Obara states as follows:

> Now, the fact that there is discrepancy between a number of theories of great experts indicates us a valuable point. Such difference may come from the individuality, disposition, nature, circumstance of each person. I think that it is not about allowing to depend on the mood but rather the value system of each person must be identified and formed[131] (the underline is added by the author).

This message would give a lot of hints and encouragement to people who are committed to education seriously.

(3) Renewing the discussion on the education content 1: absolute values (truth, goodness, beauty and holiness)

As mentioned above, Obara said that he had enhanced the content than before in regard to new "Zenjin Kyoiku Ron" (first published in 1969), and the volume doubled. Reviewing the specifics, to begin with, in regard to the discussion on the education content, education previously explained as having six aspects, namely, truth education, goodness education, beauty education and holiness education as education of mind, physical education as education of body and "practical education" was renewed to learning education, moral education, art education, religious education, health education and livelihood and wealth education. Let us quickly look at each of them.

Firstly, let us take a look at learning education. Obara's view on learning was already expressed in the lecture at the Eight Educators Educational

Advocacy Conference as follows: "I want people to free themselves from the utilitarianism and pragmatism in which learning education is provided for livelihood or convenience and return to the standpoint of truth for truth, learning for learning, science for science and arithmetic for arithmetic[132]." He stressed the necessity of freeing oneself from the utilitarianism and maintaining the purity of learning. This idea was carried on to new "Zenjin Kyoiku Ron" and the discussion on learning education to maintain the purity of learning was further developed. As the key points, it required to: (1) not destroy children's "spirit of inquiry, spirit of investigation and signs of mind of feeling wonder or surprise" by cramming knowledge into them, telling them to memorize everything and teaching for exams, as the original meaning of learning is "surprise and wonder[133]"; (2) place emphasis on "education to allow them to catch something rather than to 'give' something to them[134]"; and (3) "fire the enthusiasm for learning, teach them how to dig and temper the tools for pick work for them[135]."

Secondly, let us look at the content of moral education. In the lecture at the Eight Educators Educational Advocacy Conference, Obara criticized unnatural moral education carried out at normal schools, saying, "I want the valuable meaning of volition to be recognized more[136]," and stressed that moral education concerned "volition" in particular among mental activities (intellect, emotion and volition) of humans. In addition, he upheld affirmation of impulse, stating that "children's uninhibited, self-centered way of life driven by impulse" contained "precious signs of intellectual freedom that should be developed toward the future[137]." He argued for "special arrangement for the moral course" in new "Zenjin Kyoiku Ron" with a backdrop of the emergence of "wretched morality" and "young people poisoned by unhealthy desire for success" caused by reforms "which have gone way too far" such as the abolition of the moral training course in post-war Japan[138]. Furthermore, as the significance of moral education, he listed the following five points: (1) to allow people to understand "the preciousness of human and personality value";

(2) to allow people to "discover the solid view on life"; (3) to allow people to acknowledge "the significance of goodness, meaning of evil and deep meaning of agony" and "noble meaning of sin and confession"; (4) to allow people to completely understand "conflict between volition and intellect" and "valuable meaning of inconsistency and anguish in human life"; and (5) to allow people to create "beautiful and right human image with solid timelessness[139]."

Thirdly, school drama is worthy of special mention when talking about Obara's discussion on art education. In February 1919, about two and a half years before the lecture at the Eight Educators Educational Advocacy Conference, school dramas ("Ama no Iwato," etc.; on the day of the school play, the dramas were called "singing dramas") were performed for the first time in Japan as part of school play at the Elementary School Attached to Hiroshima Higher Normal School. At the time, Obara had already published his discussion titled "Gakko-Geki ni tsuite" (1919), in which he explained the necessity of "art education" "from the standpoint of education for the whole person[140] (the underline added by the author)" and stressed the significance of school drama in particular as comprehensive art for the whole person (art that incorporates music, painting, architecture, engraving, dancing, literature, and further lighting and sound effects). However, he did not offer the discussion on school drama in particular in the lecture at the Eight Educators Educational Advocacy Conference, but just made a critical statement on Japan's underdevelopment in that area at the beginning of the lecture, saying, "We, Japanese, are underdeveloped in the world of art as compared with advanced countries[141]." Then, he claimed that life would be nothing but a desert without art and beauty, and asked why they wouldn't let students come in touch with great dramas, great motion pictures, great music, great paintings and great novels[142] with the aim of developing a "person" as a human. Obara had already described such significance of art appreciation in *Gakko-Geki Ron* as follows: "Enjoyment (appreciation) and creation are two forms of expression of artistic activities" and "...... are ultimately the same activities[143]." In his new "Zenjin Kyoiku Ron (first published in 1969)" published after many years, Obara first turned his attention to drama and emphasized its significance stating that drama was so practical that it could give great power to the cultivation of people[144]. And he revealed that school drama had been subject to quite much oppression and vented his feelings saying that drama was "a comprehensive art and, even at the top of arts[145]."

Lines 1 through 9 on page 46 of the "Renewed Edition of Zenjin Kyoiku Ron" by Okada, which is currently the most easily available one, is an insertion from *Gakko-Geki Ron*. There, Obara's views on art and art education is expressly indicated as follows: "An aspect of artistic activities" lies in "production," "creation," "self-expression" and "demonstration of individuality." "Demonstration of individuality" in particular means "realization of the effect of creation by self-integration." The "fundamental principle of art education" is "to enable exhibition of performance as a whole person and thereby to allow the personality to be activated in a creative manner[146]." This part was not originally written in "Zenjin Kyoiku Ron" but expresses Obara's view on art education straightforwardly.

Next, let us dig into Obara's view on religious education. In the theory of the value system, Obara attached the greatest importance to the value "holiness." However, as the theory of the value system accurately indicates, Obara's standpoint is that learning, morality and art are ultimately led to the value "holiness." Obara himself was a Christian, but his explanation on religion in Zenjin Education did not represent a position of a specific religious sect. When Obara got on to the topic of holiness education in the lecture at the Eight Educators Educational Advocacy Conference, he said, "I have already published *Kyoiku Konpon Mondai toshite no Shukyo* on this topic, so there is no need to talk much about it," and argued against Kumaji Yoshida and others who argued that religion was unnecessary for school education (elementary school education in particular), by saying, "How could we educate 'a person' if we ignore the issue of valuable spirit of people?[147]"

Obara's view on religion has already been expressly indicated in *Kyoiku no Konpon Mondai toshite no Shukyo*. He explained religion as follows:

Religion is "a relationship between God and human beings." ......
Religion must have these two.

In other words, there must be extreme opposites in religious mind or religious awareness, which are subject and object. Subject is one's own self, while object is a matter to which the religious mind is devoted, a matter which has power beyond human beings, or in other words, a matter like God or Buddha. Religion is about facing with this matter, capturing this matter firmly, being engaged with, understanding and believing this matter or being inspired by this matter in various ways. In other words, religion is a sort of condition of being tied. A condition in which the subject is strongly tied to the object is called faith (the underline added by the author) [148].

As seen above, Obara's view on religion was open and not based on any specific religious sect. In his new "Zenjin Kyoiku Ron" published after many years, Obara criticized a position which argued that religious education could not be provided at public schools, and stated as follows:

It is often said that religious education cannot be provided at public schools. That is totally untrue. I hope to provide religious education which is "religious education" in every respect, not "religious sect education." What I hope for is religious education common to all human beings, a fundamental problem. Education of soul. Religious influence may be exerted wherever and as much as we like. Through music, through art, through drama in particular. Through literature, through history. Especially through science and arithmetic. Not to mention, through tea ceremony, flower arrangement, physical education, and mountain climbing[149].

Religious education which Obara discussed in the context of the theory of Zenjin Education was not education on any specific religious sect or specific religious doctrine. Rather, it was nothing else but the practice of Zenjin Education. Having "deep interest" in various aspects of human culture as well as in people and nature and being engaged in them by "devoting the entire self" beyond interests and calculation, holding "a deep devout sense" and "personality's whole mental activities targeted at personality[150]." Through the foregoing, "the spirit will be purified[151]" and "the material desire will be purged[152]." The mind will be purified. For Obara, this leads to the world of the value "holiness," or a religious state. "Pure heart[153]," which Obara told children in entrance ceremonies at Tamagawa Academy, can be said to be the core aimed for by religious education.

(4) Renewing the discussion on the education content 2: instrumental values (health and wealth)

What is important along with the aforementioned world of absolute values (truth, goodness, beauty and holiness) is the world of instrumental values (health and wealth). Active mental activities are supported by the latter. To begin with, in regard to "physical education," the subject of which is "body," the perspective of physical education for the sake of health did not come to the front yet at the lecture at the Eight Educators Educational Advocacy Conference. Rather, the context of criticizing unbalanced education, the subject of the lecture, was emphasized. Obara pointed out that "excessive physical exercises are significantly halmful[154]," taking "a physical exercise maniac school" which forces children to do physical exercise all the time from morning till night, with a lack of the "golden mean," as an example. However, he also said, "I feel that somewhat physical education is most underdeveloped[155]." In later years, Obara found Denmark gymnastic exercises as the best gymnastic exercises for health. A Denmark gymnastic team was invited in September 1931 to perform demonstration at Tamagawa Academy. In his new "Zenjin Kyoiku Ron," Obara discussed "health physical education" as the main subject, incorporating the thought of Denmark gymnastic exercises. Obara asserted that the purpose of physical education was "not a championship flag, medal, record or trophy" and we "must not mix up means and purposes[156]." And Obara proclaimed that what was aimed for by physical education was "the tough physical strength, long life, body in harmony and dexterity[157]."

Another instrumental value "wealth" was not yet organized as a specific value issue at the time of the lecture at the Eight Educators Educational Advocacy Conference. As mentioned above, it was only briefly stated that, "in addition to" education of mind (truth education, goodness education, beauty education and holiness education) and education of body (physical education), "practical education" concerning "economy, system, military affairs, transportation, politics, law, agriculture, industry and commerce, etc." was also indispensable as a "means" necessary for us as to live our lives. However, "practical education" was also rephrased as "experience education[158]." It is an expression tied to "Rosaku Education," which was not yet expressly indicated at the time. Therefore, Obara's view on "practical education" is a focus of attention as the dividing point before it branched off to later "livelihood and wealth education" and "Rosaku Education." Obara in his later years stated in his new "Zenjin Kyoiku Ron" that "bread is demanded in order to live on[159]" just like health is demanded as a means indispensable for mental activities. According to books about Obara's life, he struggled in poverty when he was young. He might be considered to have a keen interest in monetary issues due to that fact. However, he rather took wealth in a broad sense. He considered any and all means of "active mental activities" as "wealth," saying, "I give the name of wealth in a broad sense to any and all inventions, devices, transportation, politics, diplomacy, industry, military affairs, laws, etc.[160]" However, wealth per se does not have significance; the important thing is how wealth is used. As a representative philosopher who considered wealth in such a way, Obara referred to John Ruskin, an English critic and philanthropist, and "all-round genius[161]" who was the first professor of the art course at University of Oxford[162]. Further, Obara criticized that education had degenerated into "wealth for wealth, or education to gain profits," which was a "horrible defect in education in Japan," presenting "misery of becoming a slave of material desire[163]." The task of "livelihood and wealth education" is to teach "how wealth should be consumed and the true meaning of wealth[164]," so that wealth is used for the benefit of society.

This concludes the brief overview of the six aspects of the education content concerning the absolute values (truth, goodness, beauty and holiness) and the instrumental values (health and wealth), which Obara asserted in his new "Zenjin Kyoiku Ron" in his later years. One point to note is that Obara never saw them as individual, separated six types of education. He believed that a person would become unbalanced if they were merely provided with religious education, art education, moral education, etc.[165]. Obara comprehended the six aspects of education in the context of an organic interconnection for a whole person.

(5) Development of education methodology

As I already pointed out, among comments on his lecture after the Eight Educators Educational Advocacy Conference, there were some that said Obara's methodology was weak. On the other hand, he never overlooked the importance of methodology, and even stated that he would rather stress methodology if society overemphasizes fundamental issues only. However, it is true that Obara's standpoint at this lecture was clearly weighted towards "fundamental issues." Although he concluded his lecture with a heading which included "methodology," he stated that "whatever" method could be used as long as such method is rooted in the essence of "a person." He did not present any particular, specific method. And, at the end of his speech, he stated that understanding "the fundamental spirit of a method" was of importance and encouraged the audience to first start their pursuit of fundamental issues from "a person[166]." However, new development is observed in his new "Zenjin Kyoiku Ron" about half a century later, which is advent of "Rosaku Education."

The term "Rosaku Education" cannot be found in anywhere in Obara's value system diagram. However, he stressed that the fundamentals of education truly lay in Rosaku Education[167] and that Rosaku Education was in fact an integrated form of holiness education, intellectual education, moral education, beauty education, production education and health education[168]. This "Rosaku Education" is precisely the excellent method of practicing the unity of knowing and acting in which the six aspects of education are interconnected in an organic manner. Obara seemed to have struggled with how to name it at the beginning. He thought names such as "education of experience" and "education of learning from experience" were also good. But he wrote in *Tamagawa Juku no Kyoiku* (Tamagawa Academy Press, 1930), "Working is joy and pride for and duty of every person, so I want to use the character 'ro (labor)[169]' (the underline is added by the author). I also want to use the character 'saku' as is used in '*sosaku* (creation)' rather than in '*sagyo* (chore)[170]' (the underline is added by the author)." Here, Obara's view on "rosaku" is straightforwardly presented. The character "ro" is certainly related to working or labor. However, he stated that he wanted the word to mean "creation," rather than to simply mean "labor." That being said, there seem to have been some people who were against the term Rosaku Education, claiming it meant "exploitation of labor[171]." In his new "Zenjin Kyoiku Ron" published after many years, Obara changed the phrase "working is joy for every person" to "devoting oneself is joy for every person (the underline is added by the author)[172]." What is important in *rosaku* is, as Katsuyoshi Higashi pointed out, whether one can deem "the activities as their own purpose[173]." An acid test for whether the activities can be deemed as *rosaku* may be whether the activities are owned by the person "as their own," the emphasis for the activities is placed on the physical aspect as in "Learning

through one time of rosaku is worth learning through 100 times of seeing[174]"
and the purpose of the activities is creation.

Situations of rosaku are not limited to specific locations or areas. Obara
wrote in *Tamagawa Juku no Kyoiku*, in relation to Johann Heinrich Pestalozzi's
3H (Head, Heart and Hand), "It is about either working with your head, hands,
feet, heart, pen, fork, hammer or abacus[175]." Situations of rosaku are diverse.
He also discussed "learning as rosaku[176]," and cited "independent research"
as one of the "multifaceted rosaku situations[177]" in new "Zenjin Kyoiku Ron" in
his later years. "Independent research" which Obara encouraged at Tamagawa
Academy was not something superficial as people in general imagine today.
According to "Jiyu Kenkyu no Jissai (Tamagawa Press, 1947) by the Tamagawa
Academy Elementary Division, first and foremost, the thing that was important
in independent research was "voluntary activities, which are the first principle
of education that teaches everything starts from oneself[178]." It was also
important that children choose their own research project regardless of the
subject category. Teachers were expected to assist children so that they could
use creativity and devise methods on their own rather than teaching them the
most effective and efficient methods[179]. Here, thoughts of Obara, who hoped
children to demonstrate "how they are in a unique manner of their own," on
Zenjin Education are clearly presented. "I believe that, honestly, schools should
provide children with rosaku situations in the number of types that everyone
would be delighted at[180]." This statement of Obara should be an even more
important message in modern times when diversity and individual optimization
are expected.

4   In Pursuit of "True Education"

Two years after the lecture at the Eight Educators Educational Advocacy
Conference, in *Riso no Gakko* (Naigai Shuppan Kabushiki Kaisha, 1924), Obara
looked back that time when it was "overly exaggerated and advertised as 'Eight

Education' or whatever[181]." He said, "They read only stenographic notes from my lecture and criticized that that was the entire education theory of mine." and retorted. "'Zenjin Education' is not the entire education theory of mine[182]. There is nothing other than just <u>true education</u> (the underline added by the author) to which it is really hard to give a name[183]." Obara criticized unbalanced education and attended the lecture with the term "Zenjin Education" selected to express "true education." In the lecture, while he was aware of the risk that his own argument of "Zenjin Education" was to be misunderstood as unbalanced education, he even stated that it was an "theory of no-ism" and "whatever name could be used to describe it." This "just <u>true education</u> (the underline added by the author) to which it is really hard to give a name" was certainly pursued in practice at Tamagawa Academy thereafter. Tamagawa Academy has "Twelve Precepts of Education" (Zenjin Education, Respect for Individuality, Self Study, Autonomy, Highly Efficient Education, Education that is Scholarship, Respect for Nature, Trust within the School Community, Rosaku Education, Uniting Opposites, One Who Walks the Extra Mile and One Who is a Pioneer in Life, 24-Hour Education and Global Education)[184], and each of these Precepts can be deemed as a perspective of Obara on "true education" or "genuine education" acquired through practice.

How Obara explained "Zenjin Education" in his later years? In August 1973, he gave a lecture titled "Shido" at the "WEF Education Forum," an international conference sponsored by the World Education Fellowship (WEF), held in Tokyo. This Fellowship was an international organization founded in 1921 as "New Education Fellowship (NEF)," which led the New Education Movement across the globe. Obara was the President of the Japan Section of the Fellowship (then "Sekai Kyoiku Nihon Kyokai," current "Sekai Shin-Kyoiku Gakkai (The World Education Fellowship Japan Section)") at the time. On August 13, as the last lecturer, he explained "Zenjin Education" once again in front of education theorists and practitioners from around the world, discussing "ideal teachers under the concept of whole person[185]," and stated that "teachers must be a 'whole person'[186]." Then, he looked back on his own career as a teacher and summed up. "After 60 years, I feel that my Zenjin Education was right, was not wrong, and I feel really grateful for that[187]."

Now, it has been 100 years since Kuniyoshi Obara first advocated "Zenjin Education." New issues successively emerge in front of us who live in the 21st century, such as Sustainable Development Goals (SDGs), which aims to realize a world where "no one will be left behind," and efforts towards human-centered future society (Society 5.0). The educational circles are also required to realize "learning which are fairly and individually optimized and will leave no one behind." Now, as we live in an unpredictable time (VUCA time) facing an unprecedented event of the global pandemic of novel coronavirus disease (COVID-19), the importance of education in Japan, upholding development of the 'zest for living' in rapidly changing future society" is increasing. The path of thoughts and practice of Kuniyoshi Obara, who kept seeking "genuine education" or "true education" with the strong belief that each one truly demonstrating "how they are in a unique manner of their own" will lead to genuine "happiness" of one's own and others, will continue to remain a compass for our life and the basics of education where we should return.

Notes

1) Kuniyoshi Obara, "Zenjin Kyoiku Ron" in *Hachidai Kyoiku Shucho*, authored by Choichi Higuchi, Kiyomaru Kohno, Kishie Tezuka, Meikichi Chiba, Kinshichi Inage, Heiji Oikawa, Kuniyoshi Obara and Noburu Katakami, Dai Nippon Academic Association, 1921, p. 308.

2) Ibid., p. 311.

3) This can be easily confirmed by, for example, searching "Zenjin Education" on the Internet. Yoshiaki Obara remarked, "There are reportedly about 1,700 public and private schools which uphold '*Zenjin education*' as their education policy." (Yoshiaki Obara, *Kyoiku no Shimei*, Tamagawa University Press, 2019, p. 17.)

4) Central Council for Education, "Nijuisseiki wo Tenbou shita Wagakuni no Kyoiku no Arikata nitsuite–Kodomo ni [Ikiru Chikara] to [Yutori] wo (Dai–Ichiji Toshin)," 1996, (https://www.mext.go.jp/b_menu/shingi/chuuou/toushin/960701e.htm; last visited: October 21, 2020).

5) Yoshiaki Obara, *Kyoiku no Shimei*, Tamagawa University Press, 2019, p. 17.

6) Kuniyoshi Obara, "Zenjin Kyoiku Ron" in *Obara Kuniyoshi Zenshu 33: Zenjin Kyoiku Ron / Shukyo Kyoiku Ron / Shido*, Tamagawa University Press, 1975, p. 6.

7) Ibid., pp. 6-7.

8) Ibid., p. 6.

9) Kuniyoshi Obara, "Zenjin Kyoiku Ron" in *Hachidai Kyoiku Shucho*, authored by Choichi Higuchi, et al, Dai Nippon Academic Association, 1921, pp. 305-370.

10) Kuniyoshi Obara (Ajisaka), "Zenjin Kyoiku," in *Kyoiku Mondai Kenkyu*, Issue No. 19, 1921, pp. 1-53.

11) Ibid., p. 3.

12) *Hachidai Kyoiku Hihan*, co-edited by Shisui Amako, Rosei Shingyoji , Isen Okada and Hokushu Takizawa, the Dai Nippon Academic Association, 1923.

13) Kuniyoshi Obara, "Zenjin Kyoiku Ron" in *Hachidai Kyoiku Shucho* by Kuniyoshi Obara et. al., Tamagawa University Press, 1976, pp. 253-295.

14) Kuniyoshi Obara, "Zenjin Kyoiku Ron," *Obara Kuniyoshi Zenshu 33: Zenjin Kyoiku Ron / Shukyo Kyoiku Ron / Shido*, Tamagawa University Press, 1975, p. 6.

15) Kuniyoshi Obara, *Zenjin Kyoiku Ron*, Tamagawa University Press, 1969, p. 183.

16) See Kuniyoshi Obara, *Kyoiku no Konpon Mondai toshite no Tetsugaku*, Idea-Shoin, 1923. This was later republished in *Obara Kuniyoshi Zenshu 4: Kyoiku no Konpon Mondai toshite no Tetsugaku* (Tamagawa Academy University Press , 1954).

17) See Kuniyoshi Obara, "Kaihan suru ni saishite" in *Zenjin Kyoiku Ron*, Tamagawa University Press, 1969 (9th printing, 1972), p. 4.

18) The writing rules used in representing "Zenjin Kyoiku Ron" (1969) is based on the edition indicated in the bibliography. However, in addition to the foregoing, it is also used to clearly indicate the historical year when Obara's new "Zenjin Kyoiku Ron" in his later years was first published. Bokumin Tsuchiyama also used the similar writing rules in "Kaidai" in *"Obara Kuniyoshi Senshu 3: Zenjin Kyoiku Ron / Siso Mondai to Kyoiku"* (Tamagawa University Press, 1980), with respect to the "revised edition with additions and supplementations" included in the book, "This 'Zenjin Kyoiku Ron' included in 'Obara Kuniyoshi Senshu' is his work in 1969, in other words, Kuniyoshi Obara's work in his last years." (Bokumin Tsuchiyama, "Kaidai" in *Obara Kuniyoshi Senshu 3: Zenjin Kyoiku Ron / Siso Mondai to Kyoiku* by Kuniyoshi Obara, Tamagawa University Press, 1980, p. 119.)

19) Kuniyoshi Obara, *Zenjin Kyoiku Ron*, Renewed Edition, Tamagawa University Press, 1994.

20) Akira Okada, "Kaihan ni saishite ── Gakusei Shokun e" in *Zenjin Kyoiku Ron,* Renewed Edition by Kuniyoshi Obara, Tamagawa University Press, 1994, p. 183.

21) Kuniyoshi Obara, *Kuniyoshi Obara's Theory of Zenjin Education* (English/Japanese side-by-side translation of *Zenjin Kyoiku Ron*), edited by Yoshiaki Obara, English translation by Doug las Trelfa, Tamagawa University Press, 2003, p. 7.

22) Ibid., p. 137.

23) Bokumin Tsuchiyama, *Kuniyoshi Obara and the Concept of "The Whole Man,"* Tamagawa University Press, 1979. Franziska Ehmcke, *Die Erziehungsphilosophie von Obara Kuniyoshi. Dargestellt an der "Erziehung des ganzen Menschen". Ein Beitrag zur Erziehung in Japan*, Mitteilungen der Gesellschaft für Natur- und Völkerkunde Ostasiens (OAG) Band LXXII, Hamburg 1979.

24) For example, *Taisho Shin-Kyoiku no Shiso-Seimei no Yakudo,* authored and edited by Miho

Hashimoto and Satoshi Tanaka, Toshindo, 2015. Hiroyuki Sakuma, "Kuniyoshi Obara's *Zenjin education at Tamagawa Gakuen*." Yoko Yamasaki and Hiroyuki Kuno (ed.), *Educational Progressivism, Cultural Encounters and Reform in Japan*, London& New York: Routledge, 2017, pp.93–108. Kuniyoshi Obara, "West Meets East. A Well-Rounded Education versus an Angular Education in Japan". *Tiempo y Educación*, vol. 5 (2018), pp. 101–122.

25) *Seisho: Seisho Kyokai Kyodo Yaku*, Japan Bible Society, 2018, (New Testament) p. 15.

26) *Taisho Shin-Kyoiku no Shiso-Seimei no Yakudo*, authored and edited by Miho Hashimoto and Satoshi Tanaka, Toshindo, 2015, p. 165.

27) Kumaji Yoshida, "Hasshu no Kyoiku Shucho ni tsuite" in *Kyoiku Gakujutsu Kai*, Vol. 44, Issue No. 1, 1921, p. 4.

28) The ad of the Conference says, "Let's listen to what each lecturer has to say, spend time asking questions and discussions vigorously and analyze their strengths and weaknesses to the extent possible." In addition to that, an advance notice about a site tour during the day and performance after the discussion is included. (See the ad insert placed before p. 1 of *Gakko Kyoiku*, edited by Hiroshima Higher Normal School Education Research Association , Issue No. 96, Vol. 8, No. 6, 1920.)

29) Ibid.

30) However, his name as a presenter was indicated as "Kuniyoshi Ajisaka" in the ad. His name on the day of the lecture was Obara, so there was confusion observed whether Obara and Ajisaka were different persons. For example, Kohei Saruki remarkes, "I have long hoped to hear Mr. Ajisaka's speech, but it was Mr. Obara who was there on that day, and I was disappointed that the lecturer might have changed. However, I became very excited to listen to Mr. Obara's vibrant lecture" (Kohei Saruki, "Dai-Go Toron" in *Kyoiku Gakujutsu Kai*, Vol. 44, Issue No. 1, 1921, p. 80).

31) *Kyoiku Gakujutsu Kai*, Vol.43, Issue No.2, 1921, p.261.

32) Kuniyoshi Obara, "Zenjin Kyoiku Ron" in *Hachidai Kyoiku Shucho* by Choichi Higuchi et al., Dai Nippon Academic Association, 1921, pp. 308–309.

33) See Choichi Higuchi et al., *Hachidai Kyoiku Shucho*, Dai Nippon Academic Association, 1921.

34) *Taisho Shin-Kyoiku no Shiso-Seimei no Yakudo*, authored and edited by Miho Hashimoto and Satoshi Tanaka, Toshindo, 2015, p. 166. However, it is uncertain how many people actually attended on August 8.

35) Fujinshi, "Kyoiku Gakujutsu Kenkyu Taikai Kiroku" in *Kyoiku Gakujutsu Kai*, Vol. 44, Issue No. 1, 1921, p. 216.

36) According to Miho Hashimoto, Fujinshi "seems to be Koyu Sato who was appointed as the record-keeper by Amako" (Miho Hashimoto, "Hachidai Kyoiku Shucho Koenkai no Rekishi-teki Igi" in *Tokyo Gakugei Daigaku Kiyou Sogo Kyoiku Kagaku-kei*, Vol. 66, Issue No. 1, February 2015, p. 62).

37) Fujinshi, "Kyoiku Gakujutsu Kenkyu Taikai Kiroku" in *Kyoiku Gakujutsu Kai*, Vol. 44, Issue No. 1, 1921, p. 216.

38) Seiichi Hatano was assigned to the post at Kyoto Imperial University when Obara was in the third (last) year at the university (they provided three-year programs at the time). Obara was already working on his bachelor thesis. Later, he recalled those days, saying, "The greatness of

Professor [Hatano] completely struck me even I received guidance from him for only a year."
(Kuniyoshi Obara, *Kyoiku Ichiro*," Nikkei Inc., 1976, p. 64. The words within the brackets ([ ])
are added by the author.) Obara called himself as Hatano's "apprentice" (Kuniyoshi Obara,
"Hatano Sensei no Omoide" in *Tsuioku no Hatano Seiichi Sensei*, edited by Katsumi Matsumura
and Kuniyoshi Obara, Tamagawa University Press, 1970, pp. 226–227.

39) Bokumin Tsuchiyama, "*Kaidai*" in *Obara Kuniyoshi Senshu 3: Zenjin Kyoiku Ron / Siso Mondai
to Kyoiku* by Kuniyoshi Obara, Tamagawa University Press, 1980, p. 120.

40) Kuniyoshi Ajisaka, *Kyoiku no Konpon Mondai toshite no Shukyo*, Shuseisha, 1919, p. 74.

41) Ibid., p. 82.

42) Ibid., p. 83.

43) Ibid., p. 100.

44) Ibid., p. 254.

45) Ibid., p. 282.

46) Ibid., p. 293.

47) Ibid., p. 293.

48) Kuniyoshi Obara, *Shido*, Tamagawa University Press, 1974, p. 48.

49) See the ad insert placed before p. 1 of *Gakko Kyoiku*, edited by Hiroshima Higher Normal
School Education Research Association, Issue No. 96, Vol. 8, No. 6, 1920.

50) Shisui Amako, "Kanto no Ji" in *Kyoiku Gakujutsu Kai*, Vol. 44, Issue No. 1, 1921, p. 1.

51) Kumaji Yoshida, "Hasshu no Kyoiku Shucho ni tsuite" in *Kyoiku Gakujutsu Kai*, Vol. 44, Issue
No. 1, 1921, p. 4.

52) Kuniyoshi Obara, "Zenjin Kyoiku Ron" in *Hachidai Kyoiku Shucho* by Choichi Higuchi et al.,
Dai Nippon Academic Association, 1921, p. 329.

53) Ibid., p. 308.

54) Masamori Watanabe , "Dai–Nana Toron" in *Kyoiku Gakujutsu Kai*, Vol.44, Issue No.1, 1921, p.
81. Similarly, Yasaka Koshikawa, "Kyoiku Gakujutsu Kenkyu Taikai Shokan ...... Kakumei–teki
Koshukai ni Nozomite," ibid., p. 113.

55) Kuniyoshi Obara, "Zenjin Kyoiku Ron" in *Hachidai Kyoiku Shucho* by Choichi Higuchi et al.,
Dai Nippon Academic Association, 1921, p. 324.

56) Ibid., p. 313.

57) Ibid., p. 313.

58) Shisui Amako, "Kanto no Ji" in *Kyoiku Gakujutsu Kai*, Vol. 44, Issue No. 1, 1921, p. 1.

59) Kuniyoshi Obara, "Zenjin Kyoiku Ron" in *Hachidai Kyoiku Shucho* by Choichi Higuchi et al.,
Dai Nippon Academic Association, 1921, p. 309.

60) Ibid., pp. 308–309.

61) Ibid., p. 322.

62) Ibid., p. 323.

63) Ibid., pp. 323–324.

64) Ibid., p. 325.

65) Ibid., pp. 337–338.

66) Ibid., p. 338.

67) For example, Kokei Kobayashi recalled Obara's lecture, saying, "I should have been melted

by the passion in the lecture," and "I should have been just amused and excited listening to a poem read by the poet." (Kokei Kobayashi, "Kyoiku Gakujutsu Kenkyu Taikai ni Nozomite" in *Kyoiku Gakujutsu Kai*, Vol. 44, Issue No. 1, 1921, p. 145). Takumi Inoue said, "...... members were impressed and refreshed their mind which had been tired of listening lectures every day." (Takumi Inoue, "Kyoiku Gakujutsu Kenkyu Taikai Shokan" in *Kyoiku Gakujutsu Kai*, Vol. 44, Issue No. 1, 1921, p. 165). Norio Sumeragi's "Obara Kuniyoshi 'Zenjin Kyoiku Ron' no Rhetoric" (*Rinsho Kyoiku Ningen Gaku*, Issue No. 4, 2002, pp. 5-19) can be cited as research concerning Obara's "way of expression" in "Zenjin Kyoiku Ron." Sumeragi suggested to "reinterpret Obara as a person who presented to the world of education a new genre of speech which is a technique of using word tricks (rhetoric) when talking and entertaining audience by arranging such tricks effectively, in other words, 'art' of allowing audience to 'feel the sense of elegance', or as a person who created a strategic technique (attitude or method) in educational speeches, or further, as a pioneer in the field which has been called popular education." (Ibid., p. 17)

68) Morimasa Watanabe , "Kyoiku Gakujutsu Kenkyu Taikai Shokan–Iwayuru Shinshin Shoka Koen no Hihyo" in *Hachidai Kyoiku Shucho* by Choichi Higuchi et al., Dai Nippon Academic Association, 1921, p. 120.

69) Kuniyoshi Obara, "Zenjin Kyoiku Ron" in *Hachidai Kyoiku Shucho* by Choichi Higuchi et al., Dai Nippon Academic Association, 1921, p. 310.

70) Ibid., p. 350.

71) Ibid., p. 350.

72) Ibid., p. 350.

73) Ibid., p. 369.

74) Kuniyoshi Obara (Ajisaka), "Zenjin Kyoiku," in *Kyoiku Mondai Kenkyu*, Issue No. 19, 1921, p. 3.

75) Kuniyoshi Obara, "Zenjin Kyoiku Ron" in *Hachidai Kyoiku Shucho* by Choichi Higuchi et al., Dai Nippon Academic Association, 1921, p. 305.

76) Masamori Watanabe, "Dai–Nana Toron" in *Hachidai Kyoiku Shucho* by Choichi Higuchi et al., Dai Nippon Academic Association, 1921, p. 81.

77) In addition to them, Obara stated in his lecture that education of Seijo Elementary School for which he worked at the time was labeled as children–centered and liberal (in the context of tolerating teachers' sabotage and neglect) and defended that was a misunderstanding (Kuniyoshi Obara, "Zenjin Kyoiku Ron" in *Hachidai Kyoiku Shucho* by Choichi Higuchi et al., Dai Nippon Academic Association, 1921, pp. 325-326).

78) Kuniyoshi Obara, "Zenjin Kyoiku Ron" in *Hachidai Kyoiku Shucho* by Choichi Higuchi et al., Dai Nippon Academic Association, 1921, p. 330.

79) For example, "a lack of presentation of views with the proactive novelty and validity in the methodology" is listed as the "first and foremost" "weakness" of the theory of Zenjin Education in *Hachidai Kyoiku Shucho*. Furthermore, the theory was criticized as "having no unique methodology whatsoever, although its argument on fundamental problems is worthy of looking into and listening to" (*Hachidai Kyoiku Hihan*, co–edited by Shisui Amako et al., Dai Nippon Academic Association, 1923, p. 461).

80) The "Seijo Elementary School Founding Prospectus " lists "1. Education in which individuality

is respected and highly efficient education," "2. Education to commune with nature and education of sturdy and unyielding will," "3. Education of emotion and education of appreciation," and "Education based on scientific research" as the school's "aspirations and ideals at our school." (See Masataro Sawayanagi, *Shinso-ban Kyoiku Ron Sho*, Shinchosha, 2015, pp. 161-165.)

81) Kuniyoshi Obara, *Obara Kuniyoshi Zenshu 29: Obara Kuniyoshi Jiden-Yume Miru Hito (2)*, Tamagawa University Press, 1963, p. 219. The words within the brackets [ ] are added by the author.

82) Kuniyoshi Obara, "Zenjin Kyoiku Ron" in *Hachidai Kyoiku Shucho* by Choichi Higuchi et al., Dai Nippon Academic Association, 1921, p. 342.

83) Ibid., p. 342.

84) Ibid., p. 343.

85) Ibid., p. 341.

86) Ibid., p. 342. The words within the brackets [ ] are added by the author.

87) Ibid., p. 337.

88) Ibid., p. 337. In recent years, the term "whole person" is more commonly used than "whole man." See the following literature on this point. Kuniyoshi Obara (English translation by Douglas Trelfa), *Kuniyoshi Obara's Theory of Zenjin Education* (English/Japanese side-by-side translation of *Zenjin Kyoiku Ron*)edited by Yoshiaki Obara, English translation by Douglas Trelfa, Tamagawa University Press, 2003, p. 17. Hiroyuki Sakuma, "Kuniyoshi Obara's *Zenjin* education at *Tamagawa Gakuen*." Yoko Yamasaki and Hiroyuki Kuno (ed.), Educational Progressivism, *Cultural Encounters and Reform in Japan*, London& New York: Routledge, 2017, 93.

89) Iwao Koyama, *Kyoiku Tetsugaku*, Tamagawa University Press, 1976, p. 364.

90) Ibid., p. 364.

91) Ibid., p. 366.

92) Bokumin Tsuchiyama, *Kuniyoshi Obara and the Concept of "The Whole Man,"* Tokyo: Tamagawa University Press, 1979. See Bokumin Tsuchiyama, "Zenjin Kyoiku Ron wo do Rikai suru ka" in *Zenjin Kyoiku no Tegakari,* edited by Tetsuro Obara, Tamagawa University Press, 1985, pp. 67-69.

93) Ko Mitsui, *Ai no Basho-Kyoiku Tetsugaku Josetsu*, Tamagawa University Press, 1974, p. 152.

94) Ibid., p. 152.

95) Kuniyoshi Obara, *Shido*, Tamagawa University Press, 1974, pp. 47-48.

96) Kuniyoshi Obara, "Zenjin Kyoiku Ron" in *Obara Kuniyoshi Zenshu 33: Zenjin Kyoiku Ron / Shukyo Kyoiku Ron / Shido*, Tamagawa University Press, 1975, p. 7.

97) Ibid., p. 13.

98) Kuniyoshi Obara, *Zenjin Kyoiku Ron*, Renewed Edition, Tamagawa University Press, 1994, p. 10.

99) Kuniyoshi Ajisaka, *Kyoiku no Konpon Mondai toshite no Shukyo*, Shuseisha, 1919, p. 293.

100) Ibid., pp. 29-30.

101) Ibid., p. 294.

102) Kuniyoshi Obara, "Zenjin Kyoiku Ron," *Obara Kuniyoshi Zenshu 33: Zenjin Kyoiku Ron /*

Shukyo Kyoiku Ron / Shido, Tamagawa University Press, 1975, p. 26.

103) Ibid., p. 106.

104) Kuniyoshi Obara, "Zenjin Kyoiku Ron" in *Hachidai Kyoiku Shucho* by Choichi Higuchi et al., Dai Nippon Academic Association, 1921, p. 343.

105) Kuniyoshi Obara, "Zenjin Kyoiku Ron" in *Obara Kuniyoshi Zenshu 33: Zenjin Kyoiku Ron / Shukyo Kyoiku Ron / Shido*, Tamagawa University Press, 1975, p. 17.

106) Ibid., p. 17.

107) Ibid., p. 101.

108) Ibid., p. 101.

109) Ibid., p. 102.

110) Ibid., p. 102.

111) When he discussed "uniting opposites" in "Zenjin Kyoiku Ron," Obara referred to philosophers such as Giordano Bruno, Herakleitos and Georg Wilhelm Friedrich Hegel. However, he did not examine the contents of each thought particularly in detail.

112) Kuniyoshi Obara, "Zenjin Kyoiku Ron" in *Obara Kuniyoshi Zenshu 33: Zenjin Kyoiku Ron / Shukyo Kyoiku Ron / Shido*, Tamagawa University Press, 1975, p. 100. Obara discussed "uniting opposites" in *Kyoiku no Konpon Mondai toshite no Shukyo* (1919) and also presented it in the Eight Educators Educational Advocacy Conference in 1921. (Kuniyoshi Ajisaka, *Kyoiku no Konpon Mondai toshite no Shukyo*, Shuseisha, 1919, p. 345. Kuniyoshi Obara, "Zenjin Kyoiku Ron" in *Hachidai Kyoiku Shucho* by Choichi Higuchi et al., Dai Nippon Academic Association, 1921, p. 321.)

113) Ibid., pp. 99–106.

114) "Uniting opposites" presented by Obara in the Eight Educators Educational Advocacy Conference in 1921 is being criticized as follows: "This is a term used by Nicolaus Cusanus (1401-1464), and it is not about unification of two matters which are contradictory to each other, but is 'coincidence of opposites' which may seem to be 'evil' from the perspective of a person who is finite but is 'good' for God who is infinite. Coincidentia oppositorum is not 'conflict' or 'contradiction' as Obara explained, because human and god are not placed on the same level. In addition, unification of two dimensions as Obara sought is ultimately a desire of a person to become God, which may be possible in the Ancient Greek context but impossible in the context of Christianity. It is an act of blasphemy, totally godless. Obara does not understand 'coincidence of opposites' at all." (Miho Hashimoto and Satoshi Tanaka, "Dai Go Sho: Hachidai Kyoiku Shucho no Kyoiku Rinen," *Taisho Shin-Kyoiku no Shiso-Seimei no Yakudo*, authored and edited by Miho Hashimoto and Satoshi Tanaka, Toshindo, 2015, p. 188) I will just say one thing. Obara was certainly a Christian who "was baptized by the Church of Christ in Japan (reformed/presbyterian)" (Makoto Kobari, "Taisho Shin-Kyoiku Undo no Paradox-Tsusetsu no Sai-Kento wo tsujite," *Kodomo Shakai Kenkyu*, Issue No. 21, 2015, p. 31). However, he did not understand the issue of "uniting opposites" in the context of "Christianity." This issue should be understood in the context of his theory of *Zenjin* Education. It is similar to, for example, the argument of "religious education" in his theory of *Zenjin* Education is out of the context of education of a specific religious sect. The criticism of "an act of blasphemy, totally godless" is unreasonable.

115) Tsugio Ajisaka "Hantai no Goitsu" in *Zenjin Kyoiku no Tegakari*, Tamagawa University Press, 1987, p. 23. Obara clearly showed his understanding of the "existance," quoting "individuality," "perfection," and "harmony" as heObara himself said in the Eight Educators Educational Advocacy Conference lecture in 1921, "Universality is immediately particularity, perfection in individuality, individuality in harmony. This is the truth of existence (the underline is added by the author)" (Kuniyoshi Obara, "Zenjin Kyoiku Ron" in *Hachidai Kyoiku Shucho* by Choichi Higuchi et al., Dai Nippon Academic Association, 1921, p. 345.

116) Zenji Mitsui, "Obara Kuniyoshi no Zenjin Kyoiku Shiso" in *Zenjin Kyoiku Ron I / II*, Tamagawa University, The University by Correspondence, 1988, p. 75.

117) Kuniyoshi Obara, "Zenjin Kyoiku Ron" in *Hachidai Kyoiku Shucho* by Choichi Higuchi et al., Dai Nippon Academic Association, 1921, pp. 329–330.

118) Ibid., p. 330.

119) Kuniyoshi Ajisaka, "Kyoiku no Konpon Mondai toshite no Shin Zen Bi Sei" in *Gakko Kyoiku*, Vol. 6, Issue No. 67, No. 3, 1919, pp. 118–127.

120) Kuniyoshi Obara, *Shushin Kyoju no Jissai Gekan*, Shuseisha, 1922, p. 84. Fig. 2–1 is prepared by the author.

121) Kuniyoshi Ajisaka, *Gakko-Geki Ron*, Idea-Shoin, 1923, p. 7. Kuniyoshi Obara, *Kyoiku no Konpon Mondai toshite no Tetsugaku*, Idea-Shoin, 1923, p. 498.

122) Kuniyoshi Obara, *Haha no Tame no Kyoiku-gaku Jokan*, Idea-Shoin, 1925, pp. 128–129. Fig. 2–2 is prepared by the author.

123) See Kuniyoshi Obara, *Obara Kuniyoshi Zenshu 5: Haha no Tame no Kyoiku-gaku*, Tamagawa University Press, 1977, p. 90.

124) Kuniyoshi Obara, *Zenjin Kyoiku Ron*, Tamagawa University Press, 1969, p. 192.

125) See Kuniyoshi Obara, *Zenjin Kyoiku Ron*, Tamagawa University Press, 1972, p. 23.

126) See Kuniyoshi Obara, *Obara Kuniyoshi Zenshu 33: Zenjin Kyoiku Ron / Shukyo Kyoiku Ron / Shido*, Tamagawa University Press, pp. 19–24.

127) Kuniyoshi Obara, *Obara Kuniyoshi Zenshu 29: Obara Kuniyoshi Jiden-Yume Miru Hito (2)*, Tamagawa University Press, 1963, p. 84 .

128) Kuniyoshi Obara, "Zenjin Kyoiku Ron" in *Hachidai Kyoiku Shucho* by Choichi Higuchi et al., Dai Nippon Academic Association, 1921, p. 324.

129) Ibid., p. 324.

130) Kuniyoshi Obara, "Zenjin Kyoiku Ron" in *Obara Kuniyoshi Zenshu 33: Zenjin Kyoiku Ron / Shukyo Kyoiku Ron / Shido*, Tamagawa University Press, 1975, p. 15.

131) Ibid., p. 24.

132) Kuniyoshi Obara, "Zenjin Kyoiku Ron" in *Hachidai Kyoiku Shucho* by Choichi Higuchi et al., Dai Nippon Academic Association, 1921, p. 354.

133) Kuniyoshi Obara, "*Zenjin Kyoiku Ron*" in "*Obara Kuniyoshi Zenshu 33: Zenjin Kyoiku Ron / Shukyo Kyoiku Ron / Shido*," Tamagawa University Press, 1975, pp. 65–66.

134) Ibid., p. 65.

135) Ibid., p. 65.

136) Kuniyoshi Obara, "Zenjin Kyoiku Ron" in *Hachidai Kyoiku Shucho* by Choichi Higuchi et al., Dai Nippon Academic Association, 1921, p. 355.

137) Ibid., p. 357.

138) Kuniyoshi Obara, "Zenjin Kyoiku Ron" in *Obara Kuniyoshi Zenshu 33: Zenjin Kyoiku Ron / Shukyo Kyoiku Ron / Shido*, Tamagawa University Press, 1975, pp. 51–55.

139) Ibid., pp. 55–56.

140) Kuniyoshi Ajisaka, "Gakko–Geki ni tsuite" in *Gakko Kyoiku,* Vol. 6, Issue No. 69, 1919, p. 48.

141) Kuniyoshi Obara, "Zenjin Kyoiku Ron" in *Hachidai Kyoiku Shucho* by Choichi Higuchi et al., Dai Nippon Academic Association, 1921, p. 359.

142) Ibid., p. 360.

143) Kuniyoshi Obara, *Gakko–Geki Ron*, Idea–Shoin, 1923, p. 14.

144) Kuniyoshi Obara, "Zenjin Kyoiku Ron" in *Obara Kuniyoshi Zenshu 33: Zenjin Kyoiku Ron / Shukyo Kyoiku Ron / Shido*, Tamagawa University Press, 1975, p. 44.

145) Ibid., p. 44.

146) Kuniyoshi Obara, *Zenjin Kyoiku Ron*, Renewed Edition, Tamagawa University Press, 1994, p. 46.

147) Kuniyoshi Obara, "Zenjin Kyoiku Ron" in *Hachidai Kyoiku Shucho* by Choichi Higuchi et al., Dai Nippon Academic Association, 1921, p. 362.

148) Kuniyoshi Ajisaka, *Kyoiku no Konpon Mondai toshite no Shukyo*, Shuseisha, 1919, p. 2.

149) Kuniyoshi Obara, "Zenjin Kyoiku Ron" in *"Obara Kuniyoshi Zenshu 33: Zenjin Kyoiku Ron / Shukyo Kyoiku Ron / Shido,"* Tamagawa University Press, 1975, p. 38.

150) Ibid., p. 34.

151) Ibid., p. 36.

152) Ibid., p. 43.

153) Kuniyoshi Obara, *Shido*, Tamagawa University Press, 1974, pp. 45–46.

154) Kuniyoshi Obara, "Zenjin Kyoiku Ron" in *Hachidai Kyoiku Shucho* by Choichi Higuchi et al., Dai Nippon Academic Association, 1921, p. 351.

155) Ibid., p. 352.

156) Kuniyoshi Obara, "Zenjin Kyoiku Ron" in *Obara Kuniyoshi Zenshu 33: Zenjin Kyoiku Ron / Shukyo Kyoiku Ron / Shido*, Tamagawa University Press, 1975, p. 76.

157) Ibid., p. 76.

158) Kuniyoshi Obara, "Zenjin Kyoiku Ron" in *Hachidai Kyoiku Shucho* by Choichi Higuchi et al., Dai Nippon Academic Association, 1921, p. 365.

159) Kuniyoshi Obara, "Zenjin Kyoiku Ron," *Obara Kuniyoshi Zenshu 33: Zenjin Kyoiku Ron / Shukyo Kyoiku Ron / Shido*, Tamagawa University Press, 1975, p. 25.

160) Ibid., p. 26.

161) Yoshiyuki Fujikawa, "Turner Yogosha kara Senku–teki na ecologist he–Ruskin no Shogai to Sakuhin", *Kono Saigo no Mono nimo / Goma to Yuri*, authored by John Ruskin and translated by Ichiro Iduka and Masami Kimura, Chuokoron–Shinsha, Inc., 2008, p. 4.

162) Ruskin considers wealth as "ownership of beneficial things that we can use" (p. 124) and defines that the wealthiest person is "a person who perfects the functions of life of their own to the maximum extent possible, and has most widely helpful influence on lives of other people through both their personality and property." (pp. 158-159) (The citations are from John Ruskin, *Kono Saigo no Mono nimo / Goma to Yuri*, translated by Ichiro Iduka and Masami

Kimura, Chuokoron–Shinsha, Inc., 2008)

163) Kuniyoshi Obara, "Zenjin Kyoiku Ron" in *Obara Kuniyoshi Zenshu 33: Zenjin Kyoiku Ron / Shukyo Kyoiku Ron / Shido*, Tamagawa University Press, 1975, p. 93.

164) Ibid., p. 94.

165) Ibid., p. 30.

166) Kuniyoshi Obara, "Zenjin Kyoiku Ron" in *Hachidai Kyoiku Shucho* by Choichi Higuchi et al., Dai Nippon Academic Association, 1921, p. 369.

167) Kuniyoshi Obara, "Zenjin Kyoiku Ron" in *Obara Kuniyoshi Zenshu 33: Zenjin Kyoiku Ron / Shukyo Kyoiku Ron / Shido*, Tamagawa University Press, 1975, p. 109.

168) Ibid., p. 111.

169) Kuniyoshi Obara, *Tamagawa Juku no Kyoiku*, Tamagawa Academy Press, 1930, p. 64.

170) Ibid., p. 65. A similar statement is also in his new "Zenjin Kyoiku Ron." However, the sentence is changed to "I used the character 'saku' as is used in 'sosaku (creation)." (Kuniyoshi Obara, "Zenjin Kyoiku Ron" in *Obara Kuniyoshi Zenshu 33: Zenjin Kyoiku Ron / Shukyo Kyoiku Ron / Shido*, Tamagawa University Press, 1975, p. 109.)

171) Kuniyoshi Obara, "Zenjin Kyoiku Ron" in *Obara Kuniyoshi Zenshu 33: Zenjin Kyoiku Ron / Shukyo Kyoiku Ron / Shido*, Tamagawa University Press, 1975, p. 111.

172) Ibid., p. 109.

173) Katsuyoshi Higashi, "Rosaku Kyoiku Jissen no Tachiba kara" in *Zenjin Kyoiku no Tegakari*, edited by Tetsuro Obara, Tamagawa University Press, 1985, p. 213.

174) Kuniyoshi Obara, "Zenjin Kyoiku Ron" in *Obara Kuniyoshi Zenshu 33: Zenjin Kyoiku Ron / Shukyo Kyoiku Ron / Shido*, Tamagawa University Press, 1975, p. 109.

175) Kuniyoshi Obara, *Tamagawa Juku no Kyoiku*, Tamagawa Academy Press, 1930, p. 64.

176) Ibid., p. 250.

177) Kuniyoshi Obara, "Zenjin Kyoiku Ron" in *Obara Kuniyoshi Zenshu 33: Zenjin Kyoiku Ron / Shukyo Kyoiku Ron / Shido*, Tamagawa University Press, 1975, p. 107.

178) Tamagawa Elementary Division, *Jiyu Kenkyu no Jissai*, Tamagawa Press, 1947, p. 9.

179) Ibid., pp. 31–32 and 44.

180) Kuniyoshi Obara, "Zenjin Kyoiku Ron" in *Obara Kuniyoshi Zenshu 33: Zenjin Kyoiku Ron / Shukyo Kyoiku Ron / Shido*, Tamagawa University Press, 1975, p. 110.

181) Kuniyoshi Obara, *Riso no Gakko*, Naigai Shuppan Kabushiki Kaisha, 1924, p. 1.

182) Ibid., p. 2.

183) Ibid., p. 3.

184) See the following literature for changes in the Twelve Precepts of Education of Tamagawa Academy. Hiroyuki Shirayanagi, "Tamagawa Gakuen Kyoiku Juni Shinjo no Seiritsu" in *Zenjin Kyoiku Kenkyu Center Nenpo*, Issue No. 2, 2016, pp. 37–46.

185) Kuniyoshi Obara, "Shido" in *Sekai Shin–Kyoiku Kaigi Hokokusho,* edited by Kirayuki Sumeragi, Shigeo Masui, Takeshi Futami, Tomoichi Iwata, Junji Oshiman and Zenji Nakamori , *The World Education Fellowship Japan Section*, 1974, p. 152.

186) Ibid., p. 153.

187) Ibid., p. 157.

Chapter 3

Universal Validity of Zenjin Education

Introduction

I believe that if we strive to develop the aforementioned major principle from a standpoint of pure children, based on the guidance of progressing psychology, in accordance with the theory of epistemology, and in response to demands of national society, we will naturally follow the similar path even if there is more or less difference which comes from the individuality (i.e. each teacher). If we do not fix our eyes on conflicts and arguments from superficial knowledge but go back to the basics of pure educational love with knowledge obtained based on the fundamental principles and cooperation from our spirits, all kinds of formalities and methodologies would naturally return to the original place.[1]

After Zenjin Education, which was initially devised by Kuniyoshi Obara and formed the basis for the founding of Tamagawa Academy, became widespread in public, a number of schools and universities have incorporated this theory in their philosophy and other mission. For example, there is a Japanese university which cites, the idea that "fully becoming an 'individual' is a process of fostering whole person power and human quality, and freeing oneself from all values and reshaping oneself[2]" as a real strength of education provided by the university. It also stresses that in order to fully become an "individual" that can live on a global stage, it is essential to cultivate "whole person" power at the world standards through dialogue, and to provide the genuine liberal arts education. To this end, this university has required students to study abroad and live in campus dormitories for one year. This policy brought success, such as the result that half of the students reached 900 points in TOEIC test by their graduation, acknowledgement for 100% employment rate of its graduates, and recognition in the Japan University Rankings, which is the Japanese version of the World University Rankings by the Times Higher Education.

Meanwhile, is this an ideal policy of original Zenjin Education? The term "whole person power at the world standards" gives the impression that the ability of an individual can be measured on a specific scale. In general, various abilities overflowing in the world may serve as a "medal-like" function, allowing each individual to show the achievement level based on the scale created artificially (sometimes arbitral and intentionally). What is nurtured through Zenjin Education? Is this a visualized "power" or "qualification" that can also be an authoritarian symbol?

In view of Zenjin Education and practice thereof, which forms the basis of Tamagawa, the term "whole person power" cannot be interpreted simply as a pertinent expression. Similarly, it may be questioned whether "whole person power at the world standards" is an ability that can be ensured and guaranteed simply by such experiences as one-year study abroad and dormitory life, and the score of English examination at the time of graduation? Rather, it looks that aforementioned university is trying to assume the world standard by the language of English, and such attitude implicitly gives the impression that it wishes to be recognized and certified only by specific countries, regions, or organizations (mainly western countries). Hence, the university's policy is far from "universal validity[3]" in the form generally accepted in any countries and regions.

This Chapter focuses on the common points between enkyklios paideia, artes liberales and septem artes liberales, which were born in Ancient Greece, as well as well-rouded education, which is relatively used in broad form in the modern age, and the intent of the subjects devised by Obara. This Chapter then points out that the ultimate ideals of education will eventually leads to Zenjin Education, which is the very education with universal validity.

1　Historical Development of Liberal Arts

(1) Enkyklios paideia

The history of the theory of Zenjin Education is derived from the wisdom of free men in Ancient Greece, so-called, "lover of wisdom" (*philo sophia*)[4]. Like the saying of "a sound mind in a sound body," the education of free men in Ancient Greece[5] referred to human education and character building through intellectual, moral and physical development with the aim of nurturing not only universal knowledge but also human virtue, based on the philosophy of *kalokagathia* (good and the beautiful in a person), which aims at the harmony and balance between the mind and body. The specific curriculum of this education became widespread in the Hellenistic period while incorporating literature (grammar), rhetoric (speech), dialectic, physical education, arithmetic, geometry, music, astronomy, and other artistic study. The name *enkyklios paideia*, which means the education of free men, is believed to be born during this period.

"*Paideia*," a composition of enkyklios paideia, is a noun derived from the verb "*paideüein.*" This verb form is the origin of pedagogy with the meanings of (1) "child rearing," (2) "teach and train up, educate," and (3) "correct, rectify." In addition, the adjective "*enkyklios*" means (1) "circular, recurrent" and (2) "circular movement, regular." In combination of the two words, the basic meaning of enkyklios paideia basically was a circular of education or knowledge, that is, human education with subjects aligned in a circular way.

Through the subsequent shift from Greek methods (*enkyklios paideia*) to Latin methods, the word artes liberales, appeared. This Latin term, was mainly used by scholars in the Roman Republic and became the origin of "liberal arts." Marcus Tullius Cicero, who played an active role in the late period of the Roman Republic, pointed out the importance of arts that is indispensable for cultivating the mind and forming virtue by utilizing such expressions as various arts[6] and free study[7] suitable for free men. Cicero specifically listed three arts of speech, dialectic and grammar[8], and the four arts of arithmetic, music, geometry and astronomy as area of study to develop humanities[9]. On the other hand, Marcus Vitruvius Pollio, who also played an active role in the same period as an architect, listed grammar, drawing, geometry, arithmetic, history, philosophy, music, medicine, law, and astronomy[10] as the subjects that architects should learn in addition to architecture.

In any sense, the importance was likely to be placed upon the refinement of comprehensive intelligence and the harmony of comprehensiveness in this era. The concept of liberal arts that was born in Rome[11] was a symbol of freedoms that had existed with the prosperity of the Roman Empire, and was a comprehensive academic learning that includes a wide range of arts (crafts and fine arts), architecture, civil engineering, medical science, and legal studies. While the concept of liberal arts is sometimes mentioned by being interpreted as "arts that become free from practicality," separately from learning and education to cultivate professional skills, the history of development from Ancient Greece to the Roman Republic clearly shows that freedom in the pursuit of genuine learning and love of wisdom should be the original concept and interpretation.

(2) Seven liberal arts

In the next 500 years, shortly after the fall of the Western Roman Empire, Martianus Capella released *On the Marriage of Philology and Mercury* and *On the seven disciplines* (*nine books*)[12]. These books listed seven disciplines including grammar, logics, dialectic, mathematics, geometry, astronomy and music, to show the composition of the liberal arts called *septem artes liberales* (seven liberal arts) specifically. The former Latin liberal arts was replaced with this composition of the seven arts defined by Capella, leading to the birth of the seven liberal arts, which constituted the cultural formation under the Christianity.

Whereas there was no academic and creative development over the next 200 years thereafter, political academic studies were promoted by the King of the Franks during the Carolingian Renaissance in the 8th to 9th centuries. Through such trend, the seven liberal arts gained an established position as the basis of education for all disciplines, leading to the formalization and stabilization of the seven liberal arts. Thereafter, the subsequent rise of the Renaissance movement and the birth of universities prompted the transformation into today's liberal arts.

2   Today's Liberal Arts

(1) Liberal arts as general education

The previous section outlined the historical development of liberal arts from Ancient Greece to the Middle Age. This section will add a little more description on how the liberal arts acquired the today's definition as general education. As described earlier, artes *liberales*, originated from *enkyklios paideia*. While *enkyklios paideia* has a direct meaning of "circular of knowledge (education), the expression of "circular" was subsequently given the meaning of "general, universal" through interpretations by various sophists (persons with wisdom). This development created the idea that *enkyklios paideia* is understood as general education and liberal arts education, which are often compared and conflicted with skill education/specialized education today. As there is no assumption on specialized persons (like specialists) in the word "general, universal" granted to *enkyklios* and both objectives and goals of liberal arts are different from those of education aimed at developing professionals or specialists.

(2) Liberal arts education in the U.S.

With regard to the idea that the liberal arts is understood as general education, how is it embodied in the actual field of education? This section will discuss the liberal arts education in the United States (hereinafter, "the U.S."), mainly in universities, as an example. Because the actual state of liberal arts education in the U.S. is of course diverse, those which are shown relatively often as an example will be introduced.

The basic concept of liberal arts education in the U.S. consists of "concentration (one specialized area: "major") and diversification (general subjects or general education for broader knowledge: "minor"). The graduation requirements of universities are often composed of major, minor, elective subjects and general education.

In addition, the learning style of American-type liberal arts education has the following characteristics:

(i) Self-directed education by students (independent learning) and structure of curriculum selection

(ii) Specialized area is not determined at an early time

(iii) Specialized subjects as a component of liberal arts education (specialized subjects are also part of liberal arts education)

(iv) Social nature of education (expressed in general education)

(v) Development of basic skills for intellectual management, such as the development of critical thinking skills, identification of issues, and solution skills

(vi) Potential study programs such as campus life (including student's living in dormitories)

A particular characteristic of liberal arts education in the U.S. is that students leave their major undecided at the time of admission. While they usually decide on their major during the second year, "choosing a major" is different from "choosing an area of specialty" in a specialized faculty. This is rather a selection in the sense of "choosing a specific area of specialty to temporarily learn more deeply" in the course of study[13]. In addition, while an importance is placed on the content of study in the education of specialized faculty, liberal arts education rather focuses on the development of persons who study in the subject. This concept is said to originate from the philosophy of the Humboldt University: "... universities should treat learning as not yet wholly solved problems and hence always in research mode, " and "both professors and students learn by self-directed study[14]."

The principle aim of choosing a major in liberal arts education is to help students acquire a single academic way of thinking and gain confidence in their intellectual activities by giving them an opportunity to feel a sense of unity with academics and provide them with a deep learning experience. In other words, specialized study is positioned in liberal arts education as an opportunity to receive basic training to learn how to seek knowledge of major studies so as to promote essential participation in human intellectual activities (knowledge of free men) and establish self-awareness as an intellect. Studying a specialized subject is a part of specialized education but is aimed for the formation of students' personality. This may be deemed to be an element rooted in the liberal arts that was born in Ancient Greece and the Roman Republic.

Moreover, as a general education in liberal arts education, many universities offer programs that may be classified into mathematics, physics, biology, foreign languages, literature, classics, Western political history, history of philosophy, history of culture, national fundamentals and principles (social science subjects such as civics). Actually, a change was witnessed in the composition of this program around the 8th to 9th centuries when the seven liberal arts were proposed. Although music (arts) was previously included, it may be replaced with literature and classics in quite a few cases. In addition, religion-based (especially Christian) universities may include religious studies in general education, which is one of the results of the transformation of today's liberal arts education stemmed from the Renaissance movement mentioned in Section 1 and the birth of universities at that time.

3　Well-rounded Education

(1) New concept of "well-rounded education"

In recent years, the term "well-rounded education" is used in the U.S. to describe a new form of liberal arts education. What background was this term born from? For example, American high schools have previously focused on national language, mathematics, science, foreign language, civics, economics, history, geography, and arts; however, this type of subjects/program is not recognized as liberal arts subjects or liberal arts curriculum. As in Japan, main subjects have been recognized as general subjects (i.e. "subjects that everybody should learn as a matter of course"). The liberal arts for lovers of wisdom, which was once enshrined has been transformed into a framework of learning limited to specific subjects in modern times through the process of formulation of the "seven liberal arts" concept.

Even though U.S. children received a general education that actually reflects liberal arts elements, the actual results were not satisfactory in preschool, elementary and secondary education in the U.S. Taking such state into consideration, on December 10, 2015, former President Obama signed the Every Student Succeeds Act (ESSA)[15] which was proposed by both the Democratic and Republican parties and was enacted as a federal education act. The key measures of this act included financial support for areas (school districts) that need satisfactory education at elementary and secondary levels, education and training of competent teachers and principals, financial support for English learners and preschool education, and at the same time, stipulated thorough provision of well-rounded educational curriculum. As a result, in addition to the main subjects of the previous times, the U.S. is trying to offer students rich educational experiences by adding subjects such as reading, language arts, essays, technologies, engineering, computer science, career education, skills education, health and physical education in response to the tendencies and trends of the times. It is noteworthy that elements for acquiring knowledge and skills necessary to survive in highly uncertain future have been added to the liberal arts education, which has continued from Ancient Greece.

(2) Education sought by Harvard University

While gaining knowledge and skills necessary to survive in the future, studying in a well-rounded way means learning about diverse disciplines that exist in this world, and Harvard University has clearly stated such ideals in a message to applicants:

> A good high school education should do more than prepare you for the next level of education or for later employment—it should prepare you to take advantage of future learning opportunities of all kinds. You should gain particular skills and information, as well as a broad perspective on the world and its possibilities[16].

This message can also be interpreted as a warning to limit the learning potentials at an early stage and to position higher education solely for further education and employment. Looking at this message from a different angle, the University's ideals such as "learning at a university is also to explore potentials. The term "well-rounded" was therefore added by the University because it is sufficient to offer the existing liberal arts education, which has nowadays been oriented to "the-earlier-the-better, stereotyped form to faithfully embody free arts."

Following the above message, Harvard University has presented a list of recommended subjects in high school programs in order to build a strong foundation in liberal arts education of the University[17]:

(i) The study of English for four years: close and extensive reading of the classics of the world's literature

(ii) Four years of a single foreign language

(iii) The study of history for at least two years, and preferably three years: American history, European history, and one additional advanced history course

(iv) The study of mathematics for four years

(v) The study of science for four years: physics, chemistry, and biology, and preferably one of these at an advanced level

In addition to the above subjects listed as recommended subjects, which retain data that suggests that they will directly contribute to learning after the entry to the University, it places an importance on subjects such as physical education, art, and music. The University also stresses that those subjects are omitted not because they are judged unnecessary. Accordingly, although a well-rounded education for high school students sought by the University is synonymous with liberal arts education, the term "well-rounded education" is likely to imply the University's wish to further expand such framework.

4   Subjects Proposed by Kuniyoshi Obara

Then, what subject composition did Obara value and how did he position each subject in order to embody Zenjin Education? This section will introduce

Obara's perceptions on each subject based on "Kyoiku Kaizo Ron" (*Obara Kuniyoshi Senshu 4,* Tamagawa University Press, 1980).

First of all, regarding the subject of moral science (*shushin*), Obara defined it as the subject of ethics (*dotoku*). Meanwhile, attention should be paid to the point that the content of moral science defined by Obara is different from that of moral science introduced to school in Japan at that age, as he described, "intolerant national ethics, patriotism in particular, must absolutely be eliminated[18]." Obara advocated research on fundamental issues through moral science (ethics), for example, by saying that it is important to understand the essence of ethics such as "what is virtue and vice." In addition, he placed an importance upon the precise interpretation of virtues introduced in class, and the development of ethical judgment to ensure such precise interpretation. As Obara valued on the development of abilities to "discover ethics, and create ethics by oneself[19]," he believed that ethics had a nature to be transformed with the transition of civilization. He therefore sought education that does not force children to learn old types of ethics, but promoted an approach to touch the inner life and encourages both teachers and children to share the same spiritual life.

Regarding the subject of Japanese language (*kokugo*), Obara regarded it as having a value as literature and artistic meaning while avoiding a focus solely on acquiring language skills. In particular, he asked Japanese language teachers/professors to focus on the "meaning of literature, writing plan, individuality of author, criticism of personage, literature review, and the appreciation of literature[20]" to enhance knowledge of epistemology. He believed that even though students only discussed the form and content without deep knowledge of epistemology would only create individual interpretations, they would not be able to make the real examination and discussion. In addition to such reason, he placed an emphasis on Japanese language ability on the belief that language skill is a weapon of learning.

Obara actually recommended the research of foreign literature, especially foreign classical literature, in connection with the subject of Japanese language. This is based on the demand for the education of foreign language by quoting Goethe's words: "He who does not know foreign languages does not know anything about his own[21]." He believed that in order to discuss Japanese contemporary literature more deeply, knowledge obtained by studying comparable foreign literature would be required. In addition, he stated that foreign teachers in charge of such study should "focus on the development of worldwide perspective, rather than teaching language[22]."

With regard to arithmetic (mathematics), he proposed to focus on the refinement of thinking skills rather than mastery of daily calculations. This is clear because he regarded a pragmatic view as a shallow idea, and strongly opposed the use of knowledge in arithmetic and mathematics on the profit-and-loss basis that prioritizes short-time results. He found it necessary to live in pursuit of the truth and possible enough to make daily calculations if the ability of creation and the capability of thinking and examination had been cultivated. Nevertheless, it should be noted that he advocated the addition of refinement of thinking skills without neglecting the mastery of daily calculation. He asked teachers to provide students with an opportunity to discover and create established propositions and rules, instead of merely teaching the simplified method.

Similarly, Obara was worried about the situation that science was also taught for pragmatic objectives. He asked teachers to have children explore mysteriousness and mystique of science, by stressing that the object of science research is nature. He underlined the pursuit of truth for truth as objectives of science. At the same time, as his statements on the sacrifices of flora and fauna that are needed with scientific study, he stressed it important to warn human conceit through science, and to present the importance of gratitude and mercy for sacrificed experimental flora and fauna through classes. Moreover, he stressed the scientific value of skepticism for what is absolutely determined as truth, as he demanded philosophical and critical review in science. This is a reasonable teaching method that could help learners from keeping rigid attitudes and ideas.

Regarding geography, he sought an approach to deepen understanding of events in association with moral science and history as a proposal of cross-subject study. As for history, he sought an approach to understand reviews of civilizations, criticism of spirit of ages, criticism of persons, and understanding of social structure functions, and social development, while eliminating the memorization and alignment of events. In particular, he proposed the introduction of cultural history, civilization history, and life history into history classes. In addition, he advocated the ideals of the subject to pay attention to geography and history of both Japan and the world, based on the demand that "the national spirit is necessary, but hopefully students will also develop an international humanitarian conscience at the same time[23]." Finally, he also sought an opportunity for learners to learn "how to live" through geography and history, as he described: "We learn the past to understand the present and understand the future[24]."

Obara's points about art (arts and music) are diverse. First of all, he expressed doubts that only technical and expressive forms were valued, and thus proposed an emphasis on artistic and content value. As he deplored the actual state that art was disregarded, he strongly demanded approval of artistic value. He also questioned professors who just emphasized skills based on the belief that classes performed only to polish their skills would not be sublimed to art classes. Furthermore, he assured the importance of interpreting and studying arts scientifically when teaching arts. The purpose of the art is not to simply finish and complete artwork in a beautiful state, but to reflect the interior essence.

For physical education, he sought the increase of the number of children who likes physical activities through physical education. This is an opinion based on the view that the soundness of mind and body is indispensable to survive human life as there are grounds for the health maintenance and promotion even after children grow up and this view has been incorporated a healthy value in the theory of Zenjin Education. He also suggested the addition of physiology to classes. This was likely to be an attempt to encompass health and sanitation beyond the framework of the subject as physical education.

Finally, Obara encouraged both boys and girls to be exposed to contents of psychology, economics, sociology, pedagogy (including childcare law), and architecture through home economics. The exclusion of viewpoint on subjects for girls only and the provision of opportunities for children to think about diverse careers which exist in the world may be seen as a course which covers the element of so-called career education on the present day.

5   Universal Validity of Zenjin Education

Based on the simple assumption that Obara's perception of each subject described in the previous section is an educational curriculum of Zenjin Education, this section will focus on common points with liberal arts education (and well-rounded education) that still continue from Ancient Greece introduced earlier. First of all, a *"zenjin"* to be developed through Zenjin Education refers to a whole person who is in the state of harmony, balance and integration of antinomy; more specifically, *kalokagathia* in Ancient Greece, a person with arts and *humanitas* in the Roman Republic, and a person developed through well-rounded education advocated by Harvard University. The image of ideal person is likely to be very similar in any education.

Also, there are a lot of common points regarding specific subjects listed in order to realize the education. In Ancient Greece, literature (grammar), rhetoric (speech), dialectical, physical education, arithmetic, geometry, music, astronomy, and other artistic study were listed as subjects necessary for character building, and such value was then succeeded in the seven liberal arts (grammar, rhetoric, logic, mathematics, geometry, astronomy, music). Thereafter, through epochal transition of academic field becoming more detailed with the advancement of science, the development was followed by the modern liberal arts education in the U.S., which was comprised of more than seven subjects. Some changes were identified, such as the new addition of religion and a new role as an artistic subject of literature, which was an alternate of music. Nevertheless, the basic perception of subject composition necessary for human education was likely to remain unchanged.

Even in well-rounded education, which commenced to become widespread in relatively recent years, the concept of humanitas is still alive. This may be confirmed by the fact that Harvard University has listed the classics of the world's literature, foreign language, history, mathematics, science, music, art, physical education, etc. as subjects required at the level of high school education. In addition to those subjects, areas that had never been handled as subjects (e.g., computer science) are being introduced as subjects in well-rounded education with the transformation of the social structure. However, this should be understood as a derivation partly from the pursuit of character building and human education after all.

The subjects valued by Obara were comprised of morality as philosophy (moral science called shushin at that time), Japanese language, foreign language that is essential for complementing Japanese language, art (especially music in Tamagawa Academy), athletic exercise (physical education that includes training elements), arithmetic (mathematics), science, society (geography, history, politics, etc.). In addition, Obara strongly recommended both boys and girls to study home economics . While this idea may be understood as Obara's aspiration as an attempt to embody *paideia* but also *techné* in the range of his ideal education, it is not difficult at all to understand the viewpoint that a subject showing an ideal way of human life should be included.

Apparently, the infinite inquisitive spirit of exploring humanity is reflected in every education of *enkyklios paideia*, *artes liberales*, seven liberal arts, liberal arts, well-rounded education, and Zenjin Education. The truth that "education" activities are indispensable for human is the very proof demonstrated by the fact that such concept has been inherited until today's age as a result of repeated deliberations that we human sincerely and honestly carried out on the universal education for human beings in a long-lasting history.

6　Education without Name

"Enkyklios paideia," the etymology of liberal arts, basically means human education with subjects aligned in a circular way. Also, well-rounded education covers diverse subjects and represents varied and balanced education driven by the idea of liberal arts, as defined by the term "well-rounded" that was initially given such meanings as "active, mature, well-balanced, broad." Obara imaged Zenjin as a circle. In other words, as a result of pursuing the ideal education from east to west, from ancient times to today, he reached the ultimate image of education which draws a circle equal to Zenjin Education.

Actually, he mentioned in his work "Tamagawa Juku no Kyoiku" that giving a name of Zenjin Education to education valued as an ideal by Obara would hinder universality. Before wrapping up this chapter, I would like to present some passages:

> Is it appropriate to give a name to education? Is it reasonable that education has a banner such as XX-type education, XX-oriented education, or XX-ism education? ... In short, "XX-ism" ... it actually denies others.
>
> Even Zenjin Education I have advocated is baised ... XX-type, XX-oriented, and XX-ism education is much more biased towards one direction, and they are extremely far from genuine education. Needless to say, education which further boasts the looks of appearance is extremely superficial education[25].

Hence, while he severely criticized education that kind of forced a specific framework by using a lot of propagandistic words, he was aware that a name was necessary to explain his education, ideas and concepts. Although Obara faced such challenge, he consequently found it ideal to promote his education only by showing the content of his value without a name. While the ideal education (genuine education) continues to live from Ancient Greece with many different names, it should naturally return to the ultimate image because the essence is universal. Obara was strongly desirous of realizing education that is "complete and solid with permanent universality and applicable from east to west, from ancient times to today, regardless of religion and group, principle and advocacy, temporary tendency and trend, individual's principles and preferences[26]." I would like to close this chapter in wishing that genuine education and real education will be continuously be delivered from Tamagawa Academy,

Notes

1) Kuniyoshi Obara, "Tamagawa Juku no Kyoiku" in *Obara Kuniyoshi Zenshu 11; Akiyoshidai no Seija Honma Sensei, Tamagawa Juku no Kyoiku*: Tamagawa Academy Press, 1963, p. 182.

2) Times Hire Education, "Sekai Hyojun no 'Zenjinryoku' Kyoiku de Global Leader wo Ikusei Suru," March 27, 2019. (https://japanuniversityrankings.jp/college/00010/, viewed on January 5, 2021).

3) The following literature was used as a reference for this concept: "Bunka no Kosei to Fuhensei ni Tsuite," Kiyoshi Nakamura, *Utsunomiya Daigaku Kyoiku Gakubu Kiyo Section 1*, No. 48, 1998, pp. 75-78.

4) The following literature was used as a reference for writing this section (in order of the Japanese syllabary): (i) Kyoichi Tamura, "Kyoyo no Gainen to Sono Riron" in *Jobu Daigaku Keiei Joho Gakubu Kiyo*, No.32, 2008, pp. 19-38. (ii) Kohei Baba, "Hyakkajiiten to Kyoyo Shimin no Aida-18-seiki no Doitsu de Hatten Shita Shako-bunka ni Okeru Chi no Juyo wo Megutte" in *METROPOLE*, No. 35, 2015, pp. 1-16. (iii) Tomohisa Handa, "Seven Liberal Arts wa Dokokara Kitamonoka" in *Ochanomizu Daigaku Jinbun Kagaku Kenkyu*, Vol.6, 2010, pp. 149-160. (iv) Kota Yamada, "Girisha Roma Jidai no Paidea to Shujigaku no Kyoiku" in *Keiwa Gakuen Daigaku Kenkyu Kiyo*, No.17, 2008, pp. 217-231. (v) Kota Yamada, "Liberal Arts Kyoiku no Kiso to Shiteno Sakubun Kyoiku: Kodai Girisha Roma Jidai no 'Progymnasmata' ni Tsuite" in *Keiwa Gakuen Daigaku Kenkyu Kiyo*, No. 28, 2018, pp. 1-16.

5) While the education of free men who referred to professionals using languages was called *paideia*, the education of non-free men who referred to craftsmen and slaves was called *techné* (technique). Basically, the two educations were defined separately.

6) Written as *artes, quae sunt libero dignae* in Greek.

7) Written as *doctrina liberalis* in Greek.

8) Written as *trivium* in Greek.

9) Written as *humanitas* in Greek.

10) Written as *quadrivium* in Greek.

11) This may be called "Latin liberal arts" to be differentiated from "seven liberal arts" that appeared subsequently.

12) The original title is *De nuptiis Philologiae et Mercurii et de septem artibus liberalibus libri novem*.

13) Accordingly, it does not accord one's life with a specialty chosen once.

14) Masayoshi Kinukawa, "Liberal Arts Kyoiku to Gakushi Gakui Program" in *Koto Kyoiku Kenkyu*, Vol. 8, 2005, p. 16.

15) Written as the Every Student Succeeds Act in English. The following literature was used as a reference for writing this section: (i) Jimenez, L. and Sargrad, S. A,Well–Rounded Education: Rethinking What Is Expected of High Schools, Center for American Progress, (ii) Minnesota Department of Education, "Overview: Well–Rounded Education" (https://www.google.com/url?sa=t&rct=j&q=&esrc=s&source=web&cd=&ved=2ahUKEwiEurSpzaLwAhUZfnAKHTSoBac QFjAAegQIBBAD&url=https%3A%2F%2Feducation.mn.gov%2Fmdeprod%2Fidcplg%3FIdcServi ce%3DGET_FILE%26dDocName%3DMDE058763%26RevisionSelectionMethod%3DlatestRelea sed%26Rendition%3Dprimary&usg=AOvVaw1EEB3H7cajFCIC–3kxyKcy, viewed on January 5, 2021), (iii) Akio Kitano, "Gendai Beikoku no Tesuto Seisaku to Kyoiku Kaikaku" in *Kyoikugaku Kenkyu*, Vol.84, No.1, 2017, pp. 27–37.

16) Harvard College , "Guide to Preparing for College" (https://college.harvard.edu/guides/ preparing–college, viewed on January 5, 2021).

17) Ibid.

18) Kuniyoshi Obara, *"Kyoiku Kaizo–ron" Obara Kuniyoshi Senshu 4. Kyoiku no Konpon Mondai to Shiteno Tetsugaku*, Tamagawa University Press, 1980, p. 153.

19) Ibid., p. 153.

20) Ibid., p. 156.

21) Ibid., p. 158.

22) Ibid., p. 213.

23) Ibid., p. 168.

24) Ibid., p. 168.

25) Kuniyoshi Obara, "Tamagawa Juku no Kyoiku" in *Obara Kuniyoshi Zenshu 11, Akiyoshidai no Seija Honma Sensei, Tamagawa Juku no Kyoiku*, Tamagawa Academy Press, 1963, p. 220.

26) Ibid., p. 196.

Column 1

Begin with a Song and End with a Song
——What Tamagawa's Music Education Tells

"Happy Birthday to You" is listed in the Guinness World Records as the most commonly sung song in the world. This song was originally a morning greeting song sung in a kindergarten named "Good Morning to All." This song was written by Mildred, a younger sister of the Hill sisters. Mildred was a kindergarten teacher and her older sister Patti was the principal of the kindergarten. Our beautiful custom of celebrating a person's birthday by singing a song would not have taken root in the world without this song. That is because this song goes into the ears straight and very easy to sing for anyone. Also, this short song has extremely simple lyrics and is made of eight bars only. If this song were so long made of a number of pages and we were not able to sing it with lyrics without looking at a score, candles on a cake would have been burnt up before the song finished. When it comes to songs handled in the lives of Tamagawa Academy, "simplicity" has been the important keyword to live with songs that are easy to remember and can be sung by anyone. Tamagawa Academy has established such a song-filled environment because we have a wealth of teaching approaches with various ingenuity.

When talking about the characteristics of music education in Tamagawa

Academy, we cannot skip the explanation on "music in our day-to-day lives." In Tamagawa Academy, music in our day-to-day lives should not only represent the category of music, but also be deemed as a model encompassing its ideal way of music education. Our unique teaching approaches have played a major role in the course of establishing the environment of music in our day-to-day lives. It was apparently Toshiaki Okamoto, the composer of the Tamagawa Academy School Song, who built the foundation of music in our day-to-day lives. At the early stage of Tamagawa Academy, Okamoto advocated the prevalence of music in our day-to-day lives. This was the outcome of Okamoto's exploration and ceaseless efforts to respond to the expectation of founder Kuniyoshi Obara, who "strongly wished that music would blend into everyday lives[1]," and thereafter such hope became the fundamental philosophy of music education aimed by Okamoto. At the beginning of the foundation, Tamagawa Academy was just a place of practice of Rosaku Education, where students built roads, carried fecal sludge as fertilizer, and cultivated fields. According to Okamoto's essay, he was asked repeatedly by Obara, saying, "Mr. Okamoto, please show students as many songs as possible so that they would not look too muddy." To respond to such request, Okamoto resolutely worked to write so many songs that can be sung by children for fun or naturally bring everyone together. He does not even remember how many songs he wrote[2].

Okamoto asserted everywhere that the first step for the prevalence of music in our day-to-day lives is round singing[3]. Okamoto was the very person who had strongly promoted the effect of round singing on education in Japan. "Kaeru no Gassho," which is said to be synonymous with a round song, was introduced by Okamoto to children nationwide. In 1947, this song was included in the last national textbook (*kokutei kyokasho*: used in Japanese publish school until 1947) as a teaching material by Okamoto (he had been appointed as a member of Japan's textbook selection committee), and then spread to children of all over the world very quickly. Actually, this song had been sung as a favorite song in Tamagawa Academy before that year. It had already been published as a folk song of the Rhine region in the 1942 edition of *Aiginshu*[4], a song collection carried by all Tamagawa children. When this song was introduced in the Japanese national textbook, he described as follows in *Zenjin*, which was published by Tamagawa University Press:

"It is a great leap of the Japanese music education that our familiar "Kaeru no Gassho" has been included as a teaching material for Grade 4. I would like to write about more later, but the music education approach centered on "Kaeru no Gassho" will make it possible to drastically turn the direction of the future music education[5]. This value of this song may be almost overlooked as a mere play song for children at first hearing, but this sentence clearly indicates how Okamoto adopted it as a teaching material with great expectation on round singing. As a result of further interpretation of the meaning shown by the approach centered on "Kaeru no Gassho," we can understand more precisely what music in our day-to-day lives aimed for.

In 1930, which is just after the foundation of Tamagawa Academy, a pedagogist named Werner Zimmermann visited Tamagawa Academy from Switzerland. Zimmermann, completely fascinated by the education of Tamagawa Academy, stayed in Japan for six months after his arrival. During this period, he taught many European songs to children by playing the violin and piano. "Kaeru no Gassho" was also one of the songs. Okamoto, intuited the enjoyment of round singing, boldly gave Japanese words as lyrics to make it easier for children to sense the harmony created by the song, rather than simply adding translations of original lyrics. The key point of his approach is that he did not try to convey the meaning of lyrics of the original song accurately, but to help children feel the enjoyment of harmony. Okamoto resolutely took the critical attitude on chanting education implemented as a means of "moral development" and music included in the training-like art course as "inspiration of national sentiments" during the war periods. He strongly believed that music must not be a means, but something that makes human feel the joy of music itself. "If an importance of chant is excessively placed upon effects created by words, the lyrics of the song will be rigid and then the melody will also be affected by such lyrics to become rigid against the nature of music[6]." He also commented in the description of *Rinsho no Tanoshimi* edited by Okamoto , "To taste the structural beauty of music, the lyrics do not have a meaning. Just 'La La La' ... is fine. I try to pay due attention (invisible effort) to make the song easy to sing and take advantage of a rhythm of the original song[7]." In other words, he did not find the lyrics important, and yet had the great expectation for the effect of round singing as a teaching approach to make children enjoy the harmony, which is the real pleasure of singing in rounds. Moreover, he had a clear belief that human needed to taste the art only with sound, that is, pure music and absolute music, instead of being caught by titles. He believed that singing a number of round songs and being exposed to such environment every day would develop a sense of relative sound, and eventually lead to the performance of "Hallelujah Chorus" and "Symphony No. 9." He argued that Japanese music education stuck only to the melody technique, and education should seek the enjoyment of singing in chords (enjoyment of chordal music) and the enjoyment of melodic interactions (enjoyment of music in counterpoint) [8].

He also said, "Some songs in Japan's national textbook have extremely long lyrics. Some of them have four or five verses, but actually one verse is enough. A song with excessively long or accurate lyrics will only be sung in a classroom[9]." In this manner, he explained the importance of making songs that are easy to remember with familiar lyrics.

Similar to the Tamagawa Academy School Song, we have "Kangei no Uta" (score example 1), which all Tamagawa Children is familiar with. When a lead person calls out by singing "Lan La ... Lan La ... Lan," other children react immediately and start singing along the first person. This melody is based on that of "Shiawase Nara Te wo Tatako (If You're Happy and You Know it)," which has probably been a world-famous song of universal standard. Tamagawa Academy welcomes transfer students, trainees, and guests who visit the school

score example1 *Kangei no Uta*

with this song. This song plays a role in loosing up the tense atmosphere that may be created at the time of first meeting. As shown in the score example 1, the name of the welcoming person may be added in the lyrics as a modular part. Another important point is that we are able to sing immediately in any situation, such as school ground or gymnasium. Okamoto said, "Nobody starts singing a song without accompaniment—such approach will never realize the integration of music in our day-to-day lives[10]." Accordingly, he devised teaching materials that are easy to handle in daily life.

Tamagawa's familiar motto: "Begin with a Song and End with a Song" may be interpreted as an encouragement to sing not only in music classes in school but also in every scene of lives all year round. As indicated by this motto, children in Tamagawa Academy starts every morning with a song. Upon arrival at school, children in elementary school play freely on the school ground until the start of the day. When a song starts playing, they start jumping on the spot

score example2   *Yo ga Aketa*

where they were playing. Each individual actively continues a series of exercise to the music without any instructions by a teacher. Following the series of exercise, the overture of the tune called "Yo ga Aketa" (score example 2) starts playing. This 10-bar tune can be sung in rounds easily because of the very simply chord progression with two chords. In addition, inserting Einsatz[11] is not necessary as this song is arranged for singing in rounds. This tune invites children, who are scattered in different places, to gather together and set up a line up to be ready for a morning meeting without any instructions (like a cue given by a conductor). Children follow this transition activity while singing in rounds. The second part of the round song may not be able to start at the right timing, but it does not matter. This would rather create a positive effect in terms of harmony and musicality in round singing. As this round song is made of ten bars only, the length of the tune (repeated or not, where to start and end) can be adjusted immediately according to how the line ups are set up for each morning meeting. Moreover, because this activity has become a routine, children make line up neatly without a loud command by a teacher. Even if this activity is followed every day in the same kind of scene, it never becomes worn

score example3 *Sayonara*

out or out of date because of the simplicity and the playful essence of music by round singing. Such strategy is not used as widely as expected in education fields out of Tamagawa Academy.

An afterclass meeting (Kaeri no Kai) is an important period of class activity to have children review the day, and yet it may cause a serious discussion some time. In this scene, the singing power again helps regain sound atmosphere at once. Following the after-class meeting, Tamagawa children always sing "Sayonara" (score example 3) in rounds and then break up for the day. This educational round song is also made of eight bars. A dominant chord[12] and a tonic chord[13] are repeated over and over again from the first third beat to the next bar in a group of two bars. Children has mastered this chord progression sensuously and unconsciously. This sense of harmony is a basis of the harmony structure common to any major pieces of Western classical music. The repetition of such experiences has created "Tamagawa Sound," which is well recognized in all-Japan competitions of choirs and wind bands. "Kaeru no Gassho" triggered the inclusion of several other round songs in postwar school textbook for each grade; however, Okamoto did not find it enough, expressing that "children just want to sing freely. They just want to keep singing while walking and working[14]." He also tried to prepare a number of round songs associated with lives of children, such as spring round songs, cherry blossom round songs, mountain climbing round songs, autumn round songs, and snow round songs to ensure that music becomes a part of their lives and their everyday lives are full of music[15]."

Although "Kaeru no Gassho" is familiar to almost all Japanese people, it is actually not known much in Germany, the home country of this song. Rather, it is widely known in the U.S. as a Japanese traditional song under the song named "Frog's Song." What is more interesting is that a part of frog sound in lyrics is played by various sounds in Japan. This has demonstrated that this song did not stay only in the music classroom in school, travelled outside, and became widespread with words of mouth between children in a playful manner as wished by Okamoto, not as a tune that forces people to look at a score and sing without errors of lyrics. The education approach centered on "Kaeru no Gassho" played a sufficient role in spreading the enjoyment of round singing all over Japan. However, the ideal that Okamoto really wanted to spread was nothing but the spirit of "music in our day-to-day lives," which has steadily taken root in today's Tamagaku Academy. I wish Tamagawa Academy will give birth of a song that will naturally become a part of lives of world citizens, such as "Happy Birthday to You."

Notes

1) Tamagawa Academy & University, "Tamagawa Gakuen no Seikatsu Ongaku," (https://www.tamagawa.jp/introduction/enkaku/history/detail_15668.html, viewed on December 4, 2020).

2) Toshiaki Okamoto, "Okamoto Sensei to Watashitachi", *Watashi no Rirekisho*, Okamoto Sensei wo Shinobu Kai, 1983, p. 7.

3) For example, *Rinsho no Tanoshimi*, edited by Toshiaki Okamoto, Ongaku no Tomosha, 1957, p. 46.

4) *Aiginshu*, edited by Tamagawa Academy, Tamagawa University Press, 1942.

5) Toshiaki Okamoto, "Shin Ongaku Kyoka ni Arawareta Sho–Keiko" in *Zenjin*, July edition, 1947, p. 14.

6) Toshiaki Okamoto, "Katei to Ongaku" in *Zenjin*, May edition, 1939, p. 65.

7) *Rinsho no Tanoshimi*, edited by Toshiaki Okamoto, Ongaku no Tomosha, 1957, p. 142.

8) Toshiaki Okamoto, "Rinsho Ron" in *Kyoiku Ongaku*, April edition, 1956, p. 102.

9) *Rinsho no Tanoshimi*, edited by Toshiaki Okamoto, Ongaku no Tomosha, 1957, p. 46.

10) Toshiaki Okamoto, "Kando no Ongaku, Seikatsu no Ongaku" in *Zenjin*, January edition, 1966, p.

15.

11) A voice line starts playing again after a long pause in an orchestra or choir. The beginning of the theme of Fugue (*Shinpen Ongaku Chu Jiten*, co–edited by Bin Ebisawa, Yuko Kamisango, Nobuo Nishioka and Osamu Yamaguchi. Ongaku no Tomosha, 2006).

12) Also called "zokuon" in Japanese. It modulates to a tonic chord in a more definitive form than any other triads. The dominant harmonic function, so–called a dominant key, not only makes the most powerful means for preparing a tonic chord, but also creates the most commonly used key subject of tonality (George Grove, *The New Grove Dictionary of Music and Musicians 11*, edit by Minao Shibata and Kazuyuki Toyama, Kodansha, 1994).

13) The first chord of a major or minor key, and the key whose key signature name is used as the name of the key. Also called "shuon" in Japanese. (George Grove, *The New Grove Dictionary of Music and Musicians 11*, edit by Minao Shibata and Kazuyuki Toyama, Kodansha, 1994).

14) Toshiaki Okamoto, "Katei to Ongaku" in *Zenjin*, May edition, Tamagawa University Press, 1939, p. 66.

15) Toshiaki Okamoto, *Jissenteki Ongaku Kyoikuron*, Kawai Gakufu, 1966, p. 9.

Part II

An Overview of Zenjin Education
from a Global Perspective

Chapter 4

Kurt Hahn and Zenjin Education
—— School as a Place for Experience

Introduction

Kurt Hahn and Kuniyoshi Obara stand together in the great field of 20th century pedagogical reform movements. Their pedagogical thinking and acting is shaped by mutual proximity and affinity. The motif of the 'whole person', which is central to Zenjin Education, connects the two educators. A biographical approach to the person and work of Kurt Hahn will open this article. It will be demonstrated that on the one hand the notion of experience and the notion of experiencing are of central importance. On the other hand, it touches upon a new and critical perspective on the state of pedagogical institutions. In the second part, Kurt Hahn's work will be situated within the context of world education. It will be shown that the motifs of peace, human rights and international understanding were of importance for Kurt Hahn. In addition, Kurt Hahn's innovative viewpoint on pedagogial institutions will be outlined. With regard to Landerziehungsheim, Kurt Hahn developed his own concept based on a critical diagnosis of his time, and by the help of clear principles. In the concluding third part, Kurt Hahn's pedagogy as a contribution to the pedagogical program of Zenjin Education is outlined. In addition to a brief comparison with Obara's pedagogy, the concept of learning through experience comes to the fore.

1　Kurt Hahn —— a Biographical Approach

Kurt Hahn was born in Berlin on June 5, 1886. Hahn died December 14, 1974 in Hermannsberg in southern Baden-Württemberg. Hahn was known worldwide as an educator who was interested in both thinking about and acting in politics. Due to the manifold already existing literature about Kurt Hahn's biography[1], I would like to foreground some points concerning the content of Hahn's work. The main purpose is to illustrate that it is worthwhile to take a close and systematical look at Kurt Hahn's significance for comprehending both pedagogical thought and educational political action.

Overall, the intertwining of pedagogy and politics played a fundamental role in Hahn's biography. This is primarily visible in his close association with Prince Max of Baden, the last chancellor of the German Empire, and Prince Philipp, Prince Consort of Great Britain. Kurt Hahn was "[t]he man who taught Philip to think[2]." Hahn's political views were shaped essentially by the idea of a democratic coexistence. On the one hand, the yardsticks of equality, universal human dignity and entire recognition of humankind were central to his notion of democracy. On the other hand, he regarded the development of a ruling elite a significant challenge for a democratic society. This ruling elite was expected to think and act on the basis of a comprehensive responsibility for their own lives and for society in general. The development of democracy, however, was at risk and confronted with various diseases of civilization. Hahn diagnosed six societal ills: the lack of physical fitness, the decline of initiative and enterprise, of imagination, of craftsmanship, of self-discipline, and of compassion. Society hence needs to counter this by the help of an altered pedagogical thinking and educational policy.

Considering the biographical background to his commitment to democracy, Hahn was particularly involved in the ruptures of the German political systems after World War I. Hahn's clear rejection of National Socialism led to a short arrest in 1933 and his subsequent emigration to Great Britain. Hahn's standing against National Socialism was certainly influenced by his Jewish origins, but ultimately determined by his fundamental political standpoint and his commitment to democracy. Hahn had already explicitly formulated his strong rejection of National Socialism before 1933. In August 1932, he thus wrote: "Salem cannot remain neutral. I call upon the members of the Salem Federation who work with the SA or SS to either revoke their pledge of allegiance to Hitler or to Salem[3]." The incompatibility of the participation in his schools, either as a teacher or as a student, and the dull principles of National Socialism led to his emigration and the founding of the school at Gordonstoun in Scotland, which eventually had global impact[4].

If we look at the significance of his work, we can state that Kurt Hahn became known around the world for a certain pedagogical thinking as well as educational political action.

Two points can be emphasized with regard to his pedagogical thinking.

One of his leitmotifs is the idea that learning is essentially controlled by one's experiences. Pedagogy therefore needs to find ways to make the personally shaped experience the ground for all education.

Secondly, the following insight stands at the center of his pedagogical thinking: pedagogical institutions must take into account the process of learning through experience. According to Hahn, pedagogy thus only works through the interaction of personal role models and pre-arranged structures.

With regard to educational policy, two aspects in particular are to be highlighted. First, Hahn himself was a very successful founder of alternative schools. In 1919, he founded the world-famous Schule Schloss Salem in cooperation with Prince Max of Baden, which opened in Germany in April

1920. In 1932, Salem's sister school, the Birklehof in Hinterzarten, Black Forest, was founded. As mentioned earlier, Hahn founded in 1934 the British Salem School in Gordonstoun, Scotland, after his emigration from Nazi Germany in 1933.

In addition to founding his own schools, his educational political action was also impacted by his interest in setting up international network structures. On the one hand, this interest manifested itself in the network of United World Colleges, which Hahn had helped to model in the 1960s. Above all, the International Bachelor is a network of great significance and success whose objective is to make the vision of an education for global citizenship realized. The UNESCO launched this globally recognized degree qualification under Hahn's influence in the late 1960s. It is indeed a remarkable success story: "As of December 2020, there were over 7,200 programs being offered worldwide, across over 5,400 schools in 158 countries[5]."

The concepts of pedagogical thinking and educational policy can both be illustrated if we first examine Kurt Hahn in the context of the World Education movement. We will focus on his reform-oriented understanding of school. Considering his thoughts on schools, Kurt Hahn responded to important questions in his day, for example questions by Kazuhito Obara concerning the development of the educational system in Japan as follows.

"The first question asks if Japanese education is able to change, and the answer is that it is possible but may need a Copernican revolution in the educational ideology of the Japanese. In other words, considering an alternative notion of education is essential. The second question inquires as to an implementation method and process, and the answer is to return to the nature of education; that is, to get rid of current circumstances and the value system surrounding Japanese education in order to go back to basics, thinking of the true meaning of education, the real purpose of it, and the pure motivation for it. More specifically speaking, the Japanese as a whole have to confront a drastic paradigm shift from an inclination to evaluate people in terms of conspicuous yet superficial and biased information such as hensachi, gakureki, and/or occupation to a character evaluation which looks at the person as a whole[6]."

Therefore, this notion of "the person as a whole" will be dealt with in the third subchapter. Kurt Hahn's pedagogy generated stimuli for Zenjin Education. The idea of learning by experience will be in focus.

2   Kurt Hahn in the Context of World Education

Kurt Hahn's work can only be understood considering a certain conception of the worldwide reform movement in pedagogy. It is helpful to first explain the basic understanding of "New Education" (Reformpädagogik). Here, we can draw on a distinction developed by Hermann Röhrs, a former president of the World Education Fellowship (WEF). At this point, it is of crucial importance that Röhrs introduced a political distinction for the conception of "New Education" (Reformpädagogik). In this manner, Röhrs formulates an internal differentiation within the spectrum of those individuals and programs traditionally assigned to reform pedagogy. For Röhrs, the aspect of internationalism, and in its wake the commitment to the struggle for peace education, represented the significant yardstick for reform pedagogy. Yet from an outside perspective, the advocacy for the learners' own right, fed by a critical attitude towards the respective zeitgeist, interlocked different forms of reform pedagogy. "Reform pedagogy embodies a continuous, international movement in the service of mankind which promotes educational progress according to the principles of self-active and responsible development"[7]. "Reform pedagogy" is always at confrontation with "pedagogical provincialism"[8] and is constituted by the "critical inclusion of the international horizon of experience and knowledge[9]." Eventually, this is an ethical approach to understand the function of reform pedagogy[10] as a critical theory of the world under pedagogical auspices.

Today's tension between "individuality" and "globalization" demonstrates the diverse meanings of this universal label. For in this ethical perspective, reform pedagogy is committed precisely to this tension within a dual normative orientation that the individual - pointedly: every human being in its individual shape —— has the right to blossom within the world horizon and that this blooming, this unfolding requires a framework that needs to be characterized as "peace". This pedagogical understanding of peace is far more than the mere absence of war (in as much as this is an inestimable value in itself). Moreover, the pedagogical understanding —— precisely because of its reference to every human's right of individuality —— aims at realizing a social constellation in which peace is realized at least in a culture of tolerated recognition and corresponding respect.

The real test of "reform pedagogy" today is of ethical nature and, in normative terms, can be found in the pedagogical cultural criticism in the contexts of globalization. The development of pedagogical cultural criticism in the spirit of reform pedagogy includes diverse and yet interconnected issues, for instance the work of the UNESCO and its "Education for All" program, the work of the "World Education Fellowship", and documents such as the Charter of Children's Rights from 1989. The pedagogical approaches to transform the universal Human Rights into rights of the learners, and especially the political realization of children's rights, belong just as much to this field as the efforts to consolidate the anthropological site of global education concepts or sustainable learning. In this sense, it is about education for global citizenship.

Hermann Röhrs regarded particularly Kurt Hahn's work as the completion of the "genuine" reform pedagogical approach. This criterion of "genuine" reform pedagogy fulfilled ultimately a dual function. It constitutes a differene to the outside and at the same time enables a critical differentiation within reform pedagogy itself.

Within reform pedagogy, this criterion makes a differentiated reflection possible. For example, there are approaches that share certain pedagogical guidelines, such as the orientation towards the learner or the search for alternative forms of schooling, but have failed to transfer the pedagogy of the advocacy for the weak and the vulnerable into an appropriate basic sociopolitical stance. Thus, Röhrs is able to formulate the following as a guiding principle of reform pedagogy: "Fully unfolded, the reform pedagogical concept also activates its peace-educational relevance, as evident in William James, Pierre Bovet, Maria Montessori, Kurt Hahn, Friedrich Wilhelm Foerster, Elisabeth Rotten, and others[11]." For Röhrs, especially with regard to Kurt Hahn, the aspect of internationalism —— and in its wake the struggle to outline peace education —— forms an inescapable yardstick for the separation of diverse reform pedagogical mindsets. In other words, whether a practice or theory can be counted as a genuine reform pedagogy is determined by the degree to which it shares this internationalist and simultaneously pacifist attitude. Röhrs' concept implies that the consequences of reform pedagogy, in both theory and practice, remain unfinished fragments when the pedagogical approach is not transferred into a political thought. If this is the case, however, pedagogy must be open and compatible for communication within the international context.

This clearly depicts why, for Röhrs, Kurt Hahn is such an important representative of the "real", and "true" reform pedagogy. Kurt Hahn always conceived his schools as elements for international understanding and responsibility. From his school in Salem to United World Colleges, it permeates Hahn's educational thoughts and actions: we all are human beings on this earth and must therefore expose ourselves to the strangeness of the foreign. Experiencing and processing a stranger's strangeness does not make the stranger become less strange. Their strangeness, however, becomes part of one's familiarity meaning that one can share the world with them. Considering this, Hahn formulated early —— on his so-called Salem laws. These laws translate the conception of world citizenship into practical pedagogy. Hahn is concerned with the whole person on its way to becoming a global citizen. The guiding principles listed below still provide a fundamental orientation for today's pedagogical practice, for example in the boarding schools Schule Schloss Salem and Gordonstoun as well as in the United World Colleges (UWC)

"1. Give children the opportunity to discover themselves.

2. Let children experience triumph and defeat.

3. Give children the opportunity to commit themselves to the common cause.

4. Provide for times of silence.

5. Exercise imagination.

6. Let competition play an important but not the predominant role.

7. Save the sons and daughters of rich and powerful parents from the effeminating sense of privilege[12]."

Even though this education towards global citizenship is connected to an ideal of desirable personality, for Kurt Hahn the overall notion is tied to a worldy pragmatism. Hahn defined this personality ideal amid the tension field of personal inclinations, respect for human dignity, and self-commitment to universal moral law[13]. According to Hahn, the child "[needs] to comprehend its country in all the social, political, and technical facets – for no other reason than eventually becoming a morally responsible adult[14]" is the main goal of education. Hahn contrasted the dangers of the "modern urban environment[15]" with education through sports and social engagement, which are said to have a positive effect on morality. Hahn's plan of pedagogical "remedies" thus provides us with four strategies to help prevent the youth from being "victims of decay." These four elements, which Hahn wanted to be integrated into daily school life, are the following:

"1. The athletic break, four times a week in the morning,

2. The project on Saturday mornings,

3. The expeditions several times a trimester,

4. An afternoon exclusively devoted to rescue work[16]."

According to Hahn, turning towards the other, the counterpart in social structures, implies experiencing responsibility for others human beings in dangerous situations at sea or in the mountains[17]. This turning towards the other is expected to promote a general sense of recognition of others as fellow human beings and, subsequently, taking over responsibility for them. These elements are part of an "experiential therapy[18]" that intends to eventually develop a civic consciousness as a cosmopolitan consciousness. Responsibility for humankind as part of humanity itself is the ultimate goal of all possible education.

Kurt Hahn has transposed this pedagogical–political setting into a different understanding of school as an institution, as well as into a different understanding of learning. Considering World Education in this distinctive way, we will first reflect upon schools as institutions. It is crucial for Kurt Hahn that school is not only a place for cognitive knowledge transfer. School is, above all, about social learning, about learning how to behave in social structures.

When we contemplate school as a place of social learning and acting, we look at a cultural product, which means a product that has emerged from culture and, at the same time, is indispensable for the sustainment of culture. Two questions derive from this statement.

1   What happens *in* schools? This may be the first and obvious but not last question. We may not only ask what happens in the school place but also:

2   What happens *through* schools? This question points in a different direction. If we restructure the above stated perspectives in another way, we can distinguish between how social learning happens in schools and how social learning happens through schools.

With reference to Kurt Hahn's pedagogy, we can link these two perspectives:

"Social learning through the school space shapes social learning in the school place."

Undoubtedly, "school" is characterized by the staging and regulation of learning. The question, however, is how, where, and by which means this staging and regulation takes place. School is about a specific type of learning. Learning processes occur in everyday life, in front of the television, in peer groups and on various other occasions. School eventually must have special characteristics.

School does not simply exist because people decide they are ready to learn. Rather, learning is regulated, piloted. This piloting happens in different dimensions; through certain coutent, on certain occasions, and at certain times.

In other words:
· Learning content is designed and selected;
· Learning opportunities are also designed and selected, and both come to pass during a limited learning time; and
· How and what is learned consists of a conscious decision or at least a toleration.

If we conceptualize "learning" and its piloting as the centerpiece of school, we can broadly agree on the following observation that there is not only the official syllabus that regulates the learning process through the interaction of teachers and learners. This does exist, but there is something else. There is "more" to piloting learning processes, and it would be short-sighted and naive, also in Kurt Hahn's sense, it tries to hide this "more". When we think about regulating learning processes in school contexts, it certainly does not mean solely following and working through the syllabus.

Learning perhaps rather takes place outside the organized classroom with its structured transmission of knowledge. But how can learning then be described? If we assume that learning always needs certain contents, certain opportunities and certain times, the following distinctions are possible. We can distinguish three types of how learning occurs in schools —— learning that does not happen without intention, but is consciously shaped or at least tolerated. These three types of directing learning are imaginable.

First, learning, understood in its narrow sense, takes place through instructed transmission of knowledge. Teachers stand in front of the class, groups, or other forms, and present or elaborate certain subjects within a given period. In this respect, teacher-centered lessons, group work or free work do not differ ultimately. Learning at this point is always pcontrolled through diverse forms of prior instructed and determined confrontation with certain topics —— guided by professionally trained teachers.

Second, learning takes place due the organization of various forms of "Geselligkeit" (sociability). Here, sociability describes opportunities deliberately established within the school framework, and always contain a pedagogical appeal for learning such as class and school festivals, group projects that are limited in time and content, long-term study groups, the school café, field and class trips, and many more. The rules of these forms of sociability, meaning the rules applied to those intentionally formed social spaces, need to be learned. Classroom education is the staged social space par execellence, and the classroom may consist of students of the same age, with same interests or other forms. The organization of as a learning association includes learning appeals, which will be discussed later on.

Third, learning takes place due to costums which underlie all forms of school events, for example the binding and hence unifying social, temporal and spatial structures. We often use "as is the costum" as an explanation. The school "custom" also contains a pedagogically exploitable invitation to learn for example students' behavior at the playground. This behavior is influenced undoubtedly by a quantity of factors that are difficult to decipher. Nevertheless, the displayed behavior pattern can be changed and even pedagogically piloted to a certain extent. This should not be underestimated. The notion of custom is clearly more abstract and therefore more difficult to grasp than sociability. Occasions of sociability are consciously designed while custom, however, was somehow brought into or found at school. Nevertheless, the crucial point is that custom can be altered, too. When thinking about initiatives like "School without Racism", it becomes clear that the rules for social coexistence in institutions like "schools" are anything but unchangeable or given by nature. Modifying rules is possible in this case as well, and especially today the need to do so is highly visible. Even if customs are not easy to grasp, they can be changed.

During the process of teaching, it becomes clear that learning is by no means only piloted by the officially approved subject matter or by the teacher as the person in charge. Learning is significantly co-determined by social rules. In summary, we can state that not only the subject and the teachers but also the social situation in its social form control learning. This might be obvious for the case of sociability and custom, but can also be applied to the act of teaching. The main idea is that humans acquire knowledge and pick up behaviors, which in turn educate them, and this particularly happens in pre-established structures[19]. It is of importance that the place does not only exist in an abstract, non-real form but can manifest itself physically. It is this physical place, which is imbued with social rules, that pilots learning. Nevertheless, the designed, and pre-shaped place is no different from an institution. The institution, schools as institutions, are important for learners.

School as an institution, as a place of social learning and acting is not only pre-given in its social shape but is also changeable. This is of crucial importance, and these structures can be shaped in varying degrees of immediacy.

This clarification of the relationship between personal and structural education is a prerequisite to understand the special nature of the Landerziehungsheim, and it is also from Kurt Hahn's standpoint[20]. The assessment and arrangement of personal and structural education is indeed the basis for the special didactics in and through a Landerziehungsheim. Kurt Hahn took over Hermann Lietz' elementary idea of school being a place for education and of education being personality development[21]. Hahn referred to Hermann Lietz as "the greatest educator of modern Germany[22]." The arising question who the essential educator is in the Landerziehungsheim can only be answered in two interconnected ways. The key educator in the Landerziehungsheim demands, on the one hand, a certain type of teacher and, on the other hand, a certain structural arrangement. The peculiarity of the Landerziehungsheim didactic results from the tension between the individual and the surrounding structure[23]. The observation that the social space of the Landerziehungsheim is indeed a (thoroughly) pre-established environment does not mean, however, that it must involve an authoritarian, purely adult-centered overall structure. The Landerziehungsheim rather wants to be comprehended as a specific context that provides children and adolescents with "natural" spaces for their individual personality development.

The fundamental idea implies that, although education depends essentially on immediate human (inter)action, it is not at all limited to it. It is rather a shift of pedagogical stimulus concerning the piloting of learning processes towards the structures, that are consciously chosen and built. The Landerziehungsheim then comprises, above all, of a socio-cultural environment chosen and shaped by Hahn. The relationship or rather tension between the individual and the surrounding structures is the hermeneutic key for understanding the pedagogical distinctiveness of the Landerziehungsheim. Hahn wanted his school foundings to be recognized as contexts that provide children and adolescents with "natural" spaces for their development. The educational effect of the selected and designed structures should be in harmony with "personality" development cared for by the staff. The fundamental notion is that the pedagogical claim of educating morality, and the subsequent conception of a school focused on this very education, can only be achieved by the model-like interaction between individual and structure. This way only emphasizes the wholeness and completeness of children and young people as human beings. The teachers themselves eventually become a part of the socio-structural rule structure within the designed environment. Their role is to exemplify the values and corresponding attitudes.

3 Kurt Hahn and His Pedagogical Program of a Zenjin Education

Kazuhito Obara characterized Kuniyoshi Obara's guiding anthropological concept as follows, "Obara divided a person into mind and body in accordance with a philosophical notion of dualism, and therefore also divided the six values into two categories: absolute values (truth, goodness, beauty, and holiness) and instrumental values (health and wealth). [...] Truth, goodness, beauty, and holiness are included in absolute values because they are directly related to mental and spiritual aspects of humanity and thence are intrinsic values. Contrariwise, health and wealth are counted among instrumental values due to the fact that they are necessary and valuable only for realizing and sustaining absolute values[24]." Zenjin Education is about fully respecting the dignity of humans in their human completeness──this notion should also be applied when dealing with children and adolescents. Children and adolescents are full-fledged humans and not some deficient beings. This perception of children and adolescents as "whole, complete" human beings includes the appreciation of "self-education as self-development," which represent the core idea of the "Twelve Precepts of Education" for contemporary Zenjin Education[25]. Practicing Zenjin Education and its interplay between personal and structural education means primarily apprehending pedagogical institutions such as kindergarten, school, or university as arranged contexts of self-reflective experience.

In order to understand Hahn's contribution to Zenjin Education, it would suggest itself to firstly and generally define this notion of experiential learning. It will then be demonstrated how Kurt Hahn's concept of pedagogy realized this experiential learning process. To start with, we can observe that the appropriation and making available of the world by children and adolescents must and does indeed largely take place in an indirect manner. That which can be experienced directly, and experienced in close proximity to oneself only accounts for a fraction of what learning in terms of transitioning into society requires. This observation has often been labeled as "second-hand experience." Assessing the above stated fact, however, leads to many different outcomes. For some it represents the very first sin of cultural development. Rousseau's pedagogical utopia pictured in his educational novel "Émile" is an impressive example[26]. For Rousseau, who advocates in favor of direct experience, the stimuli for childhood and adolescent learning, must be, in case of doubt, available to be bodily experienced – as symbolically expressed in the punishment scene after Émile breaking a window. The opposite position argues that "second-hand experience" is not only a necessity but even a blessing of the advanced cultural standard. An unmanageable quantity and quality of information is said to be accessible to the individual for its personal and to society for its cultural development. Even if the individual can only gradually process and internalize this plenitude of information, it is said to symbolize the immeasurable richness of our culture. We shall therefore recognize the positive function of second-hand experience whose offer of information about agency is indispensable for maintaining the cultural standard of modern society. "Learning through experience" is thus a controversial claim. One of the main points of dispute over the function and role of schools, especially since around 1900s, concerned the distance, the difference between the learning subject and its life on the one hand, and the learning object and its supposed remoteness from life on the other hand. Learning through experience and providing stimuli for said experience while supporting children and adolescents in their "human wholeness" play a central role in Kurt Hahn's school conception as well as in Zenjin Education. Learning in a manifold way should be made possible in and through the help of schools. The following anthrolopological premises are the backbone to the idea that learning through experience, especially in schools, is the adequate form of learning. We only learn by doing and by doing something by ourselves.

Waltraud Neubert in particular, referencing Wilhelm Dilthey and Herman Nohl, tried to demonstrate said statements in her dissertation "Das Erleben in der Pädagogik" (1930). The premise, "We only learn by doing," leads her to distinguish between learning by experiencing and learning by working as the two basic forms of learning[27]. Thereby, the experience primarily influences the feeling, while the work primarily affects the will[28]. The underlying principle, however, is common to both experience and work: the immediacy, the unity of the learner, and the object of learning whilst self-activity.

The emphasis of the experiential side of learning, of being directly involved and affected has at least two consequences for the learning content. On the one hand, the learning content may be quickly upstaged because the learner's experience is of significance for the learning process. Without said experience, learning is said to remain pale, secondary, and ultimately ineffective. On the other hand, the above statement implies that possible learning contents are assessed in terms of value. In this logic, that which cannot be experienced must necessarily be a learning object of a lower rank. Accordingly, Neubert inititally attributes the possibility of successful experiential didactics to subjects like art, literature, history, mathematics and religious education[29]. This raises the fundamental question whether and how pedagogically regulated learning can do justice to the side of learning that highlights experience and to what extent experiential learning should be exercised.

In his book *"Reform der Erziehung"* , Andreas Flitner states that "more than ever, school lately has become a school of books and learning[30]" and thus demands a new immediacy in school learning. In terms of teaching analysis, Klaus Prange identifies in his book *"Bauformen des Unterrichts*[31]" learning through experience as one of three forms of teaching alongside lesson and work. He argues that, from a teacher's point of view, some moments during school lessons foreground the always already accompanying experience of the lesson itself and, therefore, require a special methodology about how to deal with experience. This is, however, rather the exception or should be at least.

The theorem, "learning through experience," is especially important for an understanding that regards school as a composition of directly and indirectly controlled learning processes. The design of pedagogical and experiential situations in the school is of central importance in this context. In addition, how to combine school and environment during extracurricular activities is crucial. Following Kurt Hahn, Jörg Ziegenspeck has developed the "experiential pedagogy" as a form of education that stresses the role of nature——for example mountains or the seaside. Ziegenspeck explicitly understands experiential pedagogy as an "alternative and supplement to traditional and established educational institutions[32]."

In her extensive study on Kurt Hahn's pedagogy, Hildegard Thiesen has presented in detail the peculiarity and diversity of indirect pedagogical action via pre-shaped environments in Kurt Hahn's work. Thiesen describes Hahn's pedagogy as the design of "pedagogical environment(s) between construction and connection[33]." She describes Hahn's pedagogical work as a model of pedagogical ecology in which pedagogical action mainly occurs in an indirect manner through "environments", saying: "On the one hand, Hahn sets up environments with a pedagogical intent, he creates them and constructs them (Konstruktion). On the other hand, he connects his pedagogical goals with already found environments (Anknüpfung). [...] Each of Hahn's manner to provide pedagogical environments is intended to bring those who are to be educated into a relationship with said "environment[34]." This innovative and influential proposition shows that the plausibility of a structural theory of education and the hermeneutic approach connected to it can be unfolded precisely by considering Hahn's school pedagogy.

The basis of Kurt Hahn's pedagogy is thus a "hermeneutics of pedagogical environments" that "includes the non-personal[35]" and stresses ecological and structural understanding of educational processes. Pedagogy does not only include human action in a direct and immediate manner, but also action that is accounted for by humans but rather works in a structural and indirect manner through the conscious use of environments. According to Hahn, when dealing with environments, one comes to realize that "it is possible and necessary to let the selection, design, or creation of certain environments be guided by certain educational intentions[36]." Hahn directs "his thoughts and his entire creative faculty towards the 'environments' to which he seeks to relate his students[37]." According to Thiesen, Kurt Hahn distinguished three ways in which environments intentionally come into existence: firstly by construction, secondly by linkage, and thirdly by the combination of said two aspects. Thiesen illustrates this plausible interpretation of Kurt Hahn's educational goals by analyzing known "environments": coeducation, scholarship system, training plan or finally the most complex "environment", the emergency service[38]. A possible didactic objection could be whether Hahn even assumes an "automatism of effect of his "environments[39]" and whether a "neglect[ion] of the subjective pole in the educational process[40]" can be observed.

Kurt Hahn's didactics, incorporating cultural criticism, aim at reflecting upon the human condition in the industrialized modernity. Hahn's pedagogical goal comprises of "the rescue and restitution of human qualities[41]". According to this, it is "not about the increase of forces but about the preservation of forces; not about the development but about the prevention or at least the limitation of developmental damage[42]." This pedagogical intention encounters a dramatic fundamental configuration, especially in adolescence. Hahn stated that damage in society and threats to adolescents during their puberty collide disastrously in the lived realities of adolescents. Hahn compared pedagogical with medical work at this point. According to Thiesen, a distinction can be made between the steps of diagnosis, therapy, and therapy goal[43]. A peculiarity of Hahn's position lies in his limitation of cultural criticism to a "moderate[44]" degree. There should be no limitless, no radical cultural criticism. Already in adolescence, one should rather engage oneself with the given conditions and learn to deal with them.

The reason for this didactic strategy is the idea of a global qualification that facilitates exchange and mutual recognition of school-leaving qualifications. An umbrella organization, in its role of a non-profit foundation, verifies that the participating schools comply with the relevant standards. Of course, the individual syllabi vary, depending on the profile of the participating school. Directing school-based learning towards global networking aims at creating an experience of connectedness with other students through a shared qualification. This way, Kurt Hahn's basic pedagogical concern to educate children and young people to become responsible citizens of the world has indeed spread globally. Eventually, the guiding principle of the notion of personality gains universal validity —— according to Hahn, said principle unites pedagogy in all regions worldwide. It is diametrically opposed to approaches that want to confine schools to knowledge transfer and address of the learner's cognitive abilities. Thinking of personality means including every facet —— as citizen of this world[45].

Notes

1) Hermann. Röhrs, *Kurt Hahn.*, Routledge & Kegan Paul, 1970. Jörg. W. Ziegenspeck, *Kurt Hahn: Erinnerungen – Gedanken – Aufforderungen. Beiträge zum 100. Geburtstag des Reformpädagogen*, Lüneburg 1987. Th. James, "Kurt Hahn and the Aims of Education", 2000 (http://www.kurthahn.org/wp-content/uploads/2016/04/james_final.pdf). Michael Knoll, "School reform through experiential therapy: Kurt Hahn – an effiacious educator", 2011 (https://files.eric.ed.gov/fulltext/ED515256.pdf).

2) BBC News, "Kurt Hahn: The man who taught Phillip to think", 2016 (https://www.bbc.com/news/magazine-35603975).

3) Kurt. Hahn, *Erziehung und die Krise der Demokratie. Reden, Aufsätze, Briefe eines politischen Pädagogen*, Ed. by Michael Knoll, Stuttgart, 1986, p. 54.

4) Ibid., pp. 67ff.

5) International Baccalaurate, "Facts and Figures" (https://www.ibo.org/about-the-ib/facts-and-figures/).

6) Kuniyoshi. Obara, "West Meets East. A Well-Rounded Education versus an Angular Education in Japan"., *Tiempo y Educación*, Volume 5, 2018, p. 110.

7) Hermann. Röhrs, "Die Internationalität der Reformpädagogik und die Ansätze zu einer Welterziehungsbewegung". In: Ders Lenhart & Volker Lenhart (Eds.) *Die Reformpädagogik auf den Kontinenten. Ein Handbuch*, Ein Handbuch, 1994, p. 14.

8) Ibid., p. 20.

9) Ibid., p. 19.

10) Ralf Koerrenz, *Reformpädagogik – eine Einführung*, Paderborn 2014, chap. 5. Ralf. Koerrenz, "New Education – Historical Aspects and Recent Significance", *The Journal of the World Education Fellowship*, Volume 100, 2019, No. 1, pp. 73–85.

11) Röhrs, op. cit., p. 20.

12) Salem Laws – cited from: http://www.salem-net.de/privatschule-internat/vertiefendes/salemer-gesetze.html.

13) Cf. Kurt. Hahn, *Erziehung zur Verantwortung. Reden und Aufsätze*, Stuttgart, 1958, pp. 9.

14) Ibid., p. 17.

15) Ibid., p. 30.

16) Ibid., p. 74.

17) Ibid., p. 77.

18) Ibid., p. 78; cf. also Ziegenspeck, op. cit.

19) Cf. Robert Dreeben, *Was wir in der Schule lernen*, Frankfurt/M, 1980.

20) Cf. Ralf Koerrenz, *Hermann Lietz – Einführung mit zentralen Texten*, Paderborn 2011. Juhn Yamana, "Die Struktur der "Übersichtlichkeit" des Landerziehungsheims Haubinda. Zur Interpretation des "Schulstaat"-Konzepts von Hermann Lietz"., *Zeitschrift für Pädagogik*, 42, 1996, pp. 407–421.

21) Hermann Lietz, *Schulreform durch Neugründung. Ausgewählte Pädagogische Schriften*, Paderborn, 1970. Koerrenz, op. cit.

22) Hahn, op. cit., p. 55.

23) Cf. the example of the Jena-Plan school model as an explanation of this didactic: Ralf. Koerrenz, *Reform(ing) Education. The Jena-Plan as a Concept for a Child-Centred School.*, Paderborn, 2020.

24) Obara, op. cit., p. 115; cf. Sakuma Hiroyuki, "Kuniyoshi Obara's Zenjin Education at Tamagawa Gakuen". In: Yamasaki Yoko & Kuno Hiroyuki (Eds.), *Educational Progressivism, Cultural Encounters and Reform in Japan*, Routledge, 2017, p. 105.

25) Cf. Sakuma, op. cit., pp. 101ff.

26) Cf. J.-J. Rousseau, *Emil oder Über die Erziehung*, Ludwig Schmidt (Ed.), Paderborn, 1971.

27) Waltraut. Neubert, *Das Erlebnis in der Pädagogik*, Lüneburg 1990, p. 64.

28) Neubert, op. cit., p. 65.

29) Cf. Neubert, op. cit., pp. 41ff.

30) Andreas Flitner & Doris Knab, *Reform der Erziehung, Impulse des 20. Jahrhunderts,* Piper Verlag Gmb H, 2001, p.96.

31) Cf. Klaus Prange, *Bauformen des Unterrichts,* Bad Heilbrunn, 1986.

32) Ziegenspeck, op. cit., p. 95.

33) Cf. Hildegard Thiesen, *Kurt Hahn – Pädagogische Umwelten zwischen Konstruktion und Anknüpfung,* Garamond, 2006.

34) Ibid., p. 82.

35) Ibid., p. 74.

36) Ibid., p. 62.

37) Ibid., p. 188.

38) Ibid., pp. 231ff.

39) Ibid., p. 189.

40) Ibid., p. 321.

41) Ibid., p. 155.

42) Ibid., p. 176.

43) Cf. Thiesen, op. cit., p. 135.

44) Cf. Kurt Hahn, *Reform mit Augenmaß. Ausgewählte Schriften eines Politikers und Pädagogen,* Klett–Cotta, 1988.

45) This article was translated from German into English by Sarah Ganss M.A. (Institute for Bildung and Culture, Friedrich Schiller University Jena, Germany).

Chapter 5

International Baccalaureate and Zenjin Education
——A Focus on Learner Profile

Introduction

The last page of the comprehensive brochure of Tamagawa Academy & University includes a list of accreditations——which is unusual for a Japanese school-including Tamagawa's status as an accredited International Baccalaureate World School. Accreditation, which is not yet widely known in Japan, is a review process conducted by a non-government, third-party organization for the purpose of assuring educational quality. The process demonstrates that education offered by a school is valuable from the perspective of an external party and improves the credibility of the school based on the type of accreditation obtained. This chapter examines the close ties between International Baccalaureate (IB), which is a globally recognized standard of educational excellence, and Tamagawa education.

The importance of developing globally competent human resources has been drawing attention in Japan for about a decade. The Council for Promotion of Global Human Resource Development, which was established in 2011, presented in its interim report the qualities and abilities expected of globally competent human resources as follows[1]:

Element Ⅰ : Language and communication skills
Element Ⅱ : Independence and initiative, a challenger's spirit, cooperation and adaptability, a sense of responsibility and mission
Element Ⅲ : An understanding of other cultures and a Japanese identity

The Ministry of Education, Culture, Sports, Science and Technology (MEXT) announced its plan to "increase the number of educational institutions offering an educational program that enables students to obtain IB qualifications at the time of high school graduation, or equivalent thereof, to about 200 in five years" with the aim of encouraging inward-looking Japanese students to study abroad, developing globally competent human resources, and promoting educational reform[2]. It was then that many education experts in Japan learned about IB for the first time.

1   What is International Baccalaureate?

The International Baccalaureate Organization (IB) is a nonprofit educational foundation headquartered in Geneva, Switzerland, and established in 1968. The organization has developed four international educational programs and authorizes schools to offer these programs as IB World Schools. The IB is not a school management organization; it is an accreditation body that works with schools to authorize them as IB World Schools and to award globally recognized qualifications. At present, there are over 5,000 IB World Schools in countries and regions around the world conducting educational activities in accordance with the IB's mission:

The International Baccalaureate aims to develop inquiring,

Fig. 5-1. The official IB logo licensed to accredited IB World Schools
Source: The International Baccalaureate, "Logos and programme models."
(https://www.ibo.org/digital-toolkit/logos-and-programme-models/, as viewed on December 30, 2020)

knowledgeable and caring young people who help to create a better and more peaceful world through intercultural understanding and respect.

To this end the organization works with schools, governments and international organizations to develop challenging programs of international education and rigorous assessment.

These programs encourage students across the world to become active, compassionate and lifelong learners who understand that other people, with their differences, can also be right[3].

Schools that support the IB's mission seek to qualify as an IB World School. Although they vary considerably in terms of the country of location, the number of students, cultural background, and the political, economic, and social contexts in which they operate, IB World Schools around the globe are moving in the same direction under the guidance of the philosophy of education expressed in this mission statement.

2   IB Learner Profile

The ten attributes of the IB Learner Profile express the IB's mission in terms of actions and the qualities of a young learner. The Learner's Profile and its descriptions are as follows[4]:

Inquirers: We nurture our curiosity, developing skills for inquiry and research. We know how to learn independently and with others. We learn with enthusiasm and sustain our love of learning throughout life.

Knowledgeable: We develop and use conceptual understanding, exploring knowledge across a range of disciplines. We engage with issues and ideas that have local and global significance.

Thinkers: We use critical and creative thinking skills to analyze and take responsible action on complex problems. We exercise initiative in making reasoned, ethical decisions.

Communicators: We express ourselves confidently and creatively in more than one language and in many ways. We collaborate effectively, listening carefully to the perspectives of other individuals and groups.

Principled: We act with integrity and honesty, with a strong sense of fairness and justice, and with respect for the dignity and rights of people everywhere. We take responsibility for our actions and their consequences.

Caring: We show empathy, compassion and respect. We have a commitment to service, and we act to make a positive difference in the lives of others and in the world around us.

Risk-takers: We approach uncertainty with forethought and determination; we work independently and cooperatively to explore new ideas and innovative strategies. We are resourceful and resilient in the face of challenges and change.

Balanced: We understand the importance of balancing different aspects of our lives-intellectual, physical, and emotional-to achieve well-being for ourselves and others. We recognize our interdependence with other people and with the world in which we live.

Fig. 5-2. IB Learner Profile poster
Source: International Baccalaureate. Brochures, flyers and posters
(https://www.ibo.org/digital-toolkit/brochures-flyers-and-posters/, as viewed on December 30, 2020)

Reflective: We thoughtfully consider the world and our own ideas and experience. We work to understand our strengths and weaknesses in order to support our learning and personal development.

The ten attributes of the IB Learner Profile "reflect the holistic nature of IB education. They highlight the importance of nurturing dispositions such as curiosity and empathy as well as developing knowledge and skills. They also highlight that along with cognitive development, IB programs are concerned with students' social, emotional, and physical well-being, and with ensuring that students respect themselves, others, and the world around them[5]."

Students in the IB program aim to acquire all of these ten attributes. The learner profile translates the philosophy espoused by the IB into an ideal vision of learning outcomes expected of students in the 21st century. The learner profile represents a long-term vision of education. It is a set of ideals that can inspire and motivate schools and teachers as well as focus their efforts[6]. This is consistent with Kuniyoshi Obara's view that "the purpose of Zenjin Education is to help students reach this complete state[7]." In addition, the goal of the IB is the development of international mindedness, which is accomplished by cultivating these ten attributes. In a sense, people with "international mindedness" can be described as the IB's version of the "globally competent human resources" sought by the Japanese government. Perhaps the IB Learner Profile, Zenjin Education, and the government's vision of "globally competent human resources" are all aiming toward the same goal.

3   Four IB Education Programs

The IB offers four education programs to realize its philosophy of education and to nurture its learners[8].

The Diploma Programme (DP) was the first program established by the IB in 1968 and is the most recognized IB program in Japan. The program is designed for students aged 16 to 19 and is offered in Japan as a two-year, university-preparatory program in the second and third years of high school. Along with six subject groups, the program features Theory of Knowledge (TOK) and the Extended Essay, which foster critical thinking abilities and research skills, and Creativity, Activity, Service (CAS), which emphasizes relationships with, and real-life experiences in, the community. Students take a standardized final examination marked out of 45 points and use their scores for university applications. The DP curriculum sets our certain requirements for learning contents, among other things.

Established in 1994, the Middle Years Programme (MYP) was the second program developed by the IB. The program is for students aged 11 to 16 and is generally offered in Japan as a five-year program from the sixth year of elementary school to the first year of high school. Comprising eight subject groups, interdisciplinary studies, and service activities in the community, the MYP aims to help students develop an understanding of society outside the existing curriculum framework. Some students advance to the DP after completing the MYP. The MPY curriculum framework sets no requirements for learning contents and allows schools to choose which language courses to offer.

The Primary Years Programme (PYP) was developed in 1997 for children aged 3 to 12 and is a curriculum framework that can be offered as a continuous program of at least two years at elementary schools, kindergartens, and nursery schools. The PYP is designed as a transdisciplinary study and offers

Table. 5-1. Features of IB Education Program

International education programs offered by the IB			
Philosophy of education	IB's mission		
Ideal learner profile	10 learner profiles		
Program	Primary Years Program	Middle Years Program	Diploma Program	Career-related Program
Abbreviation	PYP	MYP	DP	CP
Japanese name	Shoto kyoiku puroguramu	Chuto kyoiku puroguramu	Dipuroma puroguramu	Kyaria kanren puroguramu
Eligible age group	3-12	11-16	16-19	16-19
Aim	Development of international mindedness			
Curriculum and framework	Program of inquiry consisting of units of inquiry	8 subject groups Global context	6 subject groups and core Theory of Knowledge (TOK)	2 subject groups and a career-related study
Instruction method	6 approaches to teaching (Inquiry, concept, contexts, collaboration, inclusion, assessment)			
Learning method	5 categories of approaches to learning (Thinking, research, communication, social, and self-management skills)			
Assessment method	Internal assessment	Internal assessment Optional external assessment (eAssessment)	Internal assessment External assessment (final examination)	Internal assessment External assessment (final examination)
Experiential learning	Action	Service in Action (SA)	Creativity, Action, Service (CAS)	Service activities
Experiential learning	Exhibition	Community project/ personal project	Extended Essay (EE)	Reflective project

Source: Prepared by the author based on the curriculum models for respective programs (https://www.ibo.org/digital-toolkit/logos-and-programme-models/, as viewed on December 30, 2020)

a program of inquiry consisting of units of inquiry that aim to help children identify, think about, and communicate about social issues using familiar topics as starting points. Some students advance to the MPY after completing the PYP.

The Career-related Programme (CP) was established recently in 2012 and is designed for the same age groups as those in the DP. While the DP is designed for students advancing to university education, the CP addresses the needs of not just those planning to attend university but of a broad range of students by offering a program that combines two DP courses and a career-related study.

Thus, IB education, which began as a stand-alone DP program, is now available to students from ages 3 to 19 consistently across different countries and schools worldwide.

4   Teaching and Learning in IB Programs

Consistent approaches to teaching are employed in all four IB programs ("approaches to teaching")[9]:

1   Based on inquiry. A strong emphasis is placed on students finding their own information and constructing their own understandings.

2   Focused on conceptual understanding. Concepts are explored in order to both deepen disciplinary understanding and to help students make connections and transfer learning to new contexts.

3   Developed in local and global contexts. Teaching uses real-life contexts and examples, and students are encouraged to process new information by connecting it to their own experiences and to the world around them.

4   Focused on effective teamwork and collaboration. This includes promoting teamwork and collaboration between students, but also refers

to the collaborative relationship between teachers and students.

5　Designed to remove barriers to learning. Teaching is inclusive and values diversity. It affirms students' identities, and aims to create learning opportunities that enable every student to develop and pursue appropriate personal goals.

6　Informed by assessment. Assessment plays a crucial role in supporting, as well as measuring, learning. This approach also recognizes the crucial role of providing students with effective feedback.

IB education is designed to develop approaches to learning (ATL) and skills to "learn how to learn" with the aim of fostering lifelong learning[10].

1　Communication skills

2　Social skills

3　Self–management skills

4　Research skills

5　Thinking skills

At the heart of these approaches to teaching and learning is an emphasis on experiential learning, whereby students learn from their own actions and experiences. This experiential learning is incorporated as "action" initiated as a result of the learning process in PYP, "Service in Action" in MYP, "Creativity, Action, Service" in DP, and "Community and Service Activities" in CP[11].

5　IB and Tamagawa Academy

(1) Tamagawa Academy as a pioneer in IB education

Tamagawa Academy became an accredited IB World School when it was authorized by the IB to offer the MYP in 2009. In the following year, the school was also authorized to offer the DP. With the 2009 accreditation, Tamagawa

Academy became the second of so-called "Article 1 schools–schools recognized by Article 1 of the School Education Act–to be authorized as an IB World School in Japan. Since 1979, the Japanese government has recognized persons aged 18 or older holding IB qualifications as having academic abilities equivalent to or greater than those of high school graduates for the purpose of determining university admission eligibility under the School Education Act[12]. For many years, however, the only accredited IB World Schools in Japan were international schools. This is presumed to be due to the language barrier and the fact that it was not common practice for schools in Japan to be accredited by an external party.

The IB's official languages are English, French, and German. Thanks to the Dual Language Diploma Programme (commonly called "Japanese DP") launched through a collaboration between MEXT and the IB, many of the instruction guidelines issued by the IB have been translated into Japanese by now. When Tamagawa Academy was applying for IB accreditation, however, the school could only rely on the experience of Katoh Gakuen Gyoshu Junior & Senior High School, which was only slightly ahead of Tamagawa Academy as the first school to obtain the accreditation, and likely had to take a trial–and–error approach just to read and understand the application materials. In addition, Tamagawa was likely considered far ahead of its time when it adopted an ex-post evaluation process unfamiliar to schools in Japan called accreditation, in which educational institutions are certified or evaluated by an external body for quality assurance purposes. To be accredited as an IB World School, a school must understand the accreditation requirements described in a guideline called "Program Standards and Practices," identify the applicable programs, visualize and document them, and submit them as evidence showing that the school meets the requirements. This process requires a considerable amount of time and effort. It is a testament to a "willingness to do everything possible for education," an ideal espoused by Kuniyoshi Obara, that Tamagawa Academy was able to pursue and eventually earn IB accreditation despite these obstacles. Today, a total of 45 Article 1 schools are accredited as IB World Schools and offer one or more of the four programs[13]. No doubt Tamagawa Academy's pioneering spirit served as a good model and opened a path to many schools.

(2) Close ties between IB education and Tamagawa's Zenjin Education

The International Baccalaureate Organization emerged out of concerns shared by international schools around the world[14]. They convened for an international school conference in Geneva in 1962 to discuss common issues and agreed to develop globally recognized high school graduation requirements, which they called "International Baccalaureate." In the same year, Kurt Hahn, a German educator, founded Atlantic College, the first IB World School in the United Kingdom[15]. It is important to remember that Kurt Hahn is the founder of Round Square, an international association of private schools of which Tamagawa Academy is a member[16]. Hahn later contributed to the development of outdoor learning[17], which became the cornerstone of Tamagawa Adventure Program (TAP). This is just one of the many historical ties between Tamagawa Academy and the IB. Further, the biggest influencers on the teachers who developed the plan for the IB were John Dewey, who founded the University of Chicago Laboratory School in 1896 as an experiment in progressive education, and Alexander Neill, who founded Summerhill School in 1921 to pursue the philosophy of free learning[18]. It was around the same time that Kuniyoshi Obara founded Tamagawa Academy to implement Zenjin Education. That these educators all founded schools to practice their ideal vision of education and promoted educational reform is yet another connection between the IB and Tamagawa, and it was only inevitable, not coincidental, that Tamagawa Academy became the second Article 1 school to be accredited as an IB World School.

Tamagawa's Zenjin Education and IB share many similarities in their education philosophies, learner profiles, and approaches to teaching and

Fig. 5–3. Tamagawa brand pictogram
Source: Tamagawa University & Academy,
"Tamagawa Daigaku ni tsuite"
(https://www.tamagawa.jp/introduction/brand/,
as viewed on December 30, 2020)

Fig. 5–4. The IB Learner Profile logo
Source: International Baccalaureate, "Logos
and programme models."
(https://www.ibo.org/digital-toolkit/logos-and-
programme-models/, as viewed on December
30, 2020)

learning. First, Tamagawa has a pictogram embodying the motifs of the six values taught by Zenjin Education, namely truth, goodness, beauty, holiness, health, and wealth, the twelve precepts of education pursued to realize these ideals, and the appealing and distinguishing features of Tamagawa. Like the IB's mission statement and learner profile, the pictogram is more than just a slogan displayed above the blackboard in the classrooms. The ideas represented by the pictogram are reinforced in all kinds of educational settings and serve as a guidepost to which the school, teachers, and learners from elementary to undergraduate and graduate school return to find their way as they pursue their activities. The pictogram demonstrates that Tamagawa has an unwavering commitment to its beliefs; it allows the school to convey the beliefs in a multi-dimensional, multifaceted, and holistic approach using characters and images and to ensure that they reach people's heart in an organic, coherent way.

The IB Learner Profile represents the vision of a learner the IB seeks to nurture through its programs. This learner profile, however, did not exist when the IB was founded. The original learner profile was called the PYP learner profile. IB Learner Profile was first introduced as the "PYP student profile" when the PYP program was established in 1997 and was later adopted in all IB programs in 2006[19]. The IB and Tamagawa are also similar in that the IB Learner Profile, an essential part of IB education today, originated in elementary school education, and Tamagawa Academy started out as elementary and middle schools and not as a university-affiliated school. In addition, the only change made to the PYP student profile when it was changed to the IB Learner Profile was the addition of the "balanced" learner. This attribute used to be called the "healthy" learner in the PYP profile. Even with the addition of the "balanced" learner, however, the new profile highlighted the "importance of balancing different aspects of our lives——intellectual, physical, and emotional[20]." In doing so, perhaps the IB shared the same aspirations as Kuniyoshi Obara, who considered "health" to be one of the six values necessary for the optimal development of the human personality, noting that "a person is made up of mind and body" and "good health is needed to preserve life and to serve the mind for the realization of mental activities[21]."

Whenever I come across the "balanced" learner profile, I am reminded of a passage of the Theory of Zenjin Education which reads: "A Tamagawa student is capable of carrying a manure bucket as well as playing the piano, sweeping floor as well as performing the tea ceremony and flower arrangement, sewing a rag as well as tailoring a silk kimono, clearing the gutter as well as singing the nineth symphony, chopping wood as well as drawing, and using the abacus as well as reciting the Buddhist chant[22]." In the IB context, perhaps IB students can be described as those who pursue a self-directed inquiry but also enjoy working with others, make an evidence-based proposal but also act on their own, think in a specific, local context but also from as a broad, global perspective, maintain their linguistic and cultural identity while respecting other people's values, ask many questions but also attempt to solve problems, and value all subject areas without distinguishing between arts and science or core and practical subjects but are also proficient at integrating and reconstructing information in interdisciplinary studies. This balanced approach, shared by Zenjin Education and IB, encourages learners to

Fig. 5–5. PYP student profile
Source: International Baccalaureate Organization, History of the Primary Years Programme,
International Baccalaureate Organization, 2013, p. 28.

move beyond binary oppositions, urges them to develop higher-order thinking skills, and invites them to engage in deeper learning.

The fact that the IB changed the PYP student profile to the IB Learner Profile, and did not call it the "young student profile," is highly significant. In IB education, teachers also grow as learners[23]. The IB Learner Profile captures not just children but all stakeholders, including teachers and parents, and presents the qualities of an ideal learner applicable to all of them. It serves as a map that children and adults can turn to when they get lost in their lifelong journey in pursuit of international mindedness[24]. Kuniyoshi Obara also defined "Zenjin" as an ideal achieved when a learner reaches "the complete state[25]." Those who grew up in the hills of Tamagawa seek to realize these values even after graduating from Tamagawa. I have encountered many such Tamagawa graduates. Because Tamagawa Academy's Zenjin Education and IB education have well-defined goals, their curriculums can be developed using the "backward design" approach. Tamagawa and the IB can also manage their curriculums so that their philosophies slowly permeate every hour and every activity, not just the specified hours of educational activities. For those who are raised in Tamagawa and IB education, these philosophies are more than just teaching and learning methods; they evolve into a way of life.

As a reflection of their commitment to the constant pursuit of ideals, IB teachers regularly participate in workshops hosted by the IB with the aim of improving the quality of class instruction. During workshops, teachers are expected to reflect on their performance. In addition, IB's student unit planner include a "reflection" section[26]. The IB Learner Profile not only translates educational philosophies into attributes, but also offer a common language teachers can use when they review their class lessons and education activities . to ensure a deeper reflection process. The IB Learner Profile is different from the PYP student profile. In the theory of Zenjin Education, Kuniyoshi Obara noted that good teachers are "those who improve their skills and make progress with students." He describes his experience of learning from "Adolph Diesterweg, the director of the first teacher training school in Germany" that "only those teachers who continue to make progress have the right to teach others[27]." Tamagawa and the IB share and pursue the same vision of teaching-that education is not possible without teachers who continue to learn from their students.

One of the attributes of the IB Learner Profile is the "inquirer." Inquiry-based learning, which is one of the characteristics of IB education, is encouraged in all settings, but not necessary in pursuit of knowledge. Based on the premise that students are already equipped with knowledge, as recognized in constructivist teaching, the IB's inquiry-based learning provides students with learning experiences that let them draw on the knowledge they already possess and creates opportunities to reflect and integrate what they have learned. Students are encouraged to continually develop and understand their knowledge and learn how to transfer and apply their knowledge to a broader context[28]. The object of inquiry is what is called the concept of knowledge development, "a common principle students can apply to understand the world and achieve success in life beyond the framework of learning and school education[29]." To understand this concept, students identify the problem and build solutions using ATL, which are a set of learning skills. While exploring for answers to questions posed by teachers, students ask their own questions to delve deeper into their inquiry. Through this process, students achieve a lasting conceptual understanding[30]. Similarly, Zenjin Education is rooted in constructivist ideas: "Knowledge is gathered and built together. Rather than just copying knowledge, each person assembles, constructs, and creates knowledge[31]." In the IB's inquiry–based education, to put it in Obara's words, "teachers instill in their students a passion for learning, help them learn how to delve deep into their studies, and train their inquiry skills[32]." Further, Obara's view that "questions drive a search for truth" and his subsequent recommendation for "independent research[33]" are consistent with the IB's requirement of a major project in the programs, such as the personal project in the MYP and the Extended Essay in the DP. It is unfortunate that some schools refer to "independent research" in name only without providing any guidance on how to approach the research. At Tamagawa Academy, in contrast, Obara's "independent research" still remains as a learning tool. The school's annual exhibition of inquiry-based projects is a spectacular event worth seeing.

The term "action" is used to describe the IB Learner Profile attributes of "thinker," "principled," and "caring." Along with inquiry, action and reflection are the cornerstones of IB education. This means "a constructivist approach is taken to promote open classrooms where different views and perspectives are respected through an interplay between asking (inquiry), doing (action), and thinking (reflection) [34]." IB learners "take action at home, as well as in classrooms, schools, communities, and the broader world," and "action" includes "service learning" (learning through community service activities). A dynamic learning experience consisting of the three components of inquiry, action, and reflection——none of which can be accomplished through units of learning——allows a community of learners to tackle complex, global problems[35]. This is none other than *rosaku*, which is a component of Zenjin Education. Perhaps what one attains through "hardships, creation, experience, trials, thinking, and action[36]" matches what one gains from the interplay of inquiry, action, and reflection in IB education. When we learn about the conflicts and disputes, both large and small, occurring in modern society, we have a responsibility to take action to help find a solution instead of just sitting on the knowledge. According to the IB, we build a better, more peaceful world by fulfilling the responsibility of taking action on the knowledge we have gained. Of the six values closely related to Rosaku Education, "wealth" is one of the resources acquired through experience. Sharing wealth, in my view, will contribute to a more well-rounded development of an individual as well as the advancement of public welfare. I am reminded of this ideal vision of humanity every morning when I enter the school campus and see Tamagawa's motto, "Be the first to take on the most difficult, unpleasant, painful and unprofitable work in life with a smile," and a fountain so clear that it cleanses your soul.

6   And from Now Onward

Although IB is a product of a different time and place, the terms "*zenjin*" and "*zenjin kyoiku*," which are Japanese translations of "whole person" and "whole-person education," are used frequently in IB literature. In fact, the IB started translating instruction guidelines and other materials into Japanese in the summer of 2008, anticipating the widespread adoption of the IB programs in Japan. Members of the translation project included Kyoko Bernard, who was then an associate professor at Tamagawa University Research Institute and the IB Asia Pacific regional representative for Japan and Korea; Professor Curtis Beaverford, who is now responsible for the training of IB educators at the Graduate School of Education, Tamagawa University; Quincy Kameda, an instructor at Tamagawa University Research Institute; and myself. The other two members are my colleagues currently responsible for IB educator training at Tamagawa University's Graduate School of Education. At the time, both worked for different employers, but were invited to join the project with the other members to translate key IB terms. One of the central topics of debate was whether it was appropriate to use "*zenjin kyoiku*," a term used to describe Tamagawa education, as an IB term. Fearing that the term was too closely associated with Tamagawa, we spent considerable time searching for a different translation. But we could not find any appropriate terms and adopted "*zenjin kyoiku*" in the end. To this date, the term "*zenjin kyoiku*" remains in the translations of IB guidelines. I find it incredible——even moving——that not only do Zenjin Education and IB education match perfectly but that they found each other even though they are from different times, countries, and languages.

The relationship between Tamagawa Academy's Zenjin Education and the IB continues to evolve. It began when Tamagawa Academy (middle and high schools) was authorized to offer the MYP in 2009. In 2010, Tamagawa became an accredited IB DP World School and began offering IB-based AO-type admission to Tamagawa University. Then in 2014, Tamagawa began offering at its Graduate School of Education an IB research program, which allows students to earn eligibility for the IB Educator Certificate. In addition, the IB class, which is currently a subordinate body of Tamagawa's middle and high schools, is scheduled be reorganized as an IB vision in the spring of 2021. Further, preparations are underway to launch an online version of the IB educator training course that lets people take the course anywhere, even while remaining in their jobs. These are initiatives of a "risk-taker," one of the attributes of the IB Learner Profile, and are a testament to Tamagawa Academy's "intrinsic flexibility[37]." It is my hope that, by taking school-wide initiatives that highlight the close ties between the school and the IB, Tamagawa Academy will continue to play a central role in the community of learners that strive to create a better, more peaceful world through Zenjin Education and that it will continue to uphold the philosophy of the founder to preserve and further develop its identity.

Notes

1) The Council for Promotion of Global Human Resource Development, "Global Jinzai Ikusei Suishin Kaigi Chukan Matome, June 22, 2011," p. 7 (https://www.kantei.go.jp/jp/singi/global/110622chukan_matome.pdf, as viewed on December 30, 2020).

2) Ibid., p. 11. This target was subsequently revised to "200 or more IB World Schools by FY2020 (101 schools as of FY2016, including candidate schools)" in "Mirai Toshi Senryaku 2018-'Society 5.0,' 'Data Kudogata Shakai' e no Henkaku" (cabinet decision on June 15, 2018).

3) International Baccalaureate Organization, "International Baccalaureate (IB) no Kyoiku Towa?," 2019 (Japanese translation of the English original entitled "What is an IB education?" published in November 2019).

4) International Baccalaureate Organization, "International Baccalaureate (IB) no Kyoiku Towa?," 2017 (Japanese translation of the English original entitled "What is an IB education?" published in August 2013, revised in June 2015 and April 2017).

5) International Baccalaureate Organization, "International Baccalaureate (IB) no Kyoiku Towa?," 2017, p. 4.

6) International Baccalaureate Organization, *IB Learner Profile Booklet,* International Baccalaureate Organization, 2006, p. 1.

7) Kuniyoshi Obara, *Kuniyoshi Obara's Theory of Zenjin Education* (English/Japanese side-by-side translation of *Zenjin Kyoiku Ron*), edited by Yoshiaki Obara, English translation by Douglas Trelfa, Tamagawa University Press, 2003, p. 43.

8) International Baccalaureate Organization, "Programmes" (https://www.ibo.org/programmes/, as viewed on December 30, 2020).

9) International Baccalaureate Organization, "International Baccalaureate (IB) no Kyoiku Towa?," 2019, p. 7.

10) International Baccalaureate Organization, "International Baccalaureate (IB) no Kyoiku Towa?," 2019, p. 8.

11) International Baccalaureate Organization,"Ikkan Shita Kokusai Kyoiku ni Mukete," 2014, p. 33 (Japanese translation of the English original entitled "Towards a Continuum of International Education," published in September 2008).

12) Ministry of Education, Culture, Sports, Science and Technology IB Kyoiku Suishin Consortium, "Nihon ni Okeru IB Kyoiku" (https://ibconsortium.mext.go.jp/ib-japan/, as viewed on December 30, 2020).

13) International Baccalaureate Organization, "Find an IB World School" (https://www.ibo.org/programmes/find-an-ib-school/, as viewed on December 30, 2020).

14) Alec D. Peterson. *Schools Across Frontiers: The Story of the International Baccalaureate and the United World Colleges*, Open Court pub. Co., 1987, pp. 15-17.

15) International Baccalaureate Organization, "The history of the IB" (https://www.ibo.org/globalassets/digital-toolkit/presentations/1711-presentation-history-of-the-ib-en.pdf, as

viewed on December 30, 2020).

16) Round Square, "RS History and Heritage" (https://www.roundsquare.org/being-round-square/who/our-history-and-kurt-hahn/, as viewed on December 30, 2020).

17) Outward Bound, *HISTORY* (https://www.outwardbound.net/history as viewed on December 30, 2020).

18) International Baccalaureate Organization, "The History of the IB" (https://www.ibo.org/globalassets/digital-toolkit/presentations/1711-presentation-history-of-the-ib-en.pdf, as viewed on December 30, 2020), p. 4.

19) International Baccalaureate Organization, *IB learner profile booklet*, International Baccalaureate Organization, p. 1.

20) International Baccalaureate Organization, *IB learner profile booklet*, International Baccalaureate Organization, p. 28.

21) Kuniyoshi Obara, *Kuniyoshi Obara's Theory of Zenjin Education* (English/Japanese side-by-side translation of *Zenjin Kyoiku Ron*), edited by Yoshiaki Obara, English translation by Douglas Trelfa, Tamagawa University Press, 2003, p. 27.

22) Kuniyoshi Obara, *Kuniyoshi Obara's Theory of Zenjin Education* (English/Japanese side-by-side translation of *Zenjin Kyoiku Ron*), edited by Yoshiaki Obara, English translation by Douglas Trelfa, Tamagawa University Press, 2003, p. 117.

23) International Baccalaureate Organization, "Ikkan Shita Kokusai Kyoiku ni Mukete," 2014, p. 27.

24) International Baccalaureate Organization, *IB learner profile booklet*, International Baccalaureate Organization, p. 2

25) Kuniyoshi Obara, *Kuniyoshi Obara's Theory of Zenjin Education* (English/Japanese side-by-side translation of *Zenjin Kyoiku Ron*), edited by Yoshiaki Obara, English translation by Douglas Trelfa, Tamagawa University Press, 2003, p. 43.

26) International Baccalaureate Organization, "MYP-Gensoku kara Jissen e," 2016, p. 66 (Japanese translation of the English original entitled "MYP: From Principles into Practices," issued in May 2014 and revised in September 2014).

27) Kuniyoshi Obara, *Kuniyoshi Obara's Theory of Zenjin Education* (English/Japanese side-by-side translation of *Zenjin Kyoiku Ron*), edited by Yoshiaki Obara, English translation by Douglas Trelfa, Tamagawa University Press, 2003, p. 129.

28) International Baccalaureate Organization, "MYP-Gensoku kara Jissen e," 2016, p. 83.

29) Ibid., p. 18.

30) Ibid., pp. 73-74.

31) Kuniyoshi Obara, *Kuniyoshi Obara's Theory of Zenjin Education* (English/Japanese side-by-side translation of *Zenjin Kyoiku Ron*), edited by Yoshiaki Obara, English translation by Douglas Trelfa, Tamagawa University Press, 2003, p. 55.

32) Ibid., p. 51.

33) Ibid., p. 125.

34) International Baccalaureate Organization, "MYP-Gensoku kara Jissen e," 2016, p. 13.

35) International Baccalaureate Organization, "MYP-Gensoku kara Jissen e," 2016, pp. 13-14.

36) Kuniyoshi Obara, *Kuniyoshi Obara's Theory of Zenjin Education* (English/Japanese side-by-side translation of *Zenjin Kyoiku Ron*), edited by Yoshiaki Obara, English translation by Douglas Trelfa, Tamagawa University Press, 2003, p. 106.

37) Jeremy Breaden & Roger Goodman., *Family-run Universities in Japan*, Oxford University Press, 2020, p. 6.

Chapter 6

Round Square and Zenjin Education
—— A Focus on IDEALS

Introduction

Since its founding, Tamagawa Academy has been dedicated to promoting education for international understanding, proclaiming it as one of the twelve precepts of education. As of April 2021, Tamagawa Academy has 15 elementary and middle school affiliated campuses in 8 countries and send and accept around 300 students to and from schools outside Japan every year. In 2005, Tamagawa also became the first Japanese school to join Round Square, an international network of schools. This chapter looks at Round Square to reflect on the significance of education for international understanding, which Tamagawa has championed over the years under the guidance of Zenjin Education principles.

1   Kurt Hahn and the History of Round Square

Round Square is a global association of schools that promote character education built around IDEALS (Internationalism, Democracy, Environmentalism, Adventure, Leadership, and Service) and implement a broad range of international exchange activities, experiential learning, problem-based learning, and other programs to realize this educational philosophy. As of 2020, about 200 schools from 55 countries are members of Round Square. Tamagawa Academy became the first school in Japan to be admitted to Round Square in 2005.

(1) Kurt Hahn's philosophy of education

The German educator Kurt Hahn (1886-1974) was closely involved in the founding of Round Square. Hahn founded Salem School in Germany and Gordonstoun School in Scotland. The two schools played a major role in the establishment of Round Square.

The early 20th century saw the emergence of a new education movement that was critical of the conventional teacher-centered teaching focused on rote learning and that advocated a student-centered, and well-rounded education conducted in a rich natural environment. This movement is said to have started with the founding of Abbotsholme School in England by Cecil Reddie in 1889. Abbotsholme School[1] was established "in the countryside, free of the negative influences associated with the city, in an effort to form a community with a school dedicated to not just the development intellectual and physical abilities but a whole-person approach to education and one big family of teachers and students[2]."

Against the background of this new education movement, Hahn established Salem School as a country boarding school in Germany in 1920. The goal of the country boarding school, according to Hermann Lietz, was to "educate the children entrusted to the school into becoming German youths who are healthy and strong in body and mind, who are physically practically, scientifically, and artistically capable, who have a clear and sharp mind, who are compassionate, who are courageous and highly motivated, and who are agreeable and independent in personality[3]." Hahn also founded

Gordonstoun School in 1934 in Scotland. Hahn argued that children needed to learn about life, and, for this reason, it was necessary to provide them with various stimulating and challenging experiences. He also stressed the importance of playing leadership roles and participating in service activities to develop courage and compassion, which are vital qualities in life. In 1941, Hahn established Outward Bound School (OBS), which was the world's first organization dedicated to outdoor education and was responsible for developing Gordonstoun School's outdoor education programs[4]. In 1962, Hahn founded Atlantic College, the first United World College, which greatly contributed to the establishment of the International Baccalaureate (IB) in 1968.

The German philosopher Otto Friedrich Bollnow described the educators who played a leading role in the new education movement as follows: "...... they were a group of great educators, and these men–namely Hermann Lietz, Paul Geheeb, Gustav Wyneken, and Kurt Hahn–freed education from its rigid form in Germany by founding country boarding schools. They were essentially from the same generation, Kuniyoshi Obara is perhaps the last of this group[5]." This comment indicates that Zenjin Education envisioned by Obara and the country boarding school education established by Hahn were heading in the same direction in that they both liberated education from its rigid conventions.

(2) History of Round Square

In 1953, a devastating earthquake struck Cephalonia, one of the Ionian Islands in Greece. The following year, teachers and students from Gordonstoun School of Scotland and Anavryta School of Greece responded to a call by Salem School of Germany to join a building project to help reconstruction and recovery, spurred on to action by Hahn's philosophy of education. The great success of the building project on the Island of Cephalonia led these schools to discuss the need to continue their collaborative activities. Over time, their discussions evolved into a plan to establish an international network of schools sharing a commitment to Hahn's philosophy of education. In 1966, the headmasters of eight schools gathered at Salem School in Germany to celebrate Hahn's 80th birthday and agreed to move forward with preparations. In 1967, the first conference was held at Gordonstoun and was attended by the headmasters and board chairs of Anavryta School (Greece), Salem (Germany), Gordonstoun (Scotland), Box Hill School (England), Battisborough School (England), The Athenian School (U.S.), and Hahn. Immediately thereafter, Aiglon College of Switzerland also joined as a member[6].

Initially, it was proposed to name this school network the "Hahn Schools Conference." Hahn, however, was opposed to this, and the network was named "Round Square Conference," after the name of Gordonstoun's school building, "Round Square[7]" (Fig. 6-1), where the first conference took place.

Later, Round Square garnered the support of many schools around the world for its philosophies and activities and grew into a network of 220 schools in about 55 countries.

Fig. 6-1. Gordonstoun's Round Square
Source: Round Square Headquarters.

2 IDEALS and Zenjin Education

The philosophy of education of Round Square is centered on six IDEALS, namely Internationalism, Democracy, Environmentalism, Adventure, Leadership, and Service [8].

(1) Internationalism

Round Square schools aim to promote international understanding by encouraging students to develop a spirit of internationalism. Exchange activities are organized between students and teachers from schools around the world to foster the value of discovering and embracing the similarities and differences between themselves and people from other countries and regions, while celebrating their own identities, cultures, traditions, and heritages. In recent years, the growth of digital communication across geographical boundaries has contributed to this mutual understanding. By encouraging young people from different backgrounds to develop skills and attitudes accepted globally through a variety of exchange activities and collaborative projects, Round Square schools deepen international understanding and promote the spirit of internationalism, thereby contributing to world peace.

Obara said: "'The earth is our home.' This is what Dr. Werner Zimmermann of Switzerland said when he visited Japan for the second time in 1949. Living in the space age today, I am once again reminded of his words. To make the earth a home for all people, we must realize a true world peace. ...... The classroom is not the only place for education. Education can take place anywhere on the planet, anywhere in the universe. We have promoted international exchanges not only among university and school students but also among teachers [9]." Further, Obara noted as follows: "What we want nations around the world to do is to display their characteristics and strengths more. If they do that, they will make this world that much more vibrant[10]." He also stated: "Adopt a broad international perspective. I would like you to have the open-mindedness to 'gain extensive knowledge' when you interact with people from not just our neighboring countries but all around the world. Be friendly to them, so that they will be friendly to you[11]." The adoption of "international education" as one of Tamagawa Academy's twelve precepts of education also illustrates that Tamagawa Academy and Round Square share a respect for internationalism.

(2) Democracy

Round Square schools encourage students to develop a spirit of democracy. This means to think about equality, fairness, and justice and to embrace freedom of thought and speech. A spirit of democracy also means to volunteer to do what is right by sharing sufficient information and engaging in effective discussions while understanding public duty and the needs of others. To this end, students learn to be responsible, independent, and proactive. During international conferences and other events hosted by Round Square, students from different cultural backgrounds around the world participate in the process of working together to identify issues, find solutions based on discussions, make a decision on how to execute the solution after repeated debates and discussions, and finally take action. This experience leads to the development of democratic, global citizens of tomorrow.

Obara wrote about democracy as follows: "There is an urgent need for politicians, citizens, and educators to understand that our democracy must be founded on religion, God, compassion, and love. Never think of democracy as a superficial, legislative system[12]." Further, Obara said: "Our education is about the extraordinary conflicts, oppositions, and contradictions between individualism and socialism, nationalism and globalism, idealism and

realism, and liberalism and legalism. And yet this is the human condition."
He also urged opposing sides to be "cooperative, conciliatory, agreeable,
compromising, and accommodating[13]."

These words seem to reveal Obara's view that democracy is not a simple
decision-making process based on majority rule, but a broader action process
for seeking truth, goodness, beauty, and holiness. And his idea aligns with the
spirit of democracy advocated by Round Square.

(3) Environmentalism

Round Square schools encourage their students to develop a
spirit of environmentalism: to understand our place on the planet, the
various forces that shape our environment, and the impact we have on
the environment and to take practical action in tackling environmental
problems. By understanding the beauty, complexity, and vulnerability
of the environment, students learn to appreciate the environment. They
recognize, think about, and take action on the importance of building
sustainable communities and protecting the future of the planet.

"I want a chapel in a corner of the forest. Church bells ring in the morning
and evening. We gather in the parish hall before dawn, guided by the faint,
mysterious light of the candles glowing in the dim surroundings. There, we
pray in silence. One of us reads the scripture. A choir sings at the deep end
of the hall. In the evening, we sing 'Lord, I give myself to You again today'
and give our gratitude to God. Quietly, quietly. At a chapel in the forest. Or
by a stream. Seated at the root of a tree. This large piece of land we were
lucky to have acquired, along with birdsong, is perfect for that. How fortunate
we are! [14]" Obara considered such natural environment to be an ideal place
for education. "There, I want us to grow our own rice, barley, potatoes, and
vegetables, if possible." What was important for him was to "not to make profits
but to truly understand ...... the virtue of a grain of rice, the value of a leaf, the

nobleness of sweat, the joy of sprouting, the meaning of soil, the beauty of nature, and the preciousness of God's grace[15]." Rosaku Education taught in the natural environment of Tamagawa Academy raises awareness about the environment and inspires students to create a sustainable society.

(4) Adventure

For Round Square, a spirit of adventure is displayed by those who push themselves beyond their personal limits and build self-esteem through trial and error and successful experiences. To promote a spirit of adventure, Round Square schools offer activities that engage students to take risks and step outside their comfort zone. Students are encouraged to demonstrate courage in all settings, face a challenge, and persevere to accomplish the challenge despite unexpected situations or fear of failure. While a spirit of adventure may be effectively developed in outdoor activities, a range of other opportunities both within and outside the curriculum, such as public speaking, a performance, a mental challenge, or a new hobby or skill, allow students to set and work toward personal goals. A sense of adventure is a quality and skill necessary for the pioneers of life.

Since its founding, Tamagawa Academy has encouraged students to rise to the challenge. It was none other than the spirit of adventure that led Obara to build a school on those hills and start his education. This pioneering spirit lives on to this day at Tamagawa.

Tamagawa Academy's initiative to incorporate skiing into its education programs is also in keeping with this spirit of adventure. "A night train departing Ueno. The destination, I am told, is a place called Numajiri in Fukushima Prefecture. When I awake, I am at Kawageta Station! A powerful blizzard! There are no words to describe how incredible this is! Flower petals dancing in sync like an orchestra. It is as though the forest, farms, electric poles, and houses are all fighting the snow! Having grown up in Satsuma, I have never seen anything like it. This is it! This is it! I am going to throw it on the kids in Tokyo! [16]" Obara saw the value of skiing, which would enable students to strive for their goals in severe blizzards and train their mental resilience and skills. It is a well-known story in the history of skiing in Japan that, upon hearing a student say, "If I have to learn, I want to learn from the very best," Obara invited Hannes Schneider, the world's pioneer of Alpine skiing, from Austria.

In addition, Tamagawa Adventure Program (TAP) was launched in 2000 (see Chapter 7). TAP is Tamagawa's original program developed based on Project Adventure (PA), a derivative of the Outward Bound School (OBS) in the United Kingdom. The OBS was also founded by Kurt Hahn. The adventure education programs of Tamagawa Academy and Round Square share the same roots and are working toward the same goal of fostering a spirit of adventure in young students.

(5) Leadership

For Round Square, successful leaders are driven by personal responsibility, justice, and compassion and are capable of developing strategy and taking action to help their teams succeed. To this end, leaders must acquire skills such as the ability to analyze the current situation, decision-making, persuasion and negotiation, and creative problem solving. By gathering ideas about the problem at hand, setting direction, sharing a vision with others, and taking dynamic action with humility and confidence, leaders can inspire team members and lead them to feel valued for their contributions and take pride in their efforts and achievements.

Round Square schools provide students with training to acquire leadership skills in conferences, service projects, and a range of other activities that offer students opportunities to plan, manage, and reflect on projects.

Obara cherished the following passage of Chapter 5 of The Gospel of Matthew: "You are the salt of the earth. You are the light of the world." Yoshiaki Obara, the current president and headmaster of Tamagawa Academy, also quotes this scripture during high school graduation ceremonies to help them navigate life after high school. While Tamagawa has aimed to develop the world's leaders through Zenjin Education, the leadership roles each student is expected to play are grounded on the teachings of these scriptures.

In addition, Obara taught that teachers themselves must take leadership roles in society to develop leadership in students. He said: "An educator must be society's leader, admonitor, and bellwether. A teacher is expected to grow and acquire the skills and abilities needed to guide the politicians and citizens of the time[17]."

(6) Service

Round Square schools nurture a spirit of service and the ability to act, encouraging students to take responsible social action that is genuine and innovative. To this end, schools offer students opportunities to use familiar settings to gain a deep understanding of challenges and issues faced by individuals and communities across the world. Voluntary service activities allow individual students to engage with the local community and grow. To facilitate this growth, Round Square offers global service projects, bring together students from member schools in different countries to engage in *rosaku* in intercultural teams. Round Square's annual global conferences always include in the schedule a "Service Day," which offers students opportunities to take part in a range of service activities.

Obara said: "As Pestalozzi demonstrated by his own action, Rosaku Education is at the heart of education. As represented by the character '*ro*,' engaging in sweat-drenching physical work is a joy, pride, and duty for all of us. '*Saku*' in '*rosaku*' does not mean just work or chore. It means creative work[18]." This *rosaku*, according to Obara, "fosters virtues such as honesty, tolerance, discipline, frugality, cooperation, friendship, loyalty, bravery, liveliness, fighting spirit, independence and initiative, service, and gratitude[19]." Rosaku Education, which is at the root of Tamagawa education, nurtures a spirit of service and a heart of gratitude. Tamagawa Academy's motto, carved on the school gatepost, embodies the very spirit of service championed by Round Square: "Be the first to take on the most difficult, unpleasant, painful and unprofitable work in life with a smile."

3 Attributes and Skills Supporting IDEALS

(1) Round Square Discoveries

About half a century has passed since Round Square was born as a network of schools. Many Round Square member schools have offered a range of activities grounded on the principles of IDEALS. Recently, teachers from member schools and members of the Round Square headquarters have held many discussions and defined 12 specific attributes and skills (Table 6-1) that students should acquire based on IDEALS in the coming era (2015). These are called Round Square Discoveries[20]. Member schools offer education activities and exchanges between member schools to enable students to develop these discoveries.

Table. 6-1. 12 items of Roundsquare Discovery

Communication Skills
Students develop mutual understanding by listening to each other's ideas and sharing their own through a mutually respectful exchange. In today's digital society, developing the ability to effectively utilize a range of community tools is essential.
Inquisitiveness
Students make continuous inquiries in pursuit of truth. Develop interests, investigate, ask questions, hypothesize, challenge assumptions, judge in a critical but constructive manner, and tackle issues even when there is no single right answer. The journey of inquiry is a learning process in itself.
Appreciation of Diversity
Developing the generosity and strength to embrace all individuals regardless of nationality, race or ethnicity, culture, religion, socio-economic status, impairment, or sexual orientation allows students to overcome discrimination and prejudice and build a fair society.
Ability to Solve Problems
The ability to think logically, critically, and creatively to tackle a problem and find the best possible solutions given the circumstances.
Sense of Responsibility
Students recognize their moral obligations to themselves, others, their community and society in general and fulfill the obligations with a sense of justice. They recognize, correct, and learn from mistakes, accepting accountability for their actions and taking pride in personal effort and performance.
Commitment to Sustainability
Students learn to conserve, reuse, and recycle energy resources responsibly to repair their community and the planet and seek to develop a sustainable society, while developing an awareness of the environment and an understanding of nature, energy, waste, food, and pollution, among other things.
Tenacity
Students develop the ability to persevere when confronted with a challenge, learn from the process, and try again.
Courage
Courage is the ability and willingness to confront fear, pain, danger, and uncertainty. Courage enables students to do "what is right."
Self-awareness
Students cultivate their understanding of themselves, their personality, values, attitudes, strengths and weaknesses, as well as their environment and culture. By doing so, they develop better decision-making skills that result in better interactions with the world.
Teamwork Skills
Students recognize the strengths and weaknesses of team members and combine individual attributes, skills and talents to enhance team performance.
Inventiveness
Inventiveness means the thinking, creativity, imagination, and innovation used to produce new ideas. Inventiveness allows students to take a flexible approach to solve problems.
Compassion
Compassion must underlie the effort to promote internationalism, environmentalism, and a sustainable society. Sharing and empathizing with another person's feelings, perspectives, and opinions leads to a deeper understanding for the experiences of others.

Source: Prepared by the author based on Round Square website (http://www.round squre.org,as viewed on April 30,2021).

(2) Activities at Tamagawa

Since being admitted to Round Square as the first member school from Japan in 2005, Tamagawa Academy has sent students each year to represent the school at the Junior Conference, which is attended by Grade 9 students, and the International Conference, participated by Grade 10 to 12 students. For about a week, students engage in a range of discussions on what they can do to create a better world, take part in adventures, and experience service activities. Many Tamagawa students have also participated in service projects organized by Round Square member schools in various parts of the world. Tamagawa has worked with other member schools to organize international exchange activities, sending and accepting many students to and from other schools. Classes and programs are offered to work on inquiry-based tasks with those students.

Tamagawa's Round Square Steering Committee, made up of students in Grades 9 to 12, engages in activities with a systematic approach. Comprising about a hundred members, the committee organizes "Tamagawa Conference," the school's version of Round Square Conference, in an international conference format. Tamagawa also hosts welcome receptions for exchange students, engages in online exchanges with partner schools, and organize a variety of service activities, including collecting and sending used clothes and school supplies to developing countries.

Through these activities, Tamagawa helps students develop the qualities and skills promoted by Round Square Discoveries as well as the spirit of IDEALS. In Tamagawa's words, this leads to the nurturing of *"zenjin-sei"*, or well-roundedness.

Notes

1) Abbotsholme School is a Round Square member school and has a relationship with Tamagawa Academy today.

2) Tetsunari Ishibashi, "Shin Kyoiku Undo no Tenkai to Tamagawa Gakuen no Kyoiku," 2013.

3) Tetsunari Ishibashi, "Shin Kyoiku Undo no Tenkai to Tamagawa Gakuen no Kyoiku," 2013.

4) Project Adventure, whose programs have been incorporated into Tamagawa Academy's TAP, is an outdoor education organization established in the United States under the influence of the Outward Bound School.

5) Otto Friedrich Bollnow (Japanese translation by Masahide Hamada), *Tetsugaku teki Kyoikugaku Nyumon*, Tamagawa University Press, 1973, p. 209.

6) Peter Tacy., *IDEALS at Work*, Deerfield Academy Press, 2006.

7) Gordonstoun's Round Square is a building constructed in a perfect circle on a land owned by Sir Robert Gordon, 3rd baronet, in the 1600s. It was remodeled into student dormitories and classrooms in the 1950s after the school was founded. Currently, the building is also used as teachers' offices and a library.

8) The explanations in the boxes below are prepared based on my Japanese translations of the key contents of Round Square's official website (https://www.roundsquare. org/being–round–square/what/ideals/) as well as my experience of participating in international conferences and other events hosted by Round Square over eight years.

9) Kuniyoshi Obara, *Kyoiku Ichiro*, Nikkei Inc., 1976, p. 120.

10) Kuniyoshi Obara, *Zenjin Kyoiku Ron*, Tamagawa University Press, 1969, p. 139.

11) Kuniyoshi Obara, "Kyoiku Rikkoku Ron" in *Obara Kuniyoshi Zenshu 5: Haha no Tame no Kyoikugaku*, Tamagawa University Press, 1980, p. 397.

12) Ibid., p. 380.

13) Kuniyoshi Obara, *Zenjin Kyoiku Ron*, Tamagawa University Press, 1969, pp. 106–107.

14) Kuniyoshi Obara, "Riso no Gakko" in *Obara Kuniyoshi Zenshu 8: Riso no Gakko / Kyoiku Rikkoku Ron / Dotoku Kyoiku Ron*, Tamagawa University Press, 1980, p. 443.

15) Ibid., p. 412.

16) Kuniyoshi Obara, *Zenjin Kyoiku Ron*, Tamagawa University Press, 1969, p. 87.

17) Kuniyoshi Obara, *Kyoiku Ichiro*, Nikkei Inc., 1976, p. 181.

18) Kuniyoshi Obara, *Zenjin Kyoiku Ron*, Tamagawa University Press, 1969, p. 114.

19) Ibid., p. 115.

20) ROUND SQUARE, "Discover more .." (https://www.roundsquare.org/being–round–square/what/discoveries/, as viewed on March 2, 2021).

Chapter 7

Tamagawa Adventure Program as Zenjin Education
—— In Relation to Outward Bound School

Introduction

Driven by his conviction that the optimization of six values, namely truth, goodness, beauty, holiness, health, and wealth, was necessary for the full development of the human personality, Kuniyoshi Obara advocated Zenjin Education and adopted the twelve precepts of education to realize his ideals. Tamagawa Adventure Program (TAP) continues to evolve under the influence of the educational philosophy of Kurt Hahn, who is considered to be the father of adventure education. TAP plays an important role in realizing the philosophy of Zenjin Education and the twelve precepts of education, developing youths who will contribute to society and play leadership roles on the global stage. Readers are encouraged to study Sections 1 to 4 of this chapter for more details.

1   Tamagawa Adventure Program: Background

TAP began when Yoshiaki Obara (President and CEO of Tamagawa University and Headmaster and CEO of Tamagawa Academy) and Richard Prouty, the then Executive Director of Project Adventure, Inc. (PA, Inc.), signed an agreement to have "PA, Inc, a non-profit organization, and Tamagawa Academy collaborate in projects that promote exchanges between Japan and the United States through education activities."

In April 2000, Tamagawa Academy established the Center for Experiential Education of the Mind at Zenjin Education Research Institute based on the theme of "Zenjin Education in Action" and launched an adventure program as one of the initiatives aimed at realizing Zenjin Education. With the help of PA, Inc. and Project Adventure Japan, the center became the first school in Japan to set up an outdoor rope course on the school premises. In August of that year, Tamagawa invited an instructor from PA, Inc. to offer a training workshop on courses entitled "Adventure Programming" and "Adventure in the Classroom" for teachers at Tamagawa Academy and Tamagawa University. When the contents of these courses were modified to better suit Tamagawa's education and Japanese society, TAP was born.

In April 2002, TAP won the Project Adventure Award for Program Excellence at PA Inc.'s 30th anniversary ceremony. The prize was awarded to TAP, a program offered to K-12 students at Tamagawa, in recognition of its efforts to foster curiosity, a challenger's spirit, and an all-round personality while valuing children's self-esteem.

While the acronym of Tamagawa Adventure Program was written in lowercase (tap) from 2000 to 2014, it was changed to capital letters (TAP) in 2015. To avoid confusion, the capitalized acronym (TAP) will be used throughout this book.

(1) Concepts and principles behind TAP

"TAP" was developed based on three concepts, which have been passed down to the present day.

(1) Tamagawa Adventure Program

Employs adventure education to realize Zenjin Education and to enable students to acquire survival skills through experiential learning, in which they learn to work with and support one another as a team.

(2) Teachers as professionals

Teachers take advantage of their expertise to bring out the potential in each child.

(3) tap

"Tap" on the door (self-disclosure), "tap" to convey one's ideas (self-expression), "tap" into one's skills and resources.

The program activities are centered on (1) and (3) above. Program participants play an active role to acquire basic and general skills through experience. TAP enables students to develop a range of skills including communication skills, trust-building skills, problem-solving skills, and leadership, stressing the importance of applying what they have observed, felt, and learned to their daily lives. The program also contributes to the development of facilitation skills, which are used to help others leverage their abilities.

In addition, "TAP" represents the concept of "I am (Inter-accountable mind)." This not only serves as a statement of self-identification but also embraces the idea of holding each other accountable. "I am a challenger!" expresses the spirit of taking on challenges while respecting the ideas embodied by "I am." "Challenger" includes the following meanings:

CH: Challenge

ALL: Alternative

EN: Enrich

G: Growth

E: Experience

R: Respect

"I am a challenger!" is premised on the idea that while students have the choice to take on challenges, they must do so while being fully accountable to each other. Only then do their challenges enrich their experiences and foster their personal growth. However, even if students choose not to participate in an activity or a challenge for whatever reason, they can still be part of "I am a challenger!" by helping the team in any way they can in the spirit of "I am" and respecting each other's choices. For example, when a team works on a challenge, a student may be feeling unwell and decide not to participate in the challenge if his or her participation could affect the overall performance of the team. For some individuals, making this alternative choice in itself may be approached as a challenge. The student can still contribute to the team by cheering for the team members and taking notes instead.

The mind consists of zones that are invisible to us (C-zones: comfort, safe, known, S-zone: streched, tense, unknown, P-zone: panic). When others intrude into our safe zones without our permission or force us to step out of the zones, our psychological safety is threatened and contracts, making it difficult for us to willingly take on a challenge.

TAP mainly consists of activities in which students work in groups of about 12 or in small groups formed by dividing a larger group, depending on the goals and circumstances. Students learn from the experience of working toward group and individual goals while fulfilling their responsibilities. Rather than focusing too heavily on intellectual development, TAP stresses the importance of experiential learning and puts emphasis on the observations, insights, wisdom, sensibilities, and other learnings participants gain from experience.

(2) TAP and the twelve precepts of education

Kuniyoshi Obara developed the twelve precepts of education to realize Zenjin Education. Of these, "Rosaku Education," "Uniting Opposites," "One Who Walks the Extra Mile and One Who is a Pioneer in Life," "24-hour Education," and "International Education" are the most significant characteristics of Tamagawa Academy. In particular, "One Who Walks the Extra Mile and One Who is a Pioneer in Life," "Uniting Opposites," and "Rosaku Education" are most closely associated with TAP.

Obara used the expression "Learning through one time of *rosaku* is worth learning through 100 times of seeing" to describe Rosaku Education, which encourages students to experience, challenge, create, and act on their own. "*Rosaku*" combines "*ro*," which means to work strenuously, and "*saku*," which in this case represents creative work, rather than manual work. At its core, *rosaku* embodies the willingness and readiness to help others. In describing Rosaku Education, Kiyoaki Ishizuka noted that "the experience of accomplishing something motivates us to accomplish something else[1]." In other words, *rosaku* entails not just manual labor but initiative, action, and creativity, and TAP is the embodiment of this philosophy. In discussing the characteristics of Sumie Kobayashi's study on the philosophy of Rosaku Education, Kenichi Moriyama indicated the significance of Obara's Rosaku Education and TAP by noting as follows: "Rosaku Education has important implications on the implementation of experiential learning[2]."

The second verse of the school song of Tamagawa Academy embodies the very essence of Rosaku Education. "Under the blue stars of the morning we study" represents the importance of learning and understanding, or "knowledge," and "We plough the field where the wind blows" expresses the importance of learning something by experience, or "action." "And thus we shall grow as people" embodies the unity of knowledge and action.

The passage expresses the importance of focusing on academic studies in the bright morning light, and later engaging in strenuous, sweat-drenching physical work. That is how we grow as individuals, and that is why Rosaku Education, which aims to develop individuals equipped with both intellectual and physical abilities, is crucial.

"Uniting Opposites" means bringing together two conflicting sides, such as knowledge and experience or ideal self and actual self. For example, it is important to gain knowledge from books and learn about the means of communication, but communication cannot be realized without conveying one's thoughts and ideas to another person face to face. In other words, students must learn how to communicate through knowledge as well as face-to-face interactions. Another example of "Uniting Opposites" is refining one's values while interacting with people with different values and developing one's identity while embracing differences. TAP offers students a full range of opportunities to unite opposing views and form a consensus through problem-solving activities.

Tamagawa Academy's motto, "Be the first to take on the most difficult, unpleasant, painful and unprofitable work in life with a smile," was conceived by Obara, who was inspired by a verse in the Sermon on the Mount in Chapter 5 of the Gospel of Matthew: "If anyone forces you to go one mile, go with them two miles." Jesus taught that while those who are forced into service are free to go after a mile, they must offer to go the extra mile. Obara adopted this "extra mile" principle as one of the precepts of education. The precept can also be interpreted to celebrate the pioneering spirit of those who have the courage to go beyond the tasks they are assigned and to take on additional challenges. TAP is designed to cultivate the practical skills needed to put this pioneering spirit into action. The principle of "One Who Walks the Extra Mile and One Who is a Pioneer in Life" is exemplified by those who not only do their utmost to solve problems but are willing to work with others to achieve their goals, independently set their targets, and tackle challenges without fear of failure. TAP is the embodiment of this principle.

2　Transformation of TAP Goals

Back in 2000, the education sector faced many challenges, particularly the question of how to create an environment conducive to the development of well-rounded children. To address this social issue, Tamagawa Academy introduced TAP to build the vibrant learning community of the 21st century and made a concerted effort to support the new program.

At the time of its launch, the aims of TAP were to offer (1) programs that cultivate a strong mindset (K-12 education programs), (2) programs that cultivate more desirable interpersonal relationships (programs for K-16, teachers, and the general public), and (3) programs that develop a mindset for thriving in the global community (K-16 education programs).

As a result of the 2015 reorganization, the Center for Experiential Education of the Mind at the Zenjin Education Research Institute was renamed the Center for Tamagawa Adventure Program (TAP Center). The center aims to (1) serve as a base for education programs designed to foster spiritual well-being, interpersonal skills, and leadership through experiential learning under the guidance of the principles of Zenjin Education and (2) adopt an open-door policy for the schools of Tamagawa Academy as well as educational institutions outside Tamagawa with the goal of promoting the center's programs and research findings across society and contributing to the development and growth of education activities in Japan.

The principles of Zenjin Education are at the very heart of experiential education at Tamagawa University. For this reason, it is crucial that the implementation and development of TAP be based on the principles of Zenjin Education. After a long search for the ideal education, and informed by his journey of passion and hardships, Obara developed Zenjin Education, whose mission was to nurture a well-rounded person. The development of the human personality, according to Obara, required the optimization of six values, namely truth (ideals of academic studies), goodness (ideals of moral values), beauty (ideals of arts), holiness (ideals of religion), health (ideals of the body), and wealth (ideals of life). Twelve precepts of education were developed to realize the ideals of Zenjin Education, and TAP plays an important role in implementing them through practical and current experiential programs (Table 7-1).

The *zenjin* (whole person) flower on Fig. 7-1 represents *zenjin*, or the whole person, equipped with the six values of truth, goodness, beauty, holiness, health, and wealth. The soil for the *zenjin* flower needs nutrients, or the twelve precepts of education. For the *zenjin* flower to grow into a healthy plant, it needs to develop adaptability, resistance, and a pioneering spirit (ability to carve one's own path in life), all of which can be readily acquired through TAP. Once the *zenjin* flower grows to maturity by absorbing the skills acquired through

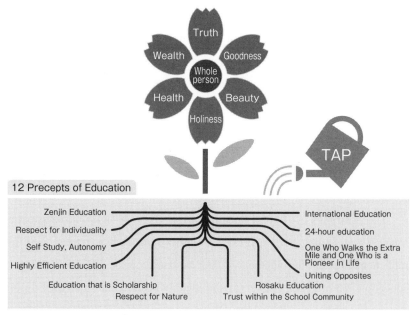

Fig. 7-1. *Zenjin* flower, 12 precepts of education, and TAP
Source: Prepared by the author based on Wataru Kudo, "TAP no Sokuseki to Korekara no Kanosei-teachers as professionals Model Kaihatsu wo Mezashite" in *Kyoiku Jissengaku Kenkyu*, No 19, 2016, p. 57.

Table. 7-1. Relationship between Twelve Precepts of Education and TAP

12 precepts of education	TAP education principles
Zenjin Education	Education for a harmonious character development Holistic approach to education Tamagawa Adventure Program, "tap" Teachers as Professionals
Respect for Individuality	Roles of individuals in ensuring complete mutual respect in a group Full Value, TAP-Commitment, embracing diversity
Self Study, Autonomy	Respect for the right of self-determination, development of self-instruction skills Rise to the challenge of learning by personal choice I am a challenger! Challenge by Choice
Highly Efficient Education	Learning style Improve efficiency by a trial-and-error, inquiry-based learning Approach based on the theory of multiple intelligences (MI)
Education that is Scholarship	Theory of experiential learning, adventure education, theory of adventure Social psychology, educational psychology, humanistic psychology Existentialism, zone of proximal development, brain science Dynamic skills theory, active learning
Respect for Nature	Outdoor education (adventure education, environmental education) Mother Nature offering great opportunities for education Education to help children make full use of their natural talents
Trust within the School Community	Relationship between facilitators and learners Community as where participants learn from each another Student instruction (instruction and support), special activities
Rosaku Education	Experiential learning, learning from experience Comprehensive learning, active moral education Initiative, action, creativity Comprehensive understanding (intellectual understanding, emotional understanding, physical understanding)
Uniting Opposites	Individual and group, theory and practice, knowledge and experience, ideal self and actual self Accepting and integrating values; thesis, antithesis, and synthesis
One Who Walks the Extra Mile and One Who is a Pioneer in Life	Pioneering spirit Leadership and fellowship, entrepreneurship Take on additional challenges, ability to take action, career education
24-hour education	Remote education In-person and online hybrid education Any time, any place
International Education	Respect for other cultures, international exchanges Communication skills

Source: Prepared and modified by the author based on Ryoji Fujikashi & Kazuhito Obara, "Tamagawa Gakuen ni okeru Round Square to Tamagawa Adventure Program no Juyosei" in *Tamagawa University Gakujutsu Kenkyusho Kiyo* No. 16, 2010, p. 7.

TAP and the nutrients from the twelve precepts of education, it blooms when the time is right and eventually yields a fruit called self-actualization.

The "experiences" mentioned in the mission statement of TAP center do not refer to the individual activities conducted as part of TAP. These include experiential and expeditionary activities conducted in the natural environment, both within and outside the Tamagawa campus, activities for environmental preservation and conservation including beautification and cleaning work, and exchange programs that enable students to interact with people from different nationalities and religions and learn about leadership and the diversity of values. The experiences offer students with opportunities to improve their communication skills, interpersonal skills, and problem-solving skills, among others.

In addition, "adopt an open-door policy for educational institutions outside Tamagawa" means actively collaborating with educational institutions outside Tamagawa, including private corporations, professional sports associations, and teacher training organizations. A range of case studies and issues pertaining to the classroom will be discussed and analyzed to ensure that research findings at TAP center are adapted for general use and application.

Based on the interpretation above, TAP Center's mission is to apply the cycle of experiential learning it promotes to reflect on its experiential education programs, adapt them for broader application and use in the classrooms and real-life settings, and publish its collection of research findings and themes. Particularly for Tamagawa University, which focuses on teacher training, one of the objectives of TAP is to develop learning styles and models for the training of education professionals.

3   Kurt Hahn's Adventure Education and TAP

The previous section outlined the relationship between TAP and Project Adventure (PA). The origin of PA is traced back to Outward Bound School

Table. 7-2. Main schools and organizations founded by
Kurt Hahn

1920	Salem school
1934	Gordonstoun school
1941	Outward Bound School
1956	The Duke of Edinburgh's International Award
1962	Atlantic College United World College
1967	Round Square
1968	International Baccalaureate

Source: Prepared by the author

(OBS) and Kurt Hahn. Hahn was a German educator of Jewish origin, who is considered to be the father of adventure education. He established many schools and education organizations, including Salem, Gordonstoun, and an OBS in Aberdovey, and his philosophy of education has had a continuing influence around the world (Table 7-2).

When "Kurt Hahn" is entered for a keyword search on CiNii Articles, a database service used to search academic articles published in Japan, only eight articles are found, indicating the limited number of studies related to Hahn in Japan. Michio Ishikawa notes that Hahn was "one of the leading educators of the new education movement, but tends to hide from our vision in the shadow of country boarding education, Rosaku Education, art education, and Wandervogel, among other things[3]." However, the database returned 57 hits when "adventure education" was entered as a keyword, indicating Hahn's significant, albeit indirect, influence in Japan (as of August 6, 2020).

OBS's adventure education program started as a training program designed to improve the survival chances of seamen working for the British shipping industry in the North Atlantic during World War II. The program was adopted as a youth education program in the post-war period. The aim of OBS is to enable youth to achieve self-development through stressful experiences in nature. The program developed remarkably quickly following its establishment in Colorado, the U. S. in 1962, resulting in a range of spin-off adventure programs.

Hahn's vision of education was to develop individuals with the ability to make morally sound and right judgments, as well as resilience. He noted as follows: "The aim of education is to enable people to develop values and maintain an enterprising curiosity, an indefatigable spirit, tenacity in pursuit, and, above all, compassion. It is culpable neglect not to impel young people into experience[4]."

The objective of education, according to Hahn, is to make students experience strict physical training and develop survival skills, experience life-threatening situations as they apply their new skills, develop the right attitudes to life, foster the ability to save others from danger to life, and cultivate a spirit of service for others.

Based on this philosophy, the fundamental principles of OBS were defined as the Four Pillars of Outward Bound (Service, Self-reliance, Craftsmanship, Physical and Mental Fitness and Compassion), the five principles of education (an enterprising curiosity, an indefatigable spirit, tenacity in pursuit, readiness for sensible self-denial, and compassion), and the Seven laws of Salem, which are the following: "First, give the children opportunities for self-discovery; second, make the children meet with triumph and defeat; third, give the children the opportunity of self-effacement in the common cause; fourth, provide periods of silence; fifth, train the imagination; sixth, make competition important but not predominant; and seven, free the sons of the wealthy and powerful from the sense of privilege[5]." These principles have been passed down to OB schools around the world today. The mission of OBS is to help students discover and realize their potential by experiencing out-of-the-ordinary challenges.

In 1967, Hahn founded Round Square with Internationalism, Democracy, Environment, Adventure, Leadership, and Service (IDEALS) as the cornerstones of its philosophy[6]. Tamagawa Academy began participating in

Round Square international conferences in 2004 and became the first school in Japan to be admitted to the network the following year. Since then, the school has cultivated relationships with Round Square schools. In light of this, Tamagawa University has promoted IDEALS as the ultimate goals in life and the fundamental principles of education.

During his visit to Japan in June 2015, Professor Ralf Koerrenz remarked, "Kurt Hahn was the true bearer of new education. What underlies Hahn's philosophy and principles is Zenjin Education. It was only inevitable that International Baccalaureate and Round Square, its present-day accomplishments, connected with Tamagawa." This comment supports the close relationship between Hahn's philosophy of education and Tamagawa Academy's experiential education, including TAP.

4   TAP's Mission

Today's youths are the future leaders of Japanese society and the world. To ensure that they will have the confidence to stride along the difficult road to their dreams, they need to develop a pioneering spirit. To this end, teachers

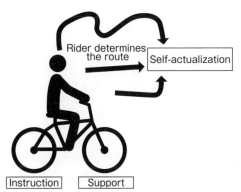

Fig. 7-2. Self-determination and self-actualization based on instruction and support
Source: Prepared by the author based on Wataru Kudo & Atsushi Fujihira, *Seito/Shinro Shido no Riron to Houhou*, Tamagawa University Press, 2019, p. 9.

need to understand and design an appropriate environment where children can learn through adventure under their instructions (direct and specific instructions by teachers to encourage character development in children) and "support (support and guidance to help each child (or group) take full advantage of their skills and talents based on an accurate understanding of the child's (or group's) talents, circumstances, processes, and other relevant factors while fully respecting the child's autonomy and goals and emphasizing teacher–student interactions)[7]."

Fig. 7-2 shows a child riding a bicycle toward their destination (self-actualization). In the process of learning how to ride a bike, the child needs someone else's instructions and support to learn riding techniques and traffic rules. At first, the child needs training wheels and someone's assistance, but slowly learns, by trial and error, to balance independently without help. As the child gradually learns to control speed and change direction, they are able to travel to more locations and bike to any destination they want on their own. If parents and teachers continue to take a leading role and give instructions, the child would never develop initiative or survival skills and would consequently face difficulty growing into an independent adult.

In TAP, a spirit of adventure means taking on a challenge even when success is not guaranteed and, as a result, discovering something new about oneself and developing a new sense of self. The theory of adventure used in TAP is based on Kurt Lewin's field theory[8], which is represented by the equation A=f (P, C-zone)[9]. A, P, and C-zone respectively stand for Adventure, Personality, and Comfort-zone (a situation or area in which the surrounding human and physical environment is perceived to be physically and psychologically safe). According to this theory, the product of personality and C-zone promotes adventure and leads to personal development (Fig. 7-3).

Teachers must take active steps to provide children with opportunities to make their own decisions and to learn by trial and error. They need to engage with children with a good balance of instruction and support to ensure that children develop self-teaching abilities and a pioneering spirit. However,

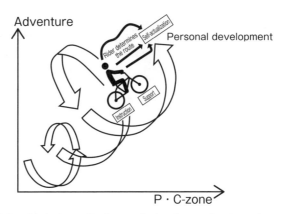

Fig. 7–3. Relationship between the theory of adventure and a pioneering spirit
Source: Prepared by the author

when this balance is lost, the bike leans to one side and causes a flat tire. Because the children have lost their balance and are unable to travel in the direction they want, the children need instructions and support catered to their individual needs. The process of learning to how to ride a bike "activates their intellect, emotion, and volition and mobilizes their mind, heart, and body. The experience enables the children to refine their intellect and sensibility as a person and gain insight and knowledge[10]."

As mentioned above, Tamagawa University adopted the aforementioned IDEALS as the ultimate goals in life, in addition to the philosophy of Zenjin Education. In 2019, TAP Center created its official logo using three colors representing the center's goals, or IDEALS. T (red) represents Leadership and Service, A (green) stands for Adventure and Environment, and P (blue) symbolizes International Perspective and Democracy (Fig. 7–4).

TAP aims to support young people so that they have the confidence to move forward on the difficult road to their dreams, equip themselves with not only specialized knowledge and skills but also moral values appropriate for independent adults, and enrich their mind and knowledge. To fulfill this mission, TAP Center will continue to balance and combine theory and practice

Fig. 7-4. TAP logo
Source: Tamagawa Adventure Program (home page: http://tap.tamagawa.ac.jp/, as viewed on March 2, 2021)

(TAP).

The philosophy of education of Tamagawa Academy is based on the idea that education enables students to learn and accomplish new things. Kuniyoshi Obara described human beings as "possessing unique talents and abilities from birth while living in a world shared by all." The mission of Tamagawa education is to realize this vision of humanity and to nurture individuals with the determination to contribute to Japanese society and the world.

Thus, Tamagawa University's mission is to develop individuals who have the determination to apply the motto of Tamagawa Academy to the challenges that lie ahead and to foster "pioneers of life" who take on new challenges without fear of failure. TAP's role, in turn, is to realize this mission.

Notes

1) Kiyoaki Ishizuka, "Rosaku Kyoiku" in *Zenjin* No. 756, Tamagawa University Press, 2012, p. 22.

2) Kenichi Moriyama, "Kobayashi Sumie ni okeru Rosaku Kyoiku Shiso Kenkyu no Tokushitsu" in *Kyoiku Jissengaku Kenkyu*, No. 15, 2011, p. 83.

3) Michio Ishikawa, "Kurt Hahn to Outward Bound" in *Kyoiku Shinsekai*, No. 27, 2011, p. 59.

4) Duke of Edinburgh International Award, "Rekishi to Rinen" (http://intaward-jp.check-sixcore. jp/history.php, as viewed on August 5, 2020).

5) Ralf Koerrenz (Japanese translation by Kaoru Yoneyama), "Denen Kyoiku Juku-Hermann Lietz to Kurt Hahn ni Okeru Kihon Rinen to Kokusaiteki Sekinin" in *Tamagawa Daigaku Kyoiku Gakubu Zenjin Kyoiku Kenkyu Center Nenpo 2015*, No. 2, 2016, pp. 16-17.

6) Peter Tacy., *IDEALS at Work*, Deerfield Academy Press, 2006, p. 63.

7) Wataru Kudo, "Teachers as Professionals to Shiteno tap-Shidosha Kara Shidosha (facilitator) e," in *Kyoiku Jissen Kenkyu*, No. 16, 2012, p. 38.

8) Kurt Lewin (Japanese translation by Daisaku Sotobayashi & Kohei Matsumura), *Topologie Shinrigaku no Genri*, Seikatsusha, 1942, p. 21.

9) Wataru Kudo, "Adventure Kyoiku ni Okeru Edgework to Dokizuke ni Tsuiteno Kenkyu– Adventure no Riron wo Motoni Shita Kyoshi no Yakuwari to C–zone ni Chakumoku Shite" in *Kyoiku Jissengaku Kenkyu*, No. 19, 2016, p. 40.

10) Masaharu Kage, *Jugyo to iu Itonami*, Kyoiku Shuppan, 2019, p. 27.

Column 2

The Precepts of Education in the Early Days of Tamagawa Academy and Their Application

Today, Tamagawa Academy (hereinafter referred to as Tamagawa) has twelve precepts of education. In this column I will examine the ideas and thoughts gave rise to these precepts in the Tamagawa's early days by examining "*Tamagawa Juku no Kyoiku*" *in Obara Kuniyoshi Zenshu 11*. Tamagawa Juku (boarding school), no longer exists today, and the education principles advocated at the time have evolved over time in both content and application. Nevertheless, the essence of Obara's philosophy from the early days has endured to this day. Obara poured his heart and soul into experiential education back in the days, and it is my hope that his early teachings will help us envision the future of the Tamagawa experiential education.

Obara lamented that young people in Japan were "spending the best time of their lives in their twenties brooding over speculative, calculated, and utilitarian exam preparations when they should be burning with passion, chasing their dreams and fantasies in the highest of spirits like a flying horse soaring into the sky[1]." Driven by a desire to "bring society into schools ...... without any intermediary in between[2]," and his commitment to the ideal that "schools should be a reflection of society[3]," Obara founded the school and Tamagawa Juku in it. Note that, in devising a plan for Tamagawa Juku, Obara believed students in kindergarten and elementary school should attend school from home. The reasons were as follows. First, it would be impossible to provide good education to children if they lived away from their parents, and it would be important for children to be in a loving family environment where they could get all the attention they want. Second, it would be virtually impossible for schools to replace parents, no matter how hard they worked and tried. And finally, schools simply could not be entrusted with kindergarten and elementary school children considering the risk of bearing the responsibility of their health and well-being. On the other hand, Obara noted that students should be admitted to Tamagawa Juku starting in middle school to help them develop social skills, among other reasons.

I will outline below the origin and evolution of the precepts of education promoted by Tamagawa today. The current precepts of education are as follows: Zenjin Education, Respect for Individuality, Self Study and Autonomy, Highly Efficient Education, Education that is Scholarship, Respect for Nature, Trust within the School Community, Rosaku Education, Uniting Opposites, One Who Walks the Extra Mile and One Who is a Pioneer in Life, 24-hour Education, and International Education. Although not all of these principles were explicitly proclaimed as the Tamagawa's precepts at the time of its founding, Obara's views described in his works in the Tamagawa's early days will help us understand the origins of the precepts and trace the path of Tamagawa education at the time.

One Who Walks the Extra Mile and One Who is a Pioneer in Life

Obara devoted many pages discussing high ambitions while referring to the words of Dr. J.C. Clark. Noting that the quality of education is not necessarily proportional to time, Obara expresses his desire to foster pioneers capable of developing new ideas on the quality of education. In addition, Obara also used the expression "pyramid foundation blocks" to encourage "unnoticed good deeds, selfless acts of kindness, those who consider themselves blessed to suffer in life, those who go the extra mile[4]." This is a vision of children who understand what it means to be "more blessed to give than to receive"– in other words, a vision of Tamagawa children who practice the Tamagawa's motto of being "the first to take on the most difficult, unpleasant, painful and unprofitable work in life with a smile[5]."

Efficient Education, Education that is Scholarship

Obara was critical of the Japanese education system for its unprincipled, unsystematic curriculum and its strict age restrictions rooted in harsh legal and systemic constraints, which result in all students advancing at the same pace despite the differences between fast-paced and slow-paced students. This may be interpreted to be an advocacy for the introduction of proficiency-based classes, in today's terms. Based on this view, Obara argued for the abandonment of age restrictions, suggesting quick learners advance to a higher grade or school without having to meet the age requirements, and allowing slower learners to take their time. Referring to the law of diminishing returns, he reasoned that "children should each be given the subjects and levels most appropriate for them at the most appropriate time[6]." Further, according to Obara, students should graduate from university before they lose their adaptability because there is a need for "people with such unspoiled enthusiasm and youthful energy that they are willing to work like trainees for about two years even after graduating university[7]." In addition, Obara proposed a smaller classroom of about 25 students per class.

As for specific methods of evidenced-based, efficient education, Obara suggested that teachers improve efficiency by studying teaching materials, organizing the system of teaching materials (units), eliminating repetitions, and refining the content. Any extra time resulting from this process should be devoted to application and so forth. I should also note that Obara's approach, unit reorganization in particular, is still used in some classes at Tamagawa.

Respect for Individuality (Education for Self-discovery)

Obara believed that the failure to recognize and respect a person's individuality is equivalent to "depriving the person of hope and pushing them down to their death[8]." He noted that "those without individuality are like machines copying and repeating others[9]." According to Obara, the ultimate goal of education is to help students make full use of their natural talents, and "there is no greater joy for them than to discover and cultivate their raison d'être, who they are, their true path, and their true self[10]." He concluded that education is not about "test scores, graduation certificates, or the amount of knowledge; it is essentially about helping students discover their own true self[11]."

Self Study and Autonomy, Juku Education

Obara believed that education did not require "large volumes of information or rote learning, cramming, scoring ...... unnatural restrictions or repetition, meaningless pacing, or teaching materials without reflection[12]." Education, according to Obara, should aim to cultivate skills "such as detection, judgment, thinking, execution, imagination, ingenuity, application, and invention[13]" with a particular focus on creativity and research techniques. Education should also foster "curiosity for academic studies ...... , an unbridled interest in knowledge, a delicate sensibility to fascination, a tireless spirit of inquiry, the joy of creation and discovery, and an academic conscience as clear as a mirror[14]," and cultivate the determination to "conquer any problems no matter how challenging[15]." Obara considered independent research to be an embodiment of these principles, noting that he wished to "give the same value to independent research as the total score of all subjects[16]."

Obara also believed that students were "completely free to choose where to study, other than when engaging in a group project[17]." He referred to initiatives in which students worked without timetables, consulted with and asked teachers for reference books, had teachers review their reports, and engaged in group projects. Further, the library was kept open from early morning to bed time during Obara's time. Obara considered the library to be the school's centerpiece and aimed to "make it a habit for not just university students but all students to use the library starting in their lower elementary grades ...... and develop them into library–loving, book–loving, and research–loving citizens[18]."

Zenjin Education, Uniting Opposites

Obara corrected the common misconception that Zenjin Education is like a mosaic of assorted wood pieces that "makes one student do anything and everything and develop the student into a generalist[19]." Rather, according to Obara, Zenjin Education is the outcome of "different elements .... sublated (aufheben) into a harmonious, coherent whole[20]." In other words, the knowledge cultivated through Zenjin Education is the embodiment of "Uniting Opposites" (aufheben). Specifically, Obara argued, the true goal of Zenjin Education is the "uniting of ...... the material and the spiritual, the heaven and the earth, perspiration and beauty, manure gathering and piano playing, the abacus and the Buddhist scripture, money and ideas, machinery and ideals, soil and philosophy, the poor and the wealthy[21]."

Respect for Nature

Obara considered the location and learning environment to be of paramount importance, as evidenced by his statement that he dedicated more effort into choosing locations for Seijo Gakuen and Tamagawa Academy than anything else. While he lamented the conditions of children who lived in city areas, Obara believed that there were "an infinite number of free classrooms under the blue sky, in the shadows of trees in the forests, in the ripples of the streams and beaches, and the green grass on the banks[22]." However, he was not proposing to insulate schools from society and mass–produce sheltered children. Rather, Obara believed that a school that maintained close ties with the real world while respecting nature was where one found the "mindset, devotion, and thriving religion, as well as the mind and heart of an unspoiled child[23]" required prior to pedagogy and methods of teaching. Note that Obara left the following words regarding his selection of Tamagawa Academy's location:

> The noble morning sun rising over the Boso Peninsula and looking over the Kanto region, the wavy peaks of the Sagami mountains poking above the sleepy morning mist, the Tanzawa mountains wrapped in gold, purple, and navy blue hues, daring us to reach high and strong like them, and the constantly changing hills on the school grounds, where Musashino's abundant weeds, dark green pine forests, and young leaves of assorted trees thrive ...... I cannot help but smile that at least the location I chose for the school was a huge success for Tamagawa education, although it is a wonder how I even came across this place, a magnificent forest filled with breathtaking natural beauty, only 40 minutes from Tokyo[24].

Rosaku Education

Since Obara discussed many concrete Rosaku Education activities offered at Tamagawa Juku, I will focus on a number of them here. For example, Obara noted that farming activities were "valuable not only from the standpoint of production but also as a source of religious and spiritual training and materials for natural history research[25]." Obara also considered rearing animals to be one of the core activities, remarking, "We cannot teach real science using dull and unoriginal specimens and obscure illustrations[26]."

However, Obara was clearly opposed to the utilitarian and calculated approach associated with vocational education. He argued that the aim of Rosaku Education was to develop self-reliance and self-actualization, and students contributed to society as a consequence. Obara's Rosaku Education "transcended self-interest, professional success, profit, and money[27]," and it was critical that "'holiness' always governed as the fundamental principle of instruction[28]."

Trust within the School Community

Tamagwa Juku was founded to "convert learning into work (*rosaku*), put theory to practical use, experience concepts, realize knowledge, bring academic studies into real life, and unite theory and practices[29]." Critical to the realization of this philosophy of education, Obara notes, are the existence of not only facilities but teachers.

Teachers who are as competent as they come! And those who are enthusiasts of Rosaku Education! Who are equipped with knowledge, ingenuity, skills, and experience ...... who love children and education! Who approach everything with a burning passion! With a spirit of generosity and love![30]

This comment can be interpreted to be a sense of urgency Obara felt toward teachers who regard only those duties specified in their contract to be their responsibilities. In particular, the contractual view of the teaching profession found in Western cultures is far removed from the precept of "Trust within the School Community" advocated by Obara.

International Education (Development of Builders of a New Japanese Culture)

Obara believed that the goal of education was to foster "Japanese people who are cheerful, brave, honorable, honest, pure-hearted, kind, deeply affectionate, stylish, artistic, devout, polite, solemn, wise, humane and peace-loving at heart[31]." To achieve this, Obara advocated that Japan incorporate thoughts from outside Japan while preserving the Japanese soul as its foundation and seedbed. Obara drew attention to Japan's flexibility and openness to other cultures: "Japan has incorporated and united Confucianism, Buddhism, and Western cultures. While universities in foreign countries outrightly reject philosophies from other countries, one of the greatest virtues of Japanese universities is their truly international and global mindset[32]."

However, he mentioned "a tendency to be overly fascinated with anything written horizontally[33]," warning against those in Japan who blindly worship Western cultures as well as those with narrow-minded, nationalistic views. It is noteworthy that Obara defined internationalism as taking a middle course between these two views, or a balanced approach.

Notes

1) Kuniyoshi Obara, "Tamagawa Juku no Kyoiku" in *Obara Kuniyoshi Zenshu 11: Akiyoshidai no Seija Honma Sensei, Tamagawa Juku no Kyoiku*, Tamagawa University Press, 1963, p. 185.
2) Ibid., p. 187.
3) Ibid., p. 400.
4) Ibid., p. 232.
5) Ibid., p. 236.
6) Ibid., p. 239.
7) Ibid., p. 240.
8) Ibid., p. 242.
9) Ibid., p. 242.
10) Ibid., p. 243.
11) Ibid., p. 243.
12) Ibid., p. 246.
13) Ibid., p. 246.
14) Ibid., p. 247.
15) Ibid., p. 247.
16) Ibid., p. 367.
17) Ibid., p. 374.
18) Ibid., p. 376.
19) Ibid., p. 252.
20) Ibid., p. 252.
21) Ibid., p. 253.
22) Ibid., p. 256.
23) Ibid., p. 260.
24) Ibid., p. 256.

25) Ibid., p. 354.
26) Ibid., p. 345.
27) Ibid., p. 390.
28) Ibid., p. 390.
29) Ibid., p. 371.
30) Ibid., p. 371.
31) Ibid., p. 210.
32) Ibid., p. 212.
33) Ibid., p. 212.

Part III
References

1   Commonalities with Tamagawa's 12 Precepts of Education

12 Precepts of Education	PA's FVC & OB Values	RS's IDEALS	IB Learner Profile
Zenjin education	Holistic education approach	Concerned with the whole man or woman	Holistic education
Respect individuality	Respect individual personality	Democracy (familiarity with a wide range of human circumstance)	Principled; Caring
Self-learning and autonomy	Challenge by choice	Self-discipline and self-confidence	Inquirers; Knowledgeable; Thinkers
Efficient education	Learning style based on multiple intelligence		Thinkers; Reflective
Education with scientific evidence	Evidence-based learning		
Appreciation of nature	Outdoor education and respect for the environment	Environmentalism; Adventure	
Mutual respect between teachers and students	Facilitator-and-learner relationship	Partnership between adults and senior pupils	
Arbeitsschule (rosaku education)	Learning based on experience	Service; Adventure	Caring; Risk-takers
Coincidentia oppositorum	Individualism and collectivism, static and dynamic learning	Democracy (awareness of domestic and foreign affairs)	Open-minded; Balanced
Pioneer spirit in human life	Adventure mind, leadership, and entrepreneurship	Leadership	Principled
Education for 24 hours	Distance-education; Any time, any place		

International education	Respect for different cultures; Communication skills; Inclusion and diversity	Internationalism	Thinkers; Communicators; Openminded; Balanced

2 Inspirational quotes from Zenjin Kyoiku Ron [Theory of Zenjin Education] by Kuniyoshi Obara (about 16 quotes)

The following are based on *Zenjin Kyoiku Ron* [Theory of Zenjin Education] by Kuniyoshi Obara (Renewed Edition, Tamagawa University Press, 1994).

1. Arguments for Zenjin Education

Everything in human culture must be incorporated in the content of education. Therefore, education absolutely must be "Zenjin Education." Zenjin means a perfect personality; in other words, personality in harmony. The more lacking a person is in human culture, the more angular he/she becomes in personality. I suspect many schools in Japan today are biased, and almost unfairly so. Or perhaps this is also the case around the world. ...

Entrance exam preparations, rote memorization, cramming, cheating, prep schools, *kyoiku mama* (disciplinarian mothers), tutoring schools, obsession with success ... they are destroying true humanity (p. 10).

2. Ideals of Education: Development of Six Cultural Values

Now, I think there are six aspects in human culture, namely, learning, morality, art, religion, body and livelihood. The ideal for learning is truth, the ideal for morality is goodness, the ideal for art is beauty, the ideal for religion is holiness, the ideal for body is health and the ideal for livelihood is wealth. The ideal for education is to create the six values of truth, goodness, beauty, holiness, health and wealth.

And I call the four values of truth, goodness, beauty and holiness as the absolute values and the values of health and wealth as the instrumental values (p. 12).

3. Harmonious Development: Like a Cosmos Flower

> I want these six cultural values to grow in harmony like cosmos flowers blooming orderly in front yards in fall. Chinese scholars translated the English word cosmos as yuzhou, or "universe." Yu means "space," and zhou means "era." The great philosopher Kant taught us that the universe consists of time and space. The Greek word kosmos means "beautiful arrangement," "harmony," and "order" (p. 14).

4. What I Expect of a Person

> In sum, I recognize the six aspects in a person. I expect a person to be equipped with these six aspects. But I do not mean to propose a half-hearted, so-called generalist education. Nor should it be a dull and uninteresting education that ignores students' individual strengths. When people are offered a truly excellent education, they develop their God-given gifts naturally. They simply create their unique worlds and, what is more, achieve a complete state in their own worlds (pp. 23-24).

5. True Education

> What I want to do is simply to go back to the people, removing all doctrines and positions. "Go back to the people, go back to the people." Simply an education for the people. From there, a true education will inevitably emerge. A person, specifically, is an individual, a member of society, a citizen, a member of the human race, a child of God, a child of humanity who works with his/her arms, thinks with his/her head, adores beauty, and performs good deeds. Above all, a person is a unique cosmos arranged in a systematic order, where he/she alone is the master above

and below the Heaven and is irreplaceable by even the entire world. When a "cosmos" completes its internal development, allowing the individual to demonstrate his/her innate gifts and abilities, he/she reaches a complete state that is unique, beautiful, and irreplaceable, just as a bamboo is a bamboo, a pine is a pine, a chrysanthemum is a chrysanthemum, and a violet is a violet. I aspire to draw a perfect circle, just as Giotto did.

Plato said harmony is a virtue. Pestalozzi demanded harmonious development. I, too, want to develop into a true "whole person" (pp. 28-29).

6. Religious Education

That is why religious education entails the optimal development of all aspects of spiritual life. It is not a one-sided, or partial, education, but the cultivation, growth, and development of the synthesis of all elements of spiritual life. Naturally, religious education is Zenjin Education. It is only when a person takes a serious interest in all matters including learning, art, morality, industry, and social issues while maintaining a deep respect for the Absolute of the universe that he/she is said to be a truly accomplished person of faith. The religious mind is a state of mind encompassing all these aspects of the human life.

Therefore, our spiritual life should be neither an artistic hobby nor a mystic tranquility; it is none other than all spiritual activities of and for our personhood. This is the very essence of Zenjin Education. The current state of Japanese education, which has neglected this and overemphasizes intellectual development, is like a truly horrific cancer destroying humanity (p. 32).

Now, it is often said that religious education cannot be provided at public schools. That is totally untrue. One can find religious inspiration anytime, anywhere. In music and art. In theater, literature, and history. Particularly in science and math. Even in tea ceremony and flower arrangement. In physical education and hiking. It is said that"mountains and streams produce great people." Hiking cleanses the soul more than it trains the body. This is why skiing is particularly emphasized in Tamagawa. The breathtaking winter wonderland. Gliding down the ski slopes, the mind completely absorbed. If anything, skiing is a religious education (p. 36).

7. Art Education

And we must not neglect education about human emotions, which help us experience the beauty of the heart and maintain loving relationships.

We need art education so that we can truly enjoy, relish, and thrive in life, nature, and art. So that we can at the very least live like a human being (p. 45).

(One aspect of artistic activity is creative work. The act of creation. To express ourselves and tap into our individuality. The absence of individuality means the absence of life.

Artistic activity involves the integration, coordination, and synthesis of one's life. The more complete this is, the more complete one's self-expression and self-fulfillment. One can, as a result, express his/her individuality to the fullest. Ultimately, expressing one's individuality involves the realization of a creative mechanism for self-integration. The free development of the self. The enhancement of life. The liberation of the self. This is what makes artistic activity precious. The fundamental principle of artistic education is to help students grow mentally and physically, maximize their performance in a well-rounded fashion, and activate their personal creative processes by relying on the artistic power that human beings are gifted with. In particular, we must not ignore children's creative instincts, imaginative instincts, inquisitive instincts, and constructive instincts.) (p. 46)

* ( ) is a quote from *Gakko-Geki Ron* [Essay on School Drama] by Kuniyoshi Obara.

8. Moral Education

A. I want all to understand the preciousness of human and personality value. Kant's principle of humanity teaches us about the inherent dignity and nobility of humanity: "Act in such a way that you treat humanity, whether in your own person or the person of any other, never simply as a means but always at the same time as an end." ...

B. Help students find a clear life vision. An unshakable life vision that transcends all——joy and sadness, pleasure and suffering.

C. I would like my students to understand the importance of virtue, the meaning of evil, the deep significance of struggles and suffering, as well as the nobility of sin and repentance.

D. Develop a full understanding of a moral life. The struggle between desire and reason. "Bandits in the mountains are easy to defeat, those in the heart are hard to break" (Wang Yangming), the contradictions in human life, and the value of suffering.

E. I want to help them create a beautiful, righteous, and enduring vision for humanity. (pp. 53–54)

9. Learning Education

Words fail me when it comes to the woeful state of learning education. Cramming, rote memorization, entrance exam preparations, obsession with success! And the worst of all, the cheating! (p. 58)

To start, there are two schools of thought in pedagogy. Either we teach students or let them study. Whether we instruct them or have them learn. Whether we provide them with knowledge or allow them to acquire it. Whether we employ rote memorization and cramming or creativity as primary learning tools.

There is no doubt that education based on having students "grab" knowledge is more valuable than one based on "giving" knowledge. Teachers who simply teach are the worst of all. Teachers must let students learn and study. University professors in particular should understand why those who study in university are called "students." Emphasize ingenuity over rote memorization, creativity over cramming, and joy of learning over quantity of knowledge learned (p. 64).

The great philosopher Kant was strict in his teaching that we must "not learn philosophy, but rather how to philosophize (philosophieren)." I would like university professors, and even K-12 teachers in Japan today to take his words to heart. Our role is to instill in students a passion for learning, help them learn how to dig deeper, and forge their "pickaxes." (p. 64)

In ancient Greece, it was said that "learning begins in wonder." The word "learning" meant "surprise" or "wonder." ... We must not kill the curiosity, inquisitiveness, wonder, and surprise sprouting in children's minds with cramming, rote memorization, and exam studies (p. 65).

10. Health Education

It goes without saying that the objectives of physical education are not championship flags, medals, records, or trophies. Do not mix up means and purposes.

I believe what is aimed for by physical education is the tough physical strength, long life, body in harmony and dexterity. To this end, students must first gain physiological knowledge. And engage in basic exercises. (I have a great respect for Denmark gymnastics, which offers a balance of three types of exercises: basic exercises, body-toning exercises, and flexibility exercises.) And various types of sports. As Japanese, students in particular should select at least one of the many types of martial arts (p. 77).

Now, I am grateful that physical education helps develop and train virtues such as restraint, courtesy, self-control, courage, team effort, and tolerance. That is why I am opposed to the excessive focus on contesting, competing for prizes, and spectatorship. My hope is to see a greater emphasis on basic exercise, its widespread adoption by the general public across the nation, and a more honorable physical education (p. 96).

11. Livelihood Education, Wealth Education

We humans have to live and survive. "Man shall not live by bread alone." Just as good health is critical for our spiritual activities, we need bread to survive. We use various means to broaden our spiritual activities effectively. Inventions, devices, politics, diplomacy, industry, military affairs, transportation, laws, and such are all called wealth, in a broad sense. Ultimately, however, wealth can only be valuable as a means to an end. At the same time, wealth is essential, just as health is. I am not in any way trying to minimize the value of wealth. I recognize the power of wealth more than anybody else. Rather, vigorous spiritual activities require a great deal of wealth. Wealth by itself has no significance. It generates value depending on how it is used. We must control our wealth, and not let wealth control us (p. 23).

Broadly speaking, wealth encompasses politics, industry, economy, transportation, military affairs, and diplomacy. Wealth is used not to produce wealth but to support, develop, and cultivate the four noble, absolute values.

The most horrific flaw of Japanese education is that it is used to produce wealth for the sake of wealth and to generate profit. A slave to material desires, a truly deplorable state (p. 98).

12. Zenjin Education and Uniting Opposites

In accordance with our noble teachings, we put particular importance on the uniting opposites from the standpoint of Zenjin Education.

Bold yet careful, cheerful yet graceful, lively yet modest, kind-hearted yet strong, studying hard while playing hard (traditional education neglected leisure education; students were not taught how to play correctly, joyfully, and properly), earning handsome money while spending it correctly (traditional education only taught students to earn, save, and conserve money and neglected to teach them to give generously to the society and country)——I want my students to grow into fine gentlemen by integrating these two opposing aspects, exhibiting both substance and style. I want them to be Tamagawa students who are capable of carrying a manure bucket as well as playing the piano, sweeping floor as well as performing the tea ceremony and flower arrangement, sewing a rag as well as tailoring a silk kimono, clearing the gutter as well as singing the nineth symphony, chopping wood as well as drawing, and using the abacus as well as understanding Buddhist scriptures (p. 105).

Ultimately, I believe a timeless, everlasting education is one that encompasses all two opposing aspects into one. At the heart of this is the ego. We must develop this ego broadly, exceptionally, profoundly, and virtuously (p. 108).

13. Zenjin Education and Respect for Indivisuality

A very good practice of Zenjin Education allows students to make the most of their individual strengths. All living things——whether it be a bamboo, a lily, a pine tree, Taro, or Hanako——are most beautiful when they display their unique features and characters.

Education is essentially about discovering a self that is precious and irreplaceable by even the entire universe and living to the fullest in a world God has blessed each one of us with.(p. 111).

If we think about it, nothing in the entire universe is as varied as human beings. All possess a unique essence and come in endless variations in terms of quality, volume, depth, speed, and timing. It seems awfully constraining to have the same curriculum and timetables, doesn't it? (p. 112)

14. Rosaku Education

As Pestalozzi demonstrated by his own action, Rosaku Education is at the heart of education. As represented by the character "ro," engaging in sweat-drenching physical work is a joy, pride, and duty for all of us. "Saku" in "rosaku" does not mean just work or chore. It means creative work (p. 114).

Some oppose Rosaku Education, saying it amounts to labor exploitation. This is a truly appalling misinterpretation, a poison for true education. Rosaku Education is in fact an integrated form of holiness education, intellectual education, moral education, beauty education, production education and health education. We sincerely hope to dedicate ourselves to true education. To be our authentic selves. To create something authentic. We are devoted and committed to true education (p. 117).

15. Teachers

Education is about connecting as much as possible. Teachers are like water wheels. They have to put themselves in students' shoes. To live and work together with students. The poem by Master Tanso, "You draw water from the river, and I will collect our firewood," is the secret to educational success (p. 56).

The outcome of education depends on teachers. Teachers decide whether an education succeeds or fails. It all boils down to people. Institutions, ideals, curriculum, textbooks, facilities, methods … they all come down to people! People! (p. 121)

本書籍をお買い上げいただいた読者の皆さまへ
特典Webページのご案内

特典コンテンツ

○全人教育論　各版の表紙
○全人教育論（全集版・日英対訳版）全文
○動画集
　・「玉川学園の教育」（1930年）
　・小原國芳：教育一筋90年
　・小原國芳の生涯
　　京都帝大・学生時代
○リンク集
　・玉川学園について
　・創立者：小原國芳
　・全人教育
　・教育12信条
　・玉川学園の歴史
　・歴史と沿革

を下記 QR コードからご覧頂くことができます。

玉川学園公式ホームページ　URL：https://www.tamagawa.jp/

執筆分担（執筆順・2021年6月現在）

小原芳明（おばら・よしあき）
学校法人玉川学園 理事長・玉川大学 学長・玉川学園 学園長
監修・「全人教育100年」

石橋哲成（いしばし・てつなり）
玉川大学 名誉教授
第1章

佐久間裕之（さくま・ひろゆき）
玉川大学教育学部教育学科 教授
第2章・資料編2

小原一仁（おばら・かずひと）
玉川大学教育学部教育学科 学部長
第3章・コラム1・資料編1

朝日公哉（あさひ・こうや）
玉川大学教育学部乳幼児発達学科 准教授
コラム2

ラルフ・ケレンツ（Prof. Dr. Dr. Ralf Koerrenz）
イエナ大学 教授（Friedrich-Schiller-Universität Jena）
第4章

星野あゆみ（ほしの・あゆみ）
玉川大学大学院教育学研究科 教授
第5章

渡瀬恵一（わたせ・けいいち）
学校法人玉川学園 理事（初等中等教育担当）
第6章

工藤　亘（くどう・わたる）
玉川大学教育学部教育学科 教授・TAPセンター長
第7章

ぜんじんきょういく　　れきし　　てんぼう
全人教育の歴史と展望

2021年8月30日　初版第1刷発行

監修者　小原芳明
発行者　小原芳明
発行所　玉川大学出版部

〒194-8610 東京都町田市玉川学園6-1-1
TEL 042-739-8935　FAX 042-739-8940
http://www.tamagawa.jp/up/
振替 00180-7-26665

装幀　水橋真奈美〈ヒロ工房〉
印刷・製本　港北出版印刷株式会社